Introduction to Counseling

INTRODUCTION TO
COUNSELING

by E. L. Tolbert

DEAN OF STUDENTS
PROFESSOR OF GUIDANCE
MADISON COLLEGE

1959
NEW YORK
TORONTO
LONDON

McGRAW-HILL BOOK COMPANY, INC.

II

To Frances, Jane, and Margaret

Preface

THE HIGH SCHOOL of today provides a great variety of courses, activities, and services which, broadly speaking, make up the educational setting or curriculum. Counseling is a part of this total educative process, yet it differs from teaching or instruction. It is an individualized learning situation in which the "subject matter" is the pupil's needs, capabilities, limitations, plans, and decisions. Counseling helps the pupil decide what other aspects of education mean for him and what he should do about them. Thus counseling is necessarily a part, in varying degrees, of the work of all educators. This book is intended to assist educators—teachers, teacher-counselors, and administrators—in effectively providing this individualized emphasis in the educational process.

Teachers, particularly, regardless of the fact that they may have no assigned responsibility for counseling, inevitably work with pupils on an individual basis, detect problems that demand individual help, and are called upon for all sorts of assistance. Pupils need help in solving problems and in making plans. Because they bring these needs and problems to teachers, teachers need some counseling skill and an understanding of what they can and cannot do in order that they may perform more effectively those counseling activities which arise in the normal course of teaching.

Teacher-counselors, who have specific time and responsibility for providing counseling or individual help, have a more clear-cut role and therefore a better-defined need for thorough knowledge of counseling techniques. The position of teacher-counselor is considered an essential one in the school. The teacher-counselor is the key person in stimulating and improving counseling services. He provides the most competent individual help that is available in the school. He must therefore know the methods of working with pupils in a face-to-face relationship and must know how to assist teachers in providing the individual help that is in their province.

The school administrator, particularly the principal, needs to understand what counseling is, what it does, and what it requires in personnel, time, and physical facilities. Without administrative understanding and support, other staff members will not be encouraged to cooperate with or utilize fully the counseling services that may be available. The administrator is, to a large extent, the determining factor in creating the proper atmosphere for effective counseling.

Two main uses of the book are visualized. First, it should be suitable as a text for a first course in counseling. Appropriate chapters could also be assigned for supplementary reading in courses in occupational information, analysis of the individual, testing, and applied psychology. Second, it should be useful for in-service education to develop counseling competencies. It should be particularly helpful for that type of in-service education which is provided regularly for all or a major group of teachers and which is conducted by the school counselor and others in the school, usually with the assistance of consultants from colleges, the state department of education, and community agencies.

Even though this text is intended primarily for secondary school educators, the principles and procedures discussed are relevant for those who work with individuals in such varied settings as community agencies, placement services, rehabilitation agencies, colleges, and business and industry.

The emphasis in this book is on what the counselor does when he is face to face with the counselee. This, it is felt, is the particular sort of help that is needed. Teachers and counselors reflect this need in such questions and statements as: "What do you actually do in counseling?" "What should I talk about?" "But I told him what to do!" In addition, a specific approach to the entire counseling process is presented. Although there are a number of approaches to counseling, this particular one appears to the author to be the most useful. On the assumption that needs and problems are essentially needs and problems of the total individual, and that no purpose is served by speaking of certain sorts of problems or limiting counseling to certain sorts of help, counseling involves the same general approach whatever the location of the problem in the pupil's life, and the same person does the counseling. Within this broad framework, variations are made to help solve the *particular* need or problem. Another aspect of this concept is that counseling is a systematic and describable process and is done at different levels, with workers at each level providing a needed sort of individual help.

The book is organized around the typical sequence of the counseling process. Early chapters deal with the information-getting or diagnostic phase. Then the use of tests and records as sources of information is taken up, with emphasis on how the counselor uses these sources rather than on setting up, maintaining, or applying these techniques. To explain why the counselor does what he does, a summary of some of the more relevant aspects of personality, learning, and environmental influences and their implications for counseling are considered. Next, the use of other sources of information about the counselee is discussed and information about occupations, educational and training opportunities, and other aspects of the counselee's present and possible future environment is covered. Since the counselor is continuously interpreting and synthesizing data about the counselee, this process is described at various points throughout the book. The final phase of the counseling process, that of helping the counselee do what he needs to do, is then described. The last chapter discusses how the counselor may evaluate and improve his work.

Each phase or technique is first discussed and then illustrated with various sorts of material, including appropriate parts of the counseling case that runs through the book. Questions are provided to help the reader review the main points that have been covered. At the end of each chapter are suggestions for activities designed to increase understanding of counseling and develop competencies. Additional reading is recommended, and references are given throughout the book.

The author is indebted to many persons who have, in various ways, helped in the preparation of this book. Dr. Donald E. Super, Teachers College, Columbia University, made many helpful suggestions, particularly in pointing out any lack of clarity in the original set of in-service education materials upon which this book is based. Dr. Ruth Strang, Teachers College, Columbia University, also helped the author in many ways, particularly in making the materials appropriate for the teacher and counselor in secondary school. Dr. Arthur Foshay, also of Teachers College, Columbia University, ably assisted the author in clarifying his ideas and adjusting the materials to the group for which they are intended. These persons deserve credit for any merits in approach and content which the book may have but cannot be held responsible for present shortcomings. In the revision of the original in-service education materials to textbook form, Dean Franklin R. Zeran, Oregon State College, has been exceedingly helpful with critical evaluation and encouragement.

E. L. Tolbert

Contents

CHAPTER 1

The Function and
Process of Counseling

A T THE ANNUAL District Z teachers' meeting, the feature address was on counseling. The speaker expounded at great length on the need for counseling, the teacher's responsibility for counseling, various concepts of counseling, experts versus amateurs, and counseling goals. The audience of teachers, supervisors, and administrators of District Z was quite enthusiastic and vigorously applauded the speaker during and after the speech. One got a mental picture of several hundred teachers, principals, supervisors, and superintendents going back to their schools and immediately providing counseling services for all pupils. However, as the teachers moved slowly out of the auditorium, one young lady was overheard to say to another, "He's a terribly interesting speaker, but what is this *counseling* anyway?"

A Pupil's Problem

Let us look at the teacher's question for a moment. What is counseling? There seems to be a great deal of mystery and misunderstanding about what it is, who does it, and how it is done. Perhaps an example of what is almost a daily occurrence in high school will provide a starting point.

When the bell rang for the end of the senior social studies period, the final period of the day at the new Center County Consolidated High School, Joe Jones thoughtfully gathered up his books. As Mr. Brown, the teacher, started to leave the room for the Tuesday afternoon faculty meeting, Joe asked a hesitant question.

I

"Er . . . Mr. Brown?"

Mr. Brown stopped. "What is it, Joe?"

Joe appeared to be at a loss of words, but Mr. Brown encouraged him.

"Something on your mind you'd like to see me about?"

"Well, if you have a minute, I thought. . . ."

Mr. Brown waited, visualizing the annoyed way the principal would look at his watch when he entered the meeting late.

"Well, you see, I'd like to ask your opinion on something. I'll finish . . . should finish school this spring. I want to go to college, . . . but I don't know if I'd have the money. It's pretty expensive, I hear. I could work, I guess, and pay part of my expenses. Or I could get a pretty good job here at the Mammoth Manufacturing Company that's building a new plant and make good money. But the other day at those assembly talks, that fellow made engineering sound good. But I don't know if I should take engineering. What's it like?"

Mr. Brown had had similar batteries of questions from other boys and girls. The word had got around that he had some scheduled time, and took some more of his own, to help students with problems.

"Well, Joe, you seem to have some pretty good questions. I'd like to talk them over with you when we have a little more time. I have a meeting coming up now. Could you drop by the Counselor's Office—Room 20, you know, next to the library—at the third period tomorrow?"

"I'll be there," Joe replied eagerly.

Mr. Brown is a teacher-counselor, one of several, in the large rural consolidated school. He comes in contact with many problems like Joe's. He is not an expert counselor, but he has had some college training in guidance and he does some reading on his own to learn more about it. He may not help Joe find all the "answers," but he has helped others to get started in working through their problems, and he will probably help Joe, too. In addition to a personal interest in Joe and his problems, members of this school staff have available an extensive file of information about Joe and a good supply of information about colleges, other educational opportunities, and occupations.

In a way Joe is more fortunate than many high school youths. He might have got a slap on the back and a hearty, "Buck up, boy. Everything will come out all right." Or his teacher might have said, "I don't know much about those things. Write to some colleges and make application to some plants."

What Is Counseling?

Joe did not say that he wanted counseling, because he had not heard that term and would not have known what it meant. But he was actually asking for counseling. Joe is not unusual or the exception; he is typical of the many pupils who stop the teacher in the hall with a question, who wait until after class to talk to the teacher about something that is bothering them, who bring up problems during the shop period, or who ask questions of the teacher visiting the farm to look over the supervised project. These pupils want real help in finding answers to their problems. They want someone with whom they can sit down and talk it over, someone who is sympathetic and understanding, and most of all, someone who can actually help them. Without knowing the professional terminology, they are asking for that type of help which is called counseling.

Now perhaps the meaning of counseling becomes a little clearer. It seems primarily to be helping people with problems. This is a very general statement, however, and it does not define counseling. A more specific definition is needed.

A Definition of Counseling. Counseling is a personal, face-to-face relationship between two people, in which the counselor, by means of the relationship and his special competencies, provides a learning situation in which the counselee, a normal sort of person, is helped to know himself and his present and possible future situations so that he can make use of his characteristics and potentialities in a way that is both satisfying to himself and beneficial to society, and further, can learn how to solve future problems and meet future needs.

In condensing a definition of counseling into a brief statement, a great deal is implied by a few words. What do these terms actually mean?

Face-to-face relationship: Counseling is carried on primarily through the face-to-face relationship of two persons, who, working together, establish a unique and personal relationship. This "working-together" process is the unifying thread of all that takes place in counseling.

By means of this relationship and his (the counselor's) special competencies: The counselor uses the relationship as the way of providing help; it is the meeting ground of counselor and counselee. However, the counselor needs to have technical competence to give effective help; he must know the science and art of his profession.

Learning situation: A unique and very personal learning situation is provided in counseling. Principles of effective learning apply here just as they do in other settings, such as the classroom. The counselee learns what he needs to know to achieve his goals, whether they be adjusting to a new situation, planning for an occupation, gaining a realistic understanding of himself, or any of the other myriad needs and problems of individuals.

The counselee, a normal sort of person: The counselees with whom secondary school counselors will work are, for the most part, essentially normal persons; these persons may profit from the type of help described. Normality is difficult to define. One way to give some meaningful boundaries would be to say that the counselees may be persons who, although they are in a troublesome situation or faced with some immediate problem, have an understanding of the cause of the difficulty. Thus they may be normally anxious or have "normal anxiety" [144, p. 23]. Those with deep-seated emotional problems, where the difficulty or problem has been repressed or shut off from awareness, should usually be referred to specialists [144, pp. 22–23].

Helped to know himself and his present and possible future situations: The counselee is helped to gain a realistic understanding of his capabilities and limitations and the effect of these on his day-to-day life. He is also helped to understand his goals, needs, attitudes, and other aspects which go to make up his concept or picture of himself and which form the basis of the roles that he desires to play in various life situations. Further, he is helped to determine how accurate his picture or concept of himself is and how realistic his desired roles are [222]. At the same time he is helped to appraise various situations or environments, such as school, job, or social activities, and to understand the factual as well as the more or less subjective aspects that should enter into his planning about them. This applies to present situations as well as prospective ones, for example, college, trade school, or a vocation.

So that he can make use of his characteristics and potentialities in a way that is both satisfying to himself and beneficial to society: Personal satisfaction should be related to the individual's contribution to the society of which he is a member. He has freedom of choice in making plans but is helped to make qualitatively good plans and decisions. Too, he accepts responsibility for his choices and plans.

And can learn how to solve future problems: The counselee has learned to accept the fact that he will face problems, and how to go about solving them. This does not mean that he now has a "built-in" problem-solving mechanism but that he knows how to use his own resources and how to obtain help from others, for example, a counselor.

One further point needs to be made here concerning the nature of problems. "Problems" may be difficulties encountered by the counselee, such as failing a course. They may also be the decisions and adjustments that the individual has to make as he grows and matures, for example, planning a suitable educational program to allow full realization of interests and potentialities, or learning how to develop suitable relationships with the opposite sex [190]. Developmental help is also preventive as it helps the counselee avoid problems that would eventually call for remedy. Thus development [131, 134, 135] is an objective of counseling as well as and perhaps more than remedial help. This developmental emphasis gives counseling a more positive aspect. There are, however, other emphases evident in counseling theory and practice today. Barry and Wolf [18] give eight current views of guidance-personnel work (counseling) in a careful analysis of the current situation.

This definition appears to be somewhat abstract; it may be made more concrete by applying it to give a running account of what one counselor did in helping a particular counselee.

Applying the Definition. John Doe comes in to see the teacher-counselor because he cannot decide what sort of work he would like to do. He is about to finish high school and has taken what is called a "general course." He is thinking about a trade school, a semiskilled job in a textile mill, selling baby furniture in an assigned district, and several other things. The teacher-counselor has a room where they can have some privacy. Just the two of them are present in a face-to-face situation.

The counselor is friendly and genuinely interested in John. The boy is somewhat in awe of adults and tries to conceal this feeling by appearing to be indifferent to others. But the counselor, by giving all his attention to John and accepting this defense of assumed indifference, aids John in speaking freely. Thus this situation is unique—both because it involves two unique people and because the counselee experiences a type of relationship that he finds nowhere else. He feels himself the center of attention and can speak freely about matters of deep concern to him.

The counselee brings out that he likes shop courses and activities and hobbies where he works with tools and equipment. However, he feels that he ought to "aim higher." He sees himself as working at a professional or managerial level, making plans for others to carry out. He likes to think of himself as having what his friends term "an excellent job." One of the factors contributing to these attitudes is the admiration of friends and parents for the technical and managerial people in the local textile mill. He states that he is interested in saleswork but shows by various comments that this interest is based primarily on a belief that salesmen are always "on the go" and have big new automobiles. John has not done much analyzing of his attitudes and goals and probably would not have been successful if he had tried. Nor does the counselor get this information quickly or in a straightforward manner. As some of these points are discussed the counselor begins to understand John's aspirations and the conflict between his fancied role and a more realistic, practical role in the world of work. He is able to help John understand his attitudes, needs, and motivations a little better.

In addition, some facts are needed—facts about training for various sorts of jobs, about activities on the job and salaries. The counselor either supplies these or helps John to locate them. Some facts about John need to be brought in too. School marks, scores on academic aptitude tests, and other data help John to understand himself better (if he accepts them). Altogether, the counselor is helping John to get a more realistic concept of himself. This is not easy because John dislikes admitting that he does not compare well with professionally trained technical people. However, he becomes better able to see himself as a skilled craftsman and requests more information about ways of getting training, the aptitudes needed for various sorts of work, the expense of training, and ways to get tryout experience. The counselor helps him to find the answers to these questions.

While the facts are important, John is able to learn to make practical plans because the counselor provides a warm, accepting, friendly setting where goals, doubts, and attitudes may be discussed freely. Learning for John, as for others, progresses most easily and effectively when the learner is personally concerned with the problem and when he is free of threat, anxiety, or extreme pressure.

The counselor, too, *is a learner* in this individual learning situation. He begins to understand what sort of person the counselee is and what sort of help he needs. He finds, as he works with the counselee, which are the more effective ways to provide the needed help. And, finally, he develops increased effectiveness in counseling; he becomes a more competent counselor.

The definition and example of counseling have shown, to some extent, the various elements of the counseling process. It would be helpful, at this point, to expand upon this definition by presenting a systematic description or an operational definition of what *may* take place as the typical counselor works with the typical counselee.

The Counseling Process

It is essential to bear in mind that counseling does not follow in routine and mechanical fashion the "steps" presented; it is instead a dynamic and flexible process that is different for each counselee. Furthermore, each counselor will work in a way that is uniquely his own. With this caution in mind and considering that what is presented is an oversimplification, the counselor may gain a mental picture of a process that *may* have certain emphases at certain times and that may proceed somewhat along the lines discussed. Even at the risk of appearing to reduce counseling to a pat formula, this approach should be helpful to give a framework or structure to the total process so that what follows in succeeding chapters will fit into a meaningful sequence.

The point of view developed in this book is that the counseling process consists of phases which are given more emphasis at particular times, rather than a series of steps, each of which takes place by itself with all other steps excluded. That is, other phases may be present but with less emphasis. Explaining or structuring counseling is placed before obtaining information. Actually information is obtained from the counselee the first time he is seen; for example, the counselor sizes him up while shaking hands. Further structuring may be done early if the counselee appears to need it or asks for it.

The use of the term *counseling process* should also be commented upon at this point. The *process* of counseling is different from the *profession* of counseling, as Tyler explains [243, p. 375], and this is one of the reasons for frequent confusion in terminology and practice. "Counseling, viewed as a process, is a term that parallels 'psychotherapy' rather than clinical psychology." Hence the emphasis is on what the counselor and counselee do when working together rather than on all the professional activities of the counselor.

The First Contact. The face-to-face part of counseling begins when the counselee first comes in to see the counselor or at the first contact between the counselor and counselee. However, the counselor or counselee may have already developed certain attitudes about each other; the counselee may have formed an opinion about counseling or the counselor, or the counselor may have learned something about the counselee. Thus it may be stated that counseling may begin before the first personal contact. Even so, the first contact is extremely important as it has a major effect on the quality of the relationship and sets the stage for further counseling. Rapport should be established at this time; it should, of course, be maintained throughout counseling and afterward. Rapport is that atmosphere of understanding, mutual trust and confidence, and good feeling that enables people to work together effectively, to talk freely, to learn, and to make plans.

Structuring or Explaining Counseling. Early in the counseling process, the counselor should get across to the counselee a concept of counseling and the kind of help that is offered. The counselor may do this by explaining what sort of help counseling provides and what it does not do; he may define the concept by his behavior, by verbal explanation, or by combination of both. The counselor defines his role and assists the counselee to comprehend the part he (the counselee) will play. This should be done early, as the counselee needs to know what to expect, even to such immediate questions as to how long the first contact can last. Structuring is not a rigid and formal procedure, however, and should not interfere with the counselee's talking about himself and expressing his feelings. In fact, it may be presented to the counselee better by the counselor's manner and by what he does rather than by what he says.

Obtaining Information. As some degree of rapport is established and as the counselee gains an adequate understanding of what counseling is like, there usually tends to be emphasis on information getting. In fact, it is quite natural for the counselee to begin to talk about himself and his problems. The counselor assists the counselee to express himself freely in bringing out what is bothering him, his goals, home life, and interests, and other personal information. The counselor makes every effort to provide as accepting and permissive a situation as possible to enable the counselee to express himself and to learn readily. Other information about the counselee is obtained outside of the face-to-face situation.

Organizing and Interpreting Information. All during counseling, from the first contact or even before, information is synthesized, and connections, patterns, and meanings are searched for. The counselor is trying to make a whole, understandable, and consistent person from the various sorts of information that have been brought out by the counselee or obtained from other sources. Counselor and counselee consider data together; meanings and patterns are inferred and evaluated by both. The counselor, however, does some synthesizing and interpreting outside of the face-to-face situation. He may follow a procedure somewhat like the following: data are studied and evaluated and meanings are searched for; inferences about meanings are derived, checked against each other, and revised, eliminated, or retained; a few of the most valid inferences are arrived at; hypotheses are set up on the basis of these inferences in order to predict how the counselee will perform in various present and future situations. The total process of bringing together data, making inferences about meanings, establishing alternative hypotheses, and arriving at predictions is a continuous process, subject to modification and change as new information is obtained and as the counselee reacts to the hypotheses and predictions. It is never final except as required by the time limitations of counseling.*

An example of hypothesizing about the counselee might be as follows: A counselee's pattern of interests and aptitudes is not of the type desirable for the college preparatory course or curriculum with emphasis on foreign language. It might also be hypothesized that this curriculum is out of line with the counselee's goals and that he would not be satisfied with accomplishment in this area. A prediction may then be made that the counselee will fail, that he will drop out, or that he will be a borderline and dissatisfied pupil if he continues in the curriculum. From further synthesis of data and hypotheses about the counselee, it may be predicted that he will like and do well in the distributive education program.

Planning and Decision Making. Usually the counseling process moves from emphasis on information getting to emphasis on planning and decision making by the counselee. The counselor may discuss with the counselee various sorts of information which have been obtained and help him to grasp meaning, relationships, patterns, and trends. Hypotheses are discussed, and the counselor helps the counselee to formulate and evaluate hypotheses. Further, the counselee is assisted in understanding the probable outcomes of various courses of action and in considering the various predictions. In the ongoing process, the counselee is aided in making plans and decisions and in taking responsibility for them.

Putting Plans and Decisions into Effect. When the counselee, working with the counselor, has evolved a plan or made a decision, the counselor assists him in carrying it out. For example, the counselor may help the counselee decide what specific steps will be taken or may contact another person with whom the counselee may work.

Evaluating the Suitability of the Decision or Plan. In many cases the counselee will be in contact with the counselor after he has carried out his decision or tried out new behavior. He may wish to discuss the results with the coun-

---

* These terms and the process were adapted from a talk made at the American Personnel and Guidance Association meeting by Donald E. Super, "The Preliminary Appraisal in Vocational Counseling," reprinted in the Veterans Administration *Information Bulletin* 7–118, Sept. 21, 1956 [224] (used by permission of the author).

selor and perhaps modify or change his plans. He has had the opportunity to try out the learning that has taken place in the counseling situation; effects upon himself and upon others have been noted; these may then be evaluated in the counseling session. It may be that no further help is needed or it may be jointly decided that further counseling is needed.

To describe counseling as a systematic and identifiable process does not mean that it should be done in a mechanical way or that all counselors will do it in the same way. The counselor keeps in mind the needs of the counselee. One counselee may have made a plan and only want to verify it; another may need extensive help. As counseling progresses, certain counselor-counselee activities assume more importance at certain times and need more emphasis. These steps or phases may occur in different sessions over a long period of time or may all take place in one session; for example, information getting may involve a half-dozen or so sessions.

Some Terms Used in Counseling

In addition to the term *counseling,* which has already been defined, there are several others which are frequently used and which have a special meaning in the counseling context. These terms are defined in the following paragraphs; other counseling terms are defined as they are discussed in the various chapters.

1. Guidance. This is the total program, or all the activities and services engaged in by the school (or other institution or organization) that are primarily aimed at assisting an individual to make and carry out adequate plans and to achieve satisfactory adjustment in all aspects of his daily life. Guidance is not teaching, but it may be done by teachers. It is not separate from education but is an essential part of the total educational program. Guidance is a term which is broader than counseling and which includes counseling as one of its services.

2. Interviewing. While there are many types of interviews for all sorts of purposes (employment, selection, research, and so on), the term as used in this book refers only to the interview in counseling. It is the face-to-face relationship that is the central part of counseling.

3. Testing. Psychological testing is the process of obtaining responses from the counselee to questions calling for information, attitudes, interests, or problem solving. The questions are presented in standardized form and in a prescribed manner. Individuals may be tested alone or in groups. Some tests are composed of apparatus; the individual responds by doing something with tools, equipment, or devices; for example, placing pegs in holes or assembling nuts and bolts. Another type of instrument is the projective test in which the individual "projects" his personality needs, attitudes, and goals in response to questions and other test materials for which he has no ready-made response. Pro-

jective tests are ". . . a method of understanding the inner world of the individual. They give the counselor a sense of the dynamic interplay of forces within each person" [218, p. 149]. A variety of materials may be used to elicit responses, for example, ink blots and incomplete pictures. These materials are ". . . ambiguous, equivocal, or in some other sense partially structured" [186, p. 108]. For a more detailed discussion, see Ref. [44, pp. 55–95].

4. Occupational Information. Under this heading comes information about occupations, industries, trends, the meaning of work, the prestige of occupations, and the like. Closely related to occupational information is information about educational and training opportunities, referred to as educational information. Other types of information that may be used with counselees are social, personal, and recreational.

Problems That Show the Need for Counseling

The need for counseling services can be amply documented [91, 177, and 264]. Verbatim recordings of counseling sessions show vividly the need of individuals for this type of help [39, 210]. Typical problems drawn from the experiences of the author and his coworkers, such as the following, further emphasize the importance of these services. The beginning counselor can, no doubt, recall others from his own experiences.

Sam Senior. Sam will finish high school this year and plans to go to State College in the fall. He doesn't know what he should take but says he thinks he would like engineering. He doesn't know what subjects he would take or what the work of the engineer consists of. Neither of his parents attended college, but they are determined that Sam go so that he will "not have the hard time we have had." They are not able to assist him in deciding what to take or what to expect in college life. Sam plans to work part time to help pay expenses and is not aware of the difficulties of trying to work and adjust to college the first year. He is not taking the college preparatory course and has made only average marks in his subjects. His only mathematics course is the first-year general mathematics course in which he received a C. About 15 per cent of the graduates of his high school attend college.

Sam's problem might be called, at first glance, a vocational one. But notice the other factors. He is selecting a field of work on the basis of the way it "sounds" to him. He is not sure why he is going to college. His course and class standing do not suggest college training. That standing, plus the need to earn part of his expenses the first year, make the situation appear rather unfavorable. There are, of course, other factors that also should be considered.

Joe Junior. Joe is the kind of boy that teachers promote in self-defense. In the formal classroom situation he does very little work unless closely supervised. In the shop, where there is less supervision and more independent work, he uses his talents to create real trouble. In spite of the fact that a number of teachers have said that Joe is the kind of boy "who ought to be in the shop," he bungles each shop job, breaks tools, wanders around, and creates a hazard around power tools. The other students do not like Joe and never include him in their group activities. Few of the teachers would be sorry to bid Joe good-by, and Joe knows it. Joe's parents, however, insist that he complete high school and that he follow in the footsteps of his sister, who was an excellent student and leader.

Joe has the misfortune to follow a bright and attractive sister. While he does have some ability and could make a fairly pleasing appearance, he could never equal his sister. From the frequent comparisons made by teachers and parents, Joe knows that, whatever he does, he will not come up to expectations. Joe's problem might be described as a personality difficulty, but educational achievement, lack of vocational choice, and family relationships complicate the problem.

Sam Sophomore. Sam is just starting in his sophomore year in school after barely passing his freshman subjects. He is having a difficult time with all his courses. He does not know how to read. He lacks any kind of an effective plan for study. He knows that he has a more difficult time than most of his friends and has come to the conclusion that something is wrong with him.

Sam's problem might be called an educational one, as his primary difficulty is lack of specific study skills. However, it is obvious that his attitude toward his poor performance will affect his whole personality, particularly his feelings about his ability. Then too, the additional time required for study interferes with his normal development in other areas such as social activities and recreation. He just has no time for recreation.

Fran Freshman. Fran is a new pupil from a nearby elementary school. In spite of the high school orientation program, she has not become adjusted to the new school. She does not feel accepted by any particular group and is lonely and unhappy. She has never been too self-confident and is daily becoming more timid and self-conscious. Her schoolwork is suffering.

Fran's problem might be described as one of social adjustment. However, her difficulties in establishing satisfying social relationships are affecting her school achievement. Adjustment and achievement in school have a direct bearing on vocational choice and adjustment.

Some Other Problems. Several other pupils who need counseling are the following:

Joe Jones's father is a tenant farmer in a rural-agricultural area. Joe is interested in farming and is now in his third year of vocational agriculture. He is doing good work and has an excellent project. However, there are no farming opportunities in the community. Joe is beginning to realize with some frustration that in his home community he cannot find the type of work he would like to do. He is beginning to get discouraged and to develop a "what's the use" attitude.

Sam Smith has been taking industrial arts and has become very interested in ceramics. He gives evidence of having real talent in this area. However, he does not know anything about occupations in this field. Furthermore, his parents are planning to send him to State University to take business administration.

Mary Doe, an average pupil in the vocational home economics department, has decided that she would like to be a home economics teacher. Overweight, unattractive, quick-tempered, and sensitive, she feels that the position of teacher would give her security and a sense of belonging. She has a need to dominate others of which she is not aware. In addition, she admires the pretty and likable home economics teacher and wants to imitate her.

Sam Jones is a new member of the scout explorer post. The other members were reluctant to let Sam join and did so only because of the persuasive ability of the post adviser. Sam is bossy, touchy, and "knows it all." He is becoming isolated; this causes him to increase his efforts to gain recognition and acceptance. Several boys have threatened to drop out if Sam is kept in the organization.

Problems in Various Settings. While these problems have been drawn from those presented by pupils of high school age, they do not differ from those presented in other settings such as colleges, trade schools, or community organizations. The recreation director, the religious education director, the YMCA secretary, and others in similar positions meet problems very much like those described. The principles and procedures of counseling apply in whatever setting the counselor is working.

Approaches to Counseling or Points of View about Counseling

In this book a point of view about counseling is presented which, to some extent, is a synthesis of techniques and procedures from other approaches. It would be helpful to the beginning counselor to realize that other points of view exist and to know a little about what is done and the reasons for doing it. He then is in a better position to read further and to evolve, through practice and study, the approach that he prefers. There is at present no one approach that has been proved conclusively to be the best.

It seems particularly pertinent that attention be given to the bases of counseling. As Shoben says [204]:

Those psychologists who deal directly with clients inevitably use theoretical ideas. Their choice is not one of theory vs. no-theory, but between notions of human conduct that are explicit and formalized against those that are implicit and the inarticulate product of experience.

Thus particular emphasis is given to the bases of the various counseling approaches.

The differing theories and processes furnish bases for identifying six different approaches to counseling. Some of these may be more accurately called therapy and are not the sort of procedure that the typical counselor would use. Concepts from each approach, however, have relevance for counseling and have played and are playing an influential role in shaping the profession of counseling.

A word should be said about the problem of classifying counseling points of view. Various authors have done this in various ways. Warters [253], Smith [209], Hamrin and Paulson [94], and Froehlich [77] use three classifications: directive, nondirective, and eclectic. Their emphasis is on the directive-non-directive continuum. Bordin [30] defines approaches as either emphasizing instrumental behavior or dynamic aspects of behavior and presents his own point of view and synthesis of personality, which emphasizes concepts from psychoanalytic theory, self-psychology, and a counseling process that involves understanding the needs of the client and a flexible approach in meeting them. Pepinsky and Pepinsky [168] identify five approaches to counseling: trait and factor, communications, self-theory, psychoanalytic, and neobehavioral. Shoben and others [204] describe four theories of behavior that may serve as bases for counseling positions: learning theory and psychoanalytic concepts; stimulus-response, reinforcement theory; client-centered theory; and a general behavior systems theory or an integration. From these classifications and from the publications about counseling available today, it appears to be useful to discuss counseling according to the six following types or points of view:

1. Directive or trait-centered approach. The assessment of psychological traits, predictions about performance, and a rather definite degree of counselor directiveness are characteristics of this approach.

2. Client-centered or self-theory point of view. Often described as "nondirective" counseling, this approach is based upon a psychology of self-actualization drives, the self-concept as a major factor in behavior, and counseling or therapy to help the individual utilize growth potential.

3. Dimensions or communications approach. This approach merits separate consideration because of the research approach which involves the study of "dimensions," the effects of the counselor varying these dimensions in the counseling process, and the adapting of dimensions and counselor roles to various sorts of counselee problems.

4. Eclectic approach. Eclectism is the systematic and purposeful utilization of procedures and techniques from other points of view to serve best the needs of the counselee.

5. Learning theory approach. Principles of learning derived primarily from experimental studies are used as bases of personality formation and change and for counselor activities to help the client relearn effective ways of behavior.

6. Psychoanalytic approach. Psychoanalytic practice has served as the source of one theory of personality or, in fact, a number of theories. The process itself,

which constitutes the most intensive and lengthy type of therapy used today, has undergone considerable modification since its origin.

Obviously, any attempt to review these counseling viewpoints in a few pages will be quite superficial. Actual typescripts or cases should be used to give the feeling, dynamics, and nuances of each process. Further reading of research and principles as well as case studies should be quite rewarding.

The first counseling viewpoint, or approach, to be taken up is the trait-centered or directive type.

The Directive or Trait-centered Approach. The best-known description of this point of view, and the most thorough development, has been done by Williamson. The discussion that follows is based on his book *Counseling Adolescents* [264]. The development of this approach is closely related to the development of psychological tests and the growth of educational and vocational counseling [227, pp. 167–169].

The Nature of Counseling. Williamson says that the counselor varies his role and techniques to present the situation needed by the client in the solution of his particular problem. "It does not seem likely that a single system of roles and techniques will suffice for all problems and all clients" [264, p. 108]. The counselor is, in fact, a ". . . 'teaching assistant' who aids in the learning process of the client-pupil" [264, p. 109]. The counselor employs the methods of science, ". . . experimental, statistical, and conceptualizational, to the process of human adjustment" [264, p. 109].

The counselor's role is an active one and he takes the responsibility for deciding what data are needed and for collecting the needed data. He then provides these data to the counselee. "Ordinarily the counselor states his point of view with *definiteness,* attempting through *exposition* to enlighten the student. If the student shows unwillingness to accept the implications of the facts or unable to think of desirable next steps, a useful technique is to tell him to think it over for a week and return for further discussion" [264, p. 230]. The role of the counselor as the source of authority is further exemplified by his actions when alternative choices are open to the client. "If there appear to be equally desirable alternative actions, the counselor says so frankly, adopting the attitude of *working with* the student in solving the problem. He avoids a dogmatic position and reveals to the student an attitude of bringing knowledge, experience, and judgment to the student's assistance" [264, pp. 230–231]. He maintains his role as the source of authority and ". . . does not at any time appear indecisive to the extent of permitting loss of confidence in the validity of his information. He maintains a varied and running discussion of the case data, constantly shifting his exposition and illustrations in terms of the student's verbal and facial reactions during the interview. In this way, the counselor seeks to arrive *cooperatively* at an interpretation of data and a program of training which will strike fire in the student's imagination and will result in a desire to achieve a goal which will be of lasting satisfaction because it is consonant with potentialities" [264, p. 231].

While the counselor does not follow a set pattern of activities, he does include certain steps or phases, only one of which is actually called counseling. Williamson says, "The work of the clinical counselor is divided into six steps; analysis, synthesis, diagnosis, prognosis, counseling (treatment), and follow-up" [264, p. 101]. But ". . . these steps do not necessarily follow in sequence . . . [264, p. 102], and each part of the process is incomplete" [264, p. 103]. The sequence is adapted to counselee needs at the time of counseling; it may involve repeating steps or phases at different stages of the individual's education, adjustment, or maturity [264, p. 103].

This sort of counseling is designed to provide help for the typical types of problems arising in educational institutions, such as selecting courses, making occupational plans, social adjustment, and emotional problems. While it is not stated specifically with what types of problems the counselor would not work, he would make extensive use of referral; for example, he would refer students to a "psychologist and psychiatrist, for specialized treatment of serious emotional conflicts" [264, p. 239]. Furthermore, Williamson says, ". . . in this book we shall not limit ourselves to emotional problems, nor shall we dismiss other types of problems such as a lack of skill or information, as having less significance for client or counselor" [264, p. 203].

Emphasis is upon the scientific and developmental nature of the counseling process rather than the therapeutic or remedial aspects. Williamson says that this approach is ". . . of a more *scientific* rather than a curative type . . ." [264, p. 107].

With this brief summary of some of the major characteristics of this approach, the process of counseling will now be discussed.

The Process. The six steps or phases of counseling—analysis, synthesis, diagnosis, prognosis, counseling, and follow-up—have already been mentioned. It has also been pointed out that this sequence is flexible and not necessarily carried out in the order given, that it may take different lengths of time for different clients. The sequence given, however, seems to be the one that would probably usually be followed, as each one is, to some extent, dependent upon the preceding step or steps. Nor is each step or phase independent or complete in itself; for example, diagnosis and counseling could actually take place in the same interview [264, p. 227]. Formulations of each step are ". . . *tentative formulations* subject to the validity test of the individual's own experiences . . ." [264, p. 104].

The first step, that of diagnosis, is the collection of all sorts of data about the individual. Williamson says, "Before a student can be effectively counseled, the student and counselor must collect *dependable,* i.e., reliable, valid, and relevant information, from which to diagnose aptitudes, interests, motives, physical health, emotional balance, and other characteristics which facilitate satisfactory adjustment in school and at work" [264, p. 127]. Many of the data are collected in personal interviews, but no counselor is informed of all needed information at the time of his first interview with the student [264, pp. 128–129].

Synthesis is organizing the data from the analysis to gain an understanding of the counselee [264, p. 101]. "After collecting analytical data, the counselor and student search for a pattern of consistency in them" [264, p. 178]. The counselor may have to assist the student in thinking clearly and in developing a state of readiness for thinking before he can participate effectively in this process.

Diagnosis involves the counselor's statement of the counselee's problem. The emphasis is on the counselor's judgment. As Williamson expresses it, "In reviewing case data to arrive at a diagnosis, the counselor seeks evidence of assets and liabilities for different types of adjustment which the student must face now or in the future" [264, p. 181]. Diagnosis is a clinical process in which all sorts of data are used, some having substantial validity and some involving ". . . hypotheses unverified as yet by research" [264, pp. 181–182]. "The method of diagnosing by patterns and characteristics we shall call the *clinical method*. The assumption is made that this method may be used by workers who make a critical appraisal of all case data, recognize errors in these data, and try to get behind the raw data to the possible factors making for a particular test score, emotional trait, or evidence of aptitude or interest" [264, p. 184]. It is important to note that "clinical hunches" are checked against the total collection of data. Furthermore, the diagnosis is tested by determining how logical it is, how well it agrees with essential information and the opinion of other counselors; by checking it with the counselee; and by determining how well it works [264, pp. 206–207].

Prognosis ". . . refers to the clinician's statement, or prediction, of the future development of the student's problem . . ." [264, p. 101]. Williamson points out that diagnosis and prognosis are separate steps [264, p. 188]. This is particularly true when data do not have the validity to enable the counselor to make dependable predictions about future behavior, but less definite when such predictions can be made [264, p. 189]. In the latter situation, the two steps may be telescoped [264, p. 189]. The counselor later explains his prognosis to the student [264, pp. 189–190].

Counseling is the actual face-to-face process for the purpose of helping the student. Williamson says that it is ". . . that part of personnel work in which a counselor helps the client to marshal his own resources, the resources of an institution and of the community, to assist the client to achieve the optimum adjustment of which he is capable" [264, p. 209]. The counselor's role is clearly described; he presents ". . . evidence for or against the student's claimed educational or vocational choice and social or emotional habit, practices, and attitudes" [264, p. 229]. He indicates which data are favorable and which are unfavorable, adds up the evidence for or against, ". . . and explains why he advises the student to shift goals, to change social habits, or retain the present ones" [264, pp. 229–230].

The counselor makes use of a variety of techniques in the counseling step or phase. Williamson classifies methods of advising under the headings of ". . . *direct, persuasive,* and *explanatory*" [264, p. 233]. Counseling techniques that may be used include "(1) forcing conformity, (2) changing the environment, (3) selecting the needed environment, (4) learning needed skills, and (5) changing attitudes" [264, p. 215].

With an adequate diagnosis completed, the counselor proceeds to move into the counseling-helping situation by ". . . (1) establishing rapport, (2) cultivating self-understanding, (3) advising or planning a program of action, (4) carrying out the plan, and (5) referring the student to another personnel worker for additional assistance" [264, p. 224].

Follow-up, the final step in counseling, ". . . includes what the clinician does to assist the student with new problems, with recurrences of the original problems, and what is done to determine the effectiveness of counseling" [264, p. 101]. With follow-up, the steps in the counseling process are completed.

Bases. Directive or trait-centered counseling draws considerable support from a trait theory of personality. That this is a theory and that it is widely accepted is pointed out by Berg when he says [24]:

The most pronounced change in our thinking about occupations occurred more than a generation ago when what Super has labeled "trait theory" began to be applied to vocational counseling. Curiously the magnitude of this change and the significance of its influence was then and still is largely unrecognized. By contrast, the chronologically parallel development of psychoanalysis was characterized by storms of controversy from the initial announcement of the Freudian system to tea-pot tempests, at least, in the present day. . . . Nobody seemed to challenge the basic ideas behind trait theory. Indeed, few persons seemed to recognize that it was a theory.

Traits are estimated by various means, including psychological tests, and predictions are made about the kind of person the counselee is and what he will do. Validity has been established for many of these traits, which allows some degree of statistical prediction. Super [220] presents descriptions of traits and instruments by which they may be measured. The process of factor analysis has been used to get at "pure" traits, that is, underlying psychological characteristics which account for various sorts of behavior. Probably the most familiar example of factored traits is intelligence. At one time it was considered to be one trait, but now it is generally recognized to be made up of a number of more specific traits such as ". . . verbal meaning, space, number, memory, word fluency, and reasoning" [196].

It has already been pointed out that this approach depends heavily upon a scientific approach to the study of the client and also upon helping him to know and understand himself and his environment so that he will have the data with which to make suitable choices and plans. Bases of counseling thus involve primarily the process of collecting valid data about a client's traits and ensuring that he uses these data correctly.

The Client-centered or Self-theory Approach. This approach, which is often referred to as "nondirective," has been developed by Carl R. Rogers and his associates and is explained and described in three publications [182, 183, 184]. It has been reviewed and commented upon in numerous other articles, monographs, and books. Counseling is considered to be a process of helping the client to use his own inner resources to solve problems. The counselor attempts to aid the client in the "self-actualizing" process by accepting him, by valuing him, by seeing the client's world as the client sees it, and by "feeling" with the client; he acts in a way to get these attitudes across to the client. The client is thus able to face his acceptable as well as his unacceptable characteristics, without fear of rejection, praise, or blame. As he begins to be more accepting toward himself, to feel more secure in his own judgments about values, he can make increasing use of growth forces and potential.

The Nature of Counseling. Rogers emphasizes that client-centered counseling is more than a set of techniques. Attitudes are of utmost importance. ". . . Individuals who are already striving toward an orientation which stresses the significance and worth of each person can learn rather readily the client-centered techniques which implement this point of view" [184, pp. 20–21]. Also, the counselor is guided by the hypothesis that ". . . the individual has a sufficient capacity to deal constructively with all those aspects of his life which can potentially come into conscious awareness" [184, p. 24].

The counselor does not collect case material nor does he make a diagnosis. Rogers says, "When the counselor assumes the information-getting attitude which is necessary for the assembling of a good case history, the client cannot help feeling that the solution of his problems is being taken over by the counselor" [182, p. 81]. Later, he emphasizes this point of view by saying, "Our experience has led to the tentative conclusion that a diagnosis is not only unnecessary but in some cases detrimental or unwise" [184, p. 223]. In a sense, the client makes his own diagnosis in this type of counseling.   ·

Earlier Rogers specified the type of clients that could profit from this type of counseling or therapy. More recently, however, he has said that ". . . client-centered therapy is widely applicable—that indeed in one sense it is applicable to all people" [184, p. 230]. It is, however, primarily for emotional problems that require therapy.

The length of the process has undergone some modification. Earlier Rogers had said that there might be ". . . six to fifteen contacts . . ." [182, p. 232] and ". . . where maladjustment is not extreme, where the individual is not deeply neurotic, two, four, or six contacts are often sufficient for the client to find the needed help . . ." [182, p. 232]. Later, in *Counseling with Returned Servicemen* [183], it was pointed out that counseling may involve only one contact [183, p. 122], and that this approach may be the best for the short-contact counseling where the counselor has limited experience and training [183, p. 6]. It is particularly important to use this approach if the contact is to be a short one [182, p. 247]. The more recent trend, however, is to have a larger number of contacts over a longer period of time.

The role of the counselor has tended to become more a matter of following the "basic hypothesis" than of using specific techniques. Rogers says that over the years the emphasis has moved from directiveness ". . . questioning, interpreting, reassuring, encouraging, suggesting . . ." [184, p. 31] to the counselor's devoting his attention to accepting and understanding the client [184, p. 31] and concentrating ". . . his whole effort upon achieving a deep understanding of the private world of the client" [184, p. 31].

The Process. In his earlier publication, Rogers gave a definite step-by-step description of the process [182, pp. 30–45]. Later, he gave another sort of description of what takes place [184, pp. 190–196], and discussed the various types of "movement" that take place in client-centered counseling. The process of counseling, as described in the earlier book, is as follows [182, pp. 31–44, 217]:

1. The individual decides that he needs help and comes in to see the counselor.

2. The counselor defines the nature of the counseling process, indicates that he does not have the answers, but that he and the client can work cooperatively to find them.

3. The counselor helps the client to express feelings and attitudes.

4. The counselor does not evaluate but accepts feelings (usually negative) and clarifies them. He attempts to understand the feelings underlying the client's statements.

5. Following expressions of negative feelings, positive feelings begin to emerge. These are indications of growth.

6. Positive feelings are recognized and accepted, as were negative feelings. The individual begins to understand the sort of person he is.

7. As he begins to understand himself and to accept himself, the client achieves new levels of adjustment. He can accept admirable self-aspects as well as the less admirable ones.

8. The client begins to gain an understanding of the possible courses of action or choices open to him. The counselor helps him to understand these choices and his feelings about them.

9. Faint positive actions are instituted by the client.

10. Further growth, insight, and positive actions are in evidence.

11. The client becomes more able to make choices and take actions, and he

becomes more self-directing. He may become interested in the counselor as a person. He is less defensive and shows considerable acceptance of himself. The counselor may supply him with information needed.

12. The counselee indicates that he feels a decreasing need for help, and while he may feel ambivalent about leaving counseling, he is actually ready to terminate contacts.

Rogers points out that these steps are ". . . not mutually exclusive, nor do they proceed in a rigid order . . ." [182, p. 41]. But, in general, this is the sequence of events in the counseling process.

In the newer publications, the author describes the process of counseling as follows [184, pp. 191–195]: The individual finds his self-structure no longer adequate or effective in meeting needs. At this point, he is ready for therapy.

As he enters the counseling relationship he ". . . experiences a freedom from threat . . . positive and negative feelings are accepted . . . the firm boundaries of self-organization relax" [184, p. 193]. The client can explore attitudes, beliefs, perceptions, but his ". . . self-structure is not sufficiently relaxed so that he can consider [faulty generalizations brought out] and contradictory experiences upon which they are based" [184, p. 193]. He goes back to his former ineffective way of looking at things and then slowly moves out to face and accept the contradictory experiences ". . . into a new and revised pattern" [184, p. 193]. Rogers describes this as a process of ". . . disorganization and reorganization . . ." and says that ". . . while it is going on it may be decidedly painful" [184, p. 193].

A new and reorganized self begins to emerge, which is based upon the client's experiences which he can now perceive without distortions [184, p. 153]. He can face conflicting attitudes and concepts and examine experiences because attitudes toward himself are accepted by the counselor as well as the client being accepted as an individual [184, p. 194]. He now has a more consistent and comfortable self-concept, one which incorporates previously denied experiences, and he can formulate his own values and face new experiences with freedom of action and with the likelihood of making more appropriate responses [184, pp. 154–155].

A number of types of therapeutic *movement* are discussed in the more recent publication. More insight, or understanding of the relationship between past experiences and present behavior, is in evidence [184, pp. 132–133]. The client begins to talk more about *self* than symptoms [184, p. 135]. Expressed feelings move from negative to positive [184, p. 134]. Repressed material becomes more available [184, p. 135], that is, he can *talk about* experiences or put them in words and can more effectively differentiate among experiences and perceptions [184, p. 147]. There is a tendency to emphasize the present more than the past as therapy progresses [184, p. 135]. The client begins to consider himself a more worthy and likable person, to be able to face and discuss all sorts of experiences, to develop his own set of values rather than taking them from others or "outside of himself" [184, p. 139]. He moves back behind the generalizations which have served as guides, to the experiences upon which these are based, to the formulation of new and more adequate guides for behavior [184, p. 146]. He comes to feel that others consider him likable, worthy, and admirable [184, pp. 159–160]. Personality becomes better integrated, there is less anxiety, and there is more effective thinking, perceiving, and problem solving [184, p. 178]. Behavior becomes more effective [184, p. 186]. A careful reading in the reference is essential, however, to understand what is meant by each of these types of movement as well as the research evidence upon which they are based.

Bases. Much of the theory upon which client-centered therapy is based is already apparent from the preceding discussion. Rogers is quite explicit on the matter of personality theory, however [184, pp. 481–533]. This theory, presented as a series of more or less tentative propositions, is summarized in part below.

The individual exists in a world which he sees in a unique and personal way. Reality for him is the way he perceives his world. No one else can know it as he does or understand just what it means for him.

An organized and consistent self is developed through his experiences—his interaction with others—and this self is made up partly from directly experienced values and partly from values taken from others. Some experiences, of course, are unimportant and ignored. Others are acceptable and incorporated in the self-structure. Others, however, are unacceptable and denied by the individual as part of the self. This denial may be a conscious act, which is a process done by everyone, but it also may be a denying to consciousness or putting into words and facing because they are too much at odds with the individual's self-concept. But these *unsymbolized* experiences and needs may result in behavior which is unacceptable to the individual. Also, needs of this sort cause tension because they are unmet. These experiences, actually of great importance to the individual, have not been organized into the self-structure.

A key concept is that the individual behaves in a way to enhance, protect, and "build up" the self. This is the basic striving for self-actualization. Now the importance of the unacceptable experiences may be recognized. They constitute a threat to the self which requires that the self protect itself. It becomes more rigid as more protection is needed. As the person's view of himself is at odds with important needs, experiences, and the like, he becomes maladjusted. Tension is present. The individual is not able to draw from his own direct experiences the values that he needs, the judgments that he should be able to make, to incorporate into the significant experiences and needs. Values taken from others, which may be quite at variance with the individual's own experiences, are quite often a source of difficulty.

In the therapeutic situation, with its acceptance of the individual and freedom from threat, the individual can examine both consistent and inconsistent experiences. As these are verbalized, they may be perceived in new and non-threatening ways and organized into the self-structure. As he learns to understand and accept himself, he becomes more understanding and accepting of others. He is able to formulate values and make judgments based upon his own experiences and values drawn from those experiences. As experiences of the individual may be recognized, verbalized, and accepted into the self, psychological adjustment becomes a reality.

The Dimensions of Counseling or Communications Approach. This approach, developed by Robinson [177], merits separate consideration because of the emphasis on the concept of *dimensions* of counseling in the face-to-face process, the determination of ways to vary dimensions based upon the kind of problem the client presents, and the ways of categorizing client problems. Robinson suggests that the counselor deals with a wide variety of problems [177, pp. 3–4], that the counselor should play a number of different roles [178], and that he should use a wide variety of techniques [177, p. 64].

The Nature of Counseling. Robinson points out that counseling is a process for helping normal people make effective adjustments [177, p. 1]. He says that the nature of client problems calls for three different types of counseling: first, to help with adjustment problems, which may be emotional or non-emotional; second, to teach a skill, such as a study skill; and third, to develop maturity, for example, increased ability to adjust in social situations [177, p. 168]. The type of problem determines, to a large extent, what the counselor will do in working with the client. Emphasis is upon flexibility in the process, however [177, p. 64].

Counseling thus has a developmental as well as a remedial emphasis, as a client may be helped to develop and make full use of potentialities as well as remedy defects and solve problems [177, p. 5].

The different ways of handling client problems and the importance of flexibility of approach in this point of view make it essential that the counselor play suitable but varying roles. In emotional adjustment problems he may help the client understand repressed or unavailable material, while in skill counseling he may actually coach the client.

The Process. The first phase of counseling, which applies to any type of counseling, is to have the counselee tell about his problem [177, p. 173]. In this process, the counselor gains information and the client is helped by talking about the problem. The counselor listens and uses acceptance, clarification, and general leads, for example, encouraging the client to ". . . tell me a little more about your job . . ." but does not take over responsibility for what is done in counseling [177, pp. 175–176]. The setting is comfortable and informal, the client unhurried. Techniques such as questionnaires or self-report documents may be used [177, p. 176]. The counselor may also make use of other information such as cumulative records to learn about the client and his problem.

While the client may expect to begin work immediately on his problem, it may be necessary for counselor and client to work together further to clarify it. As this is done, the counselor begins to use the specific approach and techniques required by the problem. He decides whether or not it is more an emotional or nonemotional adjustment problem, primarily by the determination of how available the material relevant to the problem is to the client. There is not a sharp distinction between these categories, however, because some emotional aspects, such as repressed material, may be present in all problems. Helping the client face emotional characteristics that cause difficulty in relations with others might be an emotional problem, while helping him learn about aptitudes, interests, and achievement for selecting an occupation might be a nonemotional adjustment problem. Thus the counselor uses the dimension of whether or not the needed information is unknown to the client, unrecalled, or repressed to determine what approach to use [177, p. 184]. The difference is one of degree rather than completely separate categories of problems which require completely separate types of counseling [177, p. 185].

Skill counseling is appropriate if remedial work is needed in certain areas such as social skills or study habits [177, p. 171]. A new skill may be taught as well as a deficiency remedied [177, pp. 171–172], such as ". . . constructive methods of adjusting" [177, p. 231].

What the counselor now does as he moves into the process of helping the client is partly dependent upon his knowledge of the effects of various techniques with different sorts of problems such as interpretation, degree of lead, division of responsibility, dealing with the core of the counselee's remarks, varying the working relationship. Robinson and his colleagues have studied the effects of these dimensions on client behavior and present detailed results in Refs. [177, 178] and other publications. It is not possible to discuss the extensive research here. The above publications, and others referred to in them, are recommended reading, however.

The counselor uses techniques and procedures in such ways as to help the client, aware of the effects of the ways he may vary techniques and roles. In emotional adjustment problems, he acts primarily as a "catalyst," to help the client ". . . discover and integrate the elements in his problem through his own conscious efforts" [177, p. 170]. The client is provided with a friendly and accepting setting where he can work at the recall of emotional elements of his problem; he often needs help in discovering ". . . the protective mechanisms which prevent easy access to his repressed fears and wishes" [177, p. 195]. The counselor may need to use interpretation and suggest leads that will help the client bring out repressed material [177, p. 195].

In nonemotional adjustment problems, the counselor may often give the client needed information and help him integrate it, so that the client can work out a satisfactory solution [177, p. 185]. The counselor may, to facilitate the process, give needed information [177, pp. 185–187], aid recall [177, pp. 187–188], help at decision points, including the use of test data and occupational information [177, pp. 189–191], and provide information about social customs [177, pp. 191–193]. Techniques are used which help the client obtain, synthesize, and make use of information. As has been pointed out, the counselor varies his approach along the "dimensions" studied so as to provide the most effective counseling situation, for example, dimensions of acceptance, division of responsibility, or degree of lead.

In skill counseling, the counselor takes the responsibility for making a diagnosis, which is then explained to the client. The client decides whether or not he wishes to enter upon the process of remediation. The counselor, however, plans the remedial work, supervises its being carried out, and evaluates results; he plays a major and directive role [177, pp. 224–225]. When a new and total skill is being taught, the need for which the client may not be aware, the counselor may proceed in a different manner than if the client has a specific skill deficiency of which he is aware [177, pp. 171–172]. Diagnosing immaturity and counseling to increase maturity is a new and relatively undefined area. The author suggests that more research is needed relative to this type of counseling [177, pp. 242–253].

Bases. Research has centered around the study of interaction of the counselor and client as the counselor varies his role and uses different techniques and procedures. The immediate effects of these variations is used as the criterion of counseling effectiveness, for example, the degree to which the client takes responsibility or exhibits resistance. Robinson states, however, that client behavior in the counseling situation should be related to behavior outside of counseling in everyday life as an ultimate validation of procedures [178].

Obviously, a great deal of use is made of psychological aspects of behavior and personality, such as motivation [177, p. 35], dynamics of adjustment [177, p. 54], the self-concept [177, p. 61], growth forces [177, p. 62], and normal personality [177, pp. 178–179]. Counseling thus has bases in various contemporary psychological theories. Concepts of repression and the unconscious play a part in the differentiation of the two types of adjustment counseling, and learning theory and principles are employed as bases of some aspects of skill counseling. The principles, however, are drawn from empirical evidence of what happens during the interview rather than from a specific theoretical point of view about personality.

The Eclectic Approach. Eclectism in counseling involves the adoption and use of procedures and techniques from any point of view that appears to be suitable for the particular client with his particular problem. The eclectic counselor has, in fact, a consistent philosophy and purpose to his counseling, rather than adherence to only one method or a hit-or-miss, directionless way of working. He uses what he uses for reasons that are as well verified as possible, rather than employing a completely trial-and-error approach.

Probably the most systematic development of the eclectic point of view has been done by Thorne [232]. Although he originally described his approach as "directive" (in contrast to nondirective), he now stresses directive counseling procedures as only one technique in an eclectic collection of methods. The way these methods are combined and used, however, constitutes the *art* of counseling [232, p. xiii]. Hamrin and Paulson [94] also describe what they characterize as eclectic counseling for high school age youth, and Hahn and MacLean use the term *eclectic* in identifying the approach of their illustrative counselor [91, pp. 231–232]. As an example of the eclectic point of view, the proposals of Thorne [232] will be used.

The Nature of Counseling. Thorne uses the term *personality counseling,* and defines it as follows: "Personality counseling is a face-to-face relationship in which the counselor, a person competently trained in psychological science, consciously attempts by attitudes and verbal means to help others solve problems of life in which personality factors are the primary etiologic agents" [232, p. 85]. It is for normal persons, that is, those without serious personality or organic disorders [232, p. 85], who are aware of their difficulties and motivated to do something about them [232, p. 85]. It is usually limited to ". . . the attempt to improve adaptive behavior in specific areas without altering basic personality structure" [232, p. 86].

Thorne makes a differentiation between "personality counseling" and "psychotherapy." The former would include, for example, adjustment problems of normal persons; educational problems, such as reading; marriage counseling, where serious mental disorders are not involved; problems of parent-child relationship; and more complex emotional problems under the direction of a psychiatrist [232, p. 79]. Psychotherapy would include, on the other hand, such problems as psychoses, severe psychoneuroses, and psychosomatic problems [232, p. 79].

From his knowledge of psychology and counseling methods, the counselor selects those methods which appear to be the most appropriate for the problem. Guides are provided to assist the counselor to determine whether or not counseling seems to be indicated [232, p. 91]. A set of criteria is presented by which the particular type of counseling may be selected, and which may serve as a guide to the counselor in his work [232, pp. 105–108].

The Process. The length of the counseling process varies considerably; counseling may last for a single interview or for several years [232, p. 159]. In general, the process of counseling involves making continuous diagnoses to determine the causes of the problem, formulating a plan to modify causative factors, setting up conditions for effective learning or making changes in behavior, helping the client to develop his own resources and to take responsibility, and handling other problems related to the client's adjustment [232, pp. 88–89]. The counselor must first establish communication with the client on the latter's own emotional and intellectual level [232, p. 124]; he must establish rapport [232, p. 125]; and he must engage in a mutual trying-out process, until an effective counseling relationship is established [232, p. 127].

A first step is to make a diagnosis, which includes collecting a case history [232, p. 139]. The preparation of a case history provides reassurance for the client, as this activity emphasizes the fact that he is considered important. He may also gain insight and emotional release in the process [232, ch. 9].

Usually the client will show some resistance to counseling; either active (directive) or passive (nondirective) methods may be used to reduce the defensive behavior [232, pp. 128–131].

Knowing the problem and its causes, the counselor is in a position to select a counseling approach. A number of types of counseling may be used; a discussion of these methods and indications for use of each make up a substantial portion of Thorne's book. The plan of counseling that is made may be changed, however, to fit in with what is needed as treatment progresses [232, p. 108], and there may be a varying between directive and nondirective methods in the same treatment or even in the same interview [232, p. 124].

A wide variety of methods, practically all that are used in any sort of counseling, may be employed. These methods are as follows: diagnosis and classification of problems [232, chs. 4, 9]; emotional "training and retraining," which includes providing for emotional expression, determining emotional factors in maladjustment, and helping the client to learn new emotional responses [232, chs. 15–19]; the use of suggestion [232, ch. 20], persuasion and advice [232, ch. 21], pressure, coercion, and punishment [232, ch. 22], conflict induced by the counselor [232, ch. 23] as directive methods; perceptual training and retraining, which includes helping the client formulate an adequate self-concept and make fuller use of intellectual resources [232, ch. 25]; methods of memory training and bringing to awareness repressed memories [232, ch. 26]; semantic training and reeducation, or helping the client to use verbal concepts more accurately and to eliminate faulty concepts [232, ch. 27]; helping the client to learn more effective controls over affective or emotional life [232, ch. 28]; helping the client to orient or reorient his thinking and attitudes by giving psychological information [232, ch. 29]; interpretation to foster insight into personality mechanisms [232, ch. 30], and helping the client to straighten out troublesome and erroneous attitudes [232, ch. 30]. Then, in addition, other techniques such as passive listening [232, pp. 244–245], catharsis [232, pp. 245–246], and clarification [232, pp. 253–255] may be used.

As has been mentioned, changes in procedure may be made at any time. Usually the counselor begins with simpler methods and then goes on to more complicated ones, finally trying anything if other methods fail [232, p. 108]. Thorne states that the client will usually accept almost any kind of procedure providing it is nonthreatening and used tactfully [232, p. 124]. The counselor usually employs passive (nondirective) methods wherever possible and regularly uses them in the early stages of counseling when the client is telling about himself. If these methods fail, more directive methods may be needed. As Thorne points out, however, some degree of directiveness is present in all counseling, even if it is only the decision to use passive or nondirective methods [232, pp. 112–113].

The variety of methods is much too extensive to discuss in detail here. However, each method is developed to the point of indicating when it would be used and how. Thorne states, however, that research needs to be done to validate these methods. The counselor would presumably have a repertoire of methods which he would be competent to use with a wide variety of problems.

During counseling, the client reaches a large number of insights piecemeal. These insights and emotional releases become cumulative and contribute to the solution of individual aspects of the problem. Thus since problems are solved in this way, it is desirable to have summaries from time to time and at the end of counseling to give more complete insight [232, p. 151]. Verbally expressive clients may be asked to do this for themselves [232, p. 151], but the counselor may have to provide interpretive summaries for some clients for all or a part of counseling [232, p. 151].

Structuring may be needed from time to time during counseling so that the client understands what is being done, the reasons, and his responsibility [235].

As the closing phases of counseling are reached, the client takes the lead in ". . . gradually resuming independent self-regulation" [232, p. 149]. This closing phase is reached when causes of problems have been revealed, when emotional release has been gained from talking about experiences, when the client feels less tension, and when he is ready to do something about the problem [232, p. 149]. He is now able to use his intellectual resources to solve his problem [232, p. 149]. This phase is characterized by problem-solving behavior [232, p. 149]. The counselor may be quite directive at this point [232, p. 149]. Less time is spent with the latter "half" of counseling than with the first half of release and clarification of emotional problems [232, p. 150].

The counseling usually tends to end at an optimum time, but a too early ending is bad; the counselor may need to take active steps so that counseling is not ended too soon [232, pp. 155–156]. It is probably best not to use very directive means to keep the client in counseling, however [232, p. 156].

Bases. According to Thorne, his system of eclectic counseling is based upon principles from experimental psychology [232, p. xiii], and particularly the psychology of perception and learning. Obviously, eclectism draws much of what is used from various schools of counseling and psychotherapy. While there is considerable empirical evidence to support the use of various techniques [235], the counseling position is not based upon one systematic psychological theory, nor is evidence presented to show that procedures have specific results with specific problems. It is more a logical, scientific, and objective approach, based to a large extent, it would seem, on Thorne's interpretation of the whole literature in terms of his own experiences.

As Thorne states it, while the viewpoint of his book is to be ". . . rigidly scientific and eclectic . . ." [232, p. xii], not all of what is presented has been validated to date nor will it be soon, and the most weight must be given to empirical evidence. The development of psychology is compared with the development of medicine, which he says ". . . *limits its theory and practice to scientifically established theory, fact and technical applications*" [232, p. 26]. "Schools" are not utilized as they are in psychology. In psychology, then, all methods of counseling should be rigorously evaluated to determine just how valid the techniques are [232, p. 27]. Much needs to be done in this area; little has actually been done. However, Thorne points out that scientific theory and research are sufficiently advanced in some areas (those given in treatment or process) that they can serve as a basis for "rational" counseling and psycho-therapy [232, p. 31; 234].

Field theory in psychology is given major emphasis. Thorne says, "Modern field theory in psychology with its holistic principles must become the basic reference point against which all technology is related" [232, p. 24]. Research is the way to validate hypotheses [232, p. 25]. Field theory requires a global evaluation of a person or a study of a person, past, present, future, from the standpoint of all fields appropriate, such as biology, psychology, sociology, using all known methods of science [232, p. 25]. Treatment involves not only the person but the total situation in which the person lives.

Thorne emphasizes that eclectic counseling requires an active, ongoing diagnostic process to provide the counselor with insights into what should be done therapeutically at any particular moment. He discusses the diagnostic foundations of eclectic counseling in a companion book, *Principles of Psycho-logical Examining* [233], which systematically considers the levels of organ-ization of personality integration. This system attempts to study diagnostically all aspects of the organism interacting with its environment, evaluating all possible factors contributing to maladjustment. The eclectic approach thus appears to deal with a wider range of etiologic factors than any other method.

The Learning-theory Approach. In recent years, learning theory has been used to serve as bases for counseling by a number of authors such as Dollard and Miller [61], Pepinsky and Pepinsky [168], and Shoben [203]. It offers a meeting ground for clinical work or counseling and laboratory experimenta-tion. While much of what has been done has emphasized the matter of anxiety and emotional problems, the approach appears to be relevant to counseling with all sorts of problems which the counselor meets in his daily work.

The Nature of Counseling. This approach to counseling is particularly useful for work with normal persons, those persons who can manage their lives outside of the counseling situation [168, p. 68] but who have come to be aware of a question as to whether they can make appropriate decisions or behave in an appropriate manner [168, p. 69]. The client has not learned a suitable response, he is not able to make one for some reason, or he makes other responses that are not suitable. For example, an individual cannot decide upon a choice of courses in school because he knows little about his capabilities and the demands of the courses and because he is quite dependent and cannot make decisions for himself. Very few problems involve a completely intellectual choice or action.

The counselor acts as an accepting listener and provides a setting in which the client can bring out ideas, attitudes, and emotional material. It is suggested that he may play various roles in his efforts to promote client learning, besides that of ". . . facilitator of learning . . . such as 'father,' 'friend,' or 'alter ego'" [168, p. 142]. The client views the counselor as he has learned to perceive adults in past experiences, ". . . as a figure to be feared, dominated, manipulated, or leaned upon, but not as one to trust nor from whom real concern and interest might be expected" [203]. This is particularly the case in the handling of more pronounced emotional problems. The counselor, however, is nonjudgmental and shows genuine interest in the client and his problem [203]. He does not, however, maintain a passive role but may, as will be seen later, be more active in the counseling process.

The Process. Counseling is considered to be a learning process where the results of past learnings are modified according to principles of learning. The client comes in to see the counselor for problems that represent learnings in past experiences, for example, inability to make decisions, poor opinion of self, inappropriate behavior. Pepinsky and Pepinsky point out that ". . . a client's lack of available responses for dealing with an important, external situation (or situations) is the manifest result of how he has learned to respond" [168, p. 70]. As has already been indicated, the counselor exhibits concern and interest in the client and his problem. He behaves toward the client as if he were a person of worth [200, p. 535]. He has an anonymous role, and while the client does not know him as an individual, he ". . . experiences him as the kind of person who is strong, courageous, calm, and responsible. Therefore the therapist becomes the kind of person the client would both like to know and like to be" [200, p. 536].

Usually the counselor would make use of all types of information about the client, such as that from tests and records or from other persons. Pepinsky and Pepinsky say that ". . . knowledge of the nonmanipulable circumstances of the client's learning prior to counseling can help us better to understand his behavior at the time he comes to the counselor for help" [168, p. 118]. It is thus important to know as much as possible about him. This is the source of inferences and hypotheses to be made about the client [168, p. 185]. We want to know about conditions and circumstances of prior learning. This will help the counselor, also, to understand the nature of the problem as well as the reactions of the client to counseling and the counselor.

What happens next? Shoben says that the counselor deals with ". . . these distorted expectancies and nonintegrative social behaviors as they are directed toward the clinical situation and the counselor himself" [203]. The counselor labels the client's ". . . distorted perceptions and social techniques . . ."

[203], indicates that he is aware of them (various self-defeating behaviors), and rewards the client's efforts to reveal aspects of his emotional and personal life by approving his effort to explore emotional material [203].

The counselor's manner in the early part of counseling tends to "challenge" the client's distorted perceptions about the counselor, helps to decrease resistance in talking about emotional aspects of life, and reinforces positive actions of the client, for example, bringing out of important conflicts [203]. The client feels social approval as well as some relief from emotional distress [203]. In this process, the client is learning to think about himself in a new way, and to think about others in new and positive ways [203].

As counseling progresses, the counselor may use clarification, reflection of feeling, and interpretation to facilitate insight. However, insights, or learning the connections between past experiences and present behavior, is not enough, even though the client can verbalize them fluently. It is the nature of the client-counselor relationship, the security and acceptance, which makes previously anxiety-producing cues, such as thoughts, experiences, and symbols, no longer troublesome or threatening. The client can now react in new ways to these cues [203].

The new learning, of a social sort, is transferred by generalization to social situations outside of counseling as it has been learned in the social situation of counseling, that is, involving client and counselor. Not burdened by anxiety, the client is able to behave more freely and appropriately. He has new and suitable ways to react to life situations [203]. He can make his own decisions, formulate his own values and act upon them, and can look ahead and foresee the consequences of his actions.

Counseling is considered to be an orderly process [168, pp. 197, 247; 200, p. 529; 203], and various activities are emphasized at various times. However, it must also be flexible enough for the counselor and client to work together effectively. In the latter stages, when the client is acting in a rational way to meet needs, information, such as occupational information and other types of help to enable the client to make appropriate responses (selecting an occupation), may be given.

Bases. Learning theory plays a major part in this concept of counseling. But principles have been incorporated from perceptual theory, psychoanalytic concepts, social psychology, and anthropology [203]. The learning concepts involve those of anxiety as tension that must be resolved, processes of generalization and discrimination, reinforcement or reward, conditioning, and problem-solving behavior. It is not possible here to review the total systematic theory of learning that underlies a counseling approach such as that of Pepinsky and Pepinsky [168] or Shoben [203]. Chapter 7 gives a summary of some concepts from Dollard and Miller [61]. The significant point is that counseling procedures and theory have been developed from learning theory. A theory has as its purpose explanation and prediction. Thus the counselor can explain why he does what he does and can predict what the client will do. Emphasis is put upon the formulation of testable hypotheses.

This approach to counseling is for individuals who are maladjusted, who have considerable anxiety with strong defenses, and where repression (usually not complete) is attempted. Emphasis is upon conditioning, where anxiety has been learned in connection with some cue or stimulus and where anxiety reduction results in maladaptive behavior, or where a strong conflict, out of consciousness, produces ineffective behavior. When defenses can be lessened and the faulty learning can be brought to awareness and understood, the client can develop new and effective ways of behavior.

The Psychoanalytic Approach. Probably the most intensive and long-term therapy used today is the psychoanalytic type. While this approach would be called "therapy" in the strict sense of the term, much is relevant to counseling with clients who have milder sorts of problems. The influence of psychoanalytic therapy and theory of personality is obvious in many approaches to counseling and the work of many counselors. That is, counselors draw on relevant theories of personality and techniques that offer help in their work. Particularly valuable have been the contributions emphasizing the developmental process, the effect of social experiences on development, the dynamics of personality, and personality mechanisms.

The Nature of Counseling. It may be said that psychoanalysis is not a scientific theory but rather a series of observations drawn from the experiences of therapists with clients. Much of what is advanced is not available to scientific study. Some experimentation has been done [26; 107, ch. 9; 61], and more is being done. Some concepts hold up well while others do not. Nevertheless, psychoanalysis offers a rationale and process for working with patients who are seriously emotionally disturbed.

Psychoanalysis has been modified and developed a great deal since the original work of Freud, the founder, although orthodox Freudian procedures are used today. Rank, an early therapist, developed an approach emphasizing such concepts as the birth trauma, will therapy, and the importance of the individual taking responsibility for willing and adapting to the will of the group. Allen and Rogers are among those who have been influenced by Rank. Jung, another early therapist who also broke with Freud, emphasized in his *analytical psychology* what might be called the self-actualization process, the concepts of introversion and extroversion, and the individual and collective unconscious. Adler, with his school of *individual psychology,* emphasized striving to power, self-assertion, compensation for inferiority, and style of life. His approach is not considered to be a "depth" psychology as are those just mentioned. Horney, among the "neoanalytical" group, has emphasized the social situation of the client more than the biological bases as did Freud. Other neoanalysts represent somewhat different viewpoints [26].

Psychoanalytic therapy is designed for help with emotional disorders, the neuroses. It is rarely used with psychotics but may be helpful for those with psychosomatic disabilities. The client or patient should have some healthy aspects of personality for good prognosis. The process is quite lengthy, as sessions may be held two, three, or more times a week for a period of several years; the time probably could not be much less than one year. The goal is a restructuring of the personality, which affects the patient's whole life, the way he sees himself, and his relationships with others. Such major changes, of course, take considerable time. Alexander and French [2] suggest, however, that the process may be much shorter in length.

In psychoanalytic therapy, the therapist or counselor plays an anonymous, vague, and undefined role for the patient and thus is a person upon whom the client may project inner needs, fears, and reactions or characteristic ways of dealing with others. The counselor remains in this role and does not enter into the everyday social life of the patient. He is present to serve the patient in helping him in his reactions toward others, to provide support and reassurance, and to assist in the interpretation and understanding of the meaning of the impulses, needs, and the like that are brought out. This role is quite crucial to the therapeutic process. To understand his own motives and needs, the therapist should have undergone the analytical process as a patient.

The Process.   There may be variations in the process, but in general, a diagnosis is made, and patient and therapist agree that this sort of therapeutic help is desirable. A case history is taken; early sessions may be used for this activity. After this is completed, the patient usually lies on a couch, with the therapist out of sight behind him. Free association is used; the patient reports whatever comes into his mind. He makes no effort to control or regulate his thoughts. This is not easy at first, and resistances in the form of pauses or omissions occur. Such resistances are caused by repression. Another technique to get at repressed material is dream analysis.

As therapy progresses, the analyst uses interpretation at appropriate moments to explain resistance and other behavior of the patient. The core problems are not revealed at once but appear slowly and in different ways, and a long process of *working through* is needed before defenses can be relaxed. Correct and timely interpretations assist the patient to relax defenses. Bases for these interpretations are drawn from the psychoanalytic theory of personality.

The patient is able to relax his defenses because he begins to realize that threats associated with forbidden impulses are not as dangerous or threatening as he imagined them to be. The therapist offers some support and security, even while he is urging the patient to push farther into painful emotional areas.

A crucial aspect of therapy is the attitudes which the patient manifests toward the therapist. He reacts to the therapist in the therapeutic situation as he has reacted to other important persons in his life. Bases of reactions are brought from childhood, usually from relationships with parents. This aspect of therapy is called *transference,* that is, the patient acts in a manner which is not based on the actual situation but is determined by past experiences. He may attempt to control, dominate, or otherwise gain some emotional satisfactions from the therapist. This stage, which is not reached until the minor defenses have been lessened, is considered to be an essential part of the therapeutic process. The basic emotional problem has now been brought out. It will be resolved, partly through the solution or resolution of the transference relationship. Interpretations by the therapist will assist in this process. The patient has a drive to be adjusted and happy; there is thus a force toward better adjustment that is essential for continued progress. While the resolution of the transference relationship may take considerable time, the patient, at its termination, no longer needs the therapist and now has new and more effective ways to deal with life situations. Of course, he must put these into effect in daily life, but he has become aware of the unconscious forces that affect his behavior and now can use them for effective living.

This is generally the orthodox psychoanalytic point of view. The bare outline which has been given, however, is not too different from that used in the variations of psychoanalysis.

Bases. Psychoanalytic theories of personality are quite numerous; for an adequate explanation, references such as Blum [26] should be consulted. Each of the therapists mentioned earlier utilizes some major or minor variation. Only a brief statement of some of the aspects of Freud's personality theory will be given here.

Personality is considered to be divided into three systems, the *id,* the *ego,* and the *superego.* The id is the source of all psychic energy, which must be discharged according to what Freud called the *pleasure principle. Reflex actions* and *primary processes* serve this process. In the primary processes, an image of the object needed for tension reduction is formed. The ego, in turn, is the means by which the need is gratified in contact with the world of reality. The ego plans how to satisfy the need and tests this plan by action. The superego, however, is the individual's introjection of values and restraints gained in social living. It furnishes the individual with a conscience and an ideal, and it may censor the plan of the ego to meet the need. All three systems or aspects of personality interact dynamically.

Instincts play an important role in behavior. These are needs which arouse tension that must be reduced. The means of reducing tension may vary considerably, and the individual develops an extensive and complex system of interests, habits, and activities through displacement from one source of satisfaction to another. Conflict arises when regulating forces are in opposition to forces which act to satisfy instinctual needs or drives. Anxiety arises when the instincts are too strong for control by the ego, partly in anticipation of the punishment that might ensue. Punishment may be guilt feelings originating in the superego. The ego may protect itself with various *mechanisms* like *rationalization* if it is about to be overwhelmed by the unacceptable impulse.

Emotional forces play a major role in behavior. Also, the unconscious motives which impel the individual to action and the mechanisms, including the major one of repression (in which an unacceptable object-choice or impulse is forced out of consciousness by opposing forces), are major factors in behavior and personality development.

Of great importance are the influences of childhood experiences at various stages of development. In the first five or six years [26, chs. 3–5] the infant goes through the *oral* stage where the mouth is the primary source of stimulation; then the *anal* stage where eliminative functions come in for major attention, and finally the *phallic* stage where the sex organs become the chief source of stimulation. Pleasures, restrictions, and training occur at each stage. The individual may fixate at any stage or may regress to an earlier stage. Following these stages is the *latency* period where there is a decline in the strength of instincts and less psychological activity. With adolescence, however, there is a reactivation and a resurgence of impulses which call for renewed activity on the part of the ego. With the *genital* stage, adulthood is reached. Problems at earlier stages have implications for adult adjustment [26, ch. 8].

A part of the developmental process is the *Oedipus complex,* which is a sexual attachment for the parent of the opposite sex. It is repressed at the age of five or six years but continues to have an influence throughout life.

This brief summary does not begin to do justice to the psychoanalytic personality theory. Blum [26] provides a helpful comparison of points of view at various developmental levels.

Classifying Counseling Problems

Problems are complex and defy any attempt at rigid classification. Usually all or nearly all aspects of the individual's life are involved. For example, failing a school course may affect vocational plans, relations with parents, and recreational activities.

It is possible to classify problems by using terms such as vocational, educational, social, or personal, if it is understood that the problem is simply *more* vocational or *more* personal, rather than confined to the specific area. Another way to express this classification system would be to say that the problem is one with vocational emphasis.

Another approach to classification is making use of causal factors [167]. The groupings of problems by this approach may be illustrated by the following categories:

1. Lack of assurance (the pupil wants to check on a decision which he has made)
2. Lack of information
3. Lack of skill

4. Dependence
5. Self-conflict (conflict between self-concepts or between the self-concept and some other condition)
   a. Cultural self-conflict
   b. Interpersonal self-conflict
   c. Intrapersonal self-conflict
6. Choice anxiety (need to select a course of action from several that are upsetting)

In this particular approach to classification, however, there was not complete agreement among those who analyzed the information about counselees to classify the problems. This type of classification is useful to give an idea of the sorts of problems presented by counselees, in this case, college students.

As a matter of fact, the counselor does not need to categorize or classify the problem in order to provide help. What he does need to do is to be able to get beyond symptoms to the real problem and use his resources to help the counselee, either by counseling or referral. This brings us to the question of who does counseling; what are the roles of the teacher, the teacher-counselor, and the counselor in providing counseling? One way to consider the subject is to think of counseling as taking place at various levels.

Levels of Counseling

There appear to be three levels of counseling into which persons performing counseling functions may be grouped. These levels apply not only to those in high schools but also to persons doing counseling in any setting. The description of duties, however, deals more with personnel in the school.

1. First-level counseling. This would be done by teachers, college advisers, or similar persons.

2. Second-level counseling. This is the sort of counseling that would be done by the person designated as teacher-counselor or guidance counselor. The term *psychological counselor* might be used for some counselors at this level.

3. Third-level counseling. This level of counseling would be done by persons with doctoral training in counseling or in education or psychology with emphasis in the area of counseling. The term *counseling psychologists* might apply to many counselors working at this level.

These levels are based on the education, experience, and main responsibility of the position that the individual holds. The work assignment, itself, carries considerable weight. For example, a teacher with a master's degree in guidance might be assigned a full teaching load, so that any counseling he did would be done when and if he could find the time. He would be a first-level counselor, in spite of the fact that he might have more training and skill in counseling than anyone else in the school. Bases for these three levels are explained in detail in the following paragraphs.

The First Level of Counseling. At this level are teachers, group workers, advisers, and others who have no special time or responsibility for counseling. They do have, however, interest in and some training and ability in helping individuals solve problems. Referral to specialists may be used frequently. In fact, the ability to detect the need for referral, and skill in making referrals, are two of the most essential competencies of this level.

This level of counseling is particularly important in the school. It is not a question of whether or not teachers can or should counsel—they do it every day. They provide the only sort of counseling that many pupils will receive. Thus it is important that schools ensure that this level is handled effectively.

It is up to the individual counseling at this level to recognize his competencies, to help those with whom he can be effective, and to refer those who have difficulties beyond his level. For example, a student might come to the teacher to express dissatisfaction with his mark. Counseling could involve a discussion of the factors that go to make up the mark. Possibly other matters would come up, such as attitude toward the class, time spent in studying, and so on. Or the student might have a question about the requirements for the college preparatory diploma. The teacher could supply this information. The problem is not deep-seated and there is no personality disturbance. The teacher is able to provide the needed information, and where necessary, assist the student in understanding and accepting it. It may seem that the giving of facts or information only is hardly *counseling*. However, it is difficult to imagine a situation where some feeling about the information is not present, or where there is no need to go beyond the facts and aid the student in determining what they mean for him.

While not every teacher would do counseling, there should be many who provide help at this level. Arbuckle [10, pp. 13–14, 111, 170–172] suggests that teachers may provide counseling, depending upon the sort of teachers they are. Froehlich [77, pp. 203–204] discusses ways of providing counseling in the small school and points out that, while the counselor must be competent to do the job, he may start with simple problems, working on more complex ones as he gains more competence. Shepard [202, pp. 162–164] discusses the counseling activities of faculty counselors and indicates that the college adviser should be able to do a good job of counseling. Ohlsen [163, pp. 65–68] and Willey [261, p. 42] suggest that members of the school staff counsel students. They agree with Roeber and others [180, p. 31] that counseling requires a specialized type of training and that the counselor must be competent.

There is substantial agreement that there is a need for counseling at this level. Many schools, however, appear to have overlooked or slighted it. Much of what is done is probably more harmful than helpful. For example, a pupil was told that he could get excellent marks if he "tried." He was, however, already overachieving to obtain average marks.

Counseling at this first level would usually be limited to brief contacts in whatever time was available. For example, it might be done after school in the classroom, in the shop instructor or vocational teacher's office, during a home visit, or in some other place where privacy could be obtained.

Competencies desirable at this level are discussed in later sections. For successful counseling the teacher needs to have these characteristics and competencies just as do counselors on other levels.

The Second Level of Counseling. One way to identify this second level is by the fact that specific time and responsibility for counseling are provided. The other way is by training which has been described in Refs. [3, 6, 29, 158] and by state certification requirements [209, pp. 239–258; 130, pp. 446–448]. The master's degree is considered to be the desirable level of academic training, with courses in personality, learning, counseling, and guidance as given in detail in Refs. [29, 151, 152, 153, 154, 158]. The type of training has been clearly outlined, but in practice many persons operate at this level without benefit of training. Thus, while it would be desirable for the person designated as the teacher-counselor or counselor in the school to have a master's degree in guidance and other personal qualifications, he may have been appointed to the position with little or no consideration for qualifications.

The second-level counselor in the high school usually has the title of teacher-counselor or guidance counselor [53]. He may have one, two, three, or perhaps more periods for counseling, with responsibility for other activities such as teaching. In many schools there is only one teacher-counselor, who serves as chairman of the guidance committee and director of the guidance program. In other schools there may be several teacher-counselors, each with a period or so a day for individual work.

The teacher-counselor works with pupils directly and aids teachers in helping students. Thus he may do some more or less routine counseling in such things as helping pupils select courses or evaluating educational and vocational plans. He should, however, have time for more lengthy counseling when it is needed. He confers with teachers to enable them to help pupils in their classes and home rooms. He is thus a source of assistance for first-level counselors as well as other teachers. In turn, he makes extensive use of referral to various specialists, for example, third-level counselors, reading specialists, and physicians.

Another responsibility of the second-level counselor is that of providing in-service education to enable teachers to increase their competence in understanding and helping pupils.

Thus the second-level counselor is in a key position in the provision of effective and systematic counseling for all pupils. Upon him rests the responsibility for evaluating the quality of counseling done by teachers, for providing counseling, for making referrals, for helping other staff members assist pupils, and for raising the level of counseling competence in the school through in-service education. He is perhaps the key figure in informing the public about the school guidance program and in building good public relations.

The Third Level of Counseling. This level has been rather clearly defined in recent publications [3, 7, 29]. The third-level counselor should have a doctor's degree in counseling psychology, or in education or psychology with major emphasis in counseling. The publications listed above emphasize the hospital or college counseling center setting. Not much attention is given to the third-level counselor in the high school setting. A counselor of this level, however, should be available as a source of referral and as a supervisor of a guidance system for a city, county, or other large area.

The second-level counselor might work toward this level to increase his competence in dealing with all sorts of problems and to qualify for advancement in the field. A helpful discussion of the requirements are contained in Hahn and MacLean [91, pp. 19–21]. Needed competencies for this level would include all of those for the first and second level plus others described in the references given in this section.

Qualifications of the Counselor

In discussing levels of counseling very little has been said about necessary competencies and personal characteristics of counselors. It seems necessary to point these out now and to indicate sources of more detailed information.

Statements of Counselor Qualifications. What the counselor should know is indicated by the areas covered by a series of reports prepared by the National Association of Guidance Supervisors and Counselor Trainers in 1949. These reports, in booklet form, covered duties, standards, and qualifications of counselors employed in schools, under the following topics: counselor's knowledge of occupational information [152], analysis of the individual [153], and counseling techniques [154]. Several other aspects of counselor training were covered, which indicate the nature of training and duties: administrative aspects of the guidance program [157], in-service education [155, 156], and supervised practice in counseling. About the same time the National Vocational Guidance Association published a manual, *Counselor Preparation* [158], describing a common core for all counselors and indicating special competencies for those who counsel on vocational and educational problems. Representatives of eight organizations concerned with counseling took part in the preparation of this manual. In 1956, a revision of *Counselor Preparation,* designed to set forth the program needed in the preparation of rehabilitation counselors and titled *Rehabilitation Counselor Preparation* [159], was issued by the National Vocational Guidance Association and the National Rehabilitation Association.

A recent statement of levels, and competencies for various levels, is contained in the publication, *Training of Psychological Counselors* [29]. Since the formulating of these policies, there have been further reports on the master's level program in psychology [6], on training at the doctoral level in counseling [3], and on the definition of counseling psychology [7]. A review of these reports will be of assistance in understanding the nature of counseling and the preparation required. Major points from these references are included in the following summary.

Counselor Competencies. It might seem necessary to break the competencies of the teacher and the teacher-counselor down into two levels. However, an attempt to do this would raise the problem of which ones could be left out and which ones should be held in a lesser degree by the lower level. It is suggested that the first-level counselors, that is, teachers who counsel, college advisers, and others, aim at the same types of competencies and to the same degree as the second-level counselors, even though they may have no time set aside for counseling. There seems to be no other solution to this problem unless all those below second-level counselors confine themselves to such things as collecting data on pupils and only the most routine type of program planning help. As a matter of fact, many of the first-level counselors do a great deal of counseling and will continue to do it, good, bad, or indifferent. On the other hand, there are excellent teachers who do not want to counsel pupils, who are not suited for it, and who should not have to do it.

There are *guidance* roles for all teachers which are thoroughly covered in such references as [77, 180, 219]. The following characteristics and competencies are considered to be desirable for the first two levels of counselors:

1. An understanding of one's self. Some insight into one's biases, attitudes, values, in order to be aware of these when helping others.

2. Some understanding of the causes of behavior, how personality develops, how individuals learn, and how they mature.

3. An extensive knowledge of the institutions in the community and of the community itself; for example, the customs in the community, the sources of referral help, the types of occupations and industries, and employment opportunities.

4. A warm, friendly personality, to whom others will come for help and in whom they have confidence. This is quite different from popularity. Furthermore, there does not appear to be a particular type of person who should be a counselor, but rather a variety of types or sorts of people who do a good job in helping others.

5. Finally, competence in counseling and in counselor activities, in order to be aware of just how capable he is, and what he cannot do.

It is worth noting how important most of these competencies and characteristics appear to be for the teacher or group leader who works with others. Of particular importance is the ability to establish a relationship with others as implied in (4) above. An interesting conclusion may be drawn from studies of therapy [69, pp. 296–315], in which experts from different schools of thought were found to be more alike than experts and nonexperts in the same school. Ability to understand the client and interest in helping him were among the characteristics on which expert therapists appeared to be alike. While this type of help (therapy) is different in emphasis from that discussed here, the data do suggest that in the helping situation the relationship between the two persons is of paramount importance.

The five general areas may be broken down into some more specific competencies, as follows:

1. The counselor should be able to provide a friendly, permissive, secure situation in which others will talk freely and react naturally.

2. The counselor should be able to use the results of various tests and inventories. He should either know what the instrument measures and how well it measures it or know where to obtain this information.

3. The counselor should be able to synthesize and interpret the information in the cumulative record.

4. The counselor should be able to gain a better understanding of the student by means of his own writings and reports.

5. The counselor should be able to learn about a student through observation.

6. The counselor should be able to locate, or help the student locate, information about educational and training opportunities, including information about his own school, about colleges, trade schools, on-the-job training, apprenticeship training, and opportunities in the armed forces. He should have access to information about financial aid such as scholarships and loan funds.

7. The counselor should be able to locate occupational information or to refer the student to sources of information. This would also include the ability to interpret this information to him.

8. The counselor should be able to assist the student to locate and use materials that will aid him in understanding himself and his relations with others.

9. The counselor should be able to synthesize the various sorts of information about a student to gain an understanding of him as a person. He should be able to interpret this information to the student to enable him to gain a realistic understanding of himself.

10. The counselor should be able to help others to make decisions and plans, and to assist them in taking responsibility. He should be able to refrain from taking responsibility from others by telling them what to do.

Ethics of Counseling. In discussing the qualifications of the counselor, ethics is an aspect that demands attention. It is particularly important that first- and second-level counselors be aware of the ethics of the counseling profession and apply them in their daily work. The most complete statement of ethical standards may be found in two publications by the American Psychological Association, *Ethical Standards of Psychologists, A Summary of Ethical Principles* [4], and the larger publication, *Ethical Standards of Psychologists* [5]. While these cover the whole field of psychology, they will be profitable reading for those who counsel others. Gluck [83] presented a proposed code of ethics for counselors, drawing from the fields of law, medicine, psychology, and social work. Some of the preliminary policies of the American Psychological Association are included in his report. It is not an official code but is of value to counselors in determining ethical behavior. A particularly helpful discussion of ethical problems, including those of the high school counselor, are contained in an article by Schwebel [195]. Wrenn also provides a statement of ethics particularly designed for counselors [265]. In Ref. [151, pp. 5–6] there is a code of ethics for counselors.

A review of these references will be of particular value to the counselor in formulating a code for self-guidance. Since a brief summary of these proposals would not do justice to them, the reader is referred to the original sources.

Professional Organizations

The person who is interested in counseling will find rewarding experiences in professional organizations for counselors through meetings and publications. The two most directly concerned with counseling are the American Personnel and Guidance Association and the American Psychological Association.

The American Personnel and Guidance Association. Membership in this organization entitles the counselor to receive the *American Personnel and Guidance Journal*. There are also five divisions in this organization which the counselor may join according to his special interest. They are

American College Personnel Association
National Association of Guidance Supervisors and Counselor Trainers
National Vocational Guidance Association (members of this division receive
   the *Vocational Guidance Quarterly*)
Student Personnel Association for Teacher Education
American School Counselors' Association

High school counselors will probably find the National Vocational Guidance Association and the American School Counselors' Association of most value and interest to them. There are several levels of membership. Information about membership and other details may be obtained by writing to the American Personnel and Guidance Association, Washington, D.C.

There are branches of the American Personnel and Guidance Association or one or more of the divisions in most states which offer local membership and participation. The counselor may obtain information about branches in his state by writing to the American Personnel and Guidance Association.

The American Psychological Association. Division 17, Counseling Psychology, is of particular interest to counselors. Other divisions which are related to the work of the school counselor are Division 5, Evaluation and Measurement, and Division 16, School Psychologists. While the membership requirements are high compared with those of other similar organizations, many school counselors may wish to qualify for membership in this organization. Further information may be obtained by writing to the American Psychological Association, Washington, D.C.

In addition to the publications of the above organizations, there are two journals of particular value to the counselor in keeping up with developments in the field. They are the *Journal of Counseling Psychology* [115] and *Educational and Psychological Measurement* [63]. Further information may be obtained from the publishers.

SUMMARY

Counseling is an understandable and describable process in which an individual is helped to solve problems and develop optimally. The process is flexible and adapted to the counselee's needs. The counselor works with relatively normal persons and refers to others those in need of specialized help such as therapy. Problems are unique and complex rather than easily categorized. In providing individual help there is a need for counseling by the teacher as well as for that done by specialized personnel such as the teacher-counselor. There are, however, certain competencies and characteristics which should be held by all who counsel.

CHECKS ON UNDERSTANDING

1. See if you can put in your own words the meaning of the terms counseling, guidance, testing, and occupational information.

2. Can you identify critical differences between teaching and counseling? Why may an effective teacher not be a competent counselor?

3. Describe the counseling process. What is emphasized at each stage? What is the trend as to counselee responsibility?

4. What are necessary competencies and characteristics of any person who counsels in a school setting?

THINGS TO DO

1. Talk to several teachers, group leaders, and others, and ask them what kinds of problems students bring to them. Find out what they do to help these students.

2. Ask several students if they know what kind of occupation they prefer. If they have a choice, ask what reasons they have for their choice.

3. Find out what several persons in various types of work think counseling is. For example, question teachers, businessmen, service workers, craftsmen, personnel workers, or ministers.

4. Look through several newspapers and magazines for "advice" articles or columns. Note ways of "helping" people to solve problems. Is this counseling?

5. Ask several school patrons if they think the school should provide help to students in such things as selecting a vocation, gaining self-confidence, and the like.

6. Read in the following references to learn about other counseling approaches and to broaden your understanding of counseling: Bordin [30], Brayfield [32], Colby [48], Hamrin and Paulson [94], McKinney [131], Pepinsky and Pepinsky [168], Perry and Estes [171, pp. 95–119], Robinson [177], Rogers [182, 183, 184], Sanderson [192], Shostrom and Brammer [206], Tyler [240], Williamson [264], and others given in this chapter.

Many schools have a person designated as counselor or teacher-counselor. The counselor should be the type of person to whom others go for help.

The counselor should be informed in a variety of subjects. Although he is probably not a trained psychologist, he should have a thorough understanding of human behavior. Since some of the problems brought to his attention will be severe emotional ones, which he is not equipped and should not be expected to handle, he should be able to recognize them quickly. He should also be familiar with the community facilities, such as the church and guidance clinic, to which he can refer such problems.

The counselor should know the requirements for entrance to institutions of higher learning. He should also be aware of the job opportunities both in and outside his community, and the training and abilities necessary for the various occupations. In his office he should maintain an up-to-date and readily accessible file of college catalogs and vocational-information bulletins. He should realize, however, that without skilled interpretation this information could well be confusing to the student.

It it particularly important that the counselor of high school students understand the problems of the adolescent. Many of these involve the school, which is usually the center of both social and academic development. Since failure in one area can affect the student's progress in the other, the counselor should observe both aspects of student life closely. If his duties do not include classroom teaching, he should make arrangements occasionally to sit in on classes.

CHAPTER 2

Beginning the Counseling Process

As has been pointed out, early emphasis in the counseling process is on learning about the counselee, discovering what he thinks, what he wants to do, and what he considers his problems to be. This is true whether counseling consists of one contact or many. Later on, the emphasis shifts to planning and decision making, but some characteristics of the counseling relationship such as warmth, acceptance, and respect for the individual are maintained.

In taking up this phase of counseling, examples of interviews will be presented, followed in the next chapters by principles and ways of improving the interview. Several general characteristics of the initial phase are given here; more detailed discussion is given, with illustrations, in later sections.

Characteristics of the Initial Phase

The counselor assists the counselee to bring out facts, feelings, and attitudes about himself, his relations with others, his goals, needs, and problems. The counselor strives to see things as the counselee sees them and to obtain complete enough information to understand him as a person. He searches for patterns and trends of behavior, factors affecting goals and needs, and areas of conflict, frustration, and lack of information. The counselor and counselee are both learning in this process, rather than the counselor merely collecting evidence to make his own "diagnosis." It is, further, a warm, friendly, permissive relationship, with the center of attention on the counselee's problems and questions. Gaps in information already obtained, if some has been obtained, are filled in wherever possible. Promising clues, better checked on by other techniques, are noted for later investigation. The early phase is a purposeful and dynamic process in which the two participants examine aspects of the counselee's life in an atmosphere free from tension and pressure. The counselor sets the broad limits, but within these limits the counselee is free to do as he pleases.

There is no specific point where information getting ceases and planning begins. There may be alternating from information getting to planning and back again. For example, as the counselee discusses his problems and his relations with others, he may begin to gain new understandings about himself, may make tentative decisions about what he will do, and may actually solve some of his problems. Then more information may be needed to enable him to evaluate his solutions and to begin to work out other problems. One or more sessions may be devoted to information-getting procedures. While only one such session is presented in the illustrative material, more than one would often be used in actual practice. The needs of the counselee and the progress made in obtaining information govern the amount of time used for information getting.

Additional reading about the early phase of counseling is recommended. A number of very helpful references are available. Erickson [66, chs. 3, 4] presents a list of suggestions for the counselor to follow and specific helps to get the interview started. Garrett [80, ch. 7] presents a summary of techniques with illustrations. Hahn and MacLean [91, ch. 10] give a running account of a counseling interview. Pepinsky and Pepinsky [168, pp. 171–191] describe the characteristics of the initial contacts, with emphasis on the counselee-counselor relationship. The need for obtaining data outside of the counseling session is also discussed. Many sections in Porter [173] will be helpful, but the examples and discussions in Chapter 5 should be particularly useful. Robinson [177] covers aspects of the early phase in various sections, including a helpful discussion of dimensions and techniques in Chapter 4. Emphasis in Rothney [187] is on interpretation of data but he gives an example of the interview and a helpful discussion of techniques. Shostrom and Brammer [206] discuss and illustrate techniques employed in the initial phases. Strang [218] discusses various types of interviews and different schools of thought on the interview. A helpful discussion of the process is included. The discussion of the early phase in Tyler [240, ch. 2; 241] will be of definite value to the counselor in training as well as the experienced counselor. The discussion of principles and techniques in Warters [253] should also prove to be helpful reading, as it includes a comparison and synthesis of schools of thought. A transcribed interview from Williamson [264] is provided. Steps in counseling are discussed, including the initial phase in which emphasis is placed on the obtaining of information.

To illustrate the early phase, the counselor's work with a counselee, Bill Smith, will now be described.

Bill Smith arrives at the counselor's office at the scheduled time for his first appointment. The counselor invites him in and asks him to have a chair. He knows very little about Bill except what he has learned from a survey of his partially filled in cumulative record and from talks with several of his teachers. The extent of his information so far is that Bill is in good health, has participated in a few activities, is making below-average marks, and is considered by his teachers to be rather uncooperative.

Upon the counselor's invitation to tell why he came in, Bill explains that he wants to change his mathematics section. He states very positively, "That teacher has it in for me!" The counselor accepts these feelings and encourages Bill to tell about his relations with the mathematics teacher and his other teachers. Bill is rather surprised at how freely he can talk to a "teacher" about other teachers, and his built-up resentment begins to lessen. He finds that he does not have to be on the defensive in talking with the counselor.

As the interview progresses, the counselor suggests that Bill talk about his plans, how he feels about schoolwork in general, his home life, and so on. It becomes apparent to the counselor (and to some extent to Bill) that lessons are given a "lick and a promise" and that tests are prepared for by frantic last-minute cramming. Further discussion brings out more evidence to indicate very poor study habits. Conditions such as a new television set, a room shared with a little brother, and no suitable place to study at home begin to assume importance as distracting factors. The center of attention shifts from Bill's math teacher to home conditions and habits that give Bill difficulty in preparing his lessons. Bill, however, still wants to blame his teacher. The counselor accepts this need to shift personal faults to others. At the same time Bill feels enough freedom and security in this accepting atmosphere to admit that perhaps he does not do a good job of preparing his work—an admission that he could not make to his parents or to other teachers. He finds, too, that he has never actually questioned why he is taking the courses he is now in, or just how much ability he actually has.

Bill then asks for help on these new problems—vocational choice and estimation of ability—and also wants to know what he can do about study habits. The counselor suggests that further information be obtained, such as a record of just how Bill spends his time. Activities to improve study methods are suggested; another counseling appointment is made. The counselor has noted several areas about which he wishes to obtain additional information; these include how Bill uses his time, how he compares with other students on mental ability, and more about his interests and aptitudes. Additional interviews and other information-getting techniques will be used to obtain the needed information.

While this session has emphasized information getting, some planning has taken place. However, additional information must be obtained before the counselor and counselee are ready to move to more intensive planning and decision making.

To illustrate further just what takes place in the early phases of counseling, a more complete description of a counselee, together with his first interview with the counselor, will now be presented.

A Typical Pupil

In Chapter 1 the problems of a number of pupils were discussed briefly. Each pupil was in need of counseling. In this section is presented a young fellow who has a few problems not unlike those which they had. For this average counselee the name John Doe will be used. John might be described as a typical high school boy. He is not unduly bothered by emotional problems; he has no physical handicaps; he is neither unusually bright nor unusually dull. In these and other ways he is about "average." He is the sort of pupil who make up the large middle or average group in our high schools. This group should receive counseling; in fact, they should be given most of the counselor's time. In practice, however, they often get very little attention.

The following paragraphs will tell something about John as an individual, how others react to him, and how he gets along with them. There is also some general information about his home situation, the school that he attends, the guidance service that the school provides, and the community in which he lives.

This information is not, of course, all that the counselor needs to know about John to counsel him. It is the general information that he would probably know if he had been a teacher or teacher-counselor in the school for several years. In fact, he could do very little counseling with only this information. The purpose of presenting it here is to give the setting and background for the illustrative counseling case that will be used with the discussion of the various counseling techniques. As counseling progresses, it becomes apparent that much more detailed and precise information is needed about the counselee and about the problems which he presents. The counselor particularly needs to know John's attitudes and reactions to himself as he is, and to the conditions of his home, school, and community. (It will be helpful at this point to look over case studies, such as those in White [259], for gaining an understanding of the extent of background information that is desirable.) It is assumed that the counselor already knows the information that is given here.

John as a Person. John is a sandy-haired, freckle-faced, high school junior, seventeen years of age. He is a friendly young fellow, and others say that he has a good disposition. While he is somewhat of a "wit" in the classroom, he seems to be rather shy when alone in the presence of adults, particularly teachers. He seems to be well liked by his classmates. The indications are that he gets along well with girls. Several of them admit that they think he is "cute." He attends the school parties and dances, and usually goes with a group and takes a date.

John gives the impression of being even-tempered and of being a person who would go out of his way to avoid an argument. He wants people to like him and is more concerned about approval of classmates and other peers than that of teachers. But he does offer to do odd jobs and errands for teachers and is not called an "apple polisher" for it. He dresses very much the same as the other boys. To look at him, you would not notice anything that would make him appear distinctive or different.

While our counselee is not a particularly large or strong boy, he is active, likes sports, and plays a good game of baseball. He was awarded a letter last year, as he played in the required number of games. However, he spends most of his time on the bench. Baseball is his main interest, but he also goes out for football and basketball. He is on the staff of the school paper but has not shown much interest in writing.

School marks are about average, with Latin being the lowest. John is taking the college preparatory course and states that he plans to go to college. He does not express any particular interest in school subjects and says that he thinks the teachers "work you too hard."

Work experience consists of several part-time jobs during afternoons, Saturdays, and in the summer. Most of the work has been in the stockroom or serving as a clerk in one of the chain grocery stores in town. He has done satisfactory work and his employers say that he is dependable and learns quickly.

From what we know about John, he does not appear to be particularly strong in any academic area or to have any special abilities or aptitudes. Nor does he appear to have any particular weaknesses or problems.

His Home and Family. The Doe family live in a six-room, one and one-half story frame house several blocks from school in a modest, well-kept neighborhood. Mr. Doe is a carpenter who manages to find steady work and who earns enough to have completed paying for his home, to furnish some luxuries and recreation (trips, television) for his family, and to own a five-year-old, low-priced secondhand car. He finished the eighth grade and says that he ought to have had more education. However, he declares that what he had in school has not been much use to him. He learned the carpenter's trade from an uncle. Some day he hopes to have several others working for him so that he can do some "contracting." People for whom he has worked describe him as a "good" carpenter, although they think he is a little slow and too determined to do things his own way.

Mrs. Doe, aged thirty-seven, has never worked outside the home. She married as soon as she graduated from high school. She says that she thinks her place is in the home, ". . . while the children are growing up." She does, however, belong to several women's clubs, such as the Fireman's Auxiliary, and is usually in charge of the refreshment committee as cooking is her specialty. She has very positive feelings about some things, such as education. She declares a "good education" is necessary to "get on in this world." She does not hesitate to tell her husband that he could "get ahead with more schooling," and points out his grammatical lapses such as "It ain't no use doin' that." These he accepts without apparent irritation, saying, "We didn't have none of that in school." Both parents get along well and while they have the usual little disputes and arguments, they seem to have real affection for each other and the children, and pride in the home.

Jane Doe is the only other child. She is an attractive young girl, aged fifteen, who is a freshman in the high school. Active in several clubs and often a leader, she takes school work seriously and has made excellent marks for the past several years. It would be easy for her to "outshine" John and for unfortunate comparisons to be made by teachers and parents; however, there is only friendly rivalry between them. John says that she is the "brains" in the family. In spite of her ability and achievement, the Does think it more important for the boy in the family to have the advantage of advanced education as he is the one who will have to earn a living. They expect Jane to "get married and settle down."

His School. Hometown High School, which John attends, has 435 pupils and eighteen teachers, including the principal, the coach, and the vocational agriculture teacher. The school building is crowded and it has been necessary to partition off the back end of the auditorium for classrooms. The coach teaches three periods a day and the principal has a senior mathematics class. Each teacher has five classes a day and one period for supervising a study hall or directing some activity. One teacher has three periods a day for counseling, and has the title of Guidance Director and Counselor. Three other teachers have one period a day for counseling. Most of the teachers are responsible for a home room.

The principal is interested in improving the total guidance service of the school. The present counseling service was just started last year. The guidance director, Mr. Doyle, who has had some training and experience in guidance, was brought to the school to organize and promote guidance. He has worked hard at building up good relations with other staff members and has been rather successful in getting their cooperation, in spite of some resentment because he was an "outsider" brought in for a special purpose and because guidance was looked upon as an "easy job" for some deserving member of the staff. Most of Mr. Doyle's guidance activity so far has been devoted to encouraging and helping teachers bring cumulative records up to date and to counseling with pupils who request it. He has also helped teachers with particular pupils and has organized some case conferences that have aroused considerable

interest in the guidance program and in pupils' problems. He has not neg·
lected to tell parents, by way of the PTA and service clubs, what the guidance
service aims to do. He hopes in time to reduce the pupil-counselor ratio which,
although it is now about seventy pupils per counseling hour per day, is better
than that in many schools. He also hopes to do something about the home-
room programs (or lack of them). At present, this period is used primarily for
checking the roll and for "supervised study."

Hometown High School offers the following courses: general, academic,
commercial, home economics, and vocational agriculture. Those planning to go
to college—usually about 8 to 12 per cent of the graduating class—take the
academic course, as do a number of others who have some rather vague plans
about "going away to school." A large number of girls take the home economics
course and about forty boys are in the vocational agriculture department. A
few boys and girls take the commercial course, and the remaining group take
the general course. There are not enough employment opportunities locally
for those who take the commercial course, nor do all the boys in vocational
agriculture have farming opportunities. There has been some talk about insti-
tuting diversified occupations and distributive education programs but there
are no immediate plans to do this. Dropouts, while still rather sizable as to
total number, have been reduced somewhat in the past few years.

His Community. Hometown is the only town of any size in a predominantly
farming county. Much of the business consists of retail trade to local inhab-
itants. There are the usual number of professional people, merchandisers, and
skilled workers. There is little turnover among these people except through
retirement or death. As a result there are a limited number of vocational opportunities for the young people of the town.

There are several small industrial plants in the town that provide some jobs
in semiskilled and unskilled work in woodworking and textiles. Since jobs may
be easily obtained and since a high school education is not required, students
often drop out the first or second year of high school to take jobs. Those who
want to learn a trade, such as carpenter, plumber, electrician, usually do so by
working as a helper if they can find the opportunity.

The Counselor Interviews John Doe

Mr. Doyle, the teacher-counselor at Hometown High School, is in the counselor's office that has been fixed for use by him and the other counselors.
While many of his interviews have been scheduled ahead of time, allowing
him to check the cumulative and other records, John arrives at the office without any previous request for help.

It is suggested that you look over the following questions before reading the
interview. Keep them in mind as you read it. After completing the reading,
recheck them.

1. How did the counselor open the interview? Would some other way have been more effective?

2. How did the counselor keep the interview going after the counselee had stated his problem?

3. How did the counselor respond to the counselee's request to be told what to do?

4. How did the counselor demonstrate acceptance of the counselee?

5. How did the counselor avoid taking sides on the problem of the use of the family automobile?

6. What areas of the counselee's life are covered in the interview, for example, home situation, educational experiences?

7. How did the counselor handle the situation when the counselee was attempting to get agreement and approval for his ideas?

8. How did the counselor explain the purpose of counseling to the counselee?

9. How did the counselor explain the use of tests to the counselee?

10. How did the counselor close the interview?

The Interview. When John entered the counseling room, Mr. Doyle put down the notes he was working on and began the interview as follows:

MR. DOYLE: Hello, John. How's everything going with you?

JOHN: Oh, pretty good, . . . I guess. . . . Er . . . you busy? I mean, I. . . .

MR. DOYLE: No, not at all. Come on in.

JOHN: Well, I have a study hall this period. . . . I have permission, . . . that is, Miss Brown knows where I am. I guess you're busy. . . .

MR. DOYLE: Not too busy to talk to you, John. That's what I'm here for. Here, have a seat here. (*Indicates chair by the side of the desk.*)

JOHN: Well, . . . you know, I've been talking to Bill Sampson—he said he talked to you and took a test and found out what he should do. . . . Well, I'm trying to decide now. What I mean is, I'm going to college, you know. Mother wants me to—she's all for it. She wants me to be a doctor or something like that—a professional man. Well, Dad, he says it costs a lot, and anyway a high school education's a lot more than he had, and a fellow can get almost any kind of a job if he's finished high school. . . . Well, that's it. That's my problem.

MR. DOYLE: Would you like to tell me a little more about it?

JOHN: That's all there is. So if I could take that test. . . .

MR. DOYLE: Well, tests can be helpful in assisting you to . . . well, compare yourself with others on some abilities and interests, and so on, but they don't give final answers, don't tell you what to do. There are other things about you that are equally important, you see. Maybe I can help you to know yourself and to know about some of the kinds of things there are to do . . . courses in school, jobs, so that you'll be able to make plans. Tests add only a piece of this information.

JOHN: Oh. Well, what do you want to know? I mean, I've told you about everything. . . .

MR. DOYLE: Well, suppose we talk about plans, what you want to do.

JOHN: My plans. . . . I want to go to college. That's the thing. You have to go to college today.

MR. DOYLE: How can I help you?

JOHN: I want you to tell me what I should take up in college. I should decide soon.

MR. DOYLE: The thing you want to know is the college course that's best for you?

JOHN: Yeah. That's it.

MR. DOYLE: Uh huh.

JOHN: I want to know. . . . A fellow can make a mistake.

MR. DOYLE: A bad choice might cause a lot of trouble?

JOHN: Yeah. You see, my sister Jane, she's in the first year. She's always gotten good grades, but she . . . she studies a lot. Sometimes Mother says, "John, just look at this paper of Jane's—A's, and what did you get on that paper of yours— a C!" I get sort of sore, but I don't do any better.

MR. DOYLE: Being compared with your sister doesn't please you too much.

JOHN: No! Well, mother means well, but she just don't understand that some subjects are not so interesting to boys. I can't see much point in studying some of the subjects we have. I'd rather be doing something.

MR. DOYLE: Just what kinds of things do you like to do?

JOHN: About everything except reading a lot. I like some reading, like *Life* or *True Westerns,* but I don't guess the English teacher would call that literature. I like baseball—I don't know whether I'll make the squad, but I like it. I went out last spring. Then I like to swim in the summer, and I helped the lifeguard at the pool last summer.

MR. DOYLE: Uh huh.

JOHN: I used to build models—you know, boats, cars, stuff like that. I don't do that now. Used to save stamps but I quit. I guess you do what others are doing. Now it's dates—some of us usually go around to a girl's house . . . that probably hasn't got anything to do with what I should do.

MR. DOYLE: The things that you think are important and that tell about what kind of a fellow you are are the ones that are important here. The better I know you, the better chance I'll have to help you make plans.

JOHN: Well, we just sit around, or go to the movies or go skating. But sometimes I don't go. . . . Well, I have trouble at home about the car. The other fellows get a car, and when it's my time I can't have the car. Don't you think a fellow my age should be able to drive the family car once in a while?

MR. DOYLE: You and your family don't agree on the use of the car?

JOHN: Yeah. Now my mother says that I should have it, but Dad, he says that I'm not old enough. Maybe if you talked to him about it? . . .

MR. DOYLE: Well, that may be something that you will have to work out with your family?

JOHN: Well, maybe. I'm old enough, I think, to have a voice in things. I'm old enough to make my own money!

MR. DOYLE: Uh huh. . . . Would you like to tell me a little about your work—the things you've done and what you thought about them?

JOHN: Sure. I delivered papers for a couple of years. Let's see—when I was twelve

I got a bicycle, secondhand. This took a couple of hours each afternoon. It was all right. I made about eight dollars a week. I saved half of that—I got my own bank account. Then when I was fifteen I started working afternoons and Saturdays in the Big Chain Grocery Store. I did that all year when I was a freshman, then all last year, and I'm doing it this year too.

MR. DOYLE: Uh huh.

JOHN: Well, . . . that's all.

MR. DOYLE: This grocery store work. What do you think about it?

JOHN: What do I think about it? Oh, it's all right. I don't make much—about fifteen dollars a week. You mean as a permanent job? Not that! I'm going to college. Anyway, I don't know of any full-time jobs. But I would think the manager has a good job. Yeah, I guess I'd like to be a manager. But a clerk! My uncle is a clerk in Joe's Hardware Store, and Mother says, "Look at Uncle Ed—a clerk! You don't want to be just a clerk!"

MR. DOYLE: Your mother doesn't think so much of a store clerk for you.

JOHN: No! But then a clerk has a fairly good deal. I mean it's sort of an interesting job where you see everybody and when five o'clock comes you're through, except for inventories, but that's not every night. Even the manager doesn't have to study all night like I do.

MR. DOYLE: It does have some pretty good features at that.

JOHN: Sure. Now my father would say that you make forty a week as a clerk and that's good pay. Well, he makes fifteen a day when he works but he only works off and on in the winter. If you worked steady that would be a good deal, but Father says, "You don't want to do this. Get something steady!" I don't think he thinks so much of his work.

MR. DOYLE: How do you feel about that kind of work?

JOHN: I've never thought about it. But if you asked me if I wanted to do it, I'd say no. It looks monotonous, and when I've helped a little on some jobs, I got tired of it quick. Too much measuring and sawing and stuff like that, and I never had much interest in tools.

MR. DOYLE: John, what kinds of things do you like to do best—along work lines?

JOHN: I don't know exactly. Like I told you, I helped the lifeguard at the pool last summer—didn't make much, but I had a lot of fun. Sometimes I was in charge of the checkroom. That was a lot of responsibility. I got my Red Cross lifesaving, too, so I could act as guard sometimes. Well, that was all right. Uh, yeah, that was something I liked a lot. Here at school . . . I wanted to get on the paper until I tried to write up a PTA meeting. Well, I didn't like that, but then I got put on the job of selling ads. I liked that a lot. I've been doing that, and then I see the printer to get the paper printed. But I don't like that writing. I rewrote the thing about six times, and then Miss Wilson changed it all around.

MR. DOYLE: How about other school activities? Are there any others that have appealed to you?

JOHN: Well, I told you about baseball. I hope to make the team this year. I'll have to quit work except Saturday. There aren't any other things. . . . I went to a science club meeting a few times. . . .

MR. DOYLE: Uh huh . . . what did you think of that?

JOHN: Oh, it was all right. I haven't been lately.

MR. DOYLE: Let's see. I suppose you take chemistry now?

JOHN: Yeah. It's terrible.

MR. DOYLE: Pretty bad, eh?

JOHN: It's the worst. I don't know whether I'll pass it. That and math. They're over my head. I just don't study them, I guess. They're needed for college or I wouldn't take them. Sometimes I don't know if this academic course is for me.

MR. DOYLE: Have you found any courses that particularly interest you—taken or heard about?

JOHN: History . . . civics, wasn't so bad. Maybe the teacher was easy. Then I heard some of the girls talking about the course in economics. They were griping but it sounded like it would be good if a fellow was going to start a business for himself. Now, a business like that would be good. I've thought that I'd like to have a business of my own. I've got a cousin who started a filling station in Cornerville, and he's got a new Buick now. So he must be making money. I thought I might go in with him and learn the business. Mother don't think so much of it, I don't think.

MR. DOYLE: It seems like a good thing but your mother isn't for it.

JOHN: No. She's not for a lot of things. I guess I ought to be able to say what I'm going to do. Anyway I'll probably be drafted in a couple of years. I think I'll join the Navy before that. They teach you something. I can hear what Mom will say now, but Dad says it'll be good for me.

MR. DOYLE: You're the one who will have to do the deciding, about what you're going to do?

JOHN: Yeah. Now Jane wants to be a nurse. Nobody says anything to her—she just makes up her own mind. She's pretty smart—she'd probably do better than me in college or something.

MR. DOYLE: Your sister is pretty well decided on her future plans?

JOHN: She sure is. I wish I could decide like that. Maybe there's something wrong with me. I just don't seem to be able to make up my mind at all. If I go to college what will I take? You have to decide, don't you? You don't just go in and say, "I'm going to college." I guess you've never talked to anybody who was so confused.

MR. DOYLE: Right now it's pretty hard to make up your mind.

JOHN: Pretty hard! It's impossible. With Mother telling me I should be a doctor or a lawyer, and Dad saying that I ought to be ready for work when I finish high school, and the draft. Well, I'm just in a fog!

MR. DOYLE: Hmmm. . . .

JOHN: You know that guidance day, last month, when all the people spoke on different jobs? Well, I listened to all the speeches, and they all sounded good. When I heard Mr. Smith from the bank, I thought I liked that. Then I heard the fellow from the telephone company and I thought I liked that. It sounded like each one was trying to make his work sound best. Then I went to some of the interviews and talked to some of the college people. I found out that you have to go to college eight years to be a doctor. I'd be an old man when I finished! Eight years!

MR. DOYLE: That seemed like a lot of time?

JOHN: A lot of time is right! Then I asked if there were some courses that took only four years. He—this fellow from State U—said that you could take a liberal arts course, whatever that is. But it don't make you ready for a job. I want to be ready for a special job when I finish. Like a doctor—a doctor knows what he is supposed to do.

MR. DOYLE: You'd like it better if you were preparing for a specific job, with some definite thing you could do?

JOHN: Something definite. Now suppose I was going to be a carpenter like my father. Well, if I was a carpenter, I'd know what I'd do. Or if I took training to be a pilot I'd know I'd do that. But just to take training or go to college, and when you come out where are you? . . . Then too, I don't want to spend my whole life studying. I want to make some money. I don't expect to be a millionaire. I think a fellow should do something he likes, but he's got to make some money too.

MR. DOYLE: The money is important too, as well as what you like to do?

JOHN: Uh . . . yeah. Don't you think so? You don't work for nothing. Isn't that right!

MR. DOYLE: You're wondering whether or not I agree with these things you think important?

JOHN: Well, maybe you do. You know about these things. You could tell me if I'm on the right track. Am I right?

MR. DOYLE: The important thing is what you think about it. Talking about it here will give you a chance to take a look at your ideas. But my answers wouldn't be yours, and you're the one who has to make the final decisions.

JOHN: Uh huh.

MR. DOYLE: What we've talked about so far are things that all fit into the picture. All of these things are important—if they are important to you—and enter into this business of planning what you're going to do—what plans you make. I feel that I can help you most by helping you to make your own decisions.

JOHN: You mean I'm going to have to decide for myself? Uh . . . I thought I could take a test and then you could tell me what I should do. You could tell me the best thing. Then I would know what to take in college.

MR. DOYLE: As I said, the tests, if you want to take some type and feel that it will help add information that we don't have about you, will just be a part of the picture. But other things, hobbies, work experience, things you want to do, what you want out of life, all these things are important too.

JOHN: Well, maybe we'll find that a test will help. You tell me if it would.

MR. DOYLE: Perhaps you've already taken some tests. I haven't looked at your records so I don't know whether you've taken any recently. You probably had one type when you were in the freshman class. Then, if there are things that you and I together think we can get from tests, we'll talk over that and decide on which kinds might be helpful.

JOHN: You mean there's more than one kind?

MR. DOYLE: Yes, there are several general types. In the first place there are the ones that allow you to compare your learning or problem-solving ability with that of others in the same group you're in. Then there are some that help you to see how your special aptitudes or abilities compare with those of others in work or training that calls for those aptitudes. Then there are some that try to get at the amount of learning you've picked up, for example, in a school subject. Also, some allow you to express your interests in various types of work or other activities so you can see how you compare with other people. Finally, some tests or questionnaires get at your attitudes toward other people—what you think about things and how you react to situations.

JOHN: That's quite a few. Sounds like I should have all of them.

MR. DOYLE: Suppose we talk about that after I've had a chance to look over your record a little more. How does that suit you?

JOHN: That's OK with me. When can I come back and see you?

MR. DOYLE: Let's see. I have several appointments this week, but I have next Monday open at two o'clock. If you want to, I'll see you then, and we'll talk a little more about your plans, and if tests will help. If we decide on it, you might take whatever we decide on then.

JOHN: That suits me. I want to get started.

MR. DOYLE: Well, . . . anything you've thought of that you'd like to bring up before we stop, or any questions that you'd like to ask?

JOHN: No, I don't think so. We seem to have covered just about everything. I sure hope I can get something settled on this. I'm pretty confused right now.

MR. DOYLE: We'll see. I certainly hope so too. Next Monday at two?

JOHN: OK. Good-by.

Principles Illustrated

In the following chapters, principles of counseling are discussed in detail. However, numerous illustrations of principles in action are contained in the typescript. A brief statement of the principles, together with specific illustrations, is given below. How well did the counselor apply each of these principles?

1. Showing the counselee that he is the center of attention in the interview and that his problems are important and worth considering

"Not too busy to talk to you, John. That's what I'm here for. Here, have a seat here."

2. Acceptance of the counselee and his feelings and attitudes

"A bad choice might cause a lot of trouble?"
"Being compared with your sister doesn't please you too much."
"Pretty bad, eh?"

3. Explaining the nature of the counseling, that is, structuring the situation, so that the counselee will know what to expect and what not to expect

"The important thing is what you think about it. Talking about it here will give you a chance to take a look at your ideas. But my answers wouldn't be yours, and you're the one who has to make the final decision."

4. Helping the counselee tell his own story in his own way

"Would you like to tell me a little more about it?"
"Uh huh."
"Would you like to tell me a little about your work—the things you've done and what you thought about them?"

5. Ending the interview smoothly and having the counselee leave feeling good about it

"Suppose we talk about that after I've had a chance to look over your record a little more. How does that suit you?"
"Well, . . . anything you've thought of that you'd like to bring up before we stop, or any questions that you'd like to ask?"

Additional Information Needed

Since Mr. Doyle had not looked over John's cumulative record before the interview he will do this as a matter of course. However, after his talk with John he looked at his notes and added some particular bits of information that he wished to obtain. The following items are those he noted down as John was talking and after the interview. He will endeavor to obtain more information about them, either from records, by the use of other techniques for studying the individual, or by additional counseling sessions. The comments in quotation marks are what John said, and the questions in parentheses are what Mr. Doyle noted down to check.

1. ". . . and what did you get . . . a C!" (What are actual marks?)

2. In answer to questions about vocational interests, John says, "I don't know exactly." (How about attempting to measure vocational interest?)

3. John says about his mother, "She's not for a lot of things. I guess I ought to be able to say what I'm going to do." (Need for more information about the home situation and John's attitudes toward parents.)

4. "Then too, I don't want to spend my whole life studying. I want to make some money." (What about values?)

5. "Sometimes I don't know if this academic course is for me." (How well does John compare with high school and college students in academic ability?)

6. "I guess you do what others are doing." (How does John get along with peers? Any leadership qualities?)

7. In answer to the question about what he likes to do, John says, "Just about everything except reading a lot." (What have been his interests up to now? Any consistency in these interests?)

8. "I can't see much point in studying some of the subjects we have." (What do teachers think about John as to drive, interest, work habits?)

9. "I just don't study them, I guess." (How much time does John actually put on studying? How effectively does he use his time?)

10. "So if I could take that test." (Check on tests already taken, if any.)

11. "You know that guidance day, last month. . . . Well, I listened to all the speeches, and they all sounded good." (How about checking aptitudes in several areas?)

The counselee's comments above do not represent the only ones that suggest that more information was needed. They are given as samples of what Mr. Doyle felt would be fruitful avenues for further investigation. There are a number of ways Mr. Doyle could go about finding answers to the above questions. Some of the more commonly used techniques that the counselor may employ are taken up in later chapters. Notice that, up to this point, the counselor has been slow to make definite inferences from the information. He has, however, raised questions that suggest that he is thinking along certain lines, for example, how much time does John put on study? He has thus been making some very tentative inferences and interpretations and has been doing some early synthesizing. The process of synthesis goes on continuously as new information is collected, but it receives more emphasis later on.

Practice in Interviewing and Interpreting Data

The materials presented in this chapter may be used for practice in ways that are discussed below. Other materials, listed in the following paragraphs, may also be used.

Using Case Studies to Determine Further Information Needed. There are several very useful instruments available for practice in interpreting information, determining what further information is needed, and planning ways to help the counselee. Some of these are *The Case of Mickey Murphy* [16], *A Study of Barry Black* [103], *A Study of Connie Casey* [104], and *A Study of Sam Smith* [105]. While they do not contain verbatim counseling sessions, they give the counselor practice in making judgments on the basis of progressively more complete data about the individual. They are useful in connection with this chapter and throughout the book. Two others, of a different type, are also quite helpful for practice. *Paul, A Case Study Unit* [55] and *Charles, A Case Study Unit* [59] present all the available information first and then provide for counselor judgments.

Practice in Counseling. While counseling skill is best learned in actual work with counselees, practice in role-playing situations is helpful in acquiring skill in techniques and in getting the "feeling" of the counseling situation. Reading the typescript aloud will help you to get the feel of the interview and to put yourself in the place of the counselor. You may also evaluate the counselor's responses by asking yourself such questions as, "Is this the best way to help the counselee?" "What would I have done in this instance?" Also, using the same questions, read other interviews, such as those in Refs. [10, 39, 94, 173, 182, 183, 187, 206, 264].

Another procedure that should prove helpful is to read the interview with someone taking the part of the counselee. Imagine that you are the counselor. Have your "counselee" criticize your effectiveness in this role.

A still further type of practice is to record either your reading aloud or the two-part interview. Play it back and note how effective you sound. Particularly observe such things as the degree of interest, feeling, and friendliness expressed by your voice. Ask yourself if you would like to be interviewed by someone who sounds as you do.

SUMMARY

The information-getting phase of counseling has been illustrated with a type-script of the first session with a counselee. This interview, as well as other similar material, may be used in various ways to develop counseling competence. While practice in actual interviewing is the best way to gain competence, role playing offers a "safe" way to develop skills and attitudes. From the interview, the counselor detects clues as to further information needed. This information may be collected by further counseling sessions or by counselor activities.

CHECKS ON UNDERSTANDING

1. Did John Doe's counselor ever seem to "rush things"? Explain your reaction.
2. Locate examples of the counselor "reflecting" the counselee's opinion in order to draw him out.
3. Who did most of the talking? Does this appear desirable?
4. How did the counselor
   a. define his role?
   b. explain the help that may be expected from counseling?
   c. help the counselee to see his responsibility in the counseling situation?

THINGS TO DO

1. Practice with the interview typescript as described in the chapter.
2. Select a student from your class and see how much information you can note down about him, his home, his school, and his community. Could you understand him from this information?
3. Talk to several educators—counselors, principals, or teachers—to find what sorts of counseling services are provided in their schools. Note particularly the student-counselor ratio.
4. See how many conditions in your community you can list that suggest a need for providing counseling services for "normal" people. A good starting place is to consider the local occupational opportunities.
5. Have a brief information-getting interview with another person—about ten or fifteen minutes. Explain the purpose of the practice and ask him to react naturally, that is, not attempt to be overly cooperative or uncooperative. Consciously attempt to employ the techniques discussed.

6. Record a brief interview and listen to it. Evaluate the effectiveness of your techniques.

7. Obtain permission to sit in on an interview held in a school, agency, or some other place. (While this may distract the counselee and counselor, it is sometimes permitted in training situations.)

8. Role-play an interview situation. The "counselee" may take the role of a student he knows and request help from the "counselor" on his problem.

9. Observe a counseling session by means of a one-way-vision demonstration room, a facility that many colleges have. Note how the counselor does the things discussed in this chapter.

CHAPTER 3

Objectives and Techniques of the Information-getting Phase

T HERE ARE a number of techniques that the counselor may employ to make the information-getting phase more effective. These techniques may be studied and practiced. Desirable counselor attitudes may also be learned, provided the counselor has the desire to learn them and considers them to be important. These techniques and attitudes, briefly touched upon in the previous chapters, are now taken up in more detail.

Principles of the Information-getting Phase

Principles include the attitudes of the counselor as well as the ways in which he goes about his work with the counselee. What the counselor does is primarily his way of putting his attitudes and values into operation. Thus the practices, or actual things the counselor does, should not be thought of as ends in themselves. Instead they are the means the counselor uses to show the counselee what he believes about him and to help him to do those things which the counselor considers helpful and necessary.

Since the counselor's values and attitudes are of such crucial importance, they will be considered first.

The Counselor's Values and Attitudes. To some extent counseling is an art [240]. In this respect it is particularly sensitive to the counselor's own basic attitudes, values, and his concept of his role. Yet it does not seem desirable or defensible to assert that counselors are born, not made. Attitudes and values are largely learned. While some undesirable ones may already have been learned, they may be unlearned, at least to some extent. New and appropriate attitudes and values may be learned; for example, one can come to respect the individual's right to make his own decision. However, it also seems to be true that an individual may learn, at an intellectual level, what attitudes counselors should have or what they should believe, may repeat these, but may still not actually have these attitudes and values as a part of his personality. Therefore, the reasons why the counselor feels as he does are of crucial importance. For example, he may profess and appear to believe that the counselee should be respected and valued as an individual, because he considers this to be a desirable counselor attitude and not because he sincerely has these attitudes toward others. He may, in fact, use counseling as a way to dominate others or as an expression of his own maladjustment.

Techniques and procedures, as well as attitudes and values, can be learned. Obviously some persons can learn more, and faster, and make more effective applications, than others. But the basic values, attitudes, and needs of the counselor are the foundations of his work with others. He should have a drive or desire to help others to attain fulfillment of potentialities, and a real satisfaction in seeing this accomplished. An inner feeling of respect for others is basic to success in the sort of counseling discussed here. These feelings and attitudes are a part of the personality of the counselor. They develop as his personality develops through relations with others. This relationship with others should ideally be a natural outcome of living in a democratic type of society with its emphasis on the worth of the individual. It would be assumed that a teacher who has worked with boys and girls should know very well whether or not he has such attitudes toward others.

Importance of the Counselee as an Individual. Even though the counselor has the desirable attitudes and values toward others, he needs to make them clear to the counselee. One way the counselor can do this is by showing that he is interested in the counselee. Then, in structuring the counseling situation, the counselor emphasizes the need for working together, thus making the counselee realize the importance of his role. Allowing the counselee to determine the content and direction of the counseling sessions and to move at his own speed are other ways to get across respect for him as a person. Attention to his physical comfort also helps. For example, a counselor asked a counselee, "What do you want?" while the latter stood embarrassed at the door. The conversation continued for several minutes while the counselee stood. In another case, the counselor seated counselees so that they faced the glare of a window, without realizing that he was doing so until one counselee objected. Most of these points may appear to be rather insignificant, but they demonstrate how the counselor feels toward others, particularly the counselee.

It is important that the counselee realize that he is the center of attention and that his problems are of major importance. It is difficult if not impossible to convince him of this unless the counselor really believes it. Feelings of annoyance and lack of respect for him as a person will be detected. For example, the counselee will pick up the counselor's attitudes toward him from facial expressions, tone of voice, or random activities (fumbling with mail, opening a letter, looking at his watch), of which the counselor may not even be aware. Thus to show the counselee that he actually is the center of attention, the counselor should put away papers and notes and should not engage in long telephone conversations. He does not have to look the counselee squarely in the eye, but he should keep up with what the counselee is saying and what he means and give him evidence of his attention. On this point it would be helpful to read interviews and excerpts such as those in Refs. [39, 173, 177, 182, 183] to gain an appreciation of the importance of devoting complete and sympathetic attention to the counselee.

The problem that the counselee wants to talk about may sometimes seem insignificant to the counselor. He may believe that the counselee really has some other problem and that the interview should move to this more important problem. Something that may appear trivial to the counselor, however, may be a serious problem to the counselee. Thus it is essential that the counselor look at the problem from the point of view of the counselee. If it is important to the counselee, then it is important to the counselor. For example, a student who asked for help in deciding on a college course spent a great deal of time in discussing why he thought he should be able to use the family car. He had taken driver training and apparently was competent to drive, but the aunt and uncle he lived with would not allow him to do so. It was necessary to use some time in discussing this problem, which was foremost in his mind, before much thought could be put on the matter of deciding on a college course. As it turned out, the conflict over the use of the car appeared to be one of several symptoms of a general conflict with his guardians, which was the basis of his difficulty in the selection of a college major.

The importance of the counselor respecting the counselee's right to make his own decisions needs to be continuously emphasized. Even at this early stage of counseling, it is up to the counselee to make some decisions; for example, whether he will come back for further conferences or whether he will talk about a particular topic. The need for the counselee to make his own decisions becomes more important toward the latter stages of the counseling process, however, when he may be deciding such things as what vocation he will enter, where he will obtain training, whether he will join this or that club. If his right to make decisions has been respected all along, there is no abrupt change in relationship when the planning stage is reached.

Beginning and Ending the Interview. Practice in counseling is the only way to attain ease and competence in it. The beginning counselor faces the problem of how to try out and learn suitable techniques and at the same time put the counselee at ease and help him to express his own feelings. With practice the counselor learns how to open the interview smoothly and effectively, how to keep it moving along in a productive manner, and how to close it without awkwardness and embarrassment.

For the opening, anything that will put the counselee at ease and encourage him to tell about why he came in (or was sent in) is helpful. The counselee usually has some definite purpose for seeing the counselor so it may not be necessary to discuss the latest football game or the weather, but merely to ask the counselee how you can help him. Then, since there must be an end to the interview, it might be a good idea to mention at once how much time is available so that the interview need not end abruptly when a class bell rings or the time is up. The counselor can unobtrusively keep an eye on the time, and several minutes before it is up he might say something such as, "Well, that's about all the time we have today." It would be well to make another appointment, then, if the counselee is to return.

Many counselees approach the first few conferences with some apprehension or uncertainty as to what to expect. The desire to obtain help for some problem or difficulty becomes strong enough to outweigh reluctance to approach the counselor and ask for help. No matter how approachable the counselor is, some counselees may feel that it is an admission of defeat to ask someone else for help. This feeling was expressed by a very reluctant counselee who said, "This is the first time in my life I've asked someone else to help me decide what to do." He found it initially an unpleasant feeling.

Therefore, it is quite important to make the counselee's first experience with counseling as easy and nonthreatening as possible. To accomplish this, it would be a good idea for the counselor to do what he is most at ease in doing. The more natural he appears, the more likely that he will help the counselee feel reassured and free from tension. If the counselor is an outgoing type of person, what he says and does will be different from what a more reserved person would say and do. In either case friendliness, warmth, and interest should be present. Furthermore, the counselor should try to sense the counselee's state of mind and react in an appropriate manner.

In the following excerpt, the counselee was quite ready to talk about his problem. He would very likely have begun discussing it no matter what the counselor said or did. However, the counselor provided a lead that left it up to the counselee as to what to say.

COUNSELOR: Well, what brings you in here today? What would you like to talk about?

COUNSELEE: I'd like to talk about my future, I think.

COUNSELOR: What . . . what about your future? What particular things are you interested in? . . . In talking about or finding out?

COUNSELEE: Well, other people that I talk to at school and other places always seem to have a definite thing in mind that they'd like to do, and I never seem to.

The counselor might have introduced some general topic to break the ice, but this would probably have only delayed the counselee from getting to the problem. This particular counselee had made an appointment and was interested in getting down to business. What do you think of the counselor's first and second comments? He probably could have simply waited for the counselee to continue. As a matter of fact, he may have said almost too much and thus interfered with the counselee saying what he actually had in mind.

In other cases, for example, with a counselee who is obviously awed and somewhat apprehensive (he may think the counselor can read his thoughts), it might help to begin by talking about "last night's baseball game." With a counselee who seems to be really bothered by something and ready to talk about it, however, it is often better just to start in talking about the problem.

If the counselor has let the counselee know about how much time is available, it should not be difficult to bring the session to a close. The counselee will expect it and be prepared for it. The counselor notes the passage of time and several minutes before it is up may indicate to the counselee that the time is about gone. In the interests of maintaining the counseling relationship, it is desirable to do this smoothly and with the same friendly and considerate manner used throughout counseling. Time should be allowed for the counselee to bring up any final points or questions. It is better to stop counseling when the actual session ends, rather than continue it as the counselee leaves the room or as both walk down the hall together.

An example of a counselor bringing an information-getting interview to a close is shown in the following passage:

COUNSELOR: Well, anything else that you can think of, about yourself?

COUNSELEE: No, . . . family ties would not have anything to do with what I plan to do. I wouldn't be held back by my family. I thought that might have some bearing on a career, but it wouldn't with me.

COUNSELOR: You mean . . . you could make your choice pretty much and they would go along with you on that?

COUNSELEE: I think they would. . . .

COUNSELOR: Now . . . you mentioned . . . about these fears, whether they'd bother you, occupationally speaking, or not.

(*Brief discussion of the question of leaving home, a "fear" which had come up earlier. There was no particular reason for the counselor bringing this up at the close of the interview, except that it appeared to be related to the matter of parents' influence on occupational choice.*)

.   .   .   .

COUNSELOR: Well, some of the things we've gone over certainly are important for planning for the future and possibly there are some other things. . . . Some of these things we can talk about a little more at greater length, next time.

COUNSELEE: All right.

COUNSELOR: Let's see. . . . I'll see you next Tuesday, at 10:00 o'clock?

COUNSELEE: Fine. I'll probably have some more ideas, . . . maybe some more questions.

The counselor gave the counselee the opportunity to bring up questions or points two or three minutes before the end of the session. This resulted in a new topic that would have taken additional time, and the counselor found it necessary to make a statement indicating that the time was about up.

There may be some value in a final summary made by the counselor or requested of the counselee by the counselor. However, there would not appear to be any particular need to summarize in the information-getting phase unless the counselee was to do some specific things before the next meeting and the counselor wanted to check to see if he had them clearly in mind.

The Need for Flexibility. Counseling is affected by a number of factors, chief among these being the feelings, attitudes, and personalities of the counselee and counselor. Even so, the counselor sometimes has to remind himself that no two persons are alike and that a relationship between a particular counselor and counselee is different from that involving any other counselor and counselee. Thus it would be undesirable and impossible to set up specific directions to follow in conducting the interview or to list techniques that should be employed in a specific way at a particular time. Of more importance than which technique or procedure to use is the personality of the counselor and how he goes about counseling.

For example, it is sometimes felt that note taking bothers the counselee. However, if the counselor is perfectly at ease taking notes and does it as a matter of course, the counselee will probably not think anything of it. If the counselee does comment about it, the counselor might say that he will be better able to remember what has been talked about and will be in a better position to help the counselee. Of course, if the counselee objects, it would be advisable not to take notes during the interview but to jot them down immediately afterwards. This illustrates a rather minor point in adapting counseling to the counselee. Another illustration might be the case of the counselee who has already made plans to enter college, has selected a curriculum, and wishes to confirm his choice. The counselor will begin with the counselee where he is by helping him to evaluate this goal and perhaps work backward to factors leading up to the choice and evidence for and against it. Or, for another example, the counselee who needs to "accept" counseling help may be assisted to do this before he can make intelligent use of information about jobs. It may come as a shock to some counselors that adapting counseling to the needs of the counselee may result in using no tests, no occupational or educational information, or other widely used counseling aids. In spite of the fact that the process has been described in stages of major emphasis, or because of it, flexibility needs to be an essential aspect of the counselor's work with the counselee.

Each counselor will react to the counselee and what he does a little differently. The counselor cannot detach himself from his own experiences so that they will not affect his relationship with the counselee. He gives much of his reaction to the counselee in subtle signs of which he may not be at all aware. Then the counselee reacts to the counselor in a way determined by the sort of person he is. Just as the counselor has his goals, needs, personality characteristics, and concept of his roles, the counselee, too, has his needs, unique characteristics, and goals. Counselor and counselee work together in a relationship determined by these components. Both are affected, to some extent, by the distortions caused by stereotypes. The counselee may have a concept of a counselor drawn from any of a number of sources, including the "comics." The counselor may, in turn, have a stereotype of a socioeconomic or national group of which the counselee is a member. The counselor needs to be aware of the distortions of the counselee and also of his own distortions. The relationship will probably be adversely affected by the biases or stereotypes of either participant.

To gain insight into his own attitudes and needs, it would be helpful if the counselor had himself gone through a counseling experience. Although this would not be practical in most cases, it would be desirable for the counselor to be aware of his values, needs, and goals and to realize the influence they have upon his behavior in the counseling relationship.

An illustration of how the counselor's attitudes may creep into the interview is illustrated by the following passage:

COUNSELOR: Well now, in these different activities. . . . They actually are a little different. One of them . . . in one sort of activity you dealt right much with being some sort of service to other people . . . probably not much pay. . . . The other was dealing with people in a business situation.

Notice that the counselor appears to give a little more emphasis to "service to others" occupations. The counselor later said that he did not feel that he did but admitted that the tone of his voice for the word "business" was different from that used with the term "service to other people." The counselee, though apparently not unduly influenced by the counselor, later expressed more interest in service activities.

It is difficult to illustrate this point with interview material. As a matter of fact, one can learn very little about it by observing a counseling interview. But the counselor can study transcripts of his own interviews and ask himself how he felt toward the particular counselee and why he said what he did.

The Need for a Permissive Atmosphere. The counselor develops a permissive atmosphere or climate by accepting the counselee as a person and accepting the way he feels and acts. It may be easy to be quite accepting if the counselee says, "I like school!" but not so easy if he says, "I don't think you're helping me at all, and this is just a waste of time!" However, it should be kept in mind that acceptance of the counselee and his attitudes does not mean praising "good" attitudes any more than it does condemning "bad" ones. For example, in response to the counselee's statement that he likes school, if the counselor says, "Good!" he is not accepting the counselee but evaluating him. The counselee who likes to gain approval may spend the rest of the interview period searching for "good" attitudes for the counselor to applaud. Acceptance, then, is a counseling technique that shows the counselee that he can express himself freely without praise or blame.

The counselor responds to the counselee in a way to promote a permissive atmosphere. He may reflect feelings expressed by the counselee [183, pp. 31–32] by restating them slightly or by acting as a sounding board. This is a very accepting or permissive type of response [177, pp. 83–86] and provides practically no lead for the counselee as to what direction to take or what to say next. Reflection of this sort makes use of the feeling expressed by the counselee rather than the factual statements [182, p. 133]. It is interesting to note that counselor responses may be classified as to the amount of lead they provide or the degree of permissiveness they demonstrate [182, pp. 83–95]. In this stage of counseling, emphasis is on permissive responses.

An example of the need for a permissive, nonthreatening counseling atmosphere is shown by the following problem: A counselee explained that he wanted to avoid military service. He appeared to have no concern for what others might think of him for this attitude and no feeling at all for what many would consider his responsibility and duty. The counselor accepted the counselee and his feelings and encouraged him to discuss the matter further. The counselee was, as it turned out, extremely anxious about military service, dreading everything from the first inoculation on. This was not a case of a shirker wanting to get out of something he considered unpleasant but rather an individual who actually could not control his apprehension and who would go to practically any extremes, however unpleasant, to avoid what he considered a threatening situation. The counselor's job was to help the counselee discover his reasons for this attitude and make a better adjustment to reality.

In another case, a counselee, who gave the appearance of being bored and irritated during the course of several interviews, finally stated that the counselor didn't seem to be helping him and indicated that he considered the counseling a waste of time. The counselor felt, as almost anyone would, that he should make some effort to prove the critic wrong to preserve his own feeling of status. (Instead, he should have made an effort to help the counselee understand why he felt this way.) In this particular case, the counselee had vocational plans quite beyond his capability, and in the course of the interviews it became increasingly clear to him that he would have to revise his plans downward. Thus he defended himself from the "unpleasant" counseling situation by appearing bored and hostile. The counselor, unfortunately, was not aware of the bases of the emotions and failed to help the counselee explore his attitudes. Counseling was broken off, and the counselee went on to try out his unrealistic plans.

This interview atmosphere is illustrated in varying degrees in the excerpts in this chapter. However, the following short passage may indicate how the counselor attempts to help the counselee feel free to talk about himself and about his problems. The counselee is concerned about the competition in the field of music.

COUNSELEE: Can I . . . can I ask you a few questions?
COUNSELOR: Sure. Fire away.
COUNSELEE: Well, I mean. . . . This is just what my teacher told me. Is it very tough? The competition . . . is it tough?
COUNSELOR: In music?
COUNSELEE: Uh huh.
COUNSELOR: How do you feel about it?
COUNSELEE: He said it was. I just took his word for it. (*More about difficulties stated by the music teacher.*)
COUNSELOR: Are there fields in music that there wouldn't be competition? . . . Well, what would you think about it yourself?

The counselor appears to be attempting to aid the counselee in expressing his concern about difficulties he would face in the field of music. The counselee has previously expressed confidence in his ability but seems to need to face his doubts about it. Should the counselor have answered the counselee's question or proceeded along the lines that he did above? Which do you think would promote a more permissive atmosphere?

The Need for Structuring. As a rule, counselees will not know what to do or what part to play in the counseling situation. They have had no similar experience upon which they may draw for guides to appropriate behavior. The counselee may be confused and anxious about this situation as well as about his own problems. For this reason the counselor should explain in one way or another the nature of the relationship, the role of each participant, and the sort of help offered.

Too much emphasis on letting the counselee know what to expect may, however, interfere with his bringing out what he needs [241]. What is done should fit naturally into the counseling process.

Letting the counselee know what to expect, or structuring the counseling situation, would usually be done early in the initial phases of counseling. The counselor bases his structuring on counselee needs. One counselee asks for it when he says, "What do you do here?" Another counselee may imply a need by saying, "I just want you to tell me what's wrong with me," or "I want to take those tests to tell me what to do," or "I want you to tell me what I'm interested in."

The counselor may run into difficulties, however, in getting across to the counselee what to expect. Explaining the counselee's role to him may cause resistance [177, pp. 150–152]. For example, the counselee may not want to take responsibility or to take an active role in the process. If this kind of resistance does occur, it may be necessary for counselor and counselee to explore it together before counseling can progress. Or it may be that another approach to structuring must be made. For example, the counselor may try to get across the nature of counseling by his actions and manner rather than by verbal explanation. It often is desirable to structure the counseling situation indirectly by manner and behavior rather than by verbal explanation [183, p. 26].

If verbal structuring is used, the counselor may say something such as this, "We'll talk things over, things that you'd like to talk about or that are bothering you, and I'll do all I can to help you. But the final decisions will be your own. No one can tell you what's best for you."

If there is a need to continue structuring or to restructure the counseling situation, inappropriate techniques may have been used [177, p. 152]. A good explanation of this point may be found in Ref. [39, pp. 318–320 and recorded interviews].

Needless to say, the counselor must have his concept of counseling well defined for himself before he is able to assist the counselee to understand it, either by behavior or by verbalization. It appears likely that some counselee resistance to the relationship and the type of help available may have been caused by the counselor presenting an unrealistic concept of what he does, for example, creating the impression that the counselee must accept all the responsibility for counseling outcomes.

One example of structuring or defining the help that the counselee may expect is given in the John Doe interview in Chapter 2. Another example is the following excerpt, where the counselor felt it necessary to clarify the counselee's role in counseling after a period in which extensive questioning had been necessary. The counselee seemed to be taking a passive role and appeared to need reminding that he should actively participate in the counseling process. The need for this structuring appeared to be caused by the counselor taking too much responsibility in the interview.

COUNSELOR: We've talked about a lot of different things in general. . . . It might be helpful to do this if you'd like to . . . come back in again. You're through exams now. After you've had a chance to think about some of these things a little more . . . think over some of the things we've talked about, maybe some new ideas will come to you, and maybe you'll have a chance to talk to someone. . . . But mainly think about what things are important to you in selecting an occupation. Perhaps next time we can talk a little more specifically, maybe go into some occupations and some things about your interests and attitudes a little more. I want you to work with me. We can work together in talking about what to do next.

Do you think this structuring speech would be effective? Notice how much the counselor seems to take over the responsibility for what happens in counseling.

In some cases, the counselee may profess not to like the idea of having to make his own decisions; he may actually want someone else to take the responsibility for them. The counselee's feelings of dependence may be so great that he actually is unable to face the responsibility placed upon him in this kind of situation. These attitudes should be explored in the course of the counseling. The goal of counseling includes helping the counselee to take responsibility for plans as well as to make practical and satisfying ones.

Incidentally, it is often not mentioned in discussions of structuring that the counselor should work within the sort of situation that he has structured. It is confusing to the counselee to have the counselor explain counseling one way and then do something quite different.

Helping the Counselee to Talk. In the early stages of counseling, the counselor endeavors to get the counselee to tell his own story. It is often necessary to assist the counselee to do this, as he may be reluctant to talk about some things or would not think others are important enough to bring up. General questions such as "Would you like to tell me something about your school work?" may be more fruitful than specific questions such as "What are your marks in history?" or "Do you like mathematics?" If a question can be answered with a "yes" or a "no" the counselee will usually give such a response and that may end the matter. A "yes" or "no" does not tell the counselor much about how the counselee feels about the mark or other factual information and is of little help in understanding the counselee.

In the first example, the counselor uses a question designed to help the counselee to go beyond a brief "yes" or "no" answer and to gain some insight into what he wants out of life.

COUNSELOR: Well, have you thought about any other jobs in dealing with people like that—I mean that would pay more—that you'd like?

COUNSELEE: Well, I don't know how much the jobs usually pay. I mean . . . more . . . well, for example, a school principal. . . . Of course, he doesn't do much teaching.

In another excerpt the counselor uses responses that are designed to help the counselee explore occupational goals, as follows:

COUNSELOR: Well, now, are there some other things you think you'd like to do?

COUNSELEE: Well, I think I'd like G-man work. I put that down on the sheet.

COUNSELOR: Yes, I noticed it there.

COUNSELEE: Er, . . . that's what I thought I wanted to do a long time ago when I was little. I don't know if I feel the same way about it now. But I think I'd want to do it.

COUNSELOR: Uh huh. What do you think there is about it that would appeal to you about that sort of work?

COUNSELEE: I don't know (*laughs*). Solving murders and things like that. I think I'd like that, but I think that's sort of childish. I don't know.

COUNSELOR: Yeah, looking at it from the standpoint of . . . interest years ago. . . . But how do you think about it as a practical vocational goal now? . . . Being in the Federal Bureau . . . a detective?

Not all assistance to the counselee is given by questions, however. There are two other important types of responses or interviewing techniques that should be mentioned here—the "uh huh" response and the purposeful silence [177, pp. 84–85, 126–128]. The counselor often finds it helpful to give an "uh huh" response, in an interested manner, to show that he follows what the counselee is saying and to help him to continue without running the risk of changing the subject or cutting the counselee off from something he wanted to say.

In the purposeful silence, the counselor merely does not interrupt those pauses that often occur in the interview, but rather leaves it up to the counselee to break the silence. These pauses are not actually so long as they may seem to the counselor, who feels it necessary to "do something" whenever there is a period of silence. In fact, quite often the counselee is organizing his ideas or thinking over something that has been said and does not notice the length of the silence. The counselor should keep in mind, however, that sometimes periods of silence can be threatening to the counselee. Thus the counselor should be alert for indications that he should do something to end the pause and put the counselee at ease. For example, if the counselee seems quite ill at ease, to keep the interview going the counselor might ask the counselee if he has any other matters that he would like to bring up, or might suggest a topic for discussion, such as the following: "Tell me something about what you do in your spare time," or "What other things have you thought you would like to do for a living?"

There are other instances when the counselee may normally expect the counselor to keep the interview going. If the counselee obviously has nothing to say or has exhausted a topic, the counselor may have to provide leads as to what to do next.

Helping the counselee to talk does not mean that the counselor needs to bring in personal experiences and reactions. The counseling situation might appear to be an ideal place for the counselor to tell about his own experiences and problems [240, pp. 50–51]. One beginning counselor's reaction to a counselee's problem was to "reassure" the counselee that he had had the same problem and then go on to describe in detail how he had solved it. While the counselor apparently enjoyed the conversation, the counselee very likely received little help from it. The counselee was there to tell about himself, not listen to the exploits and misadventures of others.

Many counselors, particularly those with a background in classroom teaching, seem to be unable to keep quiet and listen, or to refrain from "teaching" the counselee what he needs to think or do. These are, however, temptations that should be resisted, particularly in the information-getting phase of counseling.

Guiding the Interview. Sometimes the counselee becomes verbose, rambles extensively, and goes off on obviously irrelevant tangents. The productivity and forward movement of counseling slows down or stops. In the informal and permissive counseling situation it may be easy to forget about the fact that the counselee needs to do something about his problem, to learn about assets and potentialities, and to make plans and decisions. The counselor needs to be keenly aware of indications of getting off the track and of lack of progress. It is, after all, his responsibility that the counseling session be as effective and productive as possible.

While counseling is a joint enterprise, the counselor cannot escape his responsibility for making each session a helpful one for the counselee. He uses his counseling skill and personal attributes to provide a situation in which the counselee can learn. In the permissive and accepting setting, he keeps the interview on relevant matters. While there is considerable leeway, the counselor, by direct or indirect structuring and other ways, sets the limits and does not let the session become a social visit or a "bull session." Blocks to free expression and effective learning are recognized and reduced or eliminated.

In the information-getting phase, the various aspects of the counselee's life are considered so that a well-rounded picture of him may be obtained. The counselor does not plod steadily from one aspect or area to another, but subtly guides the interview so that all areas are covered. This coverage may seem unnecessary unless one realizes that a problem is not compartmentalized in one area of the counselee's life. For example, a counselee came in to discuss lack of interest in schoolwork. Counseling revealed that he disliked attending school and had made few friends because he was unable to afford the sort of clothes that other students wore.

The following excerpt illustrates an example of the counselor making an effort to keep the interview moving ahead:

COUNSELOR: Well, now, how about your free-time activities other than these clubs and the like . . . social activities? What kinds of things do you do when you have your time entirely your own?

COUNSELEE: Well, I go to the movies, and have friends that come around to my house and we have parties at home. We like the simple kind better when you just drop in.

COUNSELOR: Not formal and so on. . . .

COUNSELEE: No . . . informal.

COUNSELOR: Do you have time to do your schoolwork and yet keep up with social activities?

Note that the counselor uses questions and a reflective response to keep the counselee going forward in the discussion of activities. What do you think of the effectiveness of these procedures?

It may be that the reasons for the apparent random discussion and lack of movement are actually counselee resistance to the counselor and the topics being discussed. When the counselor feels that the counselee is exhibiting resistance he should check himself to determine whether or not he has been pushing the counselee or delving into a highly emotional area without realizing it. A vivid example of the latter point was the case of a counselee who, after starting on an interest test, turned it back to the counselor incompleted, saying that he would not take it. He appeared to be quite upset and refused to discuss his reasons for rejecting it. It later turned out that he was under considerable pressure at home to enter the family business and had decided to do so. However, he was intensely interested in music and had only given up the pursuit of a career in this area after what must have been violent scenes at home. He had apparently practically pushed music out of his conscious thinking. As he started on the interest test, however, he became aware that he was choosing items that indicated this desire, forbidden by himself as well as by his family. Thus he refused to complete the test.

The counselee may display various types of behavior to avoid discussing an unpleasant subject [177, pp. 105–107]. He may change the subject, become somewhat formal, silent, and uncommunicative, or appear to become disinterested in the counseling situation.

The counselor should be particularly alert for indications of resistance. The counselee may be so opposed to discussing a particular topic that there is nothing to do but leave it. In other instances, the counselor may feel that it is best to respond to the counselee's resistance by recognizing and accepting it and by helping the counselee to understand why he feels the way he does. In still other cases, referral for specialized help may be indicated.

The sort of resistance just discussed, however, is quite different from "getting off the track" because the counselor is not playing his role. In discussing this aspect, it is quite important to keep in mind that the counselor can easily become too directive and too authoritative in determining what the counselee should talk about. But when the counselee reaches a point where he wonders, "What do we do now?" the counselor needs to take some positive action, such as structuring, suggesting a topic for discussion, or providing a lead of some sort. Also, when the counseling session moves into a social visit or when the counselee becomes engrossed in a topic that may not have much value for counseling, as one counselee did in discussing his collection of coins, the counselor may subtly bring the conference back to a discussion of more appropriate matters, by a remark such as, "This is a very interesting explanation, but could we leave it for now, so that we can get to these other things?" This should be done as tactfully as possible.

It is necessary to repeat, again, the warning that the counselor can be too autocratic in directing the course of the interview as well as too passive in playing his part; the former is usually a greater danger than the latter. He, too, can easily miss the warning signs of resistance by pushing forward unfeelingly into whatever topic he wants to investigate.

Progress in counseling is evaluated by both the counselor and the counselee. The counselor may ask the counselee what he thinks he wants to get out of counseling and how far he has progressed toward his goals. Discussion of progress may come at any time, will often come up in the counseling process quite naturally, and may help as a sort of transition activity to more productive counseling when progress seems to have slowed down. The counselor, himself, should be keenly aware of where he and the counselee have come from, where they are now, and where they seem to be going.

The counselor may judge progress by the counselee's evaluation of it, and also by indications such as an increasing ability of the counselee to talk about himself, take more responsibility for introducing topics, carry out activities [11, pp. 62–65], or see relationships among various sorts of information. As the counselee makes progress in counseling, he should also become more aware of his real problem, show more insight and self-understanding, and give indications of realism in roles and goals.

If progress in counseling has slowed down or stopped, the counselor may ask himself "Why?" Has he been carrying the counselee along with little or no active participation from him? Is more information needed about the counselee? Has the counselee lost his motivation for counseling? Has the counselor been using inappropriate techniques? These are, of course, only samples of questions that the counselor should ask himself.

The counselee, too, could give his opinion about lack of progress. What does he think needs to be done? In some cases, the counselor will be surprised to find that the counselee is quite satisfied with counseling although the counselor thought it was getting nowhere.

Admittedly, the counselor does not know how fast counseling should progress, nor does he know with certainty what decisions, plans, or other goals the counselee should arrive at. On the other hand, however, he can assess growth and change, infer what needs to be done, and plan ways to help the counselee to do it. The counselor would do well to develop a critical attitude toward his work as a stimulus and a guide to self-improvement.

Being Alert to the Counselee's Feelings. The importance of the counselor being keenly alert for feelings contained in the counselee's comments has already been mentioned several times but merits repeated emphasis. Some counselors seem to classify problems as emotional and nonemotional. This appears to be an artificial classification because anything that is of concern to the counselee is going to have some emotional component. This may be illustrated by the counselee who said, "I took those tests but I still don't know what to do." He had been given some rather objective facts about measured abilities and interests, but he had not accepted them because they were not as complimentary as he had expected. The emotional aspects of this information had been ignored by the counselor.

Even in the more routine information getting, there is often an emotional reaction unsuspected by the counselor. A counselee found, in looking through a college catalogue with the counselor, that a foreign language was required for entrance to the college of his choice. As he was a graduating senior with no foreign language, this simple fact proved to have considerable emotional impact.

The counselor assists the counselee to tell his story by detecting and responding to what the counselee is trying to say and to what is really significant rather than to the literal statements only [173, ch. 4]. For example, if a student said, "I'm having a terrible time at home. I got a C last month," and the counselor inquired, "What was the C in?" he might not get any more information about the parents' attitude toward schoolwork and relations in the home. Recognition of feeling is a very important aspect of the counselor-counselee relationship. Quite often the counselor tends to overlook the really crucial information and feelings and to respond to some relatively unimportant detail.

Recognition of feeling calls for close attention to what the counselee is saying and particularly to how he says it [183, pp. 30–35]. For example, a counselee said that he had never asked anyone's help in solving any of his problems and had always taken pride in being self-sufficient. It would have been interesting to inquire if he had always made all his own decisions, even as a child. However, the counselor chose to respond to the attitudes about accepting help rather than something else. In the course of the discussion he and the counselee learned a great deal about the latter's defenses. It would have been difficult, if not impossible, to do any kind of vocational planning until the counselee gained some insight into his attitudes.

In still another example, a counselee's initial request was for information about opportunities in the electrical manufacturing industry. He said that he wanted to go to work rather than continue in college. The counselor helped him to obtain information about jobs in several plants. He also encouraged the counselee to talk more about his lack of interest in continuing his education. It turned out that the counselee was not doing too well in his classes and doubted his ability to do college work successfully. Furthermore, expenses at home were greater than could be cared for by a scholarship, which was the student's sole financial support. As the counselor recognized and responded to feelings behind the statements about wanting to stop school and lack of interest in school, he helped the counselee to bring out the real reasons for this problem and to reevaluate his college plans.

In the following excerpt the counselor appears to be trying to help the counselee evaluate various experiences in terms of their vocational significance.

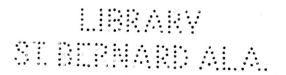

Note that the counselor responses amount to more or less of a restatement of what the counselee appears to be feeling strongly. The typescript does not, of course, show the emotional emphasis in the counselee's statements.

COUNSELOR: But they do things that, er . . . sort of annoy you? Something like that?

COUNSELEE: Well some people with their cutting remarks and, er . . . things like that. They annoy me at first, but I don't bear any grudges.

COUNSELOR: Cutting sarcastic remarks are the kinds of things that sort of get you? Is that it?

COUNSELEE: Well, not because they're about myself. For instance, er . . . in assembly . . . when the seniors march down the aisleway graduating . . . now if there's a girl in front of me that had a best friend in that class and was rather upset about her leaving, and then somebody back of me sort of laughs out of turn and makes fun of them, that annoys me very much, but it's not my place to blow up at them.

COUNSELOR: But it does sort of make you mad. You feel the pressure rising, you might say. . . .

COUNSELEE: Yes. I do (laughs).

COUNSELOR: Is that? . . . You feel more like when it's sort of making fun of someone . . . when . . . that kind of thing?

COUNSELEE: That's mostly it. Lot's of times there're people around you who have physical handicaps and people make fun of them behind their backs. I don't like that at all.

COUNSELOR: You think that's sort of a pretty mean thing to do too, and yet you like the other . . . (part not recorded).

COUNSELEE: I don't think I like it at all. I don't think much of a person who does it.

COUNSELOR: You'd like to tell 'em off or something like that?

COUNSELEE: I think I'd like to explain to them that the person was born that way and can't help it.

COUNSELOR: Well, then you feel that perhaps in a lot of things that you sort of want to . . . well, I mean understand people or take up for them, or something like that? That's something that's sort of important to you?

COUNSELEE: Yes. That might be it too, because a lot of my friends are under those particular . . . handicaps.

COUNSELOR: You mean some of your friends, er . . . for some reason or other, people make remarks about them? Something like that?

The counselor was attempting to help the counselee bring out and become aware of his basic attitudes toward other people and his personality needs that would affect vocational choice. What do you think of the counselor responses? Would you feel that he was helping the counselee to bring out feelings and attitudes that would have vocational significance?

The beginning counselor can learn a great deal about this point by recording his interviews and listening to them. This procedure provides an opportunity

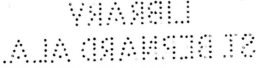

for him to study the process carefully and evaluate how well he detected and responded to feelings expressed by the counselee.

Determining the Need for Additional Information-getting Sessions

The information-getting phase of counseling shades over into the planning phase almost imperceptibly. It may be difficult to identify the period of change. Quite frequently more than one primarily information-getting session is needed. The counselor may feel that he needs to discuss further factual or attitudinal data with the counselee. Or he may feel that the counselee is not yet ready to take part in planning; it may be necessary to keep the counseling process going by continuing the discussion of various aspects of the counselee's life and plans. In other cases, there may be resistance to overcome. Perhaps the counselee has just begun to feel at ease and to be able to talk freely. It is assumed that the counselee will return for additional sessions but that it will be up to the counselor to determine the emphasis (information getting or planning) of the next session. If he decides to continue the information-getting phase, he then must make plans for the session.

The counselor's decision to continue to emphasize information getting is based on his judgments about the counselee. Some aspects of this judgment have been mentioned in the above paragraph. The counselor may ask himself, "What is the counselee ready for now?" This is not assigning the counselor the role of a traffic director. Instead he is a person sensitive to the needs of the counselee and one who *keeps up* with the counselee (not behind him or ahead of him) for determining what he is ready to do. It should be borne in mind, however, that planning is difficult or impossible unless both counselor and counselee have the material with which to plan. Thus a too hasty exit from the information-getting phase would handicap both counselor and counselee in effective planning.

When the counselor decides upon the emphasis of the next session, he uses all the information which he has available to make plans for it. In making plans, the counselor needs to consider where he and the counselee now are in the counseling process. What sorts of information have been brought out and what still needs to be covered? It is a good idea to make some brief notes on what is to be covered. The counselor may then decide upon an approach. What is the best way to start the interview? The counselor mentally reviews the general tone of the counseling so far and plans to maintain it if it is good (for example, the counselee is enthusiastic and interested), or improve it if it is poor (for example, the counselee is apathetic or lacks motivation). In what direction does the counselee appear to be going? Does this appear to be a productive direction or is it likely to be a dead end? If necessary, the counselor attempts to try to plan procedures to turn the session toward productivity. To do these things the counselor will have to summarize data that have been gathered as well as review impressions that he has received. Also, the counselor determines whether he was to do anything (for example, check on record, talk to a teacher) before the next session. Was the counselee supposed to do anything before coming back (for example, make out a time schedule, look over some information)? These responsibilities are included in the planning for the session.

It would be well to make some brief notes that can be used inconspicuously during the interview. They should include the points from the previous discussion that are to be used in starting the interview and helping it to move forward. This may include a brief summary of data already obtained. But there is one very important caution that should be kept in mind—the counselor should not have an inflexible plan that he will be unwilling to change. The counselee, too, has been doing some thinking and planning since the last session and he may come prepared to take a particular direction. Within reasonable limits the counselor should go along with him, as he has already done and will continue to do in succeeding sessions. The counselor's plan is counselee-centered and problem-centered, not counseling-process-according-to-this-book-centered.

What has been said applies to additional interviews that are primarily information getting. Planning, decision-making, and insight-promoting interviews are taken up later in the chapters devoted specifically to these procedures.

Practice to Gain Counseling Skill

Principles, procedures, and techniques assume new meaning and become part of the counselor's way of working with others when he does something with them. The remainder of this chapter, therefore, is devoted to suggestions for practice, together with some counseling tools or aids.

Practice Interviewing with Another Student. One way for counseling to be practiced or rehearsed is for students in the class or teachers in the in-service program to interview each other. While this interviewing is artificial and often seems quite humorous, it can be of real value if taken seriously and performed with a definite effort to employ techniques that have been discussed. This type of practice or role playing approaches as nearly as possible the face-to-face situation in the actual interview. However, the "counselor" does not have to be concerned with the effect of his practice on the "counselee." Too, the "counselee" can help evaluate the effectiveness of the interview. This may sound very much the same as "learning to swim on the river bank," but this sort of practice has definite value in developing counseling skill.

In the practice interview, the "counselee" also plays a role, making a conscious effort to act the part of the counselee who comes for help. (A teacher should have no trouble in recalling a student problem to use when taking the part of the counselee.) Rather than playing the role of a student, however, the "counselee" might be himself in the interview.

Before the practice interview, the counselor should look over the check list "Do's and Don't's in Counseling" on page 82 and familiarize himself with the "Interview Summary Form" on page 83. This form is provided to serve both as an interview guide and for recording information. Comments may be placed under appropriate headings as the interview progresses. As the counselee does not usually follow any particular sequence in talking about himself (there is no reason why he should), the use of a form of this type will enable the counselor to put down information in an organized way. It is also easy to make a quick check of the headings to determine whether some area of information has been omitted. For example, in the interview situation the counselor may completely overlook "work experience," which might be a crucial area of information. Another point that should be kept in mind is that the interviewer cannot put down everything that is said. Thus he will have to learn to select those items which are significant. This selectivity comes with practice; it would be better at the beginning to put down too much than too little.

When the interview information is put down in an orderly arrangement, as on the interview summary form, it is easier to get a well-rounded understanding of the individual, to see interrelationships, and to synthesize the various bits of information. Although the interview summary form does not provide a report that presents the dynamics of the interview process, it is suggested as the method of recording for this practice interviewing. Some beginning counselors attempt to take down a running account of the interview with as many direct quotations as possible. This procedure gives a more dynamic record of the process but it is difficult to do without distracting from the interview.

It would be well to have a private room for the practice interview. Approximately fifteen to twenty minutes would be suitable for each interview; a longer period of time might be used, perhaps up to fifty minutes. The counselor and counselee should change places at the conclusion of the first practice session. The practice session should begin at the time when the counselee first comes into the counselor's office, so that the role playing begins at the very first contact and the "counselor" and "counselee" have no opportunity to engage in out-of-character conversation.

Evaluation of the Practice Interview. When you have completed the practice interview, go back and rate yourself on the check list of "Do's and Don't's in Counseling." Review your notes to determine if you missed any points that you feel should have been covered. Can you see relationships among various sorts of data? Can you synthesize the data? Usually you will realize that more information is needed. Determine what you need to know and how it might be obtained, perhaps by further counseling, by testing, or by use of records.

The Interview Rating Scale

The following check list provides a self-rating for the beginning phases of counseling. Read it over before you do the practice interviewing suggested in the previous section. Then following the interview reread it and check yourself. Not all the principles of interviewing are covered, but some of the ones most useful in helping the counselee to feel at ease and to tell his own story are included. To rate yourself, place an X on the line to indicate about where you think you should be.

Do's and Don't's in Counseling

Do	Don't
1. Greet the counselee in a friendly, unhurried manner.	Give the impression of a rushed, harried, impatient person when the counselee comes in.
2. Have a chair ready beside your desk or table (not across the desk) and a clean desk (if possible).	Face the counselee across the wide expanse of a desk suggestive of the "boss-employee" relationship.
3. Have a clean, neat, uncluttered, and private office.	Have a curiosity shop that is more interesting for the counselee to look at than it is for him to talk to you; a telephone that rings every few minutes; a "reference room" where people are continually coming in to get things out of files.
4. Help the counselee to tell his story by being accepting, interested, by letting him talk.	Prod the counselee to tell all, express commendation or disapproval, and tell him about your experiences.
5. Give the counselee a chance to pause and think if he wants to.	Fill in pauses with talk.
6. Ask questions that call for discussion or explanation—that bring out how the counselee "feels" about something.	Ask questions that can be answered with a "yes" or "no."
7. Keep up with the counselee as to what he is saying, doing, or feeling that is really important.	Ask questions or make comments that cut off or divert significant statements or feelings that the counselee is expressing.
8. Meet the counselee's demand for the "answers" by defining your role as counselor.	Ignore questions that call for direct answers, or give the counselee the solution for his problems.
9. Give the counselee some idea of the amount of time you have for the interview.	Let the counselee get involved in an important discussion that has to be hurriedly interrupted when the time is up.
10. Close the interview tactfully and smoothly, with a definite time set for the next appointment, if needed.	Rush the counselee out, or otherwise close the interview abruptly and give the counselee the feeling of having been pushed out.

The Interview Summary Form

The form which follows is designed to serve as a guide for practicing the information-getting interview. It should not be used in a routine and mechanical way regardless of the counselee's needs. But it should bring out the fact that various aspects of the counselee's life need to be considered [264, pp. 133–179; 32, pp. 43–45]. In the face-to-face situation the counselor does not have time to stop and think what areas of information may be significant. He often finds after an interview session that he has overlooked a type of information which should have been covered but which the counselee did not bring up. This is a frequent occurrence with counselees who are high school pupils.

Information about the different areas should be obtained in as tactful and natural a manner as possible in the normal sequence of the interview. The principles of counseling should be kept in mind in using the form. It is an aid to obtaining diagnostic information but it does not amount to a diagnosis by itself; information from other sources will be needed. As the counselor enters information in the form and studies it he will be able to see relationships and detect patterns. Needed information will be indicated by gaps.

The summary form may be used as a record of counseling. Data are grouped in a logical manner and may be quickly reviewed before each session.

Interview Summary Form

1. Manner, physical appearance; health; attitudes toward counselor, toward others, and toward self_____

_____

_____

2. Home and family life_____

_____

_____

3. School_____

_____

_____

4. Work experience_____

_____

_____

5. Recreation_____

_____

_____

6. Relationships with peers_____

_____

_____

7. Plans for future_____

_____

_____

A form such as this gives the counselor something definite to do as he is learning to feel at ease and help the counselee to talk about himself. As the counselor develops more confidence and skill, he will have less need for such an aid. It is particularly important that the beginning counselor use this sort of aid not as a crutch but only as a guide for learning what might be done. Almost inevitably he will develop his own procedure and discard this type of guide.

Even at the beginning it is not necessary to go down the list of areas routinely. One may be taken up in some detail, another touched upon lightly, while an entire session may be spent on a third. Blum and Balinsky [27, pp. 132–133] present a similar list.

Specific Items of Information in the Summary Form. The broad headings may not give you much help in determining what sorts of questions you could ask, or what specific topics you could suggest for discussion. Therefore, the form has been expanded by adding a number of suggested points for consideration in each major area. They are not, of course, all the points that could be covered. You will think of others as you look these over. The course of a particular interview will suggest still others. This list, however, will serve as a starting point. You might abbreviate some of the items in the margin of the "Interview Summary Form" to serve as reminders. Note that many of the following points may be covered in records or other sources of information.

Expanded Interview Summary Form

I. Manner, physical appearance (observe during interview)
    Poise_____
    Self-confidence_____
    Ability to express self_____
    Reactions to new situation_____
    Mannerisms_____
    Grooming_____
    Size and build_____
    Features_____
    Facial expression_____
    Clothing_____
    Voice_____
  Health
    General state of health_____
    Children's diseases_____
    Illnesses and accidents_____
    Physical handicaps_____
    Recent physical examinations and results_____
    Vision, hearing_____
    Appetite, diet_____
    Energy_____
    Amount of rest_____
    Use of tobacco, stimulants_____
  Attitude toward counselor
    Friendly_____
    Distant_____
    Formal_____

      Hostile

      Dependent

      Familiar

    Attitude toward others

      Friendly

      Likes company of others

      Prefers to be alone

      Anxious in presence of others

      Hostile or aggressive toward others

      Dependent upon others

    Attitude toward self

      Good opinion of self

      Poor opinion of self

      Acceptance or lack of acceptance of self

      Realistic concept of self

2. Home and family life

    Location of home, type, neighborhood

    Home owned or rented

    Counselee's feeling about the circumstances

    Length of time in present home, neighborhood

    Number of rooms, whether counselee has room of his own

    Number of persons living in home, effect on counselee

    Home responsibilities of counselee, reactions to responsibilities

    Parents' ages, occupation, education, health, activities

    Which parent dominant

    Siblings' age, health, occupations, education, plans

    Attitude toward parents and siblings

    Parents' attitude toward counselee, his plans, achievements, and friends

    Appraisal of home atmosphere (secure, disrupted, tense, indifferent)

3. School

    Attitude toward school, teachers, classes

    Activities, clubs participated in, offices held

    Reasons for participation or nonparticipation

    Degree of satisfaction with school offerings

    Feeling of belonging in school

    Parents' and siblings' attitude toward school

    Participation in class activities, class discussion

    Study habits (time spent on lessons, methods of study, regular study time)

    Progress or lack of it and reactions

4. Work experience

    Jobs held, hours, pay, duties

    Attitudes toward work

    Reasons for seeking work

    Reasons for leaving work

    Interest in particular work experience as a career

    Relations with others on the job (supervisors, fellow workers, those supervised)

    Self-concept in world of work (how he sees himself, occupationally speaking)

5. Recreation

    Types of recreational activities

    Time spent on activities

    Preferred types and reasons for preference

    Other activities desired

    Parents' attitudes toward activities

    Similarities of activities to peer activities

    General nature of activities (with a large group, highly organized; with tools and
      equipment, solitary)

    Consistency and persistency of interest

    Estimate of adequacy of recreational program

Expanded Interview Summary Form (*Continued*)

6. Relationships with peers
    Attitude toward peers_____
    Consistency of attitude toward peers_____
    Emotional, social, and physical development as compared to peer group_____
    Adjustment to peers of both sexes_____
    Number of friends, close friends, casual acquaintances_____
    Accepted by others, liked by others_____
    Leadership ability, followership ability_____
    Teamwork ability_____
7. Plans for the future
    Specific plans and bases for plans_____
    If no plans, why not_____
    Consistency of plans_____
    Estimate of practicality of plans_____
    Parents' attitude toward plans_____
    Influence of others on plans_____
    Attitude toward looking ahead and planning for the future_____

A Test on Counselor Responses

The following interview was adapted from a brief session between a teacher-counselor whom we shall call Miss Jones and a student who requested help in improving poor school marks. The counselee, a girl of sixteen, is in the tenth grade. She comes from a family that places a high value on college education. Two other children, both girls, are now in college. The counselor has looked at the cumulative record and noted that Mary, the counselee, is enrolled in the academic or college preparatory course, has about a C— average, and is described by several teachers as being a hard worker. She lists as hobbies "Girl Scout handicrafts, cooking" and, in the section for future plans, states that she is going to college but has not decided what to take. At present she is very much upset by a low average and by failure in Latin and algebra. She has just arrived at the counselor's office.

NOTE: The response immediately following the counselee's statements is the counselor's actual comment. The others are added as possible alternate responses. Read the interview and check the responses that you would have used to get the information you wanted. The counselee's next statement is in answer to what the counselor actually said.

MISS JONES (*as Mary comes to the door*): Come in, Mary. You're right on time. Here, have a chair.

MARY: Thank you. I . . . I've been waiting to talk to you . . . about my work. Uh . . . I'm not doing so well.

MISS JONES: 1. Yes. I remember you told me the other day. That's too bad.
    2. Uh huh.
    3. Would you care to tell us more about it?
    4. Well, I wouldn't let it upset me. You can do better if you try.

MARY: I think it's bad too. I'm getting just awful grades in math and Latin. They're terrible! But then I do better in English . . . and history.

MISS JONES: 5. They're not as good as you'd like, but some subjects are better than others.

6. Girls often have trouble with math. I have difficulty with it myself.

7. What do you get in history and English?

8. Do you like math?

MARY: Yes, that's right. . . . The main trouble seems with certain subjects, but none are average. But the ones that are worst are required for college and I just can't seem to do anything about them.

MISS JONES: 9. Your college plans are in a little difficulty because of these grades?

10. Why don't you drop those subjects that are giving you trouble?

11. If you want to go to college you know you'll have to study.

12. Going to college is important to you.

MARY: Yes, they're in a terrible shape. I just *got* to go to college. Ann and Jane, my sisters, are both there and Mother doesn't say it but I *know* she thinks I'm dumb or something. I *just* know it!

MISS JONES: 13. What kinds of grades do your sisters get?

14. What makes your mother think you're dumb?

15. Now don't get upset about a little thing like that.

16. In your family it's pretty important for you to get a college education.

MARY: Oh, they do well. I'm not sure, but they say they get wonderful grades. A's and B's I think. . . . Are college grades the same as grades here? Is a C about average and a B good? I suppose grades are different in different places. Daddy and Mother both went to college, so I guess. . . . If you've been through something you think others can do it.

MISS JONES: 17. Well, a B here I suppose makes you above average, and I would say that . . . that is, when I was in college, I tried to get B's, at least. It was hard work.

18. Your parents are strong for you to go to college.

19. Uh huh.

20. What college did they attend?

MARY: Uh. . . . In a family like mine, where just everybody gets a college education, you stand out like a sore thumb if you don't. It's sort of a tradition, you know. . . . Isn't that right?

MISS JONES: 21. You feel that there's a lot of pressure—reasons why you should go on, that this . . . well, it's a problem, because of your grades.

22. Traditions are sometimes broken.

23. I think you're making a mountain out of a molehill, Mary.

24. Wasn't there someone in your family who didn't go to college?

MARY: That's it exactly. It *really* is pressure, and I'm in an awful situation. You know what I mean. I'm right in the middle. What can I do! . . . Well, that's what I wanted to see you about. That's my problem.

MISS JONES: 25. Well, perhaps you could take a test that would tell you whether or not you should go to college.

26. The problem is what can you work out with your family on this matter of college plans?

27. It's a problem of meeting family expectations when you're doing the best you can.

28. Maybe I could talk to your parents and tell them you're doing the best you can.

MARY: That's it! That's the answer. Then I'd know exactly what I should do. If I could just take a test that would settle everything! . . . But suppose I didn't do well; my folks wouldn't believe the test . . . I know.

MISS JONES: 29. Test scores are very accurate. If you make a certain score, that's *it*.

30. Maybe I am going a little too fast. Tests are just part of the picture, and then your family's ideas are pretty well fixed too!

31. Yes, the tests would give the answer.

32. When would you like to take the test?

MARY: That might be *it*, as you say, but it won't help much if it isn't good. It'd be just like grades; if I get low ones my folks don't say "Why," they say, "You should get better." They'd say the same thing about a test. But I don't feel. . . . I don't feel that I would do very well. I don't know. I work hard, but I just don't think I can learn some of those subjects very well. . . . There's no use hiding it from myself.

MISS JONES: 33. You're wondering if the college preparatory course is best for you after all, even if your parents think so.

34. Come now, don't give up so easily, Mary.

35. Why don't you change to some other course, then?

36. Well, the test might surprise you.

MARY: Yes, I've wondered that for some time. I wouldn't dare say it at home, because, well, what would they think? You're the only person I've mentioned this to, but I don't want to go to college—I really don't, but please don't tell my father that. . . . It's a relief to tell someone.

MISS JONES: 37. You mean you don't want to go to college?

38. This is something you've thought about for a long time but it would be hard to talk about at home.

39. Why don't you tell your parents how you feel—I'm sure they'd understand.

40. Oh, you'll get a lot out of college, I'm sure.

MARY: Isn't it awful? Well, maybe I shouldn't say that! I don't know what to do, though. What would you suggest?

MISS JONES: 41. Well, *I* would suggest that you go home and tell your parents that you don't want to go to college. See what they say.

42. It's a situation where you'd like to be told what to do.

43. Oh, it's all right to say that here.

44. Well, you do seem to have quite a problem!

MARY: But I just told you what they'd say. You see, a friend of mine finished last year. Well, she didn't want to go to school. She wanted to work, so she got a job in the Smith real estate office as secretary. She didn't even know how to type but she learned in a couple of weeks at the Rush Business School. The point is, we were talking at home about it and Mother said, "How in the world that girl can do that when she could amount to something, I can't see!" Why, she thinks that Sue is just wasting her life. Can you imagine that! Then I hear you in guidance class say that all kinds of work are honorable, and you have to have all kinds of people to do all kinds of jobs. Anyway, you can just see what I have to face.

MISS JONES: 45. It's going to be hard to get your family to see how you feel about it.
46. Does Sue like her job?
47. Maybe you could get Sue to talk to them.
48. Well, I didn't mean that all kinds of work were all right for *everyone*. It depends upon *who* you are.

MARY: Yes, and it's been worrying me a lot. It's good to talk to you about it, though. I feel better just by talking about it. I've been after my teachers to help me to get better grades and they've tried. But it hasn't made much difference. I'm going to see my math teacher again this afternoon. . . . I think I'll ask him if he thinks I can ever learn it. He ought to have some idea about it. Then I think I'd like to come back and talk to you again. I seem to see the whole thing a little clearer now, but I want to think about it. When could I see you again? Soon, I hope.

MISS JONES: How about Friday? Will that be soon enough? That's the day after tomorrow.

MARY: That will be fine. Good-by, and thanks so much.

Notice that the counselor varied a great deal in her responses; some might be considered effective and some ineffective. The following responses are considered to be the most desirable: 3, 5, 9, 16, 18, 21, 27, 30, 33, 38, 42, 45. Evaluate these responses as to how effective you think they are. Also, identify the principles violated by other responses.

Several additional counseling tests are listed in "Things to Do" on page 90. While these tests go beyond the information-getting phase and emphasize a particular point of view of counseling, they will provide valuable practice for you.

SUMMARY

The information-getting or diagnostic phase of counseling provides a setting in which the counselee can talk freely. The counselor, as a person and as a user of techniques, has an effect on the counseling relationship. The counselor accepts the counselee, respects his basic worth, and keeps his problems and needs in the focus of attention. Further, the counselor uses some specific techniques to help the counselee bring out important information. However, counseling is not a routine or mechanical process; it is adapted to the needs of the counselee. By letting the counselee talk, and by recognizing and responding to the feeling that he is expressing, the counselor helps the counselee bring out data of importance to him. The counselor has the responsibility of keeping the counseling session productive and moving forward. At the information-getting stage, preliminary and tentative interpretation and synthesizing are done, and clues as to needed information are identified and followed up.

Principles and techniques of counseling need to be put into practice to become part of the counselor's behavior. Various sorts of practice may be done prior to actually working with a counselee. Role playing offers a safe and helpful learning situation for practicing counseling techniques and procedures. The beginning counselor can evaluate his practice to detect good and poor procedures and to assist in developing competencies. To help the counselor feel he has something concrete to do in the beginning phase of counseling, an interview form may be used. The counselor needs to be aware of many possible avenues of exploration as a basis for suggesting topics for discussion but should not develop a pattern of following the same favorite lines of discussion with each counselee.

CHECKS ON UNDERSTANDING

1. How does the counselor's personality affect the counseling relationship? Why is the counselee's reaction to the counselor important?

2. What attitudes and values should the counselor hold concerning the counselee's right to make his own decisions?

3. When might the counselor remain silent during a counseling session?

4. What is a permissive atmosphere?

5. What are guiding principles for opening the interview?

6. What is structuring? Is it desirable or undesirable?

7. Explain how the feeling expressed by the counselee may be different from the actual facts of his statements.

8. Why would a counselee deliberately avoid talking about something that was bothering him a great deal? How would you recognize that he was doing this?

9. How can you determine if progress is being made in the information-getting phase of counseling?

10. What might be some effects of the counselor telling the counselee the "answers"?

11. What responses can the counselor make when the counselee demands to be told the solution to his problem?

12. What counseling techniques can be tried out in a practice counseling interview? Are there techniques that could not be effectively practiced?

13. What are the dangers of using a form, such as the interview summary form, in counseling?

14. Why does a planned demonstration interview usually appear more "spectacular" than an actual interview?

15. How might you define your role as a counselor and the purpose of counseling to a pupil who has been sent to you against his wishes?

16. Suppose you felt that a pupil should return for further counseling but you realized that he was not planning to do so. How might you go about helping him to see the need for additional counseling?

THINGS TO DO

1. Carry out the practice counseling procedures suggested in this chapter.

2. Interview several persons who work with others to find what they consider good interview techniques, for example, a personnel worker, employment service interviewer, community agency counselor, marriage counselor, and school or college counselor.

3. Obtain from several counselors or counseling agencies forms or outlines used

in the information-getting phase. Determine how they are used by counselors. Analyze them for similarities or differences.

4. Observe an interview to discover how the counselor uses techniques to keep the session on the track and moving forward. Also note the areas of information covered and how each area was brought up.

5. Look at a film showing the information-getting phase of counseling or listen to a recording of an actual counseling session. Take notes, using the interview summary form. Compare with notes taken by others.

6. Prepare a demonstration of an information-getting interview. Present it to others, or record it and play the recording.

7. Prepare a rating scale for the information-getting phase of counseling. Use it in rating yourself and others.

8. In the light of principles discussed in this chapter, review the questions about John Doe's first interview in Chapter 2.

9. Listen to a recording of a counseling session and evaluate how well the principles are carried out. Suggest alternate counselor responses.

10. Evaluate the effectiveness of counselor responses in Refs. [39, 173, 183, 187, 206, 264]. Suggest alternate responses if you think that those which the counselor made can be improved upon.

11. Make up a counselor-response test from a brief interview that you have recorded.

12. Take the counseling tests in Refs. [173, pp. 10–14] and [183, pp. 125–148].

13. Actually interview a pupil. Obtain the cooperation of a pupil who appears to be well adjusted. Ask him to help you learn about counseling by taking part in an interview. Record the interview and evaluate it.

14. There are several films that deal with the total counseling process, certain parts of which will be useful at this time. They are

Counseling—Its Tools and Techniques (22 minutes), Vocational Guidance Films, 1948.
Counseling Adolescents, McGraw-Hill, 1954. A series of three films as follows:
A Counselor's Day (12 minutes)
Using Analytical Tools (15 minutes)
Diagnosis and Planning Adjustments in Counseling (18 minutes)
Client-centered Therapy (two parts of 30 minutes each), State College of Pennsylvania, 1953.

Review these films to locate and evaluate counselor activities in the early phases of counseling. Other films dealing with adjustment problems, mental health, and the like often show various types of interviews that may be used here.

15. Play the recording, The Case of Jim [197]. Although this is an example of rather extensive psychotherapy, it illustrates many principles of value to the school counselor.

CHAPTER 4

The Cumulative Record

THE PREVIOUS chapters have dealt with the face-to-face counseling situation. However, in helping the counselee, the counselor makes use of a wide variety of sources of information. The collection and interpretation of information from these sources have already been described as counselor activities in contrast to counseling. One of the most important sources which the counselor uses is the cumulative record. In this chapter, emphasis is on interpretation of the information in the cumulative record. While some attention is devoted to using the information in counseling, it is covered more fully in Chapters 12 and 13 on planning.

Setting up a cumulative record system and keeping the record up to date are not counseling. However, a study and interpretation of the record is classified as a counseling activity which provides useful information for actual counseling. It is for this reason that the nature and use of the cumulative record are taken up. Although the record itself might be brought to the counseling session and laid out on the desk for both counselee and counselor to use, it would more typically be studied by the counselor prior to the session. Counselees often exhibit a great deal of curiosity about these records and make an effort to look for teachers' comments, IQs, and the like, which naturally distracts from the counseling session.

The Nature and Content of the Cumulative Record

Most of you are familiar with the type of record usually kept in the school in which a variety of data are collected during the school career of the pupil. For the initiation of a record system, maintenance of records, various types of forms and folders, and detailed treatment of contents, see Refs. [75, 180, 217, 218, 239, 253]. Some of you may also be familiar with personnel folders kept in college, business, industry, and the Armed Forces. These are also types of "cumulative" records; they contain important data about the individual, accumulated over a period of time.

Content of the High School Cumulative Record. There are many different forms of cumulative records, but all contain about the same type of information, such as data about the home and family, school marks, test scores, school activities, health and physical condition, and plans for the future. Strang [218] and Traxler [239], among others, give examples of record forms with pupil data included. If you have not used a cumulative record it would be a good idea to study at this time the forms in these references and those used in your school.

Often the counselor and other members of the school staff may set up a cumulative record system without careful consideration of the information needed, and space for essential facts may be left out. Then too, those responsible for providing and entering certain types of information may not have done so. As the counselor studies the record, he may find that needed information is lacking. This is a problem which the counselor, working with the school staff, can remedy.

Types of Information Provided. Strang [218, ch. 7] has pointed out that the teacher or counselor may obtain a longitudinal or developmental and a cross-sectional picture of the pupil. Both of these types of data are needed by the counselor in gaining an understanding of the counselee. When combined with other data they are extremely helpful in arriving at valid inferences about the sort of person he is and how he got that way. These two major types of information will be taken up in detail later.

The Counselor's Uses of the Cumulative Record

The counselor may use the cumulative record in a number of different ways, such as the following: to save interview time, which may be spent more profitably on counselee reactions to data than in obtaining data; to study the long-range trends in achievement, interests, activities, ambitions, or social behavior; to obtain a description of the counselee's status at the present or at some particular point of time in the past; to fill in gaps in information or to detect gaps; to locate clues for further exploration; and to suggest how to proceed in the counseling session. There are some particularly helpful references on counselor uses [78; 163, pp. 261–262, 278–279; 218, ch. 7; 240, ch. 3; 253, ch. 13; 261, pp. 369–393].

Saving Interview Time. One very useful aspect of the cumulative record is the amount of time it can save the counselor in the interview. Factual data such as age, information about parents and siblings, school marks, and work experience are available, thus eliminating the need for extensive questioning by the counselor. Interview time can much more profitably be spent in talking about those things which give insight into the personality of the counselee. A quick survey of the data contained in the cumulative record before the interview should give the counselor a great deal of factual information about the counselee and will also serve to reveal any need for information which the record does not provide or which was not entered in the space provided. The information can then be obtained during the interview. For example, the counselor may discover, by looking at the family data section, that the counselee has three older brothers and two younger sisters, what their ages are, their amount of education, and their occupations if working. Then he may spend the interview time in finding out how well the counselee gets along with siblings and how his educational and vocational plans resemble theirs. If a small amount of this information about brothers and sisters were missing, for example, amount of education, the counselor could check on this during the interview. If he found it necessary to obtain even a minor part of the data usually contained in the cumulative record during the interview, however, he would have little time for anything else.

Besides furnishing data that otherwise would have to be obtained by extensive questioning, the cumulative record may also provide information that the counselor would have to obtain by some method outside of the interview. School marks and test results are two examples. The counselee's report of his school marks is usually something less than exact. It may be helpful to find out how he represents his school achievement; however, for the actual marks, the cumulative record should be consulted. The counselee's report of test scores, if he has heard them, is even less dependable. School counselors have been known to administer tests when test results already in the cumulative record would have furnished the needed information.

Studying Developmental Trends.   The counselor may discover trends in performance, preferences, and plans by looking over entries made during successive years. For example, vocational preferences over a long period of time may show a consistency that appears to point toward a definite occupational area or may present considerable variability. School marks may show consistent performance over the years or may indicate abrupt changes at one or several points in the counselee's development. Preferences for certain types of activities, recreation, and hobbies offer clues to persistent interest patterns. Past performance offers a basis for making at least tentative inferences about future performance. Abrupt or unexplained changes or reversals in trends suggest problems that should be investigated further.

In studying the cumulative record from this longitudinal point of view, the counselor is attempting to gain an understanding of the total individual, not just his vocational plans, mental ability, or some other specific aspect. In reviewing all the developmental information, the counselor searches for major themes or patterns. For example, suppose that he finds that Joe Smith has been low in academic achievement and quite low in academic ability. He has, however, been high in ratings on industry and cooperativeness and has been quite active in minor class offices where there is more work than glory. A pattern might be inferred of an individual with low ability and achievement who puts emphasis on gaining recognition by being helpful and cooperative. This inferred pattern is only a clue, however, which should be checked against other information.

In another example, the cumulative record gave evidence that an only child had developed from a selfish, demanding, and thoroughly disliked individual into an adolescent who was well liked and who rated high on ability to get along with others. Occupational preferences, too, had tended to move toward those fields of work in which help to others plays a major part.

It is thus a good idea for the counselor to look over the cumulative record for developmental trends before the conference with the counselee. These trends may offer clues that should be followed up. If, for example, the record showed that the counselee had been a persistent underachiever, the counselor might raise a question about it or be particularly alert for counselee remarks bearing out this point. To help bring the matter up the counselor might make a comment such as, "How do you feel about what you're doing as compared with what you are able to do?" Further, underachievement provides a number of specific clues that the counselor might want to investigate, such as study habits, physical condition, attitude toward school, or future plans.

Sometimes the counselor may find that the counselee's problem is revealed by the data in the record, although the counselee himself states his problem as something entirely different. For example, a student who had consistently, over a period of years, expressed an interest in mechanical things and stated his occupational goal as a television repairman put down his educational objective as going to college. The occupational objective was unrelated to the educational plan, but the counselee stated that his problem was one of not having financial resources to attend college!

The developmental information contained in the cumulative record provides valuable data about the counselee and suggests promising leads for further investigation. Along with the study from the developmental point of view, the counselor investigates the cross-sectional or status picture.

Obtaining Cross-sectional Data. As has been pointed out, the counselor reviews data about various aspects of the counselee's life in the longitudinal study of the cumulative record. He also makes a careful check of the counselee's status at the present or at some past time. These two processes usually would go on at the same time, but they are taken up separately here for emphasis and to indicate the unique contribution of each type of information.

The cross-sectional study of the record consists of an examination of various aspects of the counselee's life to determine relationships, patterns, and balance. For example, the counselor notes that the counselee has average school marks and low-average mental ability. He further discovers that the counselee comes from a family where the highest amount of school completed is the eighth grade. The counselee has several brothers working in semiskilled jobs. He is now planning to attend college. Furthermore, the record reveals that the counselee does not participate in school activities and lists no hobbies or recreational activities. The counselor might infer that the counselee, because of the family occupation and educational status, is putting a great deal of time and effort on schoolwork and hopes to achieve more than have other members of his family. This, of course, is a very tentative inference that should be verified by checking with other data. The status picture here is one of lopsided development, however.

Filling in Gaps in Data and Locating Clues for Further Investigation. A careful study of each item in the cumulative record is made so that no significant item will be overlooked. Individual items are closely checked, of course, in the two previous approaches. However, certain aspects of the detailed study of each item are worth emphasizing again. Sometimes what appears to be a rather insignificant entry may give an important clue to a student's problem. For example, if the counselor did not notice that the counselee was a year younger than would be typical for his grade placement, he might fail to check on reasons for acceleration. At the same time the counselor would want to be alert for entries that should be carefully evaluated rather than accepted at face value. For example, if the entry "a natural leader" appeared under behavior characteristics, the counselor might wonder what a "natural leader" is and what the person making the entry had in mind. If the counselor knows the author of the comment he will probably have some idea of what was meant. However, it would not be wise to consider the student as an accomplished and effective leader on the basis of this statement alone.

In another example, the counselor failed to notice an excessive number of absences several years prior to counseling. It turned out later that the counselee had been seriously ill and had received very poor preparation during that time, with the result that he was handicapped in his present grade. Also, he still demanded the solicitous treatment that he had received during his illness. In the counseling sessions, for some reason, he had not mentioned this illness.

The potential significance of each item in the cumulative record is much too extensive to go into here. Consider, for example, the number of references on the influence of parents' occupations on the socioeconomic status, mobility, and occupational goals of the children [100]. The counselor's background of knowledge of pertinent research, his experience, and his understanding of the local situation will determine just how much interpretation he will be able to make. However, questions that a counselor might ask about typical data in the cumulative record are given below to suggest some of the significant aspects. References such as [78; 133, pp. 134–165; 187; 217; 218, ch. 7; 240, pp. 64–68; 253, ch. 13] provide excellent help in learning to interpret specific items.

1. Name. What mental picture of the person does the name suggest? Studies have shown that definite notions of personalities go with names [118, p. 486]. While these stereotypes have no basis in fact, they may determine in part the reaction of others to the counselee.

2. Date of birth. Note the age, whether retarded or accelerated in school, whether or not same age of others in class.

3. Place of birth. Is he a native of this part of the country? If not, from what section? Rural or urban? Customs of section from which he came?

4. Parents or guardians. Are parents living? Living together? Separated? Divorced? Are they about the same age? How old compared with counselee's age? Are they in good health?

5. Occupation of parents. What is the level of occupation? Amount of training required? What is the status of the occupation? What is the typical income level? Is the work seasonal or steady? Present status on the job, for example, supervisor, foreman, rank-and-file worker? Is the mother working? What kind of work? Rating of economic status of family? As is true with names, there are stereotypes of the sorts of persons engaged in various occupations [194, p. 328]. How might this affect the attitude of others toward the parents?

6. Residence. What is the section of town or country from which counselee comes? What are characteristics and attitudes of persons from this section? How many persons live in the home? Who are they? Is there adequate room or is the home crowded?

7. Brothers and sisters. Is the counselee an only child? How many siblings? Counselee's age in relation to others? Level of education of others? Level of occupation if working?

8. School progress and achievement. Has counselee progressed normally from grade to grade? Accelerated or retarded? What sort of curriculum is he taking? What subjects does he appear to do best in? Is he consistently better in these? Is there a pattern of doing well or poorly in related groups of subjects, for example, those of a verbal nature, as compared with numerical? About where does he rank in his class? What does this rank mean for further education; for example, does 10 per cent go to college, or 90 per cent attend?

These are only a few of the questions that may be raised in deriving as much significance as possible from individual items. You can, no doubt, think of many other questions about these and other items in the record. The counselor often overlooks a wealth of valuable information about the counselee by making only a superficial review of the cumulative record items. A careful study should be part of the inference-making process that the counselor uses with all data.

Cautions in the Use of the Cumulative Record

The counselor should keep two cautions in mind when using the cumulative record as a source of information for counseling. First, he should not jump to conclusions on the basis of data in the record, particularly one or two items. Second, he should evaluate with caution, if not outright suspicion, subjective items in the record. Teachers and teacher-counselors sometimes state that they would prefer not to see the cumulative record before helping the pupil. The basis for this attitude may be their uncritical acceptance of all the data in the record, particularly the subjective items. It is desirable to have as much information as possible about the counselee, but it is also essential that this information should be evaluated in a professional manner by professionally competent persons.

An illustration of the error of jumping to conclusions is the case of the counselee whose record contained a series of comments over a period of years to the effect that he was uncooperative and caused trouble in the classroom. The counselee was low in mental ability, retarded in grade, and low in school marks. Concluding that the counselee was a disciplinary problem because schoolwork was too difficult for him, the counselor began counseling with this preconceived notion and made very little progress in helping the counselee. It turned out that the counselee was a very poor reader. After remedial treatment, he showed adequate ability and motivation to do satisfactory work.

It is better to think of the cumulative record as providing *some* information which will be added to and checked against other data. It will thus help the counselor to gain a better understanding of the counselee rather than be used as the only source of information about him. It serves particularly well in providing clues to employ in searching for further information. Subjective data, in particular, should be checked against similar data from other sources. As the counselor looks over a record he will notice that a great deal of information of this type is included, for example, ratings on adjustment, leadership, or initiative. These terms have different meanings for different raters. Often the ratings are made for the entire year, without any provision for showing trends or variations or for illustrating the rating with specific examples. These ratings and comments do indicate how others react to the counselee and thus furnish data which should not be ignored.

Synthesis of Data in the Cumulative Record

While different approaches to studying the cumulative record have been taken up, it should be kept in mind that the purpose of using the record is to obtain a ". . . glimpse of a real live person" [218, p. 181]. All these approaches are combined by the counselor to enable him to obtain the maximum information from the record and to organize it into as meaningful a picture of a person as possible. A more detailed discussion of the process of synthesizing and interpreting data is given in Chapter 11.

John Doe's Cumulative Record

After the first interview, the counselor, Mr. Doyle, went to the cumulative record file and took out John's record. As you may remember, the counselor had noted several points about which he wanted more information. With these in mind, he now raises specific questions about information in the cumulative record. As he turns to the record for help, he has some definite points to check. He is not simply looking for information, but instead for information which will serve a particular purpose.

1. What are actual marks? (What is the trend in these grades? Where has he done best? Poorest?)

2. How about attempting to measure vocational interest? (Does the record contain the results of measurements of this kind?)

3. Need for more information about the home situation and John's attitude toward parents. (What about the amount of education his parents had? What effect might this have on his parents' plan for John?)

4. What about values? (What are the things that John wants most? Puts the highest values on? What are the really important things to him?)

5. How well does John compare with high school and college students in academic ability? (Does the record give any test scores that indicate academic ability?)

6. How does John get along with peers? Any leadership qualities? (Has he had any offices in school organizations? What do teachers think of his ability to influence others? Do peers accept him?)

7. What have been his interests up to now? Any consistency in these interests? (Have vocational interests been the same for a number of years? Does the record give any idea of the factors affecting his interests?)

8. What do teachers think about John as to drive, interest, work habits?

9. How much time does John actually put on studying? How effectively does he use his time?

10. Check on tests already taken, if any. (Have tests been given recently? Is there enough information about the tests taken so that the counselor can determine what group John was compared with, whether or not he took the appropriate form of the test?)

11. How about checking aptitudes in several areas? (Is there any information in the record about aptitude tests?)

The actual record that the counselor used is shown on pages 100–101.

Additional Information Needed. The counselor found that the cumulative record did not furnish all the desired information about the counselee. He still had a number of unanswered questions and made notes of the things he

Cumulative

Name : *John J. Doe*   Home address : *210 Sidestreet, Hometown*
Birthdate : *September 1, 1940*   Telephone : *543*

		Year			1955 – 56				1956 – 57				1957 – 58							
		School			Hometown				Hometown											
		Grade			9th				10th											
		Chron. age			15				16											
Notes on elem. sch. exp.	Record of classwork	Subject			Subject	1	2	Yr	Subject	1	2	Yr	Subject	1	2	Yr	Subject	1	2	Yr
					Eng.	C	C	C	Eng.	C	B	C+	Eng.	C						
					Hist.	D	C	C-	Hist.	C	C	C	Hist.	B						
					Math.	D	F	D	Math.	B	C	C-	Math.	C						
Average grades, very cooperative, good attendance record, well liked					Latin	C	D	C-	Latin	F	D	D-	Latin	C-						
	Comment				Works hard, concerned about grades				Almost a failure, plans to do better next year				Shows some improvement, but complains of lack of interest							
Academic aptitude		Test	Sc	IQ	%	Test	Sc	IQ	%	Test	Sc	IQ	%	Test	Sc	IQ	%	Test	Sc	IQ	%
						Otis		106													
Reading		Test	Sc	IQ	%	Test	Sc	IQ	%	Test	Sc	IQ	%	Test	Sc	IQ	%	Test	Sc	IQ	%
						Iowa			40												
Explan. notes on scores	Achievement and other tests	Test	Sc	Gr*	%	Test	Sc	Gr	%	Test	Sc	Gr	%	Test	Sc	Gr	%	Test	Sc	Gr	%

Notes :   * Norm group

Record

		Occupation	Education	Religion	Health	Deceased date	
	Name : *John J. Doe*						
	Birthdate : *September 1, 1940*						
Father		Carpenter	8th grade	Protestant	Good	------	Significant items about family
Mother		Housewife	12th grade		Fair	------	
Stepparent or guardian							Mother very anxious for John to finish school.
Siblings							Father questions the value of college-prep course John is taking.
Sister		Student	9th grade	Birthdate: Dec. 1, 1944	Good		

Year and age		1955 15 yrs	1956 16 yrs	1957 17 yrs	1958 18 yrs
Counselor		Smith	Jones		
Attendance		No unexcused absences	No unexcused absences		
Discipline	Academic	Good	Fair		
	Personal	Good	Good		
Interests	In school	Sports, school paper	Sports, school paper		
	Out of school	Sports, job	Sports, job		
Vocational experience		Part-time helper in grocery store, clerking, store room	Part-time clerk in grocery store		
Notable accomplishments					
Health and physical vigor		Good, very active, energetic	Good, athletic and energetic		
Educational and vocational plans		College, doctor or lawyer	College, doctor perhaps		
Behavior description	Responsibility and dependability	Good, very dependable	Very good		
	Creativeness and imagination	No special ability	Apparently no special ability along these lines		
	Influence	Follows the crowd, but has some influence	Seems to be able to get others to cooperate with him		
	Social adjustment	Well liked by classmates	Seems to be popular, takes part in social activities		
Counselor's notes					
Remarks:					

planned to check. To obtain the needed information he planned to use techniques such as those discussed in the following chapters. He first decided on what he and the counselee needed to know and then selected ways to obtain this information. The following are the still-unanswered questions which the counselor raised as he went over the cumulative record.

1. John's developing interests—how they started, what influenced them, how consistent they were.

2. More information about values.

3. Measure of academic ability.

4. An estimate of achievement in subject areas.

5. More information about how others react to John. Also, some information about his behavior in various situations. (A student can sometimes put on a pretty good "act" for the counselor.)

6. Some information about the relative strengths and weaknesses of aptitudes. What kinds of things can John do best?

7. The way John uses his time. How much time does he actually put on studying?

8. A check on reading ability, in view of John's "dislike" of reading.

9. Since the academic aptitude test and the reading test on the cumulative record were given in the freshman year, and since score, norm group (explained in Chapter 5), and form of test were not given, the counselor decided that he would not depend upon these measurements.

Several additional questions were raised by the counselor after he had reviewed the record and noted down the questions listed above.

1. Would health and physical ability be a handicap or an asset in vocational planning?

2. Is John's personality generally suited to work in which he deals with others, or is it more suited to a job of a secluded nature? Why?

3. If John went to college, how much of a financial problem would he and his family have?

The first nine questions were the unanswered parts of those that were raised by the counselor during and after the first interview. The review of the cumulative record suggested still more questions. Quite often the counselor finds that additional information gives rise to new questions.

Note that the counselor, at this point, is still raising questions and searching for information rather than making inferences about the meaning of the information. However, it is possible to see the tentative inferences behind some of his questions; for example, is poor reading ability the basis for John's dislike of reading?

SUMMARY

The cumulative record furnishes much valuable information for the counselor to use in understanding the counselee. It also provides clues for further exploration.

The counselor studies the record to obtain a picture of the whole person. He may combine longitudinal and cross-sectional methods with a detailed study of each item to obtain the most information possible. The data from the record should not be used alone but should be compared with other data. Subjective items should be appraised with caution. Snap judgments about the counselee are often erroneous and harmful and may considerably reduce the effectiveness of counseling.

CHECKS ON UNDERSTANDING

1. What general type of information about the counselee might you expect to find in the cumulative record?

2. What is meant by a developmental or longitudinal picture of the counselee?

3. What is meant by cross-sectional description of the counselee? Is this type of description dynamic or static?

4. Describe a suitable approach for the counselor to use in studying the cumulative record. What would he do first, second, and so on?

5. How might the counselor use information from the cumulative record in the counseling session?

6. Why is it essential for the counselor to combine cumulative record data with other information?

7. What cautions should the counselor observe in using the cumulative record?

THINGS TO DO

1. Obtain copies of cumulative record forms used in other schools and determine what sorts of information they contain.

2. Using the items in a cumulative record form, write out a list of significant questions about each one. Also suggest ways that items may be compared.

3. Look over an actual cumulative record of a pupil. Can you detect a problem from the information?

4. Starting with a problem exhibited by a pupil, look over the cumulative record for clues as to the cause. Formulate questions about additional data needed. Make plans for an interview with the pupil.

5. Ask an experienced counselor how he uses the cumulative record. Inquire about how he studies the record as well as what he does in the interview as a result of his study of the record. You might question several counselors and compare their answers.

6. Ask an experienced counselor if he will "think out loud" as he looks over a cumulative record. If possible, record what he says. Does he use an identifiable process? If so, evaluate it.

CHAPTER 5

Tests

THIS AND the next chapter deal with the use of tests in the counseling process and counselor activities in learning about the individual through test results. This chapter contains a brief discussion of some technical information basic to the understanding of tests, such as types of tests, meaning of test scores, reliability and validity, and norm groups. The next chapter provides a discussion of what the counselor does about selecting and interpreting tests in the counseling situation.

Testing and the Counseling Process

Testing is not in itself a counseling technique. Giving tests to a counselee, interpreting results, and combining them with other data are counselor activities. It is only when tests are selected and results interpreted in the counseling process that testing actually becomes an aspect of counseling methods and techniques. Thus topics such as setting up a school testing program, administering group tests, administrative use of test results, and others related to the school guidance program are not taken up here. There are some excellent references on these and related topics [75, chs. 1–4; 77, pp. 196–200; 78; 130, pp. 194–241; 163, ch. 6; 180, pp. 146–150; 238, chs. 1–9; 239, chs. 5–7, 9–11; 254, ch. 7; 261, chs. 7–11]. Of especial value are Froehlich and Benson [75] and Traxler [238, 239].

The use of tests is a major field of study in itself, and it may seem ambitious to present a treatment here in two chapters. However, it seems justified by emphasizing, first, a minimum of basic information that the counselor needs to know about tests, and second, learning how to use references to utilize specific tests. No particular tests are discussed in these chapters, as there are

104

excellent sources of information about tests [35, 36, 220]. A brief discussion of a number of tests here would only be misleading in that it could not treat them as comprehensively as would be necessary. Thus extensive reading and study are suggested in conjunction with this and the next chapter. The counselor should know where to go for additional information whenever the need arises.

This discussion deals primarily with the types of tests commonly used in high school and college. Performance tests, individual tests of mental ability and other clinical tests, and projective tests are omitted. Most of these tests, which require special training to administer and interpret, would be infrequently used by the typical counselor. If the counselor had occasion to use the results of these special tests, he should be furnished a nontechnical interpretation. If he plans to administer any of them, except perhaps several relatively simple performance tests of manual dexterity, he should take courses to prepare him to do so. Actually, many of the test results that the counselor uses will be from tests given routinely in the school guidance program. With particular counselees, however, the counselor will have occasion to select and use other tests.

Psychological Tests

There appears to be a great deal of misunderstanding about the meaning of the term *psychological tests,* what these tests are supposed to measure, and what should be done with the results. For example, some school counselors consider counseling not much more than interpreting test scores to the counselee. Some counselees think of tests as the "answer" to their problems. There are some counselors who consider tests as having little or no practical value. All these positions represent misconceptions of the proper use of tests in counseling. A balanced viewpoint, in which the uses as well as the limitations of tests are recognized, is the most desirable one. This "balanced" point of view is most necessary for the type of counseling discussed in this book. As has been pointed out, tests may not be needed with all counselees. Then too, with some approaches to counseling or psychotherapy, tests may not be applicable. "Schools" of counseling or counseling approaches, discussed in Chapter 1, use test results in various ways.

With this word of caution, the question of what tests are will now be taken up. Psychological tests are instruments for obtaining samples of what the counselee can do or what he thinks or believes. These behavior samples enable the counselor to make inferences about the counselee's present status and how he will react in various situations, both present and future. For example, a test of intelligence provides a basis for the counselor to make an inference about the counselee's mental ability and how much he could learn in school. Some tests are in the nature of inventories or check lists, with no right or wrong answers; others are more like the usual teacher-made tests, in that there are correct and incorrect responses. When tests are used to measure traits such as intelligence or mechanical interest, it is assumed that such traits exist in the individual, that they can be measured with tests, and that they are relatively stable or consistent from day to day. The practice of using measurements of traits in counseling is not, however, in conflict with the concept of the person as a functioning and organized whole. This is discussed in more detail in Chapter 7.

Classification of Tests. One way to classify tests is by the terms *power* or *speed.* Power tests determine how much the individual can do when not limited by time. Usually the test is organized so that it becomes progressively more difficult. Speed tests have time limits which must be strictly observed. Usually the test is designed so that no one taking it will have time to complete all the items. If many persons should get a high or perfect score, the test would not give evidence of which ones were better in the trait measured.

Most tests can also be classified as either *paper-and-pencil* or *performance.* (Not all can, however; clinical or individual tests that call for verbal response do not fall into either category.) Performance tests enable the individual to indicate ability of one sort or another with such materials as puzzle boards, pegs, or blocks which the examinee actually uses. Typical abilities measured are mechanical understanding, abstract reasoning, and finger dexterity. Paper-and-pencil tests make up a greater majority of the tests used in high school.

Tests can be classified as *group* or *individual.* Any group test may also be administered to one person. The group tests are usually paper-and-pencil tests, although a few performance tests may be given to several persons at once. Individual tests are those which must be given to one person at a time. These tests usually require special training to administer and should not be given by persons not having this training. Most of the tests used in the school are group tests, and most counseling will involve only group-test results, if test results are used at all.

The most useful way for the counselor to classify tests is by what they measure, such as aptitudes or interests. This method of grouping or classifying tests will now be taken up.

What Tests Measure

Psychological tests fit rather naturally into the following categories: intelligence, achievement, vocational aptitude, personality, and interest. An understanding of these terms is essential for the counselor in selecting and interpreting test results.

Intelligence. Actually this is not one trait but a group of traits that involves the use of symbols, such as words, numbers, or abstract symbols. Many intelligence tests give one score, which is often referred to as a global score. Some of the newer tests give separate scores for specific aspects of intelligence such as verbal or numerical. Usually intelligence is thought of as the ability to do schoolwork (academic aptitude), and many intelligence tests are evaluated on the basis of how well they predict success in academic studies. However, a helpful way to think of this type of test is in terms of the student's ability to understand and use symbols, that is, to use language, numbers, and abstract concepts both in and out of school.

Achievement. This group of tests is primarily composed of those that measure achievement in school subjects. It also includes such things as reading ability, vocabulary level, and the like. The counselor often uses achievement tests as a basis for estimating the counselee's level of achievement because his grade level and courses taken may not furnish sufficient data to compare the counselee with others. Achievement of the sort discussed here is largely a function of intelligence, but there is not a one-to-one relationship.

Vocational Aptitude. This term is used here to indicate a specific trait or ability needed in an occupation. For example, an assembly job involving small parts may require finger dexterity. Thus finger dexterity would be a vocational aptitude needed for the job. Other aptitudes would be needed, however, besides this particular one. The term *aptitude* is also used in another way, with which the counselor should be familiar, to indicate aptitude for an occupation or a type of training, which is, of course, a much broader meaning than the "specific trait" used above. For example, it may be said that a counselee has aptitude for work as an auto mechanic, meaning that he has all the various sorts of specific aptitudes needed to be successful in this occupation.

Personality. This area includes the individual's attitudes toward himself, toward others, and about various aspects of his life, including how he thinks others regard him. Personality tests of the sort frequently used in the school consist of a series of questions or statements which the individual checks as applying or not applying to him. The items may be added up to indicate problems in various areas or may be used to classify the individual as to personality traits.

Projective tests are also a type of personality test, from which more of a global approach to the total personality is obtained. The counselor should be very cautious in the use of tests of personality because the simpler personality tests that are generally used do not give as dependable information as other tests. For example, one limitation is that they do not provide much helpful information with which the counselor can predict what the counselee will do or what he is actually like. There is much overlapping of groups or classifications into which the results place the individual. Little is known as to what educational or occupational areas are best suited for types of persons, as classified by these tests.

Interest. This area, which is actually an aspect of personality, has special significance for counseling where educational and vocational problems are involved; it is therefore considered separately. The term *vocational interest* is widely used and generally understood. It is the patterning of likes and dislikes of the individual that has implications for occupational choice. Interest tests are made up of many items or questions, among which the examinee indicates a preference. These items are scored in various ways to show the counselee's occupational preferences.

These five groupings of test measurement are, of course, quite broad. Within each are more specific categories of tests. For example, in the achievement category, there are tests of achievement in English, mathematics, social studies, and other subject areas. A comprehensive listing by categories may be found in Refs. [35, 36]. To determine what a particular test measures the counselor should study the manual, check reviews in these references, and look over research and summaries of research such as contained in Ref. [220].

What Test Results Mean

Knowing the general category of the test and being familiar with the specific trait or traits measured still does not provide all the information necessary to determine the meaning of the score. The counselor also must know the following:

1. What the particular type of numerical score means
2. The group that was used as a basis for the norms from which the counselee's score was obtained
3. How consistently the test measures
4. How precisely the test measures what it purports to measure
5. The meaning of similarities or differences in test scores when two or more tests are used

Each of these topics will be taken up in one of the following sections. Before this, however, it is worth emphasizing again that the counselor needs to get firmly in mind what the test measures. This might seem to be an unnecessary caution. However, the author has personally witnessed a number of instances in which an interest test was interpreted as a measure of "what you can do best," and an aptitude battery profile was interpreted as a measure of likes and dislikes.

Types of Scores Frequently Used

Test results are usually given in percentile ranks, intelligence quotients, or mental ages. Less frequently used but also important are scores in the form of deciles or quartiles. In connection with test scores, the terms *mean* and *median* are also used. Not employed as frequently as the first three types mentioned but becoming increasingly important are various types of standard scores. The counselor should understand what each of these types means and be able to describe the score in terms that the counselee can understand.

Percentiles and Related Scores—Quartiles, Deciles, and the Median. These types of scores, particularly percentiles, are widely used. A percentile rank indicates the individual's standing compared with others. It is the percentage of persons who scored below the individual [113, p. 109]. For example, if a counselee has a percentile rank of 60 on a test, he did better than 60 out of 100 who took the test. If he has a percentile rank of 50, he is just at the middle of the group.

The centile scale is simply the division of a group of test scores (or other data) into 100 units. Each unit includes 1 per cent of the scores. This scale, with many of the centile points identified, is shown here. These centile points divide up the group of scores. The percentile rank is where the particular counselee's score places him on this scale [113, p. 109]. Notice that the units of the scale are closer together near the middle than they are at the extremes. The reason for this spacing will be given later.

The illustration shows only the divisions on the scale; it does not include the test scores of others that are needed to obtain the counselee's percentile rank. Test manuals or profile sheets furnish the data to convert the counselee's score to a percentile rank.

The counselor needs to know more than simply the centile rank to understand the meaning of the counselee's score. He needs to be able to apply qualitative terms to the rank. What is a high rank? What is an average rank? How many various ranks be described? A percentile rank of 75 or above indicates that the counselee is in the upper one-fourth of the group with whom he is compared. This would appear to be comparatively high. A percentile rank of 25 or below indicates that he is in the lowest one-fourth. This is a comparatively low rank and suggests that the counselee does not have much of what the test measures in relation to the group with which he is com-pared. In the middle area, with ranks between 30 and 70, it is difficult to say that the counselee is much different from aver-age. This, of course, does not mean that a percentile rank of 35 is not appreciably lower than one of 65. But this type of score tends to exaggerate differences in the middle ranges, in the 40s, 50s, and 60s, and to minimize differences at the extremes. The scale here illustrates this point. The centile points have been spaced according to a normal distribution (discussed later) to show more clearly the differences among various points. It is difficult to provide guides for evaluating percentile ranks with-out bringing in the concept of standard scores. Therefore some

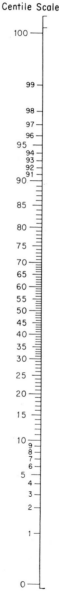

Centile Scale

additional points about percentile ranks will be discussed when standard scores are taken up.

Even if the counselee has had percentile ranks explained to him, it is not usually too helpful to tell him simply that he ranks at "the 75th percentile on mechanical ability." Some verbal explanation is also needed. Numbers are easily misinterpreted by the counselee. For example, a counselee appeared to be quite crestfallen when told that he ranked at the 74th percentile in mental ability. He explained later that he thought he had failed because 75 was the passing mark in his school! In another instance, when IQ scores were given out in a junior high school, an angry parent came to see the principal and demanded to know why her son was doing unsatisfactory work. "He ought to be passing! He got 80 on that 'test' and 75 is passing!" It should be kept in mind that the explanation should be put in words that the counselee can understand. Counselees have varying levels of ability to grasp score interpretations.

To return to the matter of describing specific scores, the following suggestions are made. If the score is 50 or close to it, that is, near the middle of the group, the score may be described as "average" or "around the middle of the group," with the counselor naming the group, for example, liberal arts college freshmen. The counselor might also say that the counselee has an adequate amount of what is measured to get along with others in the group with whom he is compared. He is neither outstanding nor weak. For example, suppose that the counselee's mental ability is being measured and he is being compared with other high school seniors. He ranks at the 50th percentile. As far as mental ability is concerned, he has about the same as the "average" senior. Furthermore, on those tasks involving mental ability he *should* be able to do about average work. This does not mean that he *will* do it, nor does it mean that he could not do better than average work. The counselor would also need to know what letter mark was considered average; for example, the average senior may receive a B. For a better comparison with his particular class or school group the counselor would need local norms (discussed later).

How about scores that do not fall near the middle of the group? Half of the individuals fall between the 25th and the 75th percentile. As has been pointed out, this is considered to be roughly in the average range. Scores around the 30s might be described as "low average" and those around the 40s as "slightly below average." The counselee could be given these descriptive terms and be told that he is "about where most people are." Then scores around the 60s could be described as "slightly above average" and in the 70s as "high average." The counselor could add that, while the counselee is about where most others are, he appears to have a little more of what is measured than the average, or that he definitely has more of what is measured, doing better than 60 out of 100 who took the test, or 70 out of 100. Thus an explanation that included the counselee's score, where it places him on the 100-point scale, and a statement about how much or how little of what is measured he possesses, would seem to be adequate. Examples of counselors' explanations are given in the next chapter.

Suppose that the counselee ranks around the 15th, 20th, or 25th percentile. The counselee may be told that he is low in what the test measures and that he would be at the lower end of the group with which he is compared. If he ranks at the 10th percentile and below, he could be described as "very low" and quite lacking in what the test measures. The illustration on page 109 gives some indication of the importance of differences of centile scores from about 10 to about 1. Then if the counselee's score is around 75, 80, or 85 he could be told that he is high in what the test measures, has more of it than three-fourths of the group, and should be able to perform very well or in an excellent manner on what the test measures. A percentile rank of 90 or above is extremely high; the counselee could be described as being at the top of the group and having a very great amount of what the test measures. He should be superior to most persons in the group in the ability or other characteristic measured. This illustration shows that there is a great difference between centile points from 90 up.

The descriptive terms given above are rather arbitrary. They seem to be accurate enough for most purposes although they may not be the same as those given in other sources. For example, some tests have profile sheets that provide specific interpretations for various percentile ranks.

Quartile and decile scores are interpreted in the same way as centile scores. Quartile points divide the group of scores into fourths, as shown in the illustration below.

Quartile Scale

```
┌──
│    Highest one-fourth
├── Third quartile point (same as 75th centile)
│    Next highest one-fourth
├── Second quartile point (or median) (same as 50th centile)
│    Next highest one-fourth
├── First quartile point (same as 25th centile)
│    Lowest one-fourth
└──
```

Quartiles, like centiles, are points on a scale. The interpretation cannot be as precise as it is for centiles but the same descriptive terms may be used. If the counselee's score was below the point dividing the lowest one-fourth and the next one-fourth, he could be described as falling in the lowest one-fourth and low in the trait measured. Note that the second quartile point is the same as the median or mid-point of all the scores. Other quartile points are given in the illustration.

Decile points divide the total group of scores into tenths. The low numbers start at the bottom of the scale; thus the first decile point is at the 10th centile, and it marks the upper limit for the lowest one-tenth. The 9th decile marks that point above which the highest 10 per cent fall. Thus to say that the counselee is above the 9th decile is to say that he is in the highest 10 per cent of the group. The same descriptive statements used for centiles may also be used for deciles. It should be kept in mind that differences near the middle of the scale are exaggerated and those at the extremes are minimized, as shown in the illustration on page 109.

Standard Scores and Similar Type Scores. These types of scores are of particular importance because they provide a basis for the counselor to understand and interpret other scores, such as percentile ranks [240, p. 113]. The use of standard scores is becoming more widespread and many of the newer tests give results in this form.

A standard score, or any of its variations, is an indication of how much the individual's score varies from the mean or average of all scores in the group. On page 113 is a curve of normal distribution with centile points, standard scores (also called "z" scores), and standard deviations. The normal curve shows the way that scores on a test usually look if they are plotted with the size of the score along the bottom and the number of persons making that score represented by the height. They do not always fall in exactly this shape, but it is possible to normalize them if they do not. Thus what we have as test scores usually represent this sort of distribution. Note that the larger area, which represents the greater majority of individuals, is near the middle, with far fewer individuals at the extremes. On the left are the lower scores and on the right are the higher ones. Centile points have already been discussed. Standard scores and standard deviations will now be explained. Standard deviations will be taken up first, as they are the basis of standard scores.

Note that approximately 34 per cent of the scores fall either one standard deviation above or below the mean or average. Thus approximately 68 per cent of the scores are in that large middle space one standard deviation above and below the mean. Note that these scores are bunched together, with the majority of test results in this area. Approximately 13 per cent of the scores fall between one and two standard deviations from the mean. When both the low and high sides are added together, this totals approximately 26 per cent. Approximately 2 per cent fall above or below two standard deviations from the mean. This makes a total of approximately 4 per cent for both sides. (The total is less than 100 per cent due to rounding.)

The standard deviation, a measure of dispersion, is the most meaningful portrayal of the individual's standing compared with the group. If the counselor has a mental picture of the normal curve and the location of standard deviations on this curve, he is in a position to make an accurate interpretation of various types of scores.

The standard deviation is derived as follows:

$$\text{Standard deviation} = \sqrt{\dfrac{\left(\begin{array}{cc}\text{each individual} \\ \text{score}\end{array} - \begin{array}{cc}\text{average or mean} \\ \text{for the group}\end{array}\right)^{2}}{\text{number of individuals in the group}}}$$

For greater ease of interpretation and to eliminate minus numbers, scores are often converted into standard scores with a mean of 50 and a standard deviation of 10; these types of scores are called "z" scores. The computation is as follows:

$$\text{Standard score or z score} = \dfrac{\text{the individual's score} - \text{mean of the group}}{\text{standard deviation}} \cdot 10 + 50$$

Many test scores are given according to the above system.

It is now possible to compare centile points, standard scores, and standard deviations. Note that the large middle group is between a standard score of 40 and one of 60. This group is also between centile points of 15.9 and 84.1. This does not mean that they are all the same or all average. However, it does suggest that they constitute a group that is neither very high nor very low, and that centile scores in this range are not as different as those below 40 or above 60 are quite low or quite high. The curve below clearly shows the differences among scores at the extremes. For example, there is as great a distance between centile scores of 84 and 97 as there is between scores of 50 and 84!

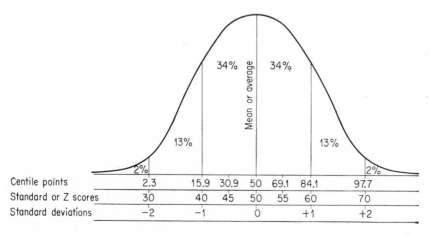

Centile points	2.3	15.9	30.9	50	69.1	84.1	97.7
Standard or Z scores	30	40	45	50	55	60	70
Standard deviations	−2	−1		0		+1	+2

How can the standard scores be described? Note that 50 is average. The descriptive terms used earlier with centiles would apply to standard scores. In fact, they were based on the standard score scale and the normal curve rather than on the centile scale. Scores from about the 30th to the 70th centiles were described as roughly in the average range. Note that these are about the same as standard scores of 45 to 55. Standard scores between 40 and 45 could be described as low to low average and those between 55 and 60 as high average to high. Those which fall below the standard score of 40 would be quite low, and those below 30 would be extremely low. On the other end, standard scores of 60 or above would be quite high, and those of 70 or above would be extremely high. The curve illustrates where the counselee stands in comparison with the total group when he has a particular percentile rank or standard score.

The Intelligence Quotient and Mental Age. The intelligence quotient or IQ is the ratio of an individual's mental age to his chronological age; it is computed as follows:

$$\text{Intelligence quotient or IQ} = \frac{\text{mental age}}{\text{chronological age}} \times 100$$

Usually the test provides a raw score which may be converted directly into the IQ. It also gives the mental age or MA from which the counselor computes the IQ. The intelligence quotient and mental age show the counselee's mental ability compared with the general population, not a select group such as high school seniors or college freshmen.

Of utmost importance in interpreting IQ scores is the fact that scores from different tests do not mean the same thing. Thus an IQ of 115 on one test does not necessarily mean the same level of mental ability as an IQ of 115 on another test. The following descriptive categories apply to one specific test, the Binet test [122, p. 97].

Above 140	Near genius or genius
120–140	Very superior intelligence
110–120	Superior intelligence
90–110	Normal or average intelligence
80–90	Dullness, rarely classified as feeble-minded
70–80	Borderline deficiency, sometimes classifiable as dull—often as feeble-minded
Below 70	Definite feeble-mindedness

While these are widely used for this particular test, they do not necessarily apply to the results of other tests [256, pp. 37–39]. One reason why they are not comparable is because the standard deviations of the various tests are different. For example, the standard deviation of the Binet test is 16 [229, p. 28]. Thus an IQ of 116 is one standard deviation above the mean, and one of 132 is two standard deviations above the mean [229, p. 42]. The counselor needs to check the test manual for the meaning of the IQ for the particular test he uses.

For some intelligence tests, scores are available in percentile ranks or standard scores. These are interpreted in the manner already discussed.

It is now time to consider another important aspect of testing, the stability of the test score.

Reliability or Consistency of the Test Score

Knowing what the test measures and what the numerical score means is still not enough to enable the counselor to interpret the results. He also needs to know whether or not the test measures consistently, or whether dependence can be put on its results. Obviously, if the counselee made one score one day and a quite different score the next on the same test, the test results would not be very useful. However, fluctuations may be caused by conditions not attributable to the test itself, for example, the physical or mental condition of the counselee, faulty test administration, or distractions during the testing session.

In the first place, a test should have a certain level of reliability to be useful. For the types of tests considered here, this reliability is expressed by a number called a *coefficient of reliability*. Several methods of determining reliability are given in Refs. [114, p. 28; 85, pp. 213–215] as follows: the coefficient of internal consistency (correlating parts of the test with each other); coefficient of equivalence (correlation between two forms of the same test given at the same time); and coefficient of stability (correlation between the same test given at two different times). The coefficient of reliability is a statistic indicating the degree of relationship. While there is no set rule as to just how large the reliability coefficient should be, a good rule of thumb is that it should be .85 or above [220, p. 65]. The test manual should be checked for information about reliability, and other sources of information [35, 36] should be reviewed.

It is particularly important to check the reliability of subtests. Many tests give scores for parts of the tests as well as for the total test. These parts of the test, or subtests, may not be as reliable as the total test; however, the test manual may give the reader the impression that they are just as reliable. Before the counselor makes use of these subtest scores he should check to determine if they are adequately reliable according to the standard given above.

Another concept that will assist the counselor in interpreting the test score is a statistic called the *standard error of measurement*. It is not an error in the sense of a mistake, but rather a variation in test results to be expected with repeated administrations of the test. Suppose that to get the counselee's *true* score the test were given over and over again. The counselee would get a slightly different score each time. The standard error of measurement indicates how much his score would be expected to vary. It is not possible, of course, to give the counselee a large number of the same type tests to measure the same thing, so the counselor has to take his results on one or two tests. It is assumed that if the counselee were given the same test many times his scores would vary on both sides of his true score, which is never known.

To explain this point further, suppose you were measuring a table with a yardstick and wanted the results to the closest one-hundredth of an inch. You probably would be a little over the exact measurement of the table one time and a little under it the next. You can, of course, obtain the exact measurement of the table if you have accurate enough instruments. In measuring psychological traits, it is not possible to get the exact measurement but only to approximate it. The coefficient of reliability tells how much dependence can be put on the counselee's score as an approximation of his true score.

The standard error of measurement has a more concrete meaning for the counselor than the coefficient of reliability. From the standard error of measurement the counselor may estimate how far the obtained or actual test score is from the counselee's *true* score. The obtained score is an estimate of the true score. The score that the counselee actually obtained may be expected to be within one standard deviation above or below the true score about two-thirds of the time. An illustration should help to make this clearer.

Suppose that Bill Smith had an IQ of 106 obtained by one of the commonly used paper-and-pencil tests. The counselor looks in the test manual and finds that the standard error of measurement is four IQ points. (This should be in the manual, but if it is not, it can be quickly computed in a manner described later.) The counselor may interpret this as follows: "Bill made a score of 106. I cannot say that this is the true score that represents Bill's intelligence, but I can say that about two-thirds, or 68 per cent, of the time his obtained score would be expected to be within four points of his true score. This gives me a fair degree of confidence that Bill is over 100 in mental ability or in the range of 102 to 110."

The counselor cannot say with much confidence, however, that Joe Jones, with an IQ of 108, is more intelligent than Bill with his IQ of 106.

Now suppose that the counselor wanted to be more precise in estimating Bill's true score. He could say that about 95 per cent of the time his obtained score would not be more than two standard deviations from his true score. This is a much better estimate of his true score, but notice what has happened to the range of scores that must be used. It is now 98 to 114! The counselor may wonder whether or not tests are worth while. The answer is that they are, if they are used correctly. Thus the counselor should understand that test results do vary and that the exact numerical score is not a fixed and absolute value.

One further point should be made in connection with the standard error of measurement. The greater the range of scores in the group, the higher the reliability is likely to be. The reason for this is obvious when the test results of a group of greatly varying ability are compared with those of a group whose abilities are almost the same. On a retest a difference of only a few points may have a marked effect on the coefficient of reliability of the group that is made up of similar individuals. In the group made up of individuals who vary widely in ability (for example, grades 4 through 8), however, the low ones would be quite low and tend to stay in their relative position. The same would be true for the high ones. Thus the counselor should consider the characteristics of the norm group when interpreting the reliability of a test. The norm group should be made up of individuals similar to the counselee.

As has been pointed out, the standard error of measurement, for the particular group with whom you wish to compare the counselee, should be given in the test manual. If it is not, it may be computed in the following way. The counselor should use data about the specific group with whom he compares the counselee.

$$\text{Standard error of measurement} = \text{standard deviation } \sqrt{1 - \text{coefficient of reliability}}$$

This formula also helps to show the meaning of the standard error of measurement. Note that the larger the coefficient of reliability, the smaller the fraction by which the standard deviation is multiplied and the smaller the standard error or measurement will be. Note too that the standard error is also affected by the units of measurement; that is, if a test has scores of from 1 to 500, with a standard deviation of 50, the standard error of measurement would be larger than that of a test with a range of scores of from 1 to 50 and a standard deviation of 5. Yet the two tests could be equally reliable.

Further study of reliability would be helpful, as this is an important concept for the counselor to keep in mind as he uses tests. There are several helpful references [52; 85, pp. 213–215; 90, ch. 17; 220, p. 651; 238, pp. 21–24].

Validity in Interpreting Test Results

While the test should measure consistently, it should also measure *something*. The degree to which it does this is called *validity*. A test can be very reliable and still not measure anything about the counselee that the counselor can use. It has already been pointed out that the counselor needs to know exactly what a test measures. He also has to know how well the test measures it.

The problem of test validity is a complex one and only a few aspects considered of particular importance for the counselor will be taken up here. Additional reading is recommended, particularly Refs. [85, pp. 215–222; 90, ch. 18; 220, pp. 32–57, 651–654].

There are four types of validity which provide data for different uses of tests, as follows [114, p. 13]: content validity (how well the test embraces items from the situation about which conclusions are to be made, for example, mathematics problems from a mathematics course); predictive validity (how well the test predicts performance, for example, school marks); concurrent validity (how well the test scores relate to the status of particular groups, for example, a group of expert mechanics); construct validity (how well test results agree with explanatory constructs, for example, lack of self-confidence, or introversion).

The validity with which the counselor is most concerned is that type for predicting performance, or some sort of external validity [220, p. 652]. This type of validity is expressed by a statistic that shows the degree of relationship, usually a correlation coefficient. The criterion traits with which the test is correlated should be clearly specified in the test manual. The correlation of the test with the criterion will usually be .20, .30, .40, or .50. The best available tests usually have validities in the vicinity of .40 to .50.

The measurement of the criterion is subject to error. For example, school marks, often used as the criterion for intelligence tests, vary according to the way the teacher marks, and for other reasons. Thus the counselor should be aware of the difficulty of setting up a useful and dependable criterion [220, pp. 32–43]. A check of the test manual and a review of Refs. [35, 36, 220] will enable the counselor to judge how well the criterion was measured.

It is important for the counselor to check the validity of the test for the particular group with whom he compares the counselee. For example, if he wishes to check the counselee for standing on mechanical aptitude, he would determine his rank compared with the appropriate group, and check the validity of the test for this *same* group.

How high should the validity coefficient be if it is to prove useful? There is no specific answer to this question [220, pp. 653–654]. It might be said that a coefficient of about .45 or better would be desirable, keeping in mind that a test with one as low as .20 or .25 might be quite useful if it measured something not estimated by any other test. Just how useful different size coefficients are is shown by the following data [90, p. 409]:

Coefficient of validity	Percentage of reduction of error in predicting the criterion from the test score	Percentage of the variance (or variability) of the criterion accounted for by the test
.20	2.0	4.0
.30	4.6	9.0
.40	8.3	16.0
.50	13.4	24.0
.60	20.0	36.0
.70	28.6	49.0

A validity coefficient of .20 enables the counselor to predict only 2 per cent better than guessing, and accounts for only 4 per cent of the amount of the variability of the criterion. To give an example, suppose that a test had a validity coefficient of .50. You can see that this increases prediction over chance by 13.4 per cent. Instead of a 50–50 chance of predicting how, for example, the counselee would perform in college, you now have, with the test results, about a 56.7 chance of being right and a 43.3 chance of being wrong.

The most useful way for the counselor to use the validity coefficient is in connection with a statistic called the *standard error of estimate*. This statistic enables the counselor to estimate the counselee's real or true score on the criterion. For example, he may predict the counselee's course mark from a test score within certain limits based upon the standard error of estimate.

Whether or not the counselor actually computes the standard error of estimate, it is essential that he understand the concept upon which it is based. If he does not, he is likely to use test results as an absolute indication of some predicted criterion, or in some other way that will nullify any potential help the test has to offer. The concept is simply that a test predicts, or enables the counselor to predict, performance within certain limits with varying degrees of certainty. The meaning of this concept may be illustrated by the way the standard error of estimate is computed, and by an example.

First, consider the way that the standard error of estimate is computed [90, p. 405].

$$\text{Standard error of estimate} = \frac{\text{standard deviation}}{\text{of what is predicted}} \sqrt{1 - (\text{coefficient of validity})^2}$$

All the needed data should be in the test manual, although they may not be. Suppose you are using an intelligence test score to predict performance in the first year of college. Performance in college is the average of all course marks for the freshman year. The test is given in the senior year of high school. The "standard deviation of what is predicted" would be the standard deviation of college marks.

The formula shows that the standard deviation or variability of what is predicted is reduced by an amount determined by the coefficient of validity. College freshman averages range from A to F. It might be assumed that the average freshman mark is C. It might be assumed further that one standard deviation above and below average would include the C— and C+ students, which would be about 68 per cent of the freshman group. Suppose these letter marks were converted to numbers in the following way:

$$A = 5 \qquad D = 2$$
$$B = 4 \qquad E = 1$$
$$C = 3 \qquad F = 0$$

It might be expected that about 68 per cent of the freshman class would have an average of from 2.5 to 3.5.

If the counselor knew nothing about test scores, he could say that the chances of a counselee making an average mark would be about 68 in 100. This is true because 68 per cent of the freshmen are in this group. It is a probability statement made with no knowledge of the counselee.

Now note again that the coefficient of validity *reduces* the standard deviation of the group (college freshmen). Even if the coefficient of validity were zero, that is, if there were no correlation between the test and college freshman marks, the standard deviation of the criterion (college marks) would not be reduced.

Assume that the test correlates .50 with freshman marks. Suppose also that the standard deviation of freshman marks is .9 and the mean is 3. Thus about 68 per cent of the freshmen receive marks of from 2.1 to 3.9, or between D+ or C— and C+ or B—. What help will the test provide to the counselor in estimating the probable first-year-college average of the counselee?

Using the formula given and inserting the standard deviation of the criterion .9 (college average) and the coefficient of validity .50, the following results are obtained:

$$\text{Standard error of estimate in predicting college average from intelligence test scores} = .9 \sqrt{1 - (.50)^2}$$
$$= (.9)(.87)$$
$$= .783$$

This statistic, .78 (rounded), is the standard error of estimate in predicting a college average from the test score. The original standard deviation of college marks was .9. Thus the standard error is .12 lower. Note that it is not much lower than the standard deviation even though the test has a rather substantial correlation with the first-year average (and about as high as is usually found). It allows the counselor to predict somewhat better than he could without any knowledge of the counselee's test score.

How much better can he predict? He can say that about two-thirds of the time the counselee's score will be within a range of plus or minus .78 rather than plus or minus .9. But to show the full use of the standard error of estimate, the predicted college average must be considered. This will be done in the next paragraph. However, if the counselor goes no farther than understanding that the standard error of measurement illustrates that test results are useful but that they have definite limitations, he should be better able to use test results effectively.

The use of the standard error of estimate with a predicted score will now be taken up.

Recall that it was pointed out that if the counselor had no information about the counselee, he could make a probability statement that there are about 68 chances in 100 that his first-year-college average would be between 2.1 and 3.9, or one standard deviation above and below the mean of all freshmen. What will the test score enable the counselor to say about the probable first-year average? It is possible actually to work out a predicted score, as will be shown later. Then it may be said that there are about 68 chances in 100 that his *actual* first-year average will be within one standard error of estimate of his *predicted* first-year average. It may also be said that there are 95 chances in 100 that his *actual* average will be within two standard errors of his *predicted* average.

The size of the standard error of estimate provides a clue as to how much help the test provides in predicting the criterion. Thus it is helpful to know it even though the counselee's predicted rating or score on the criterion is not worked out.

Computing the counselee's predicted first-year average is not difficult. If both test data and criterion data are in percentile ranks or standard scores, charts or tables may be used [128; 220, pp. 661–663]. An example of a helpful aid made for a specific group is shown in Ref. [169]. The counselor can predict the counselee's performance if he has the coefficient of validity, the mean and standard deviation for the test, and the mean and standard deviation of the first-year-college marks. It is done in the following way:

$$\frac{\text{Predicted first-}}{\text{year average}} = \frac{\text{coefficient}}{\text{of validity}} \left(\frac{\text{standard deviation of college marks}}{\text{standard deviation of tests}} \right)$$
$$(\text{counselee's test score} - \text{average test score}) + (\text{average college mark})$$

In the example used, the coefficient of validity is .50, the standard deviation of college marks is .9, and the average college mark is 3. In addition, the average test score is 100 and the standard deviation of the test is 10. Now all that is needed is the counselee's test score. Suppose he received a score of 120 on the test. What is his predicted college average and how much confidence can be put on the prediction? Insert the quantities in the formula, as follows:

$$\text{Predicted first-year average} = .50 \left(\frac{.9}{10} \right) (120 - 100) + (3)$$
$$= (.045)(20) + (3)$$
$$= 3.9$$

While 3.9 is the predicted average, the counselor does not predict an exact average but rather a range. Then he can state the chances that the counselee's average will actually fall in that range. Recall that the standard error of estimate was .78. Now the counselor is able to predict the counselee's course average. He could make statements such as the following:

The chances are about 68 in 100 that the counselee's average will be between one standard error of estimate above or below his predicted average, or 3.9 plus or minus .78 (between 3.12 and 4.78). This would be from about a C or C+ to B+ or A−.

The chances are about 95 in 100 that the counselee's average will be two standard errors above or below his predicted average, or 3.9 plus or minus 2 times .78 (between 2.34 and 5). This would be from about a C— or D+ to A.

Two very important points may be drawn from this illustration. First, tests do not tell exactly what the counselee will do. Second, they do provide helpful information that is much better than no information. Whether or not the counselor actually computes a predicted score, he improves his test interpretation by having an understanding of these concepts.

It should be pointed out before leaving the subject of test validity and prediction that local data are of great value. It would be of most help if the test results and criterion data were on the specific group with whom the counselee would be competing, for example, the freshman class in the specific college.

Norm Groups in Understanding Test Results

The term *norm group* has been used several times in previous discussions. It has been said that the counselor should be careful in selecting the appropriate norm group in determining the counselee's score. The norm group is that group of individuals upon whom the test was standardized. Their raw scores are arranged in a frequency distribution with centile points, standard scores, or some other type of scores to indicate levels of performance. The counselee's score is then compared with these scores to give an estimate of his level of performance.

The norm group is also used to determine how well the test predicts. Estimates of how well the test predicts should be made from the specific norm group. There usually are a number of different norm groups for each test.

The test manual is the source of information about norm groups. They may be a "large unselected group" or well-defined, homogeneous, and specific groups. It is particularly important to check the description of the norm groups that are used.

The norm group should be described in enough detail for the counselor to determine whether or not it is a suitable group with which to compare the counselee. Sometimes the manual does not describe the norm group adequately. In this event the counselor should use caution in interpreting the standing of his counselee when compared with a miscellaneous or unspecified group. When the counselor locates the appropriate group that will give the most information about his counselee, he compares the score on the test (the raw score) with the norm group scores and obtains a percentile rank, standard score, or other type of score. If the group is very well described the counselor can infer a great deal about the measured trait or traits of the counselee. If it is poorly described, with general terms such as "mechanical workers" or "office workers," the counselor will know considerably less about how the counselee rates on the trait measured.

The counselor faces a particularly difficult problem in determining what the counselee's test results mean in relation to the group with whom he is now or will be competing. For example, how does the senior boy compare with freshmen at State College or with trainees in auto mechanics at the local trade school? He may actually be high in mechanical understanding when compared with trainees in the local trade school but low compared with those in trade schools over the nation. Or a counselee may be high in academic ability compared with college freshmen in one college, low compared with those in another college, and average compared with a large group of college freshmen from many colleges. The answer to this problem is to use local norms. They may sometimes be obtained from schools or colleges, or the counselor may compute his own for his school, city, or county [75, pp. 91–101].

There is another caution which the counselor should observe in using norm groups and interpreting test results. The norm group may consist of persons already in an occupation or in an educational program. The counselee is usually a person who has not yet entered the educational program or occupation. Caution must be used in interpretation of the counselee's standing compared with those who may be older and more experienced. As is pointed out in Ref. [220, pp. 45–46], the counselor should know the validity of the test when given to persons prior to their entering the training or job and later checked against success on the job or in the training program.

It may appear that the counselor has a great deal to do if he wants to get as much out of tests as possible. However, developing the habit of using the manual and other references mentioned in this section will almost certainly enable the counselor to improve his skill in using tests. The more it is used, the easier this research point of view will become.

Comparability of Test Scores

The counselor often faces the question of the comparability of scores on different tests [221]. With the availability of batteries of tests given the same group, a partial answer to this question is possible [220, pp. 358–375]. An illustration of the problem is as follows: If, for example, the counselee ranks at the 65th percentile on mechanical insight and at the 35th percentile on clerical speed and accuracy, which is his strongest aptitude? Suppose the tests have been standardized on different groups. The clerical group may be a select group with very high aptitude and the mechanical group may be a miscellaneous group who are low in mechanical as well as other aptitudes. The counselee's own clerical speed and accuracy may be a great deal better than his mechanical insight. When a group of tests has been standardized on the same subjects, the counselor may better estimate the intraindividual ability or aptitude pattern. The counselor is particularly interested in the counselee's pattern of strengths and weaknesses so that he can help him to make the greatest possible use of his potentialities.

If the norm groups for the tests are the same or roughly comparable, how much of a difference in scores is needed before it can be concluded that the counselee is actually better in one area or on one trait than another? Some test profiles give an indication of how much scores should differ to be dependably different. The standard score scale shown in the curve on page 113 may be used as a guide. A difference of one standard deviation would be a dependable difference. A difference of one-half standard deviation would appear to be useful also as an indication of a fairly dependable difference. The standard error of measurement may be used to indicate the probability that the scores are dependably different. If the zone included in one standard error overlaps for two or more tests, the counselor could not put much confidence in the results being really different.

Sometimes counselors describe a difference of two or three points on two tests as being quite important. If the picture of the normal curve is kept in mind and the concept of the standard error of measurement is used, there should be less likelihood of exaggerating what are actually insignificant differences in test results.

Aids to Help the Counselor Learn about Tests

In addition to the references mentioned, there are some other aids which the counselor may use to acquire a fund of accurate information about tests. A form for evaluating a test,* such as that shown below, should prove quite helpful. The counselor would learn a great deal about the test from completing a form such as this, and the information would be available for others who use the test.

Form for Evaluating Standardized Tests

I Preliminary data: Name of test **Otis Self Administering Test of Mental Ability**
   Author   **Arthur S. Otis**   Publisher   **World Book Co., Yonkers**
   Cost per test   **5¢**   Type: Individual   Group   **X**
   Use suggested by author **Indicator of academic aptitudes, grades 4–9 and 9–13;**
   produces MA and derived IQ
   Reading level: Grade _____   MA _____   IQ equivalent _____

II   Validity indices

	Number and type of subjects	Criterion	Adequate?
.55–.59	157 to 249 H. Sch. Stud.	Sch. Marks	?
.70	?	Army Alpha	
.59	157 H. Sch. Freshmen	Scholarship	
.56	39 Machine Bookkeepers	Job Secured	No

* William C. Cottle, "A Form for Evaluating Standardized Tests," *Occupations,* vol. 30, December, 1951 [52]. By permission of the publishers.

III Reliability coefficients   Number and type of   Method used   Other data
                                        subjects

Higher exam. .92   **125 and 128; Gr. 7–12**   **Comp. forms**   **Reported by Otis**
Intermediate exam. .948   **215 and 212; Gr. 4–9**   " "   "   " "

IV Counselor's ratio   **.28**   Standard deviation   Range of scores made
     by norm group
     Percentage of forecasting efficiency   **(r = .57)**   **17.48**

V Details of administration: Untimed   Timed   **X**   Under 25
    min_____Under 45 min   **X**   Under 90 min   Over 90 min
    Materials needed: Stopwatch   **X**   Electrographic pencil   Special
    answer sheet   Punch board   Punch   Other materials

    Special training needed? Yes   No   Type
    Number of subtests and subscores   For what purposes

VI Method of scoring: Hand scored   **X**   Machine scored   Either
     Scoring stencil   Key opposite answer   **X**   Scoring time per test **I min**
     Can it be scored by client? Yes   No **X** Weighting system used? Yes   No **X**

VII Minimal interpretation needed:
_____By psychologist only
_____**X**_____By counselor with psychometric training
_____By an instructor with no psychological training
_____By client with explanation
_____By client without explanation

VIII Recommendation:
     By whom recommended:
     For what group   **Grades 4–12**
     For what purpose   **Estimating school success and employment levels**
     Use: National (Dominion)   **X**   State (Province)   Local
     References: **Manual for test; Super, D.E. Appraising Vocational Fitness; Bingham,**
     W.V. Aptitudes and Aptitude Testing; Buros
     (On the back of this sheet write a short summary)

SUMMARY

The counselor who uses tests needs to be able to employ various sources of information to determine what the test measures, what the score actually means, how much dependence can be put upon the stability of the score, how well the test measures what it measures, and what groups have been used in setting up norms. A grasp of these concepts, along with basic information about particular tests, will enable the counselor to obtain the most possible help from tests in providing effective counseling.

CHECKS ON UNDERSTANDING

1. See if you can put into your own words the five general sorts of information that tests provide.

2. What use does the counselor make of the reliability of a test?

3. What advantages do standard scores have over centile scores?

4. Where do you obtain the information to enable you to describe a particular IQ in verbal terms?

5. How can you judge the importance of the difference between two test scores on the same counselee?

THINGS TO DO

1. Take several tests, one from each of the classifications of interest, intelligence, and so on, score them, and make up a test profile. Using the manual and other references, interpret the results.

2. Administer a test (or tests) to someone else, score it, and prepare an interpretation.

3. Using test results in a pupil's cumulative record, prepare a test interpretation. Check carefully to determine if any essential information is missing, for example, the specific norm group used.

4. Use the evaluation form on pages 124–125 to summarize data about one or several tests.

5. Select a test and read the reviews in Buros [35, 36], then prepare an evaluation of the test. Note that the reviews do not always agree.

CHAPTER 6

Using Tests in Counseling

TEST DATA are potentially very helpful in counseling. They must be used effectively, however, or they will not facilitate the progress of the counseling process to the degree that they should. This chapter deals with the process of using tests in counseling and with several related matters, such as the reasons for using tests.

Why Use Tests?

When tests are used the assumptions are made that the traits they measure actually exist, that they are rather stable, and that they have importance for the counselee's life and plans. However, the counselee is not simply a collection of traits; rather he is a whole person and these traits are important only as they provide information about the total person. In order to learn as much about him as possible, tests as well as other sources of information are used. Tests furnish information which can be obtained in no other way, or which may be used to check against information obtained in some other way. They provide data from which inferences about the individual may be made and from which hypotheses about him may be formulated.

Test data thus assist the counselor in helping the counselee to learn about himself. For example, the counselee may learn that he compares well with college freshmen on academic ability. This might be an important bit of data that the counselee needs to make suitable educational plans. Then this datum, plus other information, assists the counselee to formulate and test a concept of himself and his role [222]. Test data are one sort that enables the counselee to make an adequate response, to test reality, and to develop a realistic self-concept.

The use of tests in counseling is justified if they are employed in a clinical way [220, p. 533]. Lack of data for precise predictions about specific types of work, education, and the like makes it necessary to use a clinical type of prediction rather than a statistical one, which should consist of telling the counselee his chances of success in an occupation or educational program based on test results alone. In the clinical approach, test results are combined with other data to enable the counselor to formulate hypotheses for the counselee to consider, rather than giving him a numerical prediction of his chances of succeeding, say, as an auto mechanic. Clinical and statistical predictions are explained in more detail in Chapter 11.

The use of test results, therefore, does not take from the counselee the responsibility and opportunity to make his own decisions. Note that counseling is different from "selecting," an example of which is a business using a battery of tests to furnish a numerical or statistical prediction as to how the potential worker will perform on a particular job. In counseling, one very important assumption is that the counselee has the right to make his own decisions. Tests help him to make that decision a better one than it might otherwise be. Tests furnish a particular type of data that helps the counselor provide an effective learning situation. The counselor would be neglecting a useful source of information if he did not learn about tests and use them when they can provide needed information.

Determining When to Use Tests

In spite of the potential value of tests, they should not be used routinely and automatically in counseling. Before using them, the counselor should ask himself if they will provide information that will promote the progress of counseling. He might phrase it this way, "What information do the counselee and I need that we do not have?" He would identify the information, for example, some evidence about vocational interests. Next he would ask, "Is there a test that will provide this information?" If there is a test he would use it. He might know of one that would be useful, or he might go to the test catalogues and to references such as [35, 36, 220] to locate one. The need for testing arises out of the counseling situation. Thus only one test may be used, several may be given over a period of time, or an extensive battery may be administered at one time. Whether the counselor would choose tests himself or whether he and the counselee would select tests as a joint enterprise is discussed later.

Thus far, the question of deciding whether or not to administer a test or tests to the counselee has been considered. However, in some instances, test results are already available in the counselee's records. In counseling done in high school and college, usually a number of tests have already been administered as part of the guidance program and the results have been entered in the cumulative record folder. As the counselor looks over the record he uses test data along with other data to learn about the counselee. However, test results are not brought into the counseling situation until there is a reason for doing so. For example, he may have found in the cumulative record ample evidence that the counselee can do about average college work. When the counselee comes in, he may be concerned about some other problem, such as conflict with his parents on an occupational choice. Test results about college aptitude would probably have no real meaning for him then. If he did not feel a need for the test information he would probably not learn much from a discussion of it. Thus test results should not be allowed to obscure other more important matters in the counseling process. Counselor preoccupation with tests may result in this, particularly if he brings in test results and focuses attention on them before they are needed.

Requests by the Counselee for Tests. The counselee comes in for counseling with certain expectations. Quite often he feels that he should take some tests. In fact, he may hold this belief so strongly that he thinks he is not getting what he should unless he takes some tests. If the counselee is very positive in this feeling and if it appears that not giving him tests will affect the counseling relationship and the progress of counseling, then it would seem that he should be given some tests. It will probably turn out, however, that tests will not fulfill the expectations that he had for them, and he may then be ready to proceed with counseling.

When the counselee demands tests, he may be expressing a need to avoid the responsibility of making plans and decisions or doing some thinking about himself. He may see tests as a way of being told what he should do. In effect he is saying, "The tests will give me the answer to my problems and it will not be my responsibility." For some reason he cannot or will not take responsibility for himself. In this situation the counselor may help the counselee explore his feelings about tests and why he thinks they are so important. This sort of exploration may be done in the permissive atmosphere of the information-getting phase of counseling. Until he understands his "dependency" need for someone else to make his decisions, he would probably not get much help from test results anyway. If the counselor goes ahead and administers a number of tests and discusses them with the counselee, he will probably find that they do not provide the counselee with the answers that he wants, and he will then demand additional tests or other sorts of directions from the counselor. The demand for tests may be only a symptom of the counselee's problem, and treating the symptoms would not be likely to remedy the problem.

On some occasions counselees request tests because taking a test is something they know about; it provides a familiar environment or one in which they feel secure. This point is in direct opposition to that where the test is regarded as threatening. It would appear that these counselees would be "test wise" and also reluctant to talk about themselves. Yet some counselees, those who are apparently not motivated to request counseling but are forced to do so by teachers or parents, seem to feel that taking a test is the path of least resistance to fulfilling their obligation. Thus they request tests. Actually they may be resisting a personal relationship and attempting to maintain their distance by working on impersonal tests.

Another type seems to be those who have read about "tests" in a popular magazine, heard about them in a psychology course, or obtained a smattering of information some other way. They profess curiosity in "finding out what I'm like." A test is merely a novelty that they want to try out.

Counselee Participation in Test Selection

From the foregoing discussion it may appear that the counselor decides when tests are needed and which tests are to be used. The counselor, however, does not necessarily do this alone. He may, instead, encourage the counselee to voice his feelings about taking tests and may actually work with the counselee in selecting the type of test that will be used. In this way, the counselee takes an active part in the process and may express his feelings about tests and about whether or not he thinks they will be helpful. He does not get the impression that the counselor has taken over responsibility for the outcome of counseling. The usual procedure is for the counselor to describe, in terms that the counselee can understand, what information tests will provide [30, pp. 268–272; 32, pp. 173–183]. As an example, in the following passage the counselor explains the types of test and the information which the counselee may obtain from them.

COUNSELOR: Well now, maybe at this time . . . if you'd like to, we could see if we could get a little help from using tests. We talked about a battery of tests earlier. Tests won't give you answers. They'll only give you other information about yourself that might be helpful, er . . . in estimating your abilities and seeing how well you compare with people in different sorts of work. But all these other things are important too. For example, we couldn't—no matter what tests show us—we couldn't overlook . . . the cost of training, for example. Tests don't tell you how much competition there is in the field, how many other people you're going to have to compete with to be successful. But they can offer some helpful information. . . . Now there are a number of different kinds of tests that would help perhaps, but there are generally four kinds of tests that could be helpful. One kind is mental ability or academic aptitude or intelligence, how well you can learn—how well you can do in learning from books, say. Something along that line would enable you to compare your ability with people in different sorts of schools, high school and college too . . . give you some idea of how you compare as to learning ability. Would you think something like that would be helpful?

COUNSELEE: Yes sir.

counselor: OK. We'll include something like that in the battery then. Now, there are tests that attempt to get at the things you like to do—interests. What you've stated as your interests is pretty important but the test asks you many different questions about different activities on jobs, and sometimes jobs you don't even know about. Occupations that you don't know about will show up as . . . because you picked a lot of activities in that job. Would you think that taking something along that line would be helpful?

counselee: Yes sir, it'd be nice.

counselor: Interest? OK. Well now, there are a lot of tests. . . . Some aid in estimating aptitude. It can be art aptitude, mechanical, or scientific or various types. . . . Do you think it would be helpful to have something in the way of aptitude? For instance, would you like to know how your different abilities in art compare with people who are studying art?

counselee: Yes, sir. That'd really be nice.

counselor: Some that will attempt to get at that, they might be helpful. Well, how about some other areas of aptitude? What things do you think you would like to know about yourself? How well you can do various things? Any particular things?

counselee: Besides the ones you've mentioned?

counselor: Uh huh.

counselee: Er . . . I mean. . . .

counselor: You've wondered about art aptitude. Well there're several ways to get at that, through the work you've done, opinions of your instructor . . . but I was thinking also the test will add something to that, but the test won't tell you of course, by itself.

This interview excerpt illustrates what the counselor might say about tests. It, however, does not show active participation on the part of the counselee. Since he had earlier expressed a great deal of interest in tests, his simple agreement to the counselor's suggestions could have been all that were called for. Usually, however, more active counselee participation would be desirable.

In the John Doe first interview the counselor explained the types of tests to the counselee but did not go into the test selection process.

As the types of tests are discussed, the counselee decides whether or not the sort of information provided will be of help to him in solving his problem. He is also able to express his feelings about measurement of that trait, for example, mental ability. As a matter of fact, discussion in the test selection process may open up previously unrevealed but important aspects of the counselee's personality [32, p. 179]. Since the counselor has technical knowledge about the specific tests, he actually selects the tests to be used [32, p. 175]. To do this, the counselor has to have a thorough knowledge of what the tests measure, what meaning the results have for education, occupations, adjustment, and so on, and must be able to explain them in terms that the counselee can understand. For example, it is much easier to state that a test measures "spatial visualization" than to explain this aptitude in simple words. The technical term itself, however, would have little or no meaning for the counselee. Points covered in Chapter 5 should provide the basis for an adequate description of the test.

The Usual Method of Selecting Tests

Another approach to the selection of tests in counseling, in which the counselor actually decides which sorts of tests are needed, is probably more frequently used. In this approach, the counselor recognizes that specific kinds of information are needed and that they may be obtained by tests. The information may be of the sort that can only be obtained with tests, or it may be information quite similar to data already obtained by other methods which the counselor wants to check by comparing with test results. This need would most likely be realized after a counseling session or so. For example, the counselor might have school marks, achievement test results, and comments from teachers on which to base his estimate of the counselee's chances of being able to do successful college work. But the counselor may wish as a further check to obtain an estimate of how well the counselee compares with college freshmen in academic ability.

If test selection and use actually are a part of the counseling process, the counselor will have a definite reason for using tests. The counselor should know something about the person to be tested (what sort of person he is, his background); he should know what tests can and cannot do; and he should have some idea of what the counselee wants to do or what problems he has [220, p. 534]. There is no short cut for the counselor to know whether or not tests will be useful, and which tests to use. It would appear to make a difference in the counseling relationship if the counselor himself decided whether tests were needed and which tests to use, or if the counselee helped select tests. As a matter of fact, each response the counselor makes to the counselee is a counselor decision that the response will affect the counselee in a certain way and result in certain counselee behavior. Thus in a sense, deciding to use tests is a counselor response to which the counselee reacts. If the counselor's decision has been a poor one, he may need to change his approach. But the counselor checks the suitability of what he does, of each response he makes, by helping the counselee to express his feelings about it.

With a reason formulated for using a test or tests, the counselor then brings up the matter for the counselee to consider. He may suggest that it would be helpful to have certain types of information that can be furnished by tests. For example, the counselor may say, "One way we can get at interests a little better is to use a test that compares your interest with those of other people about different sorts of activities such as mechanical things, working with people and helping them. . . ." In this instance the counselor is suggesting a specific test (an interest test). He may suggest the use of a number of tests this way:

"It looks like it would be helpful to make a survey of how well you can do in a number of different things and maybe give some leads that we can look into further. How do you feel about something like that?" In this statement the counselor was suggesting what would be termed exploratory testing.

Whether the counselor is suggesting one test for specific information or a number of tests for exploratory testing, he introduces the idea that tests may be helpful, explains why, and asks the counselee how he feels about it. The counselee should be given some idea of what the test is for, what specifically it measures, why it is suggested, and what the results could mean; he should have the opportunity to express his feelings about any or all of these aspects. Testing has a different meaning for different counselees; for example, one counselee became quite anxious when tests were mentioned because she felt sure that her high opinion of her mental ability would not be upheld by test results. Her reaction to the mention of tests was to give the appearance of indifference about them and to say that she thought it would be a waste of time. (The counselor made this interpretation from what the counselee said later and from his notes written at the time tests were suggested.) The counselor helped her to discuss and face her feelings about tests and later she expressed interest in checking her opinion of her mental ability by testing.

In both procedures, counselee participation in test selection and counselor selection, the counselee would be encouraged to react to the use of tests. In counselee participation, tests would not be given unless the counselee selected one or more types. In counselor selection, the counselor would use tests regardless of the counselee's opinion unless there was considerable resistance. It would not be helpful to attempt to force an unwilling counselee to take tests even if test data were needed.

If structuring about the use of tests has been done at the beginning of counseling, it may not be necessary to do much, or any, when tests are actually brought in. However, the counselor should be alert for indications of the counselee's understanding, or lack of it, about the values and limitations of testing. It may be that the counselor will have to do more structuring even though it has been done earlier. Possibly some would be needed to reduce the counselee's apprehension about tests, even though he wants to take them. Some counselees become quite keyed up at the thought of taking a test, even to the degree that it affects their performance. Sometimes it may help to point out that there is no passing or failing mark but that the results will give some information about how the counselee compares with others. This sort of explanation may reduce, to some degree, the counselee's feeling that he must come up to a certain mark or he will fail, as one fails a school subject. Usually some structuring about what tests measure, as previously discussed, will be necessary.

The Test Supply. Suggesting that the counselor select tests one way or another implies that he has a supply of tests on hand to use. It is quite desirable for the counselor to have a readily available supply so that he can administer the test at the time when the counselee is ready for it. References such as [75, 78, 220] will be useful in determining which tests are frequently used and which would be good ones to have on hand. Test catalogues, which may be obtained from publishers listed in Ref. [36], will also be useful. Certain references [9, 36] will probably be too extensive to use for the initial selection of tests but are extremely helpful in evaluating specific tests. Of course, selection of tests should be based on the needs of the school and of the pupils. Furthermore, the sale of some tests is restricted to persons who can give evidence of competence in their use. The counselor should be mindful of the cautions that should be observed in the handling and use of tests. One aspect of the ethics of counseling concerns the proper use of tests.

The counselor will want to keep up with new tests as they become available and with pertinent research studies. The journals listed in Chapter 1 are most useful for this latter purpose, while test catalogues will announce the publication of new tests. The counselor may find it helpful to purchase a specimen set of a new test, study the manual, and check Ref. [36] for additional information. He may take the test himself in order to understand it better. If the test appears to be a good one, considering all aspects including cost and ease of administering, he may obtain a supply for use in counseling. There are helpful references on the selection of tests [78, pp. 207–212; 238, ch. 4; 239, chs. 5–7].

As has already been mentioned, many of the test results that the counselor will use will be in the cumulative record. He will not have had the opportunity to observe the counselee taking the test and to note his way of working and his approach to the testing situation or other aspects of behavior. It would appear to be of great value for the counselor to be able to observe the counselee at work on a test. To be entirely consistent with the viewpoint of counseling given here, the counselor would go through the entire process with the counselee, including administering any tests he took. Otherwise, the counselee must face a new person, the test administrator, with whom he must establish some sort of relationship. Or he might be tested in a group—a complete change from the individual and personal nature of counseling. However, it is often necessary to use group testing even for the tests required in counseling because of financial and other limitations.

In administering the test the counselor should provide suitable conditions and follow the test directions carefully [220, pp. 72–85].

The counselor administering a test to an individual counselee has an excellent opportunity to observe the counselee's behavior. How does he act in this new situation? Does he appear to grasp directions quickly? How does he start on the test? Is he persistent? Does he appear to work calmly and effectively or does he become tense and upset? How does he react to a particularly difficult test? What are his reactions at the conclusion of a test? The counselor can infer a great deal about the counselee from observation during testing. It is unfortunate that behavior descriptions are usually made only for certain clinical tests, as they would appear to be valuable information with any sort of test. A behavior check list which the counselor may use is shown in Ref. [220, pp. 82–83].

Often the counselee seems to be ready to talk about some particular problem at the end of a test. Taking a test seems to focus his attention on some aspect of his life that gives him concern. For example, a counselee stated that he was sure that he did poorly on test items involving numbers, going on to explain that he had always disliked mathematics because his parents had checked his homework and made him keep at it until he got all problems correct. Another counselee, upset by the fact that he had to choose among several items on an interest test, revealed a great deal about conflicts in interests that might not otherwise have been brought out. The check-list type of personality test frequently seems to prepare the counselee to talk about his problms.

It would also appear desirable for the counselor and counselee to score the test and check the norms as a joint enterprise after it has been completed [220, p. 561]. This can easily be done with many tests; with some, the counselee can actually do most of the work. Thus in a real sense he is a participant in the process, and he will likely be more interested and involved in what is going on.

Using Test Results in the Face-to-face Counseling Process

From the standpoint of the actual counseling process, the most important aspect of testing is using the test results to help the counselee. The counselor's knowledge of tests and careful selection and administration will be of value only if the results are effectively used with the counselee. Thus the use of test results is taken up as a separate topic here although the presentation of all sorts of data to the counselee is covered in the chapters on planning. Also, the synthesis of test results with other data is discussed here although synthesis and interpretation of data are covered in Chapter 11.

It would be helpful at this time for the counselor to read extensively on the use of test results in the counseling process. Extremely helpful are Refs. [32, pp. 184–192; 220, pp. 556–563; 240, pp. 159–168], as well as [27, ch. 11; 75, ch. 6; 192, pp. 149–165; 206, pp. 113–124; 253, pp. 84–89].

Synthesizing by the Counselor. In any use of test results, the counselor first compares them with other data. An illustration of the counselor's mental process in doing this is given in [240, pp. 148–155]. Another good illustration of synthesis is contained in Super [220, pp. 580–584], along with further presentation and interpretation of tests and other data [pp. 590–627]. A series of brief cases with test data is presented in Ref. [22].

Some suggestions for the interpretation and synthesis of test data with other information are as follows:

1. Translate for your own thinking test data into descriptive terms about

the counselee. For example, say that the counselee seems to have the ability to do above-average high school work rather than merely stating to yourself that he is at the 85th percentile in academic ability. Require yourself actually to do this for each test and you will begin to get a better understanding of the counselee as well as check your understanding of tests.

2. Compare test data with other data similar to them. Note points of agreement and disagreement. For example, suppose that the counselee had stated that there were good relations between himself and his family, yet on a personality test he checked many items that indicated conflict with parents. Or suppose that the counselee prefers working with machines, likes shopwork, shows good mechanical understanding on a test, and also ranks high on interest in mechanical activities according to an interest test.

3. Look further for data that will help in explaining puzzling aspects. For example, if there appears to be a difference between interest and ability, look for the factors that may have affected interest. What about parent's occupation? What indications are there that the counselee is favorably inclined toward or strongly against his father's occupation?

4. Look for patterns that help you to visualize the whole individual. Data about the counselee should fit together and make sense. There is a reason for each aspect of an individual being as it is even though the reason may be obscure. For example, a pupil who had the ability to do satisfactory school-work was nevertheless failing several courses. His parents constantly urged him to do better and on many occasions compared him unfavorably with a bright older sister who had led her class. The boy finally got to the point where he made no effort because he felt he could never come up to expectations. As the counselor studied the separate pieces of data, a picture of the boy began to take shape, a boy with ability to get along all right, but one who had learned that his best was just not good enough and who felt inferior and reluctant to try.

The interpretation and synthesis of test data and other data are not mechanical processes, but ones which each counselor will approach in an individual way. They will be only as effective as his understanding of the most significant meaning of each sort of datum will allow them to be. However, the steps given above may be a useful way to start out in learning to understand the meaning and relationship of data about the counselee.

Introducing Test Results. There is an obvious and simple answer to the question of when to introduce test results: bring them in when they are needed. However, this principle is unfortunately easier to state than to explain or illustrate. If the counselor, or the counselor and the counselee, decided upon a test, the counselor administered it and worked out the score or profile with the counselee, he would probably discuss the results as soon as he had them. The counselor would relate these results to other information at that time. He would have to have a pretty good grasp of the other information because he would not have the opportunity to make a leisurely study of it. This test was given to meet a particular need, and the results should fit into the counseling process quite naturally.

If a test or battery of tests has been given in a separate session, or perhaps in several sessions, for a specific purpose, it would be natural to bring in the results during the next counseling session. It may be best, on the other hand, to introduce them during the next several sessions.

Where test results are already in the cumulative record, the counselor has a different problem, but an easier one. He can bring in test results more naturally along with other data. Furthermore, he has time to study test results. He could, therefore, introduce them when that sort of information was needed in facilitating the progress of counseling.

In general, test results would be brought in during the planning stages of counseling. This does not rule out the possibility, however, that exploratory testing may be done and results discussed early in the process or during the information-getting stage.

Using Test Results. Test results are used to help the counselee learn. Thus the setting, atmosphere, and techniques should be those which promote effective learning.

In the first place, test results should be brought into a permissive setting. This provides the best atmosphere for enabling the counselee to accept and understand them. He should feel less anxious and tense as he and the counselor discuss these measurements in which he is personally involved and which, in fact, are part of him. He will be better able to comprehend the actual meaning of the results and to bring out his feelings about them.

To assist in promoting a desirable atmosphere, the counselor is sensitive to and responds to the counselee's needs. Thus if the counselee wants to discuss the test results right away, the counselor may as well go along with this desire.

In discussing the results of a test, the counselor might first make a general statement about what the test measures. For example, he might say, "One of the things that we measured was interest. This test compared your interests with others like you on the things that you prefer to do, all sorts of activities, not just jobs. Now this is only a clue to your interests and does not tell you what you should do or can do." As an interest test has several scores, the counselor proceeds to discuss each one, explaining it in general terms and relating it to other information about the counselee. The following passage is an illustration of how one counselor presented test results.

COUNSELOR: Well, let's look at this, for example. Here are some notes I made . . . on the interests. Now when you were in the ninth grade you took an interest test. You had chosen between several items that you liked . . . you know. Well, social service in an area was one. Now you've talked about interest in social work and that's an interest that involves say, helping people, for example, working with others. When you were in the ninth grade you ranked pretty low . . . that number just means you ranked. As far as you were concerned that was a low interest.

COUNSELEE: Uh huh. Mmmmmm. . . .

COUNSELOR: This test doesn't mean that you're able to do it; it's interest, and that was low. That was one of your lowest ones. Er . . . that and science and mathematics . . . and mechanical were all low . . . you came pretty low in that one. But over here, where you just took this test, actually the twelfth grade, that came out as one of the highest interests of all, an interest in working with other people and helping them.

COUNSELEE: Uh mmmm.

COUNSELOR: That's quite a change . . . actually. What do you think of that?

COUNSELEE: I don't know . . . it's surprising. I mean I never thought it would be that low then.

COUNSELOR: Well, that was back in the ninth grade. . . .

What do you think of the way the counselor presented the information? Actually most of the discussion was about one part of the interest test, or rather two interest tests taken over a three-year interval. After this interpretation the counselee and counselor discussed the change in interest over the three-year period for about half an hour.

Test results are presented in terms that the counselee can understand. Centile ranks are perhaps the easiest for the counselee to grasp, although the counselor bases his explanation on their relation to standard scores. The counselor might say, "On mental ability you rank above average and have, in this respect, enough ability to do excellent work in high school and above-average work in college." Although the centile rank may be given and the centile system explained, it is this verbal explanation, relating the score to work or education, that provides the counselee with what he needs to know. For another example, it would not be very helpful to tell the counselee that he ranks at the 85th percentile on the social service scale of an interest test; it would be more beneficial to tell him that he expresses strong interest for activities and occupations in which he works with others for the purpose of helping them or being of service to them, such as the teacher, social worker, and so on.

In using specific occupational names, the counselor should be careful that the counselee does not take too narrow a view of the meaning of the interest. For example, he may say, "I don't want to be a teacher or social worker!" The counselor should thus have a number of illustrative occupations in mind to explain the meaning of interest, in this case, social service interest. He should also emphasize that it is an *area* of interest rather than interest for only one or two specific occupations.

Where well-designed printed profiles are provided with the test, it will probably be quite helpful to use them. They require thorough explanation, however, regardless of how "self-explanatory" they purport to be. A test profile with eight or ten scores from one test can be a very complicated affair to the counselee who knows little or nothing about tests. In using the one-test profile, it is suggested that each score be taken up separately first and adequate time be used to go into each one in detail. Then, it might be well to summarize the total profile.

As for the test profile sheets that contain the results of a number of different tests, they appear to be too complex and to contain too much information to be used with the counselee (see the profile on page 147). Furthermore, the counselee is quite often trying to find one type of information while the counselor is explaining another, for example, he often searches for his IQ.

Where no profile is provided, or even if one is, the counselor may use simple pencil sketches to illustrate the meaning of the test score. Following is one example.

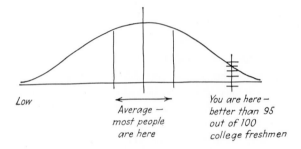

Low

Average —
most people
are here

You are here —
better than 95
out of 100
college freshmen

The counselor would make this sort of sketch as he gives the information verbally. However, it is suggested that some of the information be written on the sketch as shown. The counselor describes the group with which the counselee is compared; points out that the normal curve represents the way the scores fall from low to high; marks off ranges, such as average; and indicates the general range where the counselee scored. Note that the counselee's performance is better represented as a zone than as a point.

Following is a simpler type of sketch.

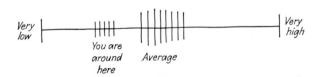

Very
low

You are
around
here

Average

Very
high

The line is described as representing the range of scores of the group, which has been defined. The counselee may or may not be told the numerical score. If it were given to him, it could also be written on the sketch.

Having something to look at often seems to help the counselee talk more freely. He may study the sketch as long as he likes without maintaining a silence that may become awkward if only verbal communications are used.

The illustration here goes beyond presenting the meaning of the score and provides information on probable performance. The previous figures also give some indication of this, but not as clearly as this type of sketch.

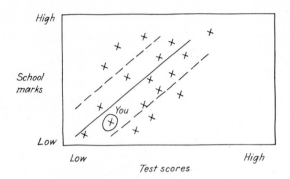

The *X*'s represent persons who took the test. Test scores are along the bottom and school marks are up the left side. No attempt is made to have the pattern of *X*'s accurately represent the correlation (the higher the correlation or coefficient of validity, the less scatter). The counselor may indicate where the counselee falls on the test. In this case he is low. The heavy diagonal line indicates that there is a tendency for grades to be associated with test scores. The dashed lines represent the range of expected performance, probably one standard error of estimate. You could explain to the counselee that he would be expected to obtain a mark close to or within the dashed lines. The sketch also shows that there is not a one-to-one relationship between test scores and school marks.

Below is another kind of sketch to aid in discussing expected performance. The data for this sort of illustration are unfortunately not frequently available, however.

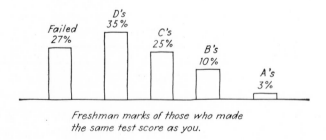

Freshman marks of those who made
the same test score as you.

This sketch illustrates the percentage of pupils obtaining each letter mark who also made the same test score as the counselee. In this case the counselee made a low score. He can gather from this sketch his chances for succeeding in this particular educational situation, for example, in engineering school.

Hasty pencil sketches such as these seem to aid the counselee in comprehending the real meaning of test results. They are neutral and objective and do not convey praise or blame. The counselee can take his time in looking at them and may thus feel less pressure to respond at once or to be defensive about the results. The counselor can probably devise other sketches. They should be kept as simple as possible and probably should be made for only one test at a time.

The counselee will react in some way to the test results. Since the counselor has provided a permissive atmosphere, the counselee should feel free to express his feelings and attitudes. Positive feelings may be as important as negative ones, although counselors usually seem to be more concerned about the latter. The counselee may begin to think of himself in a new and more highly valued way, a change which may be quite important for further counseling. Or he may only tentatively accept "good news"; for example, he may have difficulty in accepting the fact that he is more able than he had previously believed. Negative feelings and feelings of disappointment are likewise accepted. Suppose the counselee says, "I didn't do so well on that test. I thought I would have been as good as other college freshmen." The counselor would accept this feeling and might respond by saying, "You thought you stood higher than that."

If the counselee seems to reject the test results, the counselor accepts these feelings also. For example, the counselee may say, "I didn't do too well on that test, but there were too many questions about algebra and I don't need that." Another counselee may say, "I may be low but I'll work hard and make up for it." The counselor maintains an accepting attitude and helps the counselee to gain insight into his need for defenses.

The counselor does more than "accept," however. He brings in other data to show their relationship to test results and helps the counselee to see these relationships as well as to suggest some himself. The counselor might say, for example, "School marks have been in the C's and D's, and this goes along with this test which shows you in the lower one-third, or at about the 30th percentile in school ability." Or he could ask the counselee if he can think of things about himself that are related to the test result. He might ask, "This shows a high interest in scientific things. How does this agree with what you like to do in school or in your spare time?" Ideally, the counselee would see and bring out the relationships himself. However, he will probably need, in most cases, considerable help from the counselor.

There may be, however, conflicts in the various sorts of data. The counselee may lack ability in an area of strong measured interest, or he may say that he plans to do one sort of thing and show little measured interest and aptitude for it. The counselor may point out the discrepancy or help the counselee to identify it; then it would be explored to help the counselee gain some insight into the reason for it. Often these discrepancies provide clues to the counselee's basic problems.

Resistance is likely to be one of the chief problems which the counselor encounters in providing test results, and he should be particularly alert for indications of it. He would not expect much resistance when he presents test results about which the counselee is not particularly concerned. For example, many girls do not seem to be disappointed about being low in mechanical aptitude; in fact, some seem to be proud of it. However, those things in which the counselee is vitally interested, or which make up an important aspect of his self-concept, can be responsible for a considerable amount of concern and resistance. Intelligence is probably the best example. What a person thinks of his own intelligence is almost always very important to him. Thus low or below-expectation test results in this area are likely to arouse the counselee's resistance when presented to him. The same thing is true of results that suggest that a highly desired goal is unrealistic. This goal is part of the individual's self-concept. The self-concept (discussed in Chapter 7) is highly resistant to change and must be defended from what are considered threats. The counselor thus needs to have some idea of the counselee's attitudes about himself, or self-concept, so that he can present test results in a way that will enable the counselee to accept them.

In connection with resistance, the counselor may find that the counselee accepts test results intellectually but rejects them emotionally. The counselee may actually comprehend the meaning of the test results and be able to describe them accurately for the counselor. He might be able to say, for example, "That means that I am in the lowest one-tenth in ability to do academic work when compared with college freshmen. My achievement in mathematics and English is also equal to that of the bottom one-tenth. Ninety per cent of those with scores like mine fail." Yet he may completely reject this information when it comes to changing his way of thinking about himself and making more practical plans. Some counselees *will* not accept results but, psychologically speaking, turn their backs on them. It is important to keep in mind that some counselees *cannot* accept them or admit that they are part of the self. This denial of the reality of the test results may be on an unconscious level.

The actual words that the counselor uses are important enough to merit separate mention [240, p. 162]. The names of some tests may increase the counselee's apprehension. For example, part of the name of a well-known individual intelligence test is also associated by many persons with a mental hospital. Because of the effect on counselees, it is often advisable to keep the name of the test covered. In another example, a college used the term "psychology test" instead of "intelligence," in an attempt to lessen the concern of freshmen about a test of mental ability. That this attempt was not wholly successful was shown by the comment of the student who referred to it as "that test that tells you if you're crazy." In general, terms such as intelligence, personality, and interest seem to be suitable to use with counselees. But there are many terms in personality tests that should be avoided or used with caution. All that one counselee could remember from an interpretation of a battery of tests, including a well-known personality test, was that he had been told that he was "progressively deteriorating." Common sense should be an adequate guide as to which terms should be avoided.

In presenting test results, it would appear to be a good idea not to attempt to do too much at one time. When the one test is given at a time, as needed, there is less likelihood that the counselee will be swamped with details such as centiles, deciles, standard scores, mechanical interest, aptitude patterns, verbal ability, reading comprehension, and so on. It is quite easy for the counselor to forget that what is familiar to him is strange and new and probably clouded by misinformation for the counselee. When he is faced with the results of a whole battery of tests, the sheer volume of data is enough to confuse him. But he is usually expected to grasp complex patterns and relationships and to use this information right away.

Counselees frequently come from test-interpretation sessions with almost unbelievably distorted information (assuming that the tests had been interpreted correctly). The counselor should watch for signs that he is going too fast. It is possible that an entire session could be devoted to a discussion of one test score and related data. If the counselor must cover at one time a test battery, which often includes fifteen or twenty scores, the session is likely to be something less than helpful for the counselee. A hasty interpretation may also tend to emphasize test scores out of proportion to their importance compared to other data. The counselor would have a better opportunity to keep tests in the proper perspective and to play down the typical overemphasis of tests in the counselee's thinking if he intersperses test results with other information.

The Results of the Tests That John Doe Took

Mr. Doyle, John Doe's counselor, raised a number of questions about which he planned to obtain further information. Several of these questions could be at least partially answered by testing. They are:

Question (3): More information about academic ability

Question (4): An estimate of achievement in subject areas

Question (6): Some information about relative strengths and weaknesses of aptitudes

Question (8): A check of reading ability, in view of John's dislike of reading

To get some information about academic ability, Mr. Doyle gave John an intelligence test, the Otis Quick Scoring Mental Ability Test. John received an IQ of 105, which is slightly above the average (for this test) of 100. From this, Mr. Doyle concludes that the indications are that John can learn about as rapidly as the average high school boy his age, perhaps a little better. There is a question in the counselor's mind whether or not he should accept this score without an additional check. However, since it agrees with the previous IQ score of 106 in the cumulative record, he decides to see how it compares with other test scores (achievement and reading) before giving another intelligence test. Mr. Doyle plans to get some information from several colleges as to median IQs for their students, because he knows that IQs vary a great deal from college to college. He also plans to construct local norms, because this is one of the tests that will be used in the school-wide testing program which will soon be getting under way. These local norms will give him the opportunity to compare John with other students with whom he is now competing in his own high school.

The Kuder Preference Record is another test that the school is planning to use in its testing program. Mr. Doyle used it with John to get some idea of the types of activities that he preferred, that is, the general areas that he liked or disliked. At the same time, the results would give him some information as to whether John stood high, low, or average compared with other high school boys in each of several areas of interest. He was aware that hobbies and other nonvocational interests might cause some high interest scores that would not have any particular significance for future educational or vocational plans, but he felt that he knew John well enough so that he could pick out high scores of this sort. Looking at the results of the test he is not surprised to find that John scored low in mechanical, scientific, and literary interest. At the same time, high scores in persuasive interest seem to be in line with what John likes to do. Clerical interest seems a little higher than might be expected, suggesting to Mr. Doyle that this area of work might be investigated further with John. The above-average score in computational interest is also a little surprising. Mr. Doyle plans to refer to the test manual for suggestions of various types of jobs that the test maker includes in each of the interest areas. At the same time he keeps in mind that the test results do not indicate what John *should* or *can* do, but rather are suggestive of areas in which he seems to like activities and other areas in which he seems to dislike some activities.

The school has also planned to use some achievement tests but this program has not gone into effect yet. Mr. Doyle felt that it would be helpful to have results of this sort from John. He gave three achievement tests and compared John's results with those of eleventh grade students. On the test of math achievement, John was a little below average, and on social studies he was somewhat above average. Although John had not completed the eleventh grade, Mr. Doyle compared his scores with those who had completed it, which might have handicapped John somewhat. However, it could be safely assumed that results now and results at the end of the school year would not differ enough to change the picture of the counselee's achievement.

John's reading ability seems to be in line with his mental ability, but Mr. Doyle wonders if it is not advisable to check further to see if John has reading difficulty. At the same time he is aware that reading ability affects the results of the usual intelligence test to some extent. Although John seems to be about average on the different aspects of reading ability measured by the test and although there do not appear to be any weak spots that might cause particular difficulty, the counselor feels that he should investigate further the matter of dislike for reading. A referral to the county remedial reading teacher will also be suggested to John.

The aptitude tests that Mr. Doyle gave are the type that might not be used with every pupil but only in those cases where the counselor decides that they would be of help. Because of John's indecisiveness about what kinds of things he would like to do, Mr. Doyle used four of the tests in the Differential Aptitude Test Battery to see if any one area was noticeably better than the others. The results show that, when compared with eleventh grade boys, John is about average in numerical ability, below average in space relations, quite a bit below average in mechanical reasoning, and above average in clerical ability. (This test is often used in place of global intelligence tests in the school testing program. It goes farther, however, than measuring aspects of intelligence.)

The counselor learns, from information contained in the *Differential Aptitude Test Manual* [21], that numerical ability is defined as ". . . the student's ability to reason with numbers, to manipulate numerical relationships and to deal intelligently with quantitative material. . . . Educationally it is important for prediction in such fields as mathematics, physics, chemistry, engineering, and other curricula in which quantitative thinking is basic or essential." He checks the manual closely for help in the interpretation of the other scores also: Space relations is ". . . a measure of the student's ability to deal with concrete materials through visualization. . . . It is an ability which shows up in drafting and dress designing, in architecture and the arts, in die-making and decoration—wherever there is need to visualize three-dimensional space." A person with a high score in mechanical reasoning ". . . finds it easy to learn the principles of operation and repair of complex devices. . . . A student intending to major in a physical science field, or in technical or manual training courses, should make a good score on this test or anticipate some degree of difficulty." Clerical speed and accuracy indicate ". . . the student's speed and accuracy with simple number and letter combinations. . . . The ability to do routine work of the kind which this test exemplifies is important in filing, coding, stock room work and similar occupations. It is of relatively little importance for most educational purposes."

Mr. Doyle knows from the manual that all the tests were standardized on the same groups of students; therefore, the results on one test can be compared with the results on another. For this reason he concludes that John is better in clerical ability (speed and accuracy) than he is in the other three areas, that mechanical reasoning and space relations are two of his weaker areas. He also

Test

Type of test / Date	No.	Name of test	Form	Norms	Raw score
Intelligence — 2/51	1	Otis Quick Sc.	AM Gam.	Age	48
	2				
	3				
	4				
	5				
Interest — 2/51	6	Kuder Pref. R.	CH.	Boys	
	7	Outdoor			46
	8	Mechanical			35
	9	Comput.			27
	10	Sci.			31
	11	Persuasive			55
	12	Artistic			25
	13	Literary			12
	14	Musical			19
	15	Soc. Serv.			37
	16	Clerical			52
	17				
	18				
	19				
	20				
	21				
	22				
	23				
	24				
	25				
Achievement — 2/51	26	Co-op. Gen. Ach. Math.	y	11 gr.	48
2/51	27	Co-op. Gen. Ach. Nat. Sci.	y	11 gr.	46
2/51	28	Co-op. Gen. Ach. Soc. Sci.	y	11 gr.	54
2/51	29	Iowa Silent	AM	11 gr.	170
	30	Reading. Rev.			
	31	Rate			165
	32	Comprehension			171
	33	Directed Reading			169
	34	Poetry Comp.			168
	35	Word Meaning			172
	36	Sentence Meaning			172
	37	Par. Comp.			170
	38	Use of Index			169
	39	Selection of Key Words			169
	40				
	41				
	42				
Aptitude — 2/51	43	DAT - Numer. Abil.	A	11 gr.	22
	44	Space. Relat.	A	Boys	34
	45	Mech. Reas.	A	Boys	35
	46	Clerical	A	Boys	60
	47				
	48				
	49				
	50				
Personality — 2/51	51	Bell Adj. In.	Stu.	HS boys	
	52	Home			10
	53	Health			3
	54	Social			6
	55	Emotional			7
	56	Total			

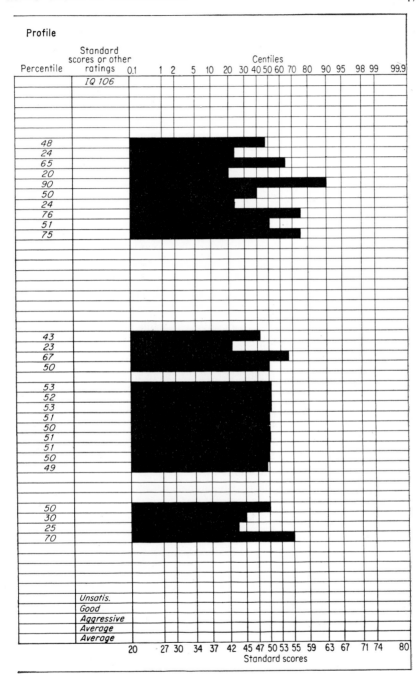

concludes that John has more clerical ability than the average in the norm group, that he is about average compared with this same group in numerical ability, and that he is below the average on space relations and mechanical reasoning. However, he does not know how John's clerical and numerical ability compare with those of persons employed in occupations requiring these aptitudes.

Another test that the school plans to give to all pupils is the Bell Adjustment Inventory. Mr. Doyle decided to use this with John in the hope that it would tell a little more about adjustment, particularly in the home. He expected, too, that a survey of the answers to specific questions might give some information that he had not obtained in the interview or cumulative record. As shown on the profile sheet the results on this test were as follows: "health," good; "social," excellent; "emotional," average; "home," poor. Mr. Doyle felt that he had a good idea of the factors involved in the home adjustment, and a review of the "home" items on the test confirmed his suppositions.

In summing up the results of the testing, Mr. Doyle notes down the following on the back of the test profile sheet: "The counselee seems to be of about average mental ability. In the subject fields, his achievement has been highest in social studies, with knowledge in this area being above average for his grade. His achievement in math is about average, while achievement in natural sciences is low. Reading ability seems to be about at the level that might be expected in view of his mental ability and achievement. He has more ability in handling numbers and number concepts than in understanding mechanical principles and visualizing how objects fit together or how they work. He is above average in working rapidly and accurately with numbers and other printed material. His interests seem to be predominately in persuasive and clerical types of activities. Indications are that he dislikes activities involving mechanical work, scientific work, and literary work such as reading and preparing written material. Adjustment seems to be good except in the "home" area, where he indicates some conflict with parents over independence and plans for the future."

The results of the tests are shown in the test profile on page 147. Note particularly that the name of the test is given in complete detail, that the form of the test is specified, and that norm groups are given and raw scores included. The profile is designed to show the relative importance of scores at the extremes as well as near the middle, that is, based on the standard score scale.

SUMMARY

Tests furnish valuable data for counseling, but their potentialities as well as limitations should be understood by the counselor. Tests may be used in the sort of counseling process described here without disrupting counseling or taking responsibility away from the counselee. They may be selected by the counselor or by the counselor and counselee together; the counselor is responsible, however, for ensuring that the most useful tests are actually employed. Tests may be used to satisfy the counselee's need to take a test. Observing the counselee as he takes a test furnishes useful behavioral data. Tests appear to fit into the counseling process best when they are given when the need arises, one or two being given at a time unless there is a reason to administer an extensive battery. Test results are related to other data and presented to the counselee in a neutral and nonevaluative way. Sketches may help in getting the meaning across. The counselee's feelings about the test results are recognized, accepted, and explored in a permissive atmosphere.

CHECKS ON UNDERSTANDING

1. What are the advantages of having the counselee decide that tests are needed and having him determine the general areas in which tests will be administered?

2. How would you justify the use of tests in counseling?

3. What should the counselor know about the counselee before he uses tests?

4. What is meant by relating test data to other information?

5. Why might the counselee not accept test results?

6. How does the counselor present test results to the counselee?

7. What aspects of the counselee's behavior might you observe when he takes a test?

THINGS TO DO

1. Prepare an interpretative summary of a test you took or that you gave to someone else. (Include as much nontest data as available.)

2. List some terms that should not be used in test interpretation.

3. Read and evaluate examples of test selection and interpretation of test results to the counselee in Refs. [32, pp. 176–179, 189–191; 39, various passages in the five recorded cases; 94, ch. 6].

4. Listen to a recorded interview where tests are selected or results are presented, and evaluate its effectiveness.

5. Using a case study with test results, prepare in written form, with sketches, the report that you will give the counselee.

6. Observe a counseling session where tests are selected or test results are presented. Evaluate the effectiveness of the session according to the points in this chapter.

7. Interview a counselor (or several counselors) to obtain his opinion on how tests should be selected and interpreted to the counselee.

8. Give several tests to a pupil, make notes using the manual and other references on the meaning of the test and other essential points, and interpret the results to the pupil. Record the session and play it back for self-evaluation.

9. The following multiple-choice test will show you how well you have grasped some of the main points covered in Chapter 5 and this chapter.

1. Scores on intelligence tests are affected by school experience
   (a)_____To an appreciable degree
   (b)_____To so great a degree that a person's IQ is determined by these experiences
   (c)_____In so far as the material in the tests is the same as that studied in courses
   (d)_____To some degree

2. The score on an aptitude test gives some indication of
   - (a)_____How much experience the individual has had in the activity being measured
   - (b)_____Whether or not the individual is suited for a certain kind of work
   - (c)_____Promise for certain types of work
   - (d)_____The individual's IQ
3. A personality test will tell
   - (a)_____Whether or not a person is suffering from a mental disease
   - (b)_____The reasons why the individual acts as he does
   - (c)_____The counselor a little about how well-adjusted the individual is, and may suggest problem areas that need further investigation
   - (d)_____Nothing about the individual, except the activities he likes or dislikes
4. Test scores can be used
   - (a)_____Only for comparing the individual with others
   - (b)_____Only for determining the individual's strong and weak areas, compared with himself
   - (c)_____As an adequate indicator of the type of work the individual should select
   - (d)_____To help the individual compare himself with others, and also to determine his strong and weak areas
5. Test validity means
   - (a)_____The extent to which the test resembles the activity it is supposed to measure
   - (b)_____The extent to which the test has been used with other persons similar to the individual being tested
   - (c)_____How well the test measures what it is supposed to measure
   - (d)_____How nearly alike a person's scores will be if he takes the same test twice
6. The best source of critical reviews about all types of tests is
   - (a)_____A test manual
   - (b)_____The Mental Measurements Yearbook
   - (c)_____The test publisher's catalogue
   - (d)_____Guidance Testing, by Froehlich and Benson
7. If you were giving a test and found that you had accidentally allowed five minutes too much time, the best thing to do would be to
   - (a)_____Count the scores made as accurate and let the students have the advantage of the error in timing
   - (b)_____Subtract the number of items that you estimated they answered in the last five minutes and count as the score the remaining items
   - (c)_____Tell the students about it so that they would know the scores were better than they should be
   - (d)_____Consider the score void
8. A test designated as an interest test measures
   - (a)_____The kinds of activities the individual prefers
   - (b)_____The kinds of activities the individual can do best
   - (c)_____How many different activities the individual knows about
   - (d)_____What the individual does in his spare time
9. A person scoring at the 75th percentile on a test has
   - (a)_____Made a rather poor score
   - (b)_____Made about an average score
   - (c)_____Made a score well above average
   - (d)_____Answered seventy-five out of a hundred questions right
10. In discussing test results with the counselee, it is usually best to
    - (a)_____Give him a copy of the numerical scores, along with the name of the test
    - (b)_____Tell him that you cannot give him the results, as he would not understand them
    - (c)_____Discuss the results in general terms, and if possible, in relation to types of work or training
    - (d)_____Give him the test to look at, so he can see his mistakes

Correct answers are as follows: 1 (d), 2 (c), 3 (c), 4 (d), 5 (c), 6 (b), 7 (d), 8 (a), 9 (c), 10 (c).

A student enters the counselor's office for the first time. The counseling sessions should be held in a location which is both comfortable and private so that the counselee will feel at ease.

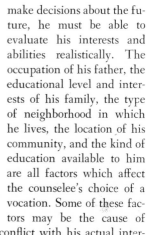

Before the counselee can make decisions about the future, he must be able to evaluate his interests and abilities realistically. The occupation of his father, the educational level and interests of his family, the type of neighborhood in which he lives, the location of his community, and the kind of education available to him are all factors which affect the counselee's choice of a vocation. Some of these factors may be the cause of pressures which conflict with his actual interests and abilities. Since the counselee may be unaware of these pressures or their role in his vocational choice, the counselor must have sufficient information about his background to help him make realistic decisions.

The counselee learns that his feelings about his schoolwork, extracurricular activities, and after-school job are important considerations in deciding upon an occupation. These factors provide a practical guide to his interests and abilities, and thus enable him to evaluate his choice in a more realistic light. A profession that merely sounds glamorous to him, for example, may require a high degree of proficiency in a skill in which his ability is only average or may not make use of skills in which he excels.

CHAPTER 7

Bases of Counseling

A T THIS POINT in a discussion of the counseling process questions are likely to arise as to why the counselor does what he does. On what is the particular approach to counseling based? These are really important questions to ask. All counseling is based on some point of view about human behavior. The point of view may be quite definite or it may be entirely a matter of what the counselor "feels" is right. Since each action of the counselor is done because he expects it to have a certain effect on the counselee and to help him in some way, it is important that the counselor have reasons for what he does. It is also important that these reasons be as good ones as the counselor can formulate.

In this chapter, bases for the counseling approach used throughout this book are given. These are drawn from various areas of behavior study and related to the process and techniques of counseling. This presentation begins with a discussion of adjustment.

The Concept of Adjustment

Perhaps the first and most important concept about human behavior for the counselor to have is one of adjustment, or the characteristics of the normal person. This concept is needed for a guide in what the counselor aims to help the counselee to do and for evaluating the effectiveness of the help given, whether the counseling is remedial or developmental.

In setting up a concept of adjustment, two essential aspects should be mentioned at the outset. The first is that adjustment is an ongoing and continuous process rather than a static condition, to be once arrived at and thereafter maintained. The second is that the limits of normal adjustment are wide, with exact boundaries unclear and undefinable. Many sorts of behavior may be included in the normal range; many day-to-day variations are possible. There are, however, criteria that the counselor may use to estimate the adjustment of the counselee. The following appear to be useful: *

1. The individual is able to face the long-range consequences of his actions and control his behavior according to these consequences. He can look into the future and anticipate the results of plans and choices.

2. The individual is able to control himself and thus is less concerned with external controls. He does what he does because he decides to do it for thought-out reasons. He is honest with himself about the reasons and he takes responsibility for his actions.

3. The individual can form and maintain good personal relationships. He has a positive attitude toward others, can admit his need for them, and demonstrates concern for them.

4. The individual recognizes his obligations to others, to his immediate group, and to mankind in general. He is aware of his social responsibility.

5. The individual has ideals and standards which serve as guides, even though he may fall short of reaching them many times. He recognizes that he has imperfections and limitations yet he strives to act in accordance with the best ideals that he can formulate. His concept of the ideal is neither so high that it can never be attained nor so low that he is self-satisfied, complacent, and, in fact, has no meaningful standards or values.

The normal person is thus not always a happy person. He experiences doubts and anxiety as he decides on courses of action. He falls short of his ideals. He may feel guilt at times. But he is an integrated and consistent person who can find reasons to respect himself, can relate to others, and can learn better ways of behavior from experiences. Whatever the problem presented by the counselee, the counselor may use a concept of adjustment such as this one as a guide to what he is trying to help the counselee to do; for example, get along with parents, select a vocation, or decide on the meaning of a college education for him.

Implications for Counseling. Probably the most important meaning that may be derived from this concept of adjustment is the positive or developmental emphasis that it gives to counseling. The counselor helps the counselee to make use of strengths, develop potentialities, meet and deal with problems, and make effective plans. This is a more important emphasis in counseling than simply helping the counselee to remedy problems after they have developed.

To be more specific, this concept implies that the counselee formulates goals

* Adapted from E. J. Shoben, "Toward a Concept of the Normal Personality," a paper given at the 1956 American Personnel and Guidance Association meeting in Washington, D.C., reprinted in the *American Psychologist*, vol. 12, pp. 183–189, April, 1957 [205].

and chooses among these goals. He accepts responsibility for his choice. If the counselor set up goals for the counselee or imposed his own goals upon him, he would not be helping the counselee toward normal adjustment.

This concept of adjustment implies, too, that the counselor helps the counselee to foresee as accurately as possible the probable outcome of various courses of action. Many of the skills and information that the counselor has are used for this purpose. The counselee is usually not too well equipped to do this himself. Even so, the counselor needs to be aware of the large margin of error that must be taken into account in predicting future outcomes. Even more important, the counselor needs to help the counselee accept the valid predictions that can be made.

A further implication may be drawn from this concept. A specific problem or need cannot be dealt with in isolation from other aspects of the counselee's life in his environment. Thus the counselor cannot say that a problem or need is *only* a vocational or personal one, or some other sort. The total individual has the problem or need. If he is maladjusted vocationally he is maladjusted as a total person. It is quite true that difficulties or needs may come into sharp focus in one area of the person's life. This means, however, that a number of aspects about the individual and his environment have raised this problem or need. Following this concept of adjustment, the counselor helps the counselee muster all resources or strengths for the solution of the problem [131].

A further point should be made here that has to do with the counselor's responsibility to the counselee. As the counselor is aware of the total and interacting nature of behavior, he attempts to detect difficulties or needs in any area of the counselee's life rather than centering on the specific difficulty presented. For example, a person with no direction or purpose in his life may request help from the counselor because he finds it difficult to study effectively. The counselor's responsibility extends beyond simply helping the counselee learn effective study habits.

Many of these points about adjustment and the resulting implications for counseling may seem to be obvious and hardly worth repeating; several have already been covered in earlier discussions of counseling. The effort is made here, however, to show the sources of counseling principles.

Other concepts relating to behavior which are of importance to the counselor include those involving the ways behavior emerges, develops, and changes. These are now taken up.

Turning now from the nature of adjustment, the process of how adjustment is achieved will be discussed. This process will be examined from the standpoint of personality dynamics, learning, and environmental influences. The effects of innate characteristics must also be considered. The counselor is concerned with all these aspects as they serve as guides to understanding the counselee, in deciding how to help him modify or improve behavior, and in determining what specific things to do or say when face to face with him.

Without some bases for counseling, the counselor is more or less "shooting in the dark" when he formulates an explanation for the counselee's behavior and plans what to do to help him. While it is true that no existing bases or principles will provide incontrovertible evidence on exactly what to do and guarantee that techniques and procedures will have a specific effect on the counselee, it is better to use available knowledge about behavior than not to use it. The alternative (which unfortunately some seem to take) is a "this seems to work" set of procedures for which the counselor has no rationale nor explanation. The counselor, furthermore, cannot effectively evaluate what he has done because he has not set up hypotheses about what will happen. He does not have a basis for explaining what has happened. A counselor, however, is a professional worker rather than a technician who follows instructions with little or no concern for the theory—the why—of the procedures. He should have carefully thought out bases for what he does [242].

The science of behavior furnishes bases of varying degrees of validity. Some theories are rather well supported while others are only tentatively supported. This is true of those given here and others described in the references below. Only a brief introduction of bases of counseling is given in this chapter, and further extensive reading is strongly recommended. As the counselor reads various points of view and practices counseling, he should begin to formulate his own approach and bases for counseling to the degree that he can state what he is doing and why he is doing it. As new developments are arrived at in personality theory and counseling theory, he can incorporate these into his particular approach and thus improve the quality of his help to others.

What the Counselor Needs to Know

It was previously pointed out that the counselor needs to have a definite concept of adjustment to serve as a guide in his work with others. It has also been pointed out that he should have an understanding of the way personality develops and the influence of various environmental conditions and innate characteristics. Of what do these areas of information consist? Tyler [242] describes the contributing areas and the way a counselor might draw upon them.

Of first importance is the area of personality. How is personality understood? How is it organized? How does it operate? What are the forces that move the individual to action, that determine the way he sees the world and himself? What is done in counseling needs to be related to answers to these and similar questions.

The counselor is also concerned with the process by which personality develops, expands, and is modified. Most of the individual's personality is learned, particularly those aspects with which the counselor is concerned. The counselor thus needs to have some idea of how learning takes place and how to promote effective learning in the counseling process. He needs further to be able to detect and help remove blocks to learning and personality development.

The individual's personality has developed in a particular context, subject to some extent to the effects of innate characteristics. Thus the counselor needs to understand how environmental factors affect learning and the development of personality, which factors should be explored, and what probable effects they have had or are having on the counselee. But he also needs to understand the role of innate characteristics in the development of the individual. To some extent innate characteristics act as limiting factors, or factors predisposing the individual to one trend or another of development, for example, sex, physical characteristics, and mental ability.

These aspects of the individual operate in a unique and dynamic way to produce the individual who comes in for counseling, and will continue to operate thus during the counseling process. They are taken up in the following discussion separately not because they are unrelated and compartmentalized aspects of life but simply for ease of presentation. The unity and wholeness of the individual should be kept in mind; if this is done, the following fragmented discussion should not prove harmful or give an unrealistic picture of the individual.

Personality Dynamics and the Counseling Process

There is more to the term *personality* than is indicated by everyday statements, such as, "She has no personality," or "He has a good personality." Personality is a highly complex, organized, and functioning entity; it is the way the individual is. Each person has a unique personality, but there are aspects that are characteristic of all personalities. These aspects have particular significance for the counselor and are the ones now taken up. Later in the chapter, concepts of personality are related to counseling procedures and techniques.

Personality Is Learned. Of foremost importance in counseling is the concept that the individual's personality is learned primarily in relations with other people. This learning process begins very early and continues all through life. Innate characteristics may have an effect, for example, physical size and build; but what the individual thinks or feels about himself is more important than his actual physical attributes. These reactions, as well as the way he reacts to others and perceives their reactions to him, his goals, defenses, and values, are almost completely the product of social living.

For the counselor, this concept has several important implications. First, he recognizes that there is a reason for the counselee being the sort of person he is. The counselee's personality is the result of a great many conditions and experiences; each aspect has personal meaning for him. The counselor needs to know as much as possible about these factors to understand the counselee, for example, experiences of success, relationship with others. He needs, too, to know about the counselee's present situation. It is quite significant that, since the counselee's personality has developed through experiences, he can be helped to modify or further develop it through experiences, such as the counseling experience.

Responses. The experiences that the individual has had and the way that he has reacted to these experiences have resulted in the individual forming a concept of the sort of person he is or a self-concept [148, p. 479]. This self-concept is patterned in a unique way and is highly organized, stable, and resistant to change. The pattern of habits, tendencies, and attitudes that make up the self-concept functions in a way to improve, protect, and increase the value of the self as the individual sees it. Thus those things that enhance or improve the self are more readily acceptable as part of it than those which would detract from or be unacceptable to the self-concept. For example, if a pupil thinks of himself as able to do college work, he would have difficulty in accepting evidence that he could not, even if there were rather conclusive evidence. Not all things about him are equally important. He might admit quite readily that he could not crochet; this is no detraction from the sort of person that he thinks he is.

The individual's self-concept may vary from one that is quite realistic to one that is highly unrealistic. The further his concept is from reality, the more difficulty he will have in living a satisfying life and the poorer his adjustment will be. It is also possible for a person to consider himself to be one sort of person or have one concept about himself and wish he were another sort. If he were thus dissatisfied with the way he is or thinks he is, his adjustment would be poor.

The individual's concept of himself is the basis of occupational roles [222, 223], as well as roles in other life situations. If the individual plays or fills the role that he considers to be in line with his self-concept, he will be meeting his needs and expectations. If he must take what he considers to be an unacceptable or inferior role, he will probably be dissatisfied, frustrated, and unhappy.

The individual has a unique self or a ". . . personal pattern of tendencies . . ." [258, p. 140], and he sees the world about him in a unique way [161, pp. 99–108]. This individual and personal perception is a result of his experiences, needs, and goals [145, p. 30; 148, p. 332].

Just as the individual develops a concept or idea of the sort of person he is, so he also develops or learns a pattern of motives or needs. Some needs can be described as primary or innate, such as the need for water, food, air, and other physiological needs. Of much greater importance for the counselor is the complex system of "secondary" or learned needs of motives. These learned needs determine the behavior of the individual as a human, socialized, and sociable being. Both types of needs are the result of tensions in the individual. They motivate the individual to do something to relieve them.

Social or learned needs may be grouped under general headings as well as quite specific ones. Some general headings are: maintaining the self, enhancing the self, preserving maximum integration. These show the over-all goal or motive. More specific needs might be making a good mark in school or earning a regular place on a team. There does not seem to be a conflict between the concept of specific needs and that of over-all general needs. The crucial point is that needs or goals are for the most part learned.

When the individual cannot meet needs or reduce tension, various sorts of behavior may appear, such as the "mechanisms" discussed in a later paragraph. All behavior serves the individual in some way, but some may be ineffective or inefficient. For example, the boy who cannot do satisfactory work in a course and thus satisfy his need for prestige, recognition, or acceptance may concentrate on disturbing his fellows in class and may eventually be expelled from school.

The pattern of needs or motives of the individual is stable and highly organized. Just as some aspects of the self are more important than others, so some needs or motives are more important than others and take priority over others. This ranking of needs is the result of learning.

The relative importance of needs may be changed by experience. Furthermore, when one need is met, another comes to the forefront. For example, a boy who has developed a pattern of depending upon his parents, goes away to college and learns new patterns of needs which he must satisfy. A boy who has valued the respect of others nevertheless cheats so that he will not fail. It is obvious, however, that under relatively normal circumstances, the basic underlying needs are rather consistent. The way the person meets them or his responses are much more modifiable, however.

A helpful concept related to the needs of the individual and the setting of goals is that of the level of aspiration [107, ch. 10; 161, pp. 90–99]. Based on past experience, particularly successes or failures, the individual's concept of himself, and his present situation, the individual sets a goal or level that he feels he should attain. This goal may be practical and closely related to reality or it may be too high or too low. The level of aspiration has a pronounced effect on how much the individual will attempt to accomplish.

Each individual has certain types of behavior that are more likely to occur in a given situation and other types that are less likely to occur. The preference for a particular response or pattern of responses has been learned. This learning has taken place because the response meets needs and reduces tension. If the response does not meet needs it will be replaced by another that does. The behavior pattern is changed. For example, a pupil's need for acceptance is met by being friendly and helpful. Suppose, however, that he were thrown into a new environment where one had to be aggressive and vicious to be accepted.

To meet his need for acceptance he would have to behave differently than in the past. If no appropriate behavior were available or if the individual had no idea of what sort of behavior was appropriate, he might show maladaptative or ineffective behavior. An example of this situation was the "Invasion from Mars," when many persons, after hearing a fictitious but vivid account by radio of an invasion from another planet, reacted with extremely disturbed and erratic behavior. On the other hand, some persons made more effective responses, such as checking other radio programs to determine the validity of the "news" broadcast [161, pp. 619–628].

Even though behavior or responses are arranged in order of preference, there is always some competition among several responses that could be made; only one can actually be made. Until the response is actually made there is some conflict present. For example, the pupil may be considering dropping out of school and going to work, changing to another high school course, or asking for counseling help. Whichever response he makes will, at least temporarily, eliminate the others.

In the relatively normal individual there is some degree of awareness of needs. Some needs or motives are not so readily identifiable or available to awareness; these unconscious needs or motives are extremely important for behavior [228, p. 198]. Individuals are not aware of why they are doing many of the things they do every day (ask yourself why you are studying counseling). If the individual is faced with a conflict of needs or motives and has some awareness of the conflict and of the needs involved, he may feel normal anxiety [144, pp. 17–18]; he can usually identify the conflict and do something about it. If, however, the conflict is intense and unacceptable to the individual, he may attempt to repress it or deny it to consciousness. Dissociation or shutting out of the needs and conflict from conscious thought may follow [144, pp. 20–21; 148, p. 408]. When this happens the individual may be quite unable to make any progress in resolving the conflict or in meeting needs.

Not all repression is harmful, however [228, pp. 199–200]; some is necessary in everyday life. In the discussion of personality mechanisms it is pointed out that while they are the result of repressed conflicts, some may be adaptive and some maladaptative.

Traits and the Total Personality. In the discussion of tests, it was pointed out that these instruments may be used to measure specific aspects or "traits" of the individual. Also, in Chapter 1, in the review of counseling approaches, trait theory was mentioned as one of the major types of counseling. Actually, it is more helpful to think of traits as psychological aspects of the individual which may be measured but which make up aspects of the total individual and are meaningful only when considered in relation to the unique pattern or configuration of the individual. Thus it does no violence to a theory of a "self-concept" or a total personality to speak of "traits"; it is necessary, however, to point out that the individual is not considered to be only a collection of separate and independent traits.

Personality Mechanisms. The concept of personality mechanisms is useful for understanding personality and behavior that are the result of unconscious conflict [228, p. 154]. Mechanisms are not to be thought of as maladaptive only but may be seen in everyday life in normal individuals [228, pp. 143–144]. Even though the individual is aware of what he is doing in the behavior involved in these mechanisms, he is not aware of his motivation or reasons for doing it [228, p. 154]. If he is aware of the motivation he is not demonstrating a defense or personality mechanism. For example, if the pupil knows that he is blaming the teacher for his failure because he did not prepare his assignments, he is not exhibiting a mechanism. Some of the more common mechanisms which have significance for the counselor are as follows:

1. Projection. This is that process in which the individual attributes to others feelings and characteristics based upon his own needs. Projection may be slight or it may be extensive and greatly distort reality. A helpful discussion is provided by Symonds [228, pp. 223–239], in which he points out the occurrence of this behavior in the classroom and counseling situation.

2. Transference. This is a mechanism by which the individual transfers his attitudes and feelings from one individual to another. It is a term used primarily in the therapeutic relationship to indicate or explain the client's attitude toward the therapist. It also appears to be an example of overgeneralization [61, p. 260]. It would seem to be a mechanism, however, that would operate in other situations, including counseling, though perhaps to a lesser degree.

3. Rationalization. By this mechanism the individual explains or justifies his behavior with reasons that are not in line with facts. His explanation may sound "good" but it is incorrect. However, this mechanism enables the individual to justify his actions and to preserve his self-esteem. Symonds [228, pp. 321–335] provides a helpful explanation of the process.

4. Sublimation. The use of this mechanism enables the individual to divert his energies from an unacceptable goal or activity to one that is acceptable. The substitute activity provides a means of meeting a need and reducing tension. This is frequently used in everyday life. Among other uses, it has significance for occupational choice [228, p. 299].

5. Repression. This mechanism, which has already been mentioned, is the one by which a need or conflict is "pushed out" of awareness and denied to the conscious mental process of the individual. Symonds [228, pp. 181–204] gives a helpful discussion of the process and points out that it serves useful purposes in social living. Where the conflict is intense, however, repression may result in serious maladjustment. Therapy may be necessary to help the individual recognize the repressed conflict and arrive at some solution to it.

6. Reaction formation. In this mechanism the individual does the opposite

of what he has a need or desire to do. The unacceptable impulse is replaced by one which is acceptable and which enables the individual to maintain his good opinion of himself [148, p. 551].

There are also other mechanisms besides those briefly noted here. Helpful discussions may be found in Refs. [40, 148, 228, 258].

Mechanisms, such as those discussed here, have been brought into sharp relief through the study of maladjusted persons. These concepts, however, are also helpful in understanding normal persons. Mechanisms occur in normal persons in everyday life [259, p. 316], as has been mentioned. It is when the conflict is severe, the behavior is maladaptive, and the results are emotional maladjustment that mechanisms result in abnormal behavior.

This elementary discussion of personality is far too brief and incomplete to provide the counselor with the foundation he needs, but it presents some aspects with which the counselor should be familiar and provides bases from which counseling procedures discussed in the last section of this chapter may be drawn. It also provides a starting point for further reading.

Learning

Counseling has been described as a learning process. Thus it is necessary to consider how learning takes place and what this means for counseling. As in the case of personality, specific counseling procedures which may be drawn from this discussion will be presented in the last section of this chapter.

As has already been pointed out, the counselee's personality has been developed through a process of learning. It seems reasonable to assume that learning is an orderly process. It also appears to be essential that some consideration of learning be included in a discussion of bases of counseling. The point of view developed by Miller and Dollard [141] and later applied to psychotherapy [61] has been utilized as the basis for this discussion. There are other points of view about learning [98] and other applications to counseling (see Chapter 1). The one selected for use here, however, appears to offer valuable suggestions for the counselor. Like the others mentioned, it is not a complete and thoroughly validated theory but rather is made up of some substantially verified principles, some hypotheses, and some highly tentative concepts [61, preface].

Four Fundamentals of Learning.* It is desirable to consider the learning process and its application to everyday behavior. In the point of view used here there are four essential parts to the learning process. These are as follows:

First there is a *drive*. The drive impels the person to do something. He has

* This concept and those about learning which follow have been adapted from Neal E. Miller and John Dollard, *Social Learning and Imitation*, New Haven, Conn., Yale University Press, 1941 [141], and John Dollard and Neal E. Miller, *Personality and Psychotherapy*, New York, McGraw-Hill Book Company, Inc., 1950 [61] (used by permission).

a need which causes tension and which must be met. The drive is toward need reduction or tension reduction.

Then there is a *cue*. This cue gives the individual some idea of what kind of response to make. For example, a pupil is in a new school building and is looking for his next classroom. He has a strong need to find the right room before the tardy bell rings. He notes where other students are going and looks for signs on doors. He is searching for cues to help him to decide which classroom to enter.

Next, a *response* is made. The response, in this case, is to enter a room and take a seat. If it is the wrong room, no doubt the pupil will leave hastily amid laughter and comments of "dumb freshman" when the teacher announces the name of the class and calls the roll. If it is the right room, he will come to it again; he will have made the correct response.

Finally, the response is *rewarded*. Tomorrow the pupil will go to the same room, more quickly and directly than he did today. Responses of looking in other rooms and looking for other students that he knows are in the same class will have dropped out. The response of finding the right classroom has met a need, and the drive to find the right classroom has been reduced.

The Origin of Needs or Motives. Of particular importance to the counselor is the source of needs, drives, or motives. Why does it make a difference to the pupil whether or not he gets to the right classroom? It is a learned or secondary drive rather than a primary need, such as the need for food or water. The learned or secondary needs have their origin in the satisfaction of primary needs in social situations, for example, in the home; primary need reduction and approval of others have taken place at the same time. Thus the approval of others, being associated with gratification of needs (physiological), becomes in itself need reducing. In the same way, the individual can learn to need the approval of others.

Learned drives or needs are the basis for social behavior. For example, the hungry individual who has a job to finish may work well past lunchtime. The dinner guest who is not at all hungry will nevertheless make efforts to appear to be eating and enjoying the meal. The very hungry guest does not immediately grab the largest steak; he waits until they are passed to him and may actually get the smallest! These persons are behaving according to learned needs.

It is possible for the individual to perceive as a reward something that was previously of no value to him. A check or deposit slip from the bank assumes value when it represents the individual's monthly salary. The piece of paper, however, has no intrinsic value. The same thing is true of currency. It can serve as a reward for work done. The individual has learned what it can do, for example, pay the rent. He would not, however, accept any kind of currency; if he were paid in Confederate currency, he would not feel rewarded.

Fear, guilt, and anxiety are learned drives, the reduction of which can be rewarding. For example, during a severe thunderstorm an individual is sitting in front of an open window. He recalls that he once heard about a person who was struck by lightning as he sat before an open window. He immediately feels sharp anxiety, which is not reduced until he closes the window; the reduction of anxiety is rewarding. After this incident he makes a habit of closing all windows during electrical storms. While fear is usually considered a strong learned drive, it is obviously not the strongest. Witness the behavior of some individuals in extremely dangerous situations.

It seems reasonable to assume that the individual's pattern of learned needs or drives is rather stable. The student who does good work in school tends to do it consistently. When the drive is reduced, however, it may motivate the individual very little. For example, when the lesson is completed, the individual may then go to the movies, as there is no immediate need for further study.

The behavior or responses that needs or drives elicit show more variability than the drives themselves. The relative strength of responses will now be taken up.

The Pattern of Preferred Responses. Behavior or responses may be thought of as arranged in a hierarchy according to their effectiveness in reducing tension. When a need is present, the individual makes the top response in the hierarchy to reduce it. If the top response is not rewarded, the next one is made. Others farther down will be made if higher ones are not effective. The hierarchy is revised if lower ones prove to be more effective in meeting needs; the individual then has a new hierarchy of responses to meet needs.

What happens to the responses that do not meet needs? If they are not rewarded and do not meet needs, they are less likely to be given. They will tend to drop out of the individual's behavior pattern.

Certain conditions affect the speed with which the response is dropped. If the response is a strong habit, it will resist extinction or dropping out. But if it is a difficult response to make, it will tend to drop out more quickly. Also, if the strength of other competing responses is great, the response will drop out more readily.

An example will show how a new and difficult response could drop out. A student who is trying to set up a time and study schedule may be tempted to go to the movies as he has been in the habit of doing rather than studying. However, the need to study is quite strong because he is in danger of being dismissed from school if he does not make a satisfactory average. Making a study schedule and sticking to it is hard work; later, after a few attempts, he may end up at the movies and fail his courses. It was difficult to make the new response of sticking to a study schedule. Furthermore, this response had not actually been rewarded. Even if it had, it might have dropped out.

In the above illustration, the result of what is called spontaneous recovery of a response is shown. The old response appeared in full force after it had been discarded. This happens because the inhibition or the holding down of the behavior weakens faster than the strength of the habit or response. The response itself does not disappear. In the illustration, the determination not to go to the movies weakened faster than the liking to attend the movies during study time.

It is important for the new response to be rewarded so that it will have the strength to replace the old one. As the old response weakens, the individual has the opportunity to learn new ways of behavior. If the boy who is quite shy can gain some success and satisfaction at the school party, that is, if he can make the new response of actually going and taking part in some of the activities, the new behavior of going to parties may hasten the dropping of the old habit of staying away. Not rewarding an old response provides a way for the individual to make a new one; in fact, it actually puts pressure on him to make a new response. If old responses were rewarded, the individual would probably not change or learn. A very self-satisfied person is a poor learner.

The learner must be able to make the new and desirable response; he needs also to have a situation in which it may be made. He can be helped to master the response and to have it ready to make at the appropriate time and the appropriate time can often be arranged. If it is rewarded, it will move to a high rank on the response hierarchy.

Generalization and Discrimination. How does learning in one situation transfer to another? How does the individual learn to make different responses in different situations? The concepts of generalization and discrimination provide help in answering these questions. In these two processes, however, occur many of the errors in learning, or ineffective learning.

In generalization, the individual gives a response that was rewarded in one situation in another situation that appears to be similar. For example, in one class the teacher gives the best marks to those who participate in class discussion. In another similar class the pupil will be likely to continue this rewarded response. In this case, the good mark is the reward. Reduction of fear or anxiety can also be rewarding. Thus a pupil who has learned to reduce anxiety in one classroom by presenting an indifferent appearance may make the same response in other classes. The similarity of the situations depends upon the cues that the individual notices. The more similar these cues are in different situations, the more likely the individual will be to generalize behavior from one situation to another. If he notices unimportant cues or assumes that cues are the same when they actually are not, he may overgeneralize and behave in an inappropriate manner.

In the principle of discrimination, the individual distinguishes among situations that are actually different and responds in a manner appropriate to the situation. For example, spectators at a baseball game shout encouragement to their team and heckle the opposing pitcher. Then some individuals go to another event that could also be labeled a sports contest, but this time it is a golf tournament. They know that they do not shout encouragement to their favorite as the participants are about to drive or direct insulting remarks at the opposing players. Thus discrimination is needed if behavior is to be appropriate. Too much generalization would get the individual in trouble. The individual needs to be able to discern cues that will indicate that different situations are actually different. Too much discrimination, on the other hand, based on insignificant aspects of situations, reduces the probability of making appropriate responses in new situations. Suppose that the recruit had to learn by many different experiences that he is supposed to salute a person with a gold bar, a silver bar, two silver bars, and so on, rather than understand that he salutes a person with any of a number of different insignia indicating officer status.

The Effect of Reward. As has been pointed out, learning takes place when there is a reward of some sort. How does this reward affect the learner when it is near as compared to when it is far away? Many counseling rewards are far in the future, for example, a good job for which many years of preparation are required.

The closer the reward, the more strength it has for behavior. If the reward immediately follows the behavior, it will be more effective. The individual's level of maturity plays a part in the effects of a reward. Children appear to need the reward to be quite close to the behavior. In adults, the reward may be farther away. Even so, immediate rewards are helpful and in some cases necessary, or the far-distant goal may lose its appeal. Language plays a part in bridging the gap between what the individual is doing now and the distant reward. For example, the college freshman may have the ultimate goal of obtaining a B.A. degree. This goal is far away and may never be reached. However, he receives many intermediate rewards such as quiz and exam marks, completing courses, moving from freshman to sophomore level. Further, he may tell himself from time to time, "I will get that degree. I'll be a college graduate." Thus, to some extent, he can maintain the strength of the goal by telling himself about it. He can look ahead and anticipate a far-distant reward.

As the individual nears the goal he makes anticipatory responses; some of these are ineffective and are not rewarded. In later behavior for reaching the same goal, he may eliminate the nonrewarded and ineffective responses. For example, the pupil who looked in other classrooms and searched for pupils he knew, as he tried to find the correct classroom, will eliminate these responses and go directly to the room the next time. Another pupil may feel apprehensive when he has to make an oral report. He may prepare an elaborate set of notes and rehearse his talk over and over. When he makes the talk, however, he finds that elaborate notes do not help. The next time the ineffective behavior (elaborate notes) will probably be dropped.

Thus the individual drops ineffective behavior and takes a short cut to the goal with the most effective responses. If fear is present, however, maladaptative behavior may occur as the goal is neared. For example, as the beginning driver approaches a crowded intersection he may act quite ineffectively, stalling his car, then choking the motor and flooding it as he attempts to start up again.

The Effect of Conflict. Why does an individual not do something he professes that he wants to do? Why does a boy climb to the high diving board and then hesitate to dive in? He says and feels that he wants to do it. Why does he appear to be more and more reluctant the closer he actually gets to doing it? The situation is one of conflict between what he wants to do and what he wants to avoid. The drive to do something that the individual wants to do does not increase as much as the drive to avoid something that he does not want to do. At the point where these drives are equal, he will stop, for example, as he arrives at the top of the diving board. If the drive to perform the response is quite strong, it may be greater than the drive to avoid it and he may go ahead anyway without hesitation. Conflicting drives are often the cause of difficulty in planning for the future and in adjusting to present circumstances. The repressed conflict, as has been mentioned, may result in rather serious emotional maladjustment.

Thinking and Problem Solving. How do individuals go about solving problems, thinking, and making decisions? These activities may be classified as higher mental processes. Up to now the discussion of learning has been primarily concerned with instrumental behavior, or that behavior which produces an immediate change in the external environment, such as getting out books and preparing a lesson.

Suppose that the individual has a problem which involves a considerable amount of thinking or mental manipulation of verbal, numerical, and other symbols. Action is withheld until some solution is reached. It may be an emotional problem or one that is largely intellectual. Several examples may help to illustrate the process.

A pupil may want to decide on a course of study to take at college. He may simply pick one out at random and then announce his decision to his parents, without being aware of why he made the choice. But suppose he has done a considerable amount of thinking about it. He may have considered the State University at first. This thought or response may have suggested to him that State is too near home and he would like to attend a college more distant. Thinking about a distant college may remind him that he has never been away from home for any length of time, and he might not like it. On the other hand, he may decide it would be a sign of growing up to be able to be almost completely on his own. All this has been a mental activity, but the pupil has not actually done anything about it so far. This use of language in thinking could be described as a series of cue-producing responses, as each response provided a cue for a new idea. Language used in this manner seems to play a major role in the higher mental processes of thinking and problem solving. As counseling is carried on primarily through verbal communication, it is important for the counselor to have some concept of the use of language and think-ing, even if it is only at the stage of hypothesis.

These cue-producing responses can assist in discrimination or generalization or can cause problems. For example, an individual may be driving in a strange city and become anxious about meeting the rush of after-work traffic. He recalls the day of the week and tells himself that it is Saturday and that there will not be an afternoon traffic rush. Thus his anxiety at being lost in a strange city and looking for route markers in an impatient tangle of traffic is reduced; he can now calmly look for road signs and stop to check his map. In this way a series of cue-producing responses has helped the individual to take effective action. As an example of faulty generalization, the case of a pupil who con-siders all teachers unfair may be used. He had one teacher who was unfair and indifferent to his needs. He applies the label "unfair" to each new teacher and proceeds to act as if this opinion were based in fact. He may not actually apply the label but he more or less automatically acts as if all teachers are unfair.

For effective thinking and problem solving, a series of cue-producing responses (reasoning) is more effective than a series of instrumental acts or "doing something" with no foresight. By reasoning, it is possible to foresee what will happen. Suppose the pupil wants to make a good mark in a difficult course. He knows by past experience, and from what others say, that objective tests are given on questions from the lectures. He tells himself that he does not know the material in the lecture notes. Then he reminds himself that he ought to use good study habits to learn the material. Eventually he should decide upon a way of study and put it into effect.

There are other details of the learning process; the ones given here, how-ever, appear to have the most significance for counseling. Reading in Refs. [61, 141] and other similar references will be helpful in gaining an under-standing of other points of view.

The Importance of Innate Characteristics

In a discussion of those aspects of the individual and the environment which have significance for counseling, innate endowment should not be omitted. These innate characteristics include physical size and physical characteristics, build, temperament, and ability [107, chs. 16, 17; 258, pp. 208–239]. These characteristics are of more importance in the way that they have been modi-fied by experience and by the way the individual regards them than as causes of certain sorts of behavior. There is not much evidence to indicate how dif-ferences in temperament, which seem to be innate, affect the development of personality [107, ch. 17; 258, p. 144]. Neither is there much help from studies of physique and specific aspects of temperament [107, pp. 541–545; 258, p. 148]. The overwhelming influence of experience is more important in behavior [107, pp. 516–518, 539–540; 258, p. 148].

Differences in initial mental ability, while affected by experiences, are innate [107, pp. 511–512]; there are limits to how much the individual may develop. These differences have a pronounced effect on behavior; for example, one individual learns rapidly while another has difficulty in following simple directions.

Differences in physical characteristics are, of course, in evidence everywhere; of more importance than the actual physical characteristics is the way the individual regards them. His attitude is, to some extent, a reflection of how others regard his characteristics, for example, being unusually short and fat. Growth rates vary also, but again this does not cause a certain sort of personality development or directly account for certain personality characteristics.

Environmental Effects

The particular individual with whom the counselor is working is a unique personality and different from any other counselee, because of experiences that he has had and the innate characteristics and previous learning that he has brought to those experiences. The earliest experiences are primarily in the home. Later experiences involve those outside the home to a greater degree. As the individual approaches adulthood, his experiences involve a wider setting including a variety of persons, many institutions, and the occupational world. The culture and the subculture of which the individual is a member exert an influence on behavior, somewhat indirectly through the family at first [148, p. 843] and then directly upon the individual as he moves about in them. Not to be overlooked is the over-all influence of the wider political or national unit, with its ethical, economic, and social customs and laws. The influence of each of these characteristics of the environment is not separate; they work together to make the world in which the individual lives.

To each new experience in this environment, the individual brings his own unique personality. He perceives and reacts toward conditions, persons, and situations in a personal and individual way. It is obvious that each individual is almost unbelievably complex. In order to begin to comprehend the meaning of his behavior, the counselor should have an understanding of the possible effects of various circumstances on individuals. He then uses this knowledge to assist him in understanding and helping the particular counselee with whom he is working.

Some of the environmental effects that have particular significance for counseling will now be taken up. The first of these is the early home situation.

Early Life in the Home. The infant is completely dependent upon adults for meeting his needs. He soon learns what attitudes and treatment to expect from them, whether it be love, coldness, harshness, and so on. Thus he formulates his expectations of how others react to him. With security and support, he feels free to try new experiences; with other sorts of treatment he may feel unloved, anxious, or tense. He may experience overprotection or he may feel rejected. He perceives, too, one way or another, the psychological climate of the home. Strain or tension, even if not expressed in quarrels and open hostility, has an effect on him [107, pp. 621–622]. Lack of affection may cause behavior problems [107, p. 633]. Thus the individual is learning ways to react that affect his behavior at that time and later.

In the process of socialization, the child cannot possibly have every wish gratified [107, p. 88]. The love and affection present in the home will make it easier for him to give up those things that he must relinquish. He has mixed feelings, however, toward parents who both reward and deny. He begins to form a concept of the sort of individual he is, based largely on how others react to him but also on innate characteristics [107, p. 633]. What is expected of the infant or child is influenced by the customs of the particular subculture of which the home is a part [107, p. 92], and by the experiences the parents have had as children.

Other members of the family are a part of the child's world. To some extent there is rivalry with brothers and sisters. If he is an only child he has a quite different situation than if he is one of four or five.

Thus the child learns in the home how others meet his needs and how they react to him, how they make demands and enforce regulations, and what authority means. He learns, too, that parents and other persons are interested in other things besides him. He learns how to react to others and how to meet his own needs. He moves into an ever-widening environment, involving more people and more situations [12, chs. 2, 3]. As he moves into other groups outside the home, he has new adjustments to make. He finds that he is more on his own, that he is more valued for what he can do than by his adherence to adult standards. These experiences, too, have an effect on the way he reacts to others and what he thinks of himself.

Later Childhood Experiences. As the child's environment expands, he forms friendships and engages in more activities out of the home. Play makes demands for ability and cooperative activities. What he has learned so far may assist or retard his success. He is finding his role in activities with peers. The school makes new demands. The child must submit to authority and it may be any of a number of types of authority. Emphasis is put upon certain behavior in the classroom and other behavior on the playground. The influence of the peer group begins to carry more weight. There may be conflicts between home values, school values, and peer values.

The Adolescent Environment. The adolescent's environment expands far beyond that of childhood and new adjustments need to be made (12, chs. 6, 7). Interest in the opposite sex is developing. The peer group and its standards and values becomes more significant in his life. As he approaches physiological and psychological maturity, he faces the need to act as an adult yet at the same time he needs to depend upon the home. Plans must be made for the not too distant adult role; for example, he must choose a vocation. The way the individual has developed up to now, and the degree of acceptance by home and family, will have an effect on how well he is able to meet the demands of his new roles. Peer groups have rather definite values, attitudes, and customs, which in some cases conflict sharply with those of the home. Excessive demands upon the adolescent are often made by parents; some friction with parents is almost inevitable. New interests and demands seem to be largely responsible for what is called the emotionality and instability of adolescence [107, p. 693].

The Cultural Environment. The indirect effect of cultural customs and beliefs through the home has already been mentioned [148, ch. 37; 161, pp. 494–501]. The effects of the cultural group or subgroup are also apparent in the neighborhood. If, for some reason, the individual has different values and beliefs from others in his community or subculture, there will likely be a conflict between the individual and the group.

The cultural subgroup has a pervasive influence on what the individual does and thinks, on the educational level he attains, on his occupational goals and the occupation he enters, on his recreation, and on the organizations to which he belongs [100; 125; 126; 161, pp. 467–475; 251]. Members of a class or group can identify and describe the characteristics of those in their own and other classes; attitudes toward other classes are known and understood. Class membership goes beyond attitudes and actually has an effect on what the individual can do, enforced by unwritten customs in the community. It would be extremely helpful to the counselor to read in the above references to gain an understanding of the effect of class membership on the development of attitudes, values, self-perception, and perception of others. The counselor will be able to look about his own community with increased understanding of the groups that exist and the effects of these groups on the counselee.

There are some effects of the wider culture that, to some extent, override those of the specific cultural group and to some extent are nullified by them. For example, in this country, much emphasis is put upon initiative, getting ahead, and accumulating material possessions. The competitive spirit is rewarded and each person is expected to stand upon his own feet. Yet fairness and sportsmanship are emphasized. These values appear to be quite pervasive, although they are more typical of some subcultures than others.

There is also a belief in the good judgment of men and a faith in the collective judgments of the people. Education is generally accepted to be of great value. Yet, again, not everyone would give complete allegiance to these values.

This has been only the briefest review of a few of the aspects of the environment that affect the development of the individual. The counselor needs to be aware of the significance of the counselee's experiences and to be able, through a background of study and experience, to assess the effects of these experiences. Any plan or method of counseling must take into account the fact of these experiences and the effect that they have had on the counselee.

Choice of Occupation

Of particular interest to counselors are hypotheses and theories of the way an individual goes about the matter of choosing an occupation. Various points of view utilize in different ways concepts of learning, personality development and structure, environmental influences, and innate characteristics. Considerable attention is given to cultural demands and expectations and to the degree of physiological maturity of the individual as well as other aspects of behavior. As further research is completed, counselors may expect to have available substantial evidence as to how vocational choices are made and thus to have guides for better ways of helping individuals to make more effective choices. The following is an adaptation of concepts from several different theories [82; 102, ch. 7; 207; 223; 227, part 2].

1. First, there is a growth stage during childhood where interests, roles, and the like are formed.

2. Next, there is an exploratory stage, consisting of a fantasy period; a tentative stage, where interests alone are first emphasized, followed by emphasis on ability as well as interest; and then a movement toward more realism. This may be during early and middle adolescence.

3. Next comes the realistic phase where a compromise is made between the desired role in work and the actual demands and conditions of the world of work. This may be during later adolescence.

4. Next comes the establishment and maintenance stage where the individual first tries out his plans, arrives at what seems to be the best area of work, and becomes more or less stable or settled in this area. This would usually start during early adulthood and continue through the major part of the individual's working life.

5. Finally, there is the stage or period of decline where the individual experiences decreasing physical and intellectual capacities. He may need to revise occupational activities and plan for retirement.

This brief review does not do justice to the carefully worked out theories from which the concepts were drawn. It is presented to indicate what is meant by the process of vocational choice and to stimulate the counselor to read further in the references. It is an interesting example of the application of some aspects of what is known about human behavior and its determinants to one particular problem which the individual faces.

Implications for Counseling

From what has been covered in this chapter, a number of theories about counseling procedures and techniques may be drawn. These will be briefly described in the following paragraphs. The essential point is that counseling should be based on what is known or what seems to be reasonably hypothesized about behavior.

The Counselor as a Person. The counselee perceives the counselor in a unique way, based upon his past experiences and other persons in his life. He assigns the counselor a role. As he probably has had little experience with counselors, he may project needs in assigning the counselor his role. Subcultural influences and values play a part. His reaction to the counselor may be distorted by ineffective generalization; he transfers attitudes held toward others to the counselor and acts as if they are true.

Obviously, then, the quality of the relationship is affected by the sort of person the counselor is and even more by the way the counselee perceives him. The counselor's job is to help the counselee gain a realistic understanding of the role of the counselor and to accept it.

While the counselee reacts to the counselor as a person and as a member of a professional group (counselors), the counselor also reacts to the counselee. Thus the counselor should be aware of his own needs and defenses as he works in the personal counseling situation. He too may overgeneralize about the counselee because of past experiences, biases, and the like. He may "use" the counselee in some way to satisfy his own needs, for example, to dominate others.

The Counselee's Expectations. Just as the counselee will bring certain attitudes toward others, including the counselor, to the counseling situation, he will have certain expectations about what counseling is and what it does. These expectations are based on needs, on past experiences (for example, he may expect to be told what to do), and on what he knows about counseling. He may be under the impression that counseling and testing are synonymous and that tests will predict the future.

The counselee may experience ambivalence, or a need to request counseling competing with a need to deny it. Also, he may feel anxiety in approaching a new and strange situation. It is quite easy for the counselor to forget that counseling is a different and undefined experience for most adolescents.

The counselee's expectations may be expressed verbally and by his behavior, or they may be carefully hidden, as behind a mask of friendliness or humility. The counselor needs to be aware that the counselee has some sort of expectations and help the counselee to express them. The counselor would not, of course, force the counselee on the defensive about his expectancies but rather would accept them just as he accepts the counselee as a person.

The Physical Setting. Privacy and comfort are important in the counseling situation to help reduce tension, eliminate distractions, and provide an atmosphere for effective thinking. The counselor can help reduce threat if he and the counselee are alone. Many counselees feel that other students may think they are in trouble, lacking in self-sufficiency, or odd, if they are seen talking to a counselor. They may become more tense and anxious than they would otherwise be and have difficulty in expressing themselves or in planning.

Physical comfort usually helps to reduce mental strain and tension. It would augment what the counselor does to establish a permissive and accepting atmosphere. Thus seating, lighting, and ventilation should add to the comfort of both the counselor and counselee. The actual location of the counselee's and counselor's chairs makes a difference. They can be so arranged that both appear to be working together, or in such a way that the counselor is more or less a judge and decision maker.

Beginning in a Permissive Atmosphere. It has been pointed out that the counselor needs to find out what the counselee's conception of counseling is. This is one reason for beginning in a permissive manner. The counselee is, to some extent, testing the limits and characteristics of the counseling situation. He wants to discover how much he can become involved and how much he can safely reveal of his self. If he feels lack of acceptance or threat (criticism, blame) he must defend his self; he must maintain his self-respect. He is not ready to learn to make plans and decisions and to find new ways to behave. Practically all the concepts of personality and learning discussed in this chapter would support the principle of a permissive beginning in counseling.

There is also a permissive and accepting atmosphere to later stages in the counseling process; in this sort of atmosphere the counselee can try out new and more desirable responses, can face new ideas about himself, and can talk about emotionally charged subjects. More effective learning is possible; for example, the counselee may perceive new and important cues or may gain insight into the elements causing conflict. As emotional tension is lessened, he can consider a wider range of possible behavior.

Information about the Counselee. From the discussion of factors affecting behavior, a large number of reasons for collecting data about the counselee may be drawn. It is advisable that all available information be used and to as great a degree as practical. The counselee is helped to make a choice or decision. The fewer "unknowns" involved in the plan, the more possibility there is that it will be a good one. Accurate information about the counselee tends to reduce the unknowns.

Information about the individual includes more than data about psychological traits such as intelligence and interests, and physical characteristics such as health and physical handicaps; of primary importance is the way the individual sees himself and his world. What is his concept of himself? How does it compare with the way he really is? What role is he playing and what roles does he want to play? What are his goals? Only with such comprehensive data can the counselor begin to understand the counselee.

The purpose of using a variety of information-getting techniques is to collect the sorts of data needed. Some techniques obtain somewhat the same types of information, but usually they involve a different view of the individual, for example, the autobiography and anecdotal records.

Psychological traits are relatively stable and knowledge of them gives some basis for predicting behavior. Physical characteristics are of primary importance according to the way the individual sees them. All these traits, characteristics, and so on are organized into a unique personality. The counselee acts in predictable ways based upon the organization of his personality. He will accept certain information based on what he thinks is acceptable and reject other that he considers unacceptable. He will find satisfaction in playing certain roles and will experience frustration and discontent in others. The counselor must know as much as possible about these aspects if he is to help the counselee.

The collection of information about the counselee assists the counselor in determining what the real problem or need is. The process also enables the counselor to plan ways of helping the counselee and to formulate hypotheses or expectancies about what the counselee may do in counseling as a result of the counselor's actions. For example, the counselor may decide that he needs to provide occupational information to the counselee to help him understand how unrealistic his plans are.

Importance of Past and Present Environment. Learning about the counselee includes learning about his environment. Several aspects need additional emphasis and are worth mentioning separately. The outstanding point is that the environment characterized by a subculture has values and customs that may be meaningful and important to the counselee but not to the counselor. To understand the counselee, the counselor has to have some understanding of what the counselee is adjusting to and what is acceptable to his environment.

Certain other environmental factors in the community and home may amount to limiting factors, for example, not enough financial resources for the counselee to attend college, no suitable place for study in the home. Group or class membership may set up barriers to education, occupations, or social activities. These, of course, must be understood if the counselee is to be given realistic help.

Need for Structuring. It has already been pointed out that the counselee has certain expectations about counseling when he comes in for help. It was also pointed out that the counselor should know what these expectancies are. It also seems desirable to let the counselee know what to expect if the learning situation (counseling) is to be as effective as possible. The counselee will, as he tries to get his bearings in the counseling situation, draw upon past experiences and past relationships, none of which are apt to be at all like the counseling experience. Structuring is simply a way to help the counselee learn as directly and effectively as possible what he can expect from counseling.

Providing Information. It has been pointed out that the counselee needs to enhance and protect the self. It has also been brought out that he perceives according to experiences and needs. Furthermore, he learns when he has a need or motivation to learn. Thus in getting information across to the counselee, the counselor needs to find the moment when it is needed, to present it in a way that will allow the counselee to consider it rather than force him to defend himself from it, and to check on counselee distortions. A neutral way of presenting data would appear to allow the counselee the most freedom in reaction to it. If he feels it necessary, the counselee can reject the information without rejecting the counselor.

It seems reasonable to assume that information about the counselee and his present and future environments is very frequently of concern to him and seldom without any emotion-arousing content. It also appears reasonable to assume that the counselor will often not be able to judge whether or not the information will be received as threatening or enhancing, even though he understands the counselee rather well. Thus, very seldom should information be considered purely "factual." In presenting any sort of information, the counselor should be alert for signs of emotional reactions.

Referral. In the discussion of behavior, it was pointed out that conflicts and mechanisms may be out of the awareness of the individual and may be the cause of maladaptive behavior. Help for these problems is a long-term process and one that requires the services of a specialist; referral is usually needed. To build a relationship with a really maladjusted person may cause all sorts of difficulties beyond the skill of the counselor. For example, a strong dependency may develop which the counselor is unable to end without psychological damage to the counselee.

Referral for other problems, such as for occupational information or help with a physical handicap, may be necessary. Usually, however, the need for referral in these situations is more obvious than with emotional problems, and it is usually easier to make the referral.

Resistance to Change. The self-concept is rather stable and resistant to change; the pattern of needs and responses has been built up over a long period of time and is modified slowly. Thus the counselor should not expect new responses or patterns of behavior to emerge quickly. Furthermore, he should not feel frustrated or that he has failed to help the counselee if effective plans and decisions are not made quickly and easily.

Even when the counselee tries new ways of behaving, old responses will return, particularly if new ones are not immediately rewarding. It is often difficult to ensure that the new and more appropriate responses will be rewarded.

Defenses may be strong; the counselee may reject what appear to be reasonable plans and persist in following some impractical course. These defenses are of importance to the counselee and serve some purpose in his behavior. The counselor cannot expect the counselee to drop them quickly, without something to replace them in maintaining his opinion of himself.

Possibility for Learning or Relearning. In spite of what has been said about slowness of change, it can and does take place; otherwise, there would be no point in counseling services. It has already been pointed out that needs are learned and new ones can replace old ones. The process of establishing and changing the response hierarchy shows how new and more productive behavior may be developed in and through counseling.

Perceiving new cues, or perceiving old cues in a different way, can help the counselee in making effective generalizations and discriminations. The counselor can assist the counselee in this process. He can also help to identify conflicts and to bring out the elements involved in the conflicts as a means of resolving them. He can bring the needed elements for learning to the counselee's attention by reflection, interpretation, or questioning, and can help the counselee to identify the appropriate cues for behavior and to find the sorts of responses that will be rewarded. For example, the counselee can be helped to find rewarding aspects of skilled trade work although he has previously thought of it as an inferior type of work fit only for those who could not attend college.

The learning process can result in new goals, new levels of aspiration, a new concept of self, and new strength of motivation. Short cuts to effective behavior may be developed. Some of the reward may come in the counseling situation; for example, feeling satisfied that a definite plan has been made, finding a way to develop potentialities in a training program, or finding suitable alternatives to an unsuccessful plan. The major rewards, however, must come outside the counseling situation in everyday life, for example, recognition and acceptance by peers, success in school, or feeling of satisfaction in work.

Motivation. It has been pointed out that the individual learns when he has a drive or need to learn. Without motivation, no value can be expected to be derived from counseling. The counselor needs, therefore, to discover what motives or needs the counselee has. It is possible, also, to help the counselee build motivation toward worthwhile goals.

Each individual has some needs that he is trying to meet and goals that he is attempting to achieve. He may not be aware of what he is trying to do or why he is trying to do it. Thus the counselor must try to understand how the counselee's behavior serves him. Motivation must be understood and capitalized upon. For example, an attempt to gain recognition by disruptive behavior can be channeled into new ways of behavior that will be more effective in reaching the goal.

The counselor can help the counselee develop motivation. Formulating and setting up desirable goals is one way. Since near goals have more strength, intermediate goals may be set up. Some success strengthens reward value; the counselor can help the counselee achieve success and increase motivation toward desirable behavior.

Whatever progress is made in counseling depends upon the counselee's motivation; the counselor should be constantly aware of its influence. He must realize that the counselee's goals may be quite different from counselor goals, and that the drive to do something must come from within the counselee rather than from the counselor.

The Counselee's Decisions. It is an important principle of counseling that the counselee should make his own decisions. This is related to motivation, which has just been discussed. For goals to be really effective, the counselee must, himself, choose them. He will not give his wholehearted energies to attain a goal or plan imposed by others. He has no reason to feel personally involved in a decision that was made by someone else; he can shift the blame for failure and cannot expect much real credit for success. If the pressure to accept the goal is great, the counselee may display various sorts of personality mechanisms that retard or prevent progress toward the goal. At the same time he may give the appearance (and may believe) that he is trying as hard as he can. He may not actually be aware of the effect of the conflict between his personal desires and those of others which he is forced to follow.

The counselee's concept of himself and his roles are revised by him based on his own learning. If he sees himself as a failure he usually cannot be argued or coerced out of this belief. He must reorganize his perceptions of himself to make a real change in the way he thinks of himself.

The role of counseling in a democratic society makes it essential that the individual have freedom of choice. He even has the freedom to make mistakes. It would, of course, be best if he made a good decision and made it the first time.

Worth of the Counselee's Decision. Even though the counselee makes his own decisions, the counselor uses his ability to help him arrive at a good decision. He makes skillful use of information about the counselee himself, but more than this, he needs to help the counselee project himself into the situations or environments about which decisions are to be made. This makes essential the use of occupational and other information. The situation should be understood in all its psychological, sociological, and physical characteristics, and the counselee needs to be able to relate these aspects to information about himself.

It is apparent, too, that the counselor needs to acquaint the counselee with situations or information of which he may not be aware, for example, occupations which will enable him to play a preferred role.

It is also apparent that the counselor must point out or help the counselee identify probable difficulties in carrying out plans. Some prediction is possible, although it cannot be done as precisely as desirable. Furthermore, all eventualities cannot be anticipated.

The counselor must further help the counselee accept information that has a bearing on the counselee's plans. It is not enough to merely present "facts" to the counselee, without being concerned about whether he uses these facts.

Occupational Choice. The way individuals select occupations may provide suggestions for counseling and indicate types of help needed. It is reemphasized here because of its relevance to counseling. It points up the fact that help, including counseling help, should be given over a period of time and furnishes bases for the sort of help that may be given at various stages in the life of the individual. Also apparent from studies of theories of occupational choice are the levels of development the individual should have reached at various stages in growth and education. The concept of occupational choice as a developmental process adds weight to the statement that counseling should be more of a developmental help than a remedial one. It also has implications for where counseling should be available in the school and what its aims should be.

Counselor Roles. In order to help the counselee learn effectively, the counselor actually takes different roles at different times during the counseling process. All roles are, however, in the general framework of counseling as defined in Chapter 1. At the early stages, the counselor helps the counselee to speak freely about himself; later, he helps the counselee gain understandings and attitudes that will enable him to develop effective plans and make wise decisions. Each role is designed to help the counselee do most effectively what he wants and needs to do at that time. For example, if information is needed to facilitate the progress of counseling, the counselor obtains the information or ensures that it is obtained. If the counselee is hazy and confused about his attitudes or interests, the counselor assists him to clarify them.

The concept of changing roles is based upon the assumption that in the counseling process or the learning process the individual needs different sorts of help at different stages. The counselor acts as the helper. It is felt that early in counseling the counselor helps the counselee to get used to the situation and the relationship, to become oriented, and to bring out and discuss all sorts of relevant data. These are the data with which they work later in the process.

The learner (counselee), it could be assumed, would expect the helper (counselor) to play the role that is most helpful. He does not know just what that role is, but will very likely recognize that it is "right" if it is helpful. Needless to say, the role of authority never fits naturally into this learning or counseling process, as it does not promote the sort of learning that should be characteristic of counseling.

Counseling as Verbal Help. Counseling is largely symbolic behavior. Language is the primary method of experiencing in counseling. The past can be reviewed, events can be relived emotionally, and new situations can be vicariously experienced. The future environment can be explored at the symbolic level. Expressions, gestures, and similar nonverbal behavior also play a part in counseling. The importance is determined by the symbolic meaning attached to them by the counselor or counselee.

The process of thinking can occur in the counseling situation. Plans may be weighed; action may be suspended until decisions are carefully evaluated. Experiences may be reexamined and new interpretations made. For example, threatening cues in an experience may be reassessed as actually nonthreatening.

The importance of the principle is simply that the primary medium of counseling communication—language—enables the individual to learn more effective behavior, some desirable attitudes, more balanced emotional reactions, and new roles for satisfactory self-expression.

This is only a brief summary of what the science of behavior implies for counseling. The discussion could, of course, be elaborated in considerable detail. It should be adequate, however, to indicate bases for the particular approach to counseling described in this book.

SUMMARY

The counselor needs some bases for what he does to help the individual. Bases may be derived from concepts about personality, learning, innate characteristics and their effect on behavior, and environmental influences. These bases provide the framework for a way of working with the individual to help him. Within the framework variations are made to adapt counseling to the needs of the particular counselee.

CHECKS ON UNDERSTANDING

1. What is meant by the term, *concept of self?*
2. Why does an individual see a situation or person in a unique way?
3. Why is the individual's personality not due entirely to experiences?
4. What is a learned need?
5. Why might a pupil have a poorer opinion of himself than the facts in the case would warrant?
6. Why does the culture or class of an individual affect personality?
7. How can size, appearance, and physical maturity help or hinder adjustment?
8. Why does the counselor collect information about the counselee?
9. Why does the counselor refrain from telling the counselee what to do?
10. Define adjustment. Describe a person you would classify as normal.
11. How does the counselor as a person affect the counseling process?
12. Why is it so important for the counselor to recognize counselee feelings and emotions?
13. What are some basic considerations which the counselor should keep in mind as he helps the counselee plan and make decisions?

THINGS TO DO

1. Read a case study and prepare a personality description from it.

2. Observe a situation in which an individual is learning something. Can you infer from his behavior what the learning process is? Ask him to "think aloud" and see if you can identify the process.

3. See if you can identify classes or levels in your own community.

4. Interview several counselors to determine what concept of personality they use as a basis for their counseling.

5. Read a case study and identify the effect of environmental conditions and of innate characteristics. The case studies in Ref. [259] will be of considerable value as examples of what to look for and how to interpret it.

6. Analyze the group structure and influences in your community. Identify as many of these groups as you can. What effect does group membership have on success in schoolwork? A group may be a club, an organization, or a social class [100].

Select a pupil who is making low grades or is about to drop out of school. See if you can place him in one or more of the groups that you identified. Then formulate your answers to the following questions:

a. What effect does his group membership have upon his educational opportunities?

b. Does his group membership have any effect on vocational opportunities in the community? How?

c. How might a teacher tend to rate a student who was a member of a less favored group than the teacher? Who was a member of the same group as the teacher? Who was a member of a more favored group? ("Rate" may be interpreted in such ways as grading on written work, grading on oral comments in class, and ratings on such traits as responsibility, tact, cooperativeness. The "group" may be interpreted as socioeconomic.)

7. Read a typescript of a counseling case, such as those in Refs. [39, 94, 264], and describe the process that the counselor appeared to be using.

8. Observe a counseling session and see if you can infer the counselor's approach and what he is trying to do. Interview him later to discover why he did what he did.

9. As the most important purpose of this chapter is to indicate that counseling procedures and techniques should have bases and to provide some bases for counseling, one of the most helpful activities that you could do would be to study and evaluate bases for counseling and procedures and techniques derived from these bases. The data for study may be obtained from observation and interviewing of counselors, and from books and research studies by counselors. You might prepare an outline based upon points covered in this chapter as a means for organizing data. You will also find it helpful to do some reading about therapy and interview a therapist. The ultimate objective is to enable you to formulate rather definite reasons for the sort of counseling you do.

10. Evaluate a recording of a counseling session or sessions that you have conducted. Can you give reasons for doing what you did?

CHAPTER 8

Other Sources
of Information
about the Student

THE COUNSELOR has available, in addition to those types already discussed, a number of other very useful sources of data about the individual. Usually he will study these sources outside of the actual face-to-face relationship; they may not be used in the counseling process itself. The counselor may, however, ask the counselee to furnish the information while they are together in a counseling session. Furthermore, the counselor may bring a portion of the information, such as the completed time schedule, to the counseling session, lay it on the desk, and discuss it with the counselee.

There are four aspects of these sources of information about which the counselor should know: first, when to use them if the information is not already available; second, how to use the techniques; third, what the information obtained by these techniques means; and fourth, how to use the technique and information in the counseling process.

The details of setting up and using these techniques in the school guidance program are beyond the scope of this chapter. Excellent discussions on the guidance program use of the techniques may be found in Ref. [77] and other similar books.

In this chapter, emphasis is on collecting and interpreting the information; while some attention is given to using the data with the counselee, more detailed discussion of this process is reserved for Chapters 12 and 13.

Anecdotal Records

The anecdotal record is a brief, factual report of pupil behavior made by someone who actually has observed his behavior. Comments, suggestions for action to be taken, as well as interpretation may be added but should be kept separate from the factual objective report of the behavior.

When to Collect Anecdotal Records. Assuming that there are no such reports in the cumulative record folder or that the ones available are quite old or incomplete, the counselor might feel that the sort of information provided in anecdotal records would be helpful. For example, suppose that he needed indications of consistent patterns of behavior in dealing with others. A typical question might be how the counselee reacts to other pupils and teachers. How does he express his needs? Does he attempt to dominate situations, does he play a passive role, or does he try to escape from competition? Then the counselor often needs to know how others react to the counselee. Is he involved in group activity? Do others look to him for advice? Is his opinion valued? When there is a need to know more about behavior in everyday life situations, the anecdotal record provides helpful information. This is the sort of information that cannot be obtained very well in the face-to-face counseling situation where the counselee, for a short period of time, may act quite differently from his usual behavior.

It would be best if the anecdotal records covered a rather substantial period prior to counseling. After counseling has started there would be less time to obtain a desirable number of observations. However, the counselor might obtain the help of several teachers in collecting a series of records after counseling has begun.

Using Anecdotal Records. Usually the counselor would not collect anecdotal records on the counselee, but there might be times when the counselor would actually make the observation himself. He may also help teachers learn how to obtain them. Furthermore, being familiar with the way that observations are made provides assistance to the counselor in interpreting anecdotal records.

The anecdotal record is a factual, objective, "photographic" account of a specific example of behavior. The observer sets down exactly what happened, including quotations of what was said, if possible. Evaluative words and expressions are not used. The result is an account of what happened as accurately as the observer can describe it. The reader can "see" the behavior almost as if he had been present. If there is an evaluation or interpretation of the incident, it is kept separate.

The most difficult aspect of writing anecdotal records is to keep personal opinion out of them. For example, suppose that the counselor read an anecdote such as the following: "This morning John came into class late, deliberately slammed the door, acted in a very unruly manner to me, and made it plain to everyone that he was not interested in the lesson." All you know is that John was late (not how late), and that the door was closed with some unknown amount of noise (how many high school students close a door silently?). The counselor may imagine that the teacher was rather perturbed by John's behavior, but he might have some difficulty in determining whether the teacher was in an irritable mood or John was particularly annoying.

Instead of this, suppose the teacher had written the following: "John came in the room about five minutes after the tardy bell, pushed the door closed without attempting to hold it, dropped his books on the desk, not picking up one that fell on the floor, and sat looking out of the window during the remainder of the period." While John might not have looked out of the window *all* of the period, this at least seems to be a factual and objective report on what happened. Reading the latter report one gets quite a different impression of John from that given by the former.

Comments and interpretative statements should be labeled as such and kept separate from the factual report. For example, under comments, the teacher might say, "John seemed to be quite upset or angry about something, and presumably used disturbing activities and deliberate inattention to 'blow off steam.'" This is the particular teacher's *interpretation* of the incident. It may be quite accurate or it may not. The teacher or counselor may use the interpretation to help in understanding John, but he is aware that it is the meaning given to the incident by another person.

The observer might have suggestions to make concerning the pupil and these, too, should be reported separately from the incident itself. For example, the teacher might say: "It would seem to be helpful for the counselor to talk to John to find the causes of his present attitude."

Anecdotal records may be made in any of a number of different forms. A suggested form is shown on page 183. An entire sheet is to be used. A smaller form could be employed, but the standard size sheet of paper fits into the cumulative record quite nicely, and records may be clipped together in sequence. The incident is identified by the observer's name, when it was made, and where it was made. Space is provided for the factual report, and places are designated for interpretation and recommendations. When the teacher is making the record, the sheet could be folded to leave only the anecdote section exposed. Thus it would not be necessary to use a conspicuously large form in recording the observation on the spot.

A number of behavior incidents reported over a period of time will give more information about persistent patterns of behavior and will enable the counselor to discern trends in behavior. The more extensive (and dependable) data the counselor has, the more confidence he can put in his conclusions about the counselee. Thus if the records are collected only after the pupil entered into counseling, they may cover only a short period of time and may not reflect persistent patterns or indicate the direction of trends. There is a

Anecdotal Record Form

Pupil_____ Date _____

Class and time_____

- -

Anecdote: _____

_____

_____

_____

_____

- -

Observer_____

Interpretation: _____

_____

Suggestions: _____

_____

_____

definite advantage in collecting anecdotal records systematically as part of the guidance or personnel program. References, such as the one already given, will provide help to the school in setting up such a system.

Interpreting the Information. In searching for the meaning of the anecdotal descriptions, the counselor would first evaluate the objectivity with which they appear to be written. If they seem to be largely opinion, evaluation, criticisms, and judgments, the counselor can tell very little or nothing about the counselee.

If the records appear to be factual enough for use, the counselor then needs to consider the scope of the records or the amount of behavior that has been sampled. He cannot arrive at conclusions about the counselee from two or three records. They may be good samples of behavior or they may not. From the most valid representation of the counselee, the records should cover a substantial period of time and should reflect behavior in different sorts of situations.

Data about the counselee from anecdotal records need to be interpreted in combination with other data obtained by other means. They should not be used alone as a basis for understanding why the counselee does as he does and what can be done to help him. The counselor may get clues and ideas to follow up from these types of observations, as well as information about what the counselee actually does, but he should check these against other data, rather than accept them as proved facts.

Since anecdotal records give behavior descriptions of the counselee in life situations, the counselor looks for behavior that will indicate what the counselee is really like in his dealings with others. He might begin to study the collection of records by asking questions such as: "Is there evidence that the counselee is accepted by others?" "Does he give indications of having ability to influence others and to lead them?" "What sorts of situations cause him to withdraw?" Or he may begin to read over the anecdotes and search for behavior patterns and trends. As these emerge, the counselor may look for confirming evidence. He searches particularly for evidence of strengths and positive aspects of the counselee, but at the same time he notes weaknesses and areas of difficulty. He formulates a description of the individual and tries to make it a consistent and understandable one. He compares the meaning or inferences he has drawn from the data with those from other data. For example, if the counselee has said he dislikes school, is low in mental ability, and shows a pattern (in anecdotal records) of inattentiveness in class and resentment of teachers, the counselor may suspect that this is an individual who finds schoolwork too difficult and is defending himself by this behavior. Thus anecdotal behavior descriptions are compared with other data. A pupil may exhibit the same sort of behavior in the classroom for a number of reasons, including emotional conflicts in the home.

Several anecdotal records that the counselor found in John Doe's cumulative record folder will illustrate what is meant by interpretative comments rather than factual reporting. Read them over and identify observer comments that would not be very useful. Then look for evidence which could be used to answer the following questions:

1. How does John get along with other students?
2. How does John react to the unsympathetic attitude of teachers?
3. Are there any indications of leadership ability?

Record #1 (undated)
Today in class recitation John said that he had not had time to prepare his lesson. I asked him why he couldn't if everyone else could. He was offended by this, began to whisper and tell jokes to other students in order to disturb them. I stopped this immediately.

Miss Swift, Latin I

Record #2
John came to me after class and asked if I would help him with the math lesson. He said, "I would sure appreciate it, because I can't go out at night until I get all the homework. Everybody else gets them and I don't." I replied that others were having trouble too, and that I was having a special session that afternoon. He said that he would be glad to come. Comment: John is a hard worker, and is trying to learn. His family probably are checking up on him at home, but this does not seem to be the only reason for his concern.

Mr. Brown, Math I

Record #3
John Doe is a lazy student. Today he had not finished his English theme, and when I asked him why, he used the well-worn excuse that he had spent too much time on other lessons. What he needs is some discipline at home.   John Sharp, Eng. I

Record #4
Today, in class meeting to plan for the Junior-Senior party, there was a discussion as to whether the party should be held in the school auditorium or in the Half-Moon Dance Hall. The discussion was getting heated when John got up and said, "Everybody who wants to pay three dollars instead of one please hold up your hands with the money." Everyone laughed at this, and after a few more comments, the school auditorium was selected.

Comment: John seems to be able to influence others and get them to agree with him.

Jane Jones, Junior Home Room

These anecdotal records illustrate varying degrees of objectivity in reporting what actually occurred. Rate them as "factual," "fact and opinion," and "opinion." Note too that the counselor would need more records than these few to learn much about John. The school has no plan for collecting anecdotal records and so very few were actually made.

Using the Information in Counseling. The sort of information collected by anecdotal records is of particular value to the counselor as it helps him to understand how the counselee reacts to real life situations. However, it is not the sort of information that would be brought directly into the counseling situation. In the first place, since the counselee very likely did not know that his behavior was being observed and recorded, he might be somewhat embarrassed or resentful if he were confronted with the actual records. The most important use is to add to other data in order to make inferences about the counselee's patterns and trends in behavior and to formulate hypotheses about his probable behavior in other situations.

Valuable clues for further investigation may be obtained from anecdotal records. For example, if the counselee seems to show aggressive behavior toward certain classmates, the counselor may want to search for the bases for the behavior. An illustration may help show the sort of clues that may be obtained from anecdotal records. A pupil, who seems to be quite likable and who seemed to exhibit leadership behavior in the classroom and in activities, was nevertheless disliked by other pupils. Anecdotal records pictured his behavior and the reactions of others. The counselor looked further into this puzzling situation and found that, because of an incident that had occurred years before, the pupil's family (and the pupil) were disliked and distrusted by people in the community.

Anecdotal records are particularly useful to the counselor in that they show persistent patterns of behavior and the duration and direction of trends. For example, a counselee was only moderately skilled in getting along with others. He would not be judged very successful in interpersonal relations when only his present status was considered. However, a series of anecdotal records extending over several years showed that he had made a great deal of progress in this respect and that the trend was one of increasingly greater social competence. Then, too, anecdotal records give indications of the effect of counseling both while it is in progress and after it has been completed, so that the counselor is able to estimate what changes have taken place. For this purpose the counselor may take some records himself or request others to keep anecdotal records on the counselee during and after counseling.

The Autobiography

The autobiography is an account of the counselee's life as he sees it. Usually likes and dislikes, interests, plans, reasons for behavior, and similar topics are requested of the counselee rather than merely a chronological listing of events. In a sense, the autobiography is a projective technique. The counselee describes events, people, and his actions from his own point of view. While his report may not be factually accurate and may even be intentionally distorted, it usually gives the teacher or counselor insight into the counselee's personal and private world. This is particularly true for the counselee who writes better than he talks. Such counselees may give information in the autobiography that the counselor would have great difficulty in obtaining otherwise. On the other hand, the counselee who does not express himself very well in writing may not produce a very helpful autobiography. However, elegance in style is not a prerequisite for a useful autobiography.

Obtaining the Autobiography. Sometimes pupils write autobiographies as an assignment in a class, such as an English class. If an autobiography were already available, the counselor would use it along with other records and reports. However, this source of data is infrequently used [199] and often it will be up to the counselor to decide whether or not he wants it and to request that the counselee write an autobiography. Then, too, in many instances the available autobiography may be a brief, superficial page or so that was obviously done with little thought or effort. In this event the counselor would want to obtain a more extensive and carefully prepared one.

It would appear desirable to have an autobiography on each counselee, which should be written early in counseling. The autobiography provides information which supplements other types of data and which may not be obtained in any other way. It is particularly useful when the counselor wishes to get at aspects of the counselee's inner world, his feelings about others, his view of himself, his goals, fears, and problems. Thus when the counselor feels that he needs to know how the counselee perceives the world about him and to gain an understanding of the way he sees events and people, he would particularly want to obtain an autobiography. This need is often felt with the counselee who seems to be introverted, who keeps his problems and needs to himself, and who does not say too much about inner feelings. On the other hand, counselors are often surprised to find that every individual has unexpected facets to his life that are revealed by the autobiography. Thus it is difficult to say that the autobiography should be used with this or that sort of person and at a certain time in some cases and not in others.

Collecting Information. There are two general approaches to having the counselee write an autobiography. In the unstructured approach the counselor would give him only a few directions, such as asking him to put down the story of his life and to indicate experiences in certain areas such as family relations, education, and so on. The directions would be so brief and general that the counselee would have to decide what to include. An example of a rather brief set of directions is given with the excerpts from John Doe's autobiography. The second approach is to structure the autobiography by giving the counselee an outline to follow or a list of questions to answer [189, pp. 11–14; 217, pp. 14–16]. Although there is not a great deal of evidence as to which approach is of the most value, the structured autobiography might obtain more information than the unstructured [56].

The usefulness of the autobiography is dependent upon the counselee's freedom and sincerity in expressing himself and his degree of motivation to write about himself. Therefore the counselor should have established rapport with the counselee before asking for the autobiography. It might be helpful to have the counselee write several short accounts of experiences, interests, and plans as a kind of warm-up for the writing of an autobiography.

The counselor might want to emphasize a particular type of information, for example, experiences that have helped to build self-confidence. He might include in the directions the statement that the counselee should try to recall times when he felt that he did especially well in something, when he had feelings of accomplishment and satisfaction, and when he felt particularly happy and well liked. At the same time he would want the counselee to explain why he felt as he did and what effect these experiences have had on his development. If the counselor is interested in developing vocational interests, he might ask the counselee to name activities that he has liked, how he became interested in them, and why he has enjoyed them. He might also want the counselee to tell about the kinds of jobs he has thought about preparing for and why. Some high school students will have a great deal of difficulty with this sort of introspective reporting, so adequate directions may be of great help. Some directions as to length should be given. Usually an autobiography should be 4,000 to 5,000 words in length. This may seem to be quite long, but if the writing is extended over a period of time and the counselee becomes interested in it, it will probably not appear too demanding a project.

Interpreting the Information. The autobiography provides information about the inner world of the counselee and thus enables the counselor to understand his needs, fears, and ambitions. The counselor uses the information to gain an understanding of the way the counselee perceives people, events, and circumstances rather than as a technique for obtaining factual information. The counselor compares information in the autobiography with other data. He may, in reading it over, pose several questions as guides for arriving at inferences about the counselee. Questions may be of the following sort:

1. What appear to be dominant needs of the counselee?
2. How does he regard others, such as peers, teachers, parents?
3. What does he think of himself?
4. What topics or aspects of his life are conspicuous by their absence?
5. In what sorts of situations does he appear to be happiest?

Other questions could be formulated on the basis of what the counselor needs to know to understand the counselee. The autobiography tends to give information as to why the counselee behaves as he does, as contrasted with other techniques, such as anecdotal records, which give more of the "how" of behavior. But the counselor should use great care in making judgments about the counselee from the autobiography. Often he finds what appear to be excellent explanations for behavior, or detects what appear to be serious emotional problems; he might presume that he has the counselee "figured out." But the data in the autobiography should be regarded very tentatively until he has additional information to back up his hypotheses. Then, too, the kind of data in the autobiography should be viewed in relation to the counselor's own level of understanding of dynamics of personality. The better his understanding in this area, the more meaning he may obtain from these data. With a limited knowledge, he should be particularly careful not to jump to diagnostic formulations about the counselee or to feel satisfied that he knows what sort of person the counselee is and why.

As an example of the directions for writing an autobiography and for parts of an autobiography, the following data from the John Doe case are presented.

My Autobiography (Directions)

This is to be an account of your life as you see it. Try to remember as far back as you can. Tell about the experiences you had that seem to stand out in your memory. Include both pleasant and unpleasant ones, and tell why you felt about them as you did. Include something about your family life, the neighborhoods in which you have lived, friends, groups that you have been a member of, school, hobbies, work experience, ambitions. Naturally you cannot include everything but try to include the high spots, particularly those events that caused some change in your life, like moving to a new neighborhood or getting a job. See if you can recall your reactions or feelings about the events. If you can, tell something about the events, people, conditions, that have had a great deal of influence in making you the way you are today—in making your personality what it is—in helping you make your plans for the future.

There is no set limit to this autobiography, but you will probably need ten to fifteen pages really to tell something about yourself. Don't try to write it all at once, but do a little at a time, over a period of about two weeks.

These directions were given to John Doe by the counselor and John wrote, with a great deal of effort, a paper that was somewhat shorter than was called for. However, he gave some very descriptive accounts, the most revealing of which are presented below:

When I was about four years old I was very sick with scarlet fever. I remember Mother looking after me day and night, and after I was able to get out, she was always telling me to be careful and didn't let me do anything for a long time. She was still this way after I had been to school a couple of years, and I guess she is still this way some.

When I was in the eighth grade, I was elected class president. I was proud of this, but some of the others said I wouldn't make a good one. I tried to make friends with them because I wanted to get them all on my side.

I have never thought very seriously about plans for the future. I guess I thought things would just happen. Part of it, I think, is having other people make choices for me, like taking the college preparatory course. I never thought about going to college in a practical way. In fact, when I think about it now, I guess I thought it meant not having to make any definite plans for work for another four years, and having a good time. Now I realize I'll have to decide something myself. When I think of this, I get worried and confused and don't see how I can do it. But I think I would feel more worried if I didn't.

When I got the job of selling ads for the paper I was afraid that I might not be able to sell any. Some of the others had tried it and didn't do so well, although it was a chance to get out of class and go downtown. I knew most of the men I saw but I guess they thought of me as a kid more than someone to do business with. I had to do a lot of talking with some of them, even though they said they always helped the school. After awhile I got used to it, and now I like it.

As a guide to interpreting these autobiographical excerpts, look for data about the following points:

1. John's reactions to others telling him what to do
2. The importance he puts on good relations with peers
3. The fears and conflicts caused by his striving for independence

Using the Information. The autobiography itself, or data from it, would usually not be brought directly into the counseling session. If the counselor had requested the counselee to prepare the autobiography he might, however, use it during the conference. Typically, the data from the autobiography are used to round out the picture of the counselee and to provide clues for further exploration by other methods, including the counseling session itself. Suppose, for example, that the counselor found evidence in the autobiography that the counselee had a very low opinion of himself and felt quite inferior to others. Very likely the counselor would also find clues as to the bases of these feelings. He could compare the counselee's opinion of himself with what reasonably objective observers would say about him as a way of checking the reality of his opinion, and could combine the counselee's opinion of himself with other data to aid him in understanding the counselee as a person.

The autobiography often provides promising clues about the writer that the counselor may wish to follow up. For example, the counselee may appear to prefer scientific activities, courses, and hobbies. This could be followed up by checking other indications of interest.

Since the counselor may gain an understanding of the counselee's point of view, he will be able to provide a more accepting and permissive counseling atmosphere than might otherwise be the case. It would seem likely, too, that the act of writing an autobiography would aid the counselee in becoming aware of and talking about significant aspects of his life. The autobiography would not take the place of any of the face-to-face aspects of counseling, but it does provide supplementary data that cannot usually be obtained as well in any other way.

Comments of Others Who Know the Counselee

A valuable source of information, often overlooked, are other persons who know the counselee. Sometimes a question or two may be asked of teachers, or perhaps a parent, but usually there is no planned or systematic collection of data from persons such as employers, parents, medical persons, past and present teachers, friends, and classmates. Admittedly this procedure takes time and may, in some cases, arouse counselee resentment as he may feel that the counselor is checking up on him behind his back. Usually the counselor discusses with the counselee his plans for contacting others prior to doing so. The information obtained may be obviously biased or hastily formed opinion. Nevertheless, the counselor would do well to tap this source to aid him in gaining an understanding of the counselee.

When to Use This Source of Information. It would be difficult to state that there would be any time that comments of others who know the counselee would not be useful. In general, it would appear most helpful to contact teachers, parents, and others early in the counseling process. The nature of some of the questions that the counselor raises about the counselee as he attempts to understand him would indicate whether or not he needs to contact one or more of these sources, and which ones. Suppose that the counselor wanted to know how the counselee performed on a job. The employer and immediate supervisor would be the logical ones to contact. If the counselor had to ration his time and establish priorities on what he could do for each counselee, he would have to judge which cases required contacting some outside source of information. For example, if the counselee's problem appeared to center around relations with several teachers, it would appear to be essential to talk to those teachers. Or if the home situation appeared to be a crucial aspect, the counselor would likely want to visit the home and talk to the parents. It might be possible for the counselor to overlook the need for contacting one of these sources, however, simply because it does not seem to be very important. For example, he may decide, on the basis of what he knows about the counselee, that there is no need to visit the home and get information from parents, when, in fact, the home is the central factor in the counselee's problem. Valuable information may not be obtained. It may be well, therefore, for the counselor to contact some of these sources even if there seems to be no definite need for the sort of information that could be obtained.

Gathering the Information. Once the counselor has decided to contact parents, employers, friends, or others, it would seem to be advisable to discuss this with the counselee to allow him to react to the idea. Of course, it would be better if the counselee suggested that the counselor make the contact. But if he does not, the counselor might bring up the matter and ask him what he thinks of it. Quite often the counselee will react in such a way as to tell something about his relations with the suggested person, as, for example, the counselee who objected to the counselor talking to his parents with this comment, "I know what they'll say and they'll make you agree with them like they do everybody else." The counselor probably should not follow up the plan if the counselee objects to it. The same principle would seem to hold here as with other techniques, that is, the counseling relationship is more important than the use of a specific technique and should not be endangered by attempting to force the counselee to accept something to which he is definitely opposed. The counselor may feel sure that it would aid counseling for him to contact, say, an employer, but if the counselee is opposed to the counselor making the contact, it would be advisable not to do it. The counselor, however, would have the obligation of helping the counselee understand the advisability of obtaining needed information from the employer or some other person. Thus it is not a matter of the counselor leaving the matter entirely up to the counselee.

In contacting the person or persons for information, the counselor should have specific questions in mind. However, in actually talking to the individual it would appear advisable to provide a lead and encourage him to talk, rather than ask him a series of questions. It would be necessary to avoid loaded or slanted questions. At the same time the counselor would not reveal any information that the counselee had given him. This is usually a problem in talking to parents, as they are naturally very curious to know just what the counselor and the counselee have been discussing. It would appear, too, that it would be better to use a personal contact or interview with the individual rather than sending him a form to fill in.

Interpreting the Information. It would be well to keep in mind the limitations of this source of information as data are evaluated and interpreted. In the first place the counselor would want to estimate how much opportunity the individual actually had to observe the counselee and to know something about him. Then the counselor would want to consider how objective the individual's information was. (Parents would not be expected to be very objective in talking about their son or daughter.) Knowing the individual who provides the information will help the counselor to evaluate its meaning. What the counselor finds is compared with other data about the counselee.

This source is not usually much help in discovering what the counselee thinks of the situation but is more useful for learning what he does, how he affects others, and how they react to him. For example, the parents of a counselee stated that he was unusually bright and said that he had plans to attend a technical college. The counselor had substantial evidence that the counselee was in the dull range of mental ability, that all college plans originated with his parents, and that he actually had no plans for education beyond high school. The parents were not the best source of information about the counselee's mental ability or desires. But they were the best source of information about their own overly optimistic rating of their son. This information was quite important for the counselor to know.

Information from peers, classmates, and the like can be quite revealing. A remark such as, "Everybody had a good time at the Hi-Y meeting because Joe was master of ceremonies," tells a great deal about Joe. Most of the information from this source will probably be from casual comments, as it usually is not advisable to question pupils directly about other pupils.

Using the Information in Counseling. As in the case of similar types of data, such as items on the home situation in the cumulative record, the counselor usually would not bring the information directly into the counseling process but would synthesize it with other data about the counselee. It would often provide verification for inferences and hypotheses about the counselee drawn from other data. In some cases, it would conflict with other data and the counselor could investigate this conflict further by looking for additional data and by exploring the conflict during the counseling situation. There would be some cases, of course, when the information might be brought directly into the counseling situation. For example, a counselee's parents were planning to send him to college to take a course in business administration. Later he was supposed to enter into the family business. The counselee had said very little about this plan, but the parents stated that it was settled and that the counselee was in favor of it. It was necessary for the counselor to discuss the parents' attitudes and plans with the counselee in the counseling session as they were a major factor in any educational and occupational goals that the counselee would formulate. In some cases, however, the person giving the information would not want any of it disclosed to the counselee. The counselor would naturally respect this desire.

Counselors may make extensive use of the information of others who know the counselee, keeping in mind that this sort of data must be evaluated very carefully and that it may be highly subjective, biased, and based on hasty judgments.

Informational Forms

A source of information extensively used in the collection of data for a guidance program but sometimes neglected in the actual counseling process is the informational form. Various sorts of forms will very likely be familiar to the counselor as he may have collected data from pupils or employees with them. The form is usually made up of a number of questions about the individual, his experiences, preferences, and so on. The items should be included for a definite purpose and should furnish needed information.

When to Use This Source of Information. As a general rule the counselor would use this technique prior to the actual counseling process. It appears to be an economical way to obtain a great deal of data from the counselee with little expenditure of the counselor's time and effort. Counseling time is thus made available to a larger number of counselees and for obtaining information that cannot be obtained in any other way. Frequently the school has pupils fill out an informational form routinely and thus it is available for the counselor. If this is not done and if needed data are not in some other place, such as the cumulative record, the counselor might obtain or devise a form providing for the collection of data that he needs and have counselees fill it in prior to the beginning of counseling, or at least quite early in the counseling process. An example of a form, already mentioned as a structured autobiography, is given in Ref. [217, pp. 14–16].

Interpreting the Information. The type of data collected by means of the informational form is quite similar to that collected by other methods such as the cumulative record and the conference with the counselee. Data about the home situation, such as socioeconomic conditions or occupation of parents, would be interpreted in the same way as already discussed in the section on the cumulative record. Information about interests, choices, and plans would also be interpreted the same way as information obtained in other ways directly from the counselee. Usually this sort of information would be further taken up with the counselee in the counseling process; for example, a hobby of electronics would be discussed to discover what he does and how strong his interest is.

The data in the information form should be checked against other data. For one thing, the counselee may be inclined to put down what he thinks is a desirable response, or he may not give the meaning that he intends to. For example, a counselee may state as an occupational preference "scientist" because he thinks this is the same as "mechanical repair work." Then, too, the data should be checked for misinformation on the part of the counselee. For example, he may say that he is in the academic curriculum when he is actually taking a general course. Pertinent bits of data in the informational form are compared and synthesized with data from other sources. As in the interpretation of data obtained by any information-getting technique, conclusions should not be formulated on the basis of only one type of information.

Using the Information in Counseling. Data from the form may be used to understand the counselee better and to provide leads for further discussion in the counseling session. The form itself would probably not be brought into the counseling session, although there may be times when the counselor would have it before him and ask the counselee to discuss one or more of the items. The counselor would want to be careful not to ask the counselee a question that he had already answered on the informational form, or he would probably wonder why he had been asked to spend his time and effort filling it out.

Informal Projective Methods

Much counselee behavior is projective in nature; it can be interpreted as an expression of inner needs, tensions, and conflicts. The autobiography often presents a great deal of projective material. There are, however, several techniques not previously mentioned which provide for counselee projection and which the counselor and teachers may use. These are role playing and sociodrama, pictures, and lists of words or incomplete sentences.

The more specialized projective tests are not covered here, as they require training to administer and interpret correctly. In fact, sentence-completion techniques have been standardized and developed a great deal. Uses of projective techniques suggested here are limited to simpler applications of the techniques. Even with these, however, caution should be used in making interpretations.

Obtaining and Interpreting the Data. Pictures may sometimes be used to encourage the student to talk about himself. The counselor might find that a collection of pictures, such as may be obtained from a magazine, will help a reticent or shy student to talk in the interview situation. The purpose here is not to attempt to interpret the comments that the person makes about the picture but rather to use these to get him to start talking. If the counselee appears to have a great deal of difficulty in expressing himself, the counselor might present a picture and ask him to talk about it—to tell what is happening. Such pictures might be of sports, social activities, and other appropriate scenes.

Sociodrama [218, pp. 243–244] is a projective method well suited to the classroom situation as it involves role playing in groups. A number of persons take roles, for example, students take the roles of teachers or parents and deal with some group problem or situation. Role playing may also be used with the individual playing "himself" in a group situation. The situation is presented to the group, each member of which knows the part he is supposed to play. There are no further directions, and no solution is presented by the teacher or leader. The members then play their parts, projecting themselves into the situation. For example, a group of adolescents who are having difficulty with their parents over the time they are required to come in at night might take the part of their parents and discuss the matter. Besides having the opportunity to express feelings that otherwise might be bottled up, the adolescent might develop some insight into the parents' attitude about the problem and be able to think of the matter in a much more objective way.

The counselor might request the teacher to have a sociodrama session including the counselee if he felt that he needed more information about the way the counselee perceives various situations and persons. In some cases, this may have already been done in the classroom and the counselor could obtain information about the counselee from the teacher. The counselor should be alert for the sorts of projective behavior that occur in everyday activities and be aware of the meaning and importance of this behavior.

Incomplete sentences may be used to obtain projective data about the individual [218, pp. 166–167]. The counselee completes a sentence from one or several given to him. Several examples are: "Money . . . ," "My best friend . . . ," and "My home. . . ." The results provide clues to the coun-selee's feelings and attitudes about himself and others.

While not a technique, observation in the classroom and in other situations provides helpful data about the individual. For example, during a discussion, the teacher may observe which students do a great deal of talking. What does this behavior tell about the individual? Does he seem to be demanding atten-tion from the teacher, or is he seeking to achieve some recognition from class members? If he is generally snubbed by his peers, does this behavior take on any particular meaning? What about the student who offers no comment in a session of relatively free class discussion? Does the fact that he appears quite fearful of attracting attention to himself tell anything about his personality needs? Projections can occur at many other times, such as during study periods or when the teacher is out of the room.

Behavior that is more clearly projective is that in which a student interprets a situation or the actions of others according to his own needs. For example, in social studies class where delinquent behavior and its causes are being dis-cussed, a student who is neglected by his father and who has been delinquent or near-delinquent might explain that parental neglect is responsible for ado-lescent delinquency. If the teacher were not aware of the parent-child relation-ship, this explanation would be a clue to the reasons for the pupil's behavior. However, the statement should be compared with other information about the pupil, particularly that of the home situation. If the teacher or counselor were aware that this particular student was neglected by his father, the projections revealed by the statement would give indications of the way the student feels about the situation.

Another illustration is as follows: In an English class during the discussion of the story of a boy who "made good," a student makes a comment such as, "He was a success because he worked hard and did not let bad treatment by bosses discourage him. The world is a tough place and it's everybody for him-self." A statement of this kind might be the reporting of something that the pupil had heard, and one which does not represent any particular deep-seated attitude. On the other hand, it might be an attitude that plays a major influ-ence in the student's interpersonal relationships. The need to know more about the student before interpreting the comment is obvious. It should be pointed out here, however, that even if the student's statement is a stereotyped response that he has obtained from someone else, the fact that he remembered it and selected it as an explanation of someone else's behavior is in itself significant.

In the halls between classes, during recess and lunch period, and on the playground, a great deal of information about the student can be obtained by the careful observer. The free play or activity periods are particularly useful times for making observations. Note which students take the lead in games or other activities. How does the leader express his leadership: by dominating others, or by representing the group opinion? How does this fit in with other data, such as relations with parents and teachers, success in schoolwork? What about heterosexual activities? Adolescents often find difficulty in making adjustments in this area, and behavior gives information about these heterosexual drives and conflicts. The club meeting, conducted by a student officer, is often a very fruitful source of observational material about students.

The interpretation of data involving projection can be only as good as the counselor's background in the psychological bases of behavior. Thus references given in the chapters on bases of counseling will be helpful. Many of the references on projective techniques deal almost exclusively with specific instruments or therapeutic procedures designed for the specialist. A useful discussion, however, is provided in Ref. [218, ch. 6].

Using the Technique and Data in Counseling. In the actual counseling situation the counselor will have the opportunity to observe examples of projection, for example, the way that the counselee reacts to him and to the total counseling situation. The counselor should be alert for indications of projection and look for significant meaning. The counselor does not change anything in the counseling process by doing this but merely attempts to learn more about the counselee by utilizing this approach to understand him. The use of pictures, already mentioned, may help the counselee to start talking and may provide some useful data.

Information about the counselee drawn from many sources, such as informal observations in and out of class and sociodrama, could be compared and synthesized with other data to provide the counselor with a better understanding of the counselee. There would probably be no occasion when the counselor would bring these sorts of data directly into the counseling process; for example, they would not discuss the counselee's opinion that the world of work is a "tough place." Rather, they would be combined with other data and used in ways discussed in the chapters on planning.

Sociometric Data

There appears to be an increasing use of sociometric techniques and data in school guidance programs. The term sociometrics means measuring social preferences, dislikes, and so on, in a group. The teacher or group leader may use this method for obtaining data to be used in understanding the group structure and may employ this knowledge to do more effective teaching. The counselor is primarily interested in what sociometric data tell about the counselee. Sociometric data show the way the individual regards others and how they in turn regard him, what subgroups or cliques he is a member of, what his status is in the group, and whether or not he is a "lone wolf."

When to Collect the Data. While these sorts of data would almost always be useful, the counselor would have particular need for them when he has questions as to how well the counselee gets along with others, whether he is accepted or rejected, whether or not he is a member of a particular clique or subgroup, and how much influence he has on others or how much leadership ability he has. The counselor would, however, probably not obtain this sort of information until counseling had progressed to the point where he felt that he needed it. If, as it is in some cases, the information were already in the school record, the counselor would use it at the beginning along with other data to aid in understanding the counselee.

How to Collect the Data. The counselor might have an opportunity to obtain sociometric data in his own class or in whatever group work he is doing. Usually, however, he would have to enlist the help of others. Teachers might be well acquainted with the technique and thus be able to provide the data, or the counselor might help them to understand and apply the technique.

A very simple way to discover social preferences is to ask pupils or members of a group to select two persons with whom they would like to work on a project or some other real situation. You might also ask for names of those with whom each would least like to work. Pupils should feel that they are doing something that has real significance and should not be given reason to think that it is procedure to study the group structure and the place of individuals in the group. The activity on which pupils are asked to express preferences would depend upon the particular sort of information the counselor wanted. For example, if he wanted to assess the counselee's status in social activities, he might ask for names of those with whom pupils would prefer to attend a social affair or to plan a class party.

Interpreting the Information. The counselor is primarily interested in what the sociometric study tells about the counselee. However, he would also need to know something about the structure of the group to interpret the data about the individual. Thus the counselor would need to study the individual's place in the group as well as the group structure.

Probably of first importance would be the actual preferences of others for the counselee. Is he accepted by some members of the group? Is he completely rejected and an isolate? Who accepts him? Is he a member of a small group of outsiders to the main group? Or does he appear to be accepted in the major group? If the group is actually a number of more or less independent subgroups or cliques, with which sort of subgroup is he identified? Does he appear to be the popular choice of most of the other members of the total group?

It would also be important to keep in mind the basis of the choices. To be chosen to work on a class presentation might indicate different capabilities than being chosen to take part in a social activity or go on a camping trip. Different attributes would influence selection for different activities. Thus the counselor must infer from the choices (or rejections) what particular qualities others see in the counselee.

The counselor would not put too much emphasis on or draw very extensive conclusions from the results of only one sociometric study. A series, over a period of time, should give more reliable information about the counselee and also show trends. Also, a number taken in different groups would be of great value as to how he is chosen in different situations and by different persons.

Using the Technique and Data in Counseling. The technique itself could not be used in the counseling process. The counselor might request that some-one obtain the data or he might obtain them himself if he had the counselee in a group or class. The primary use of the data would be to combine them with other sorts of information to learn about and understand the counselee's behavior, and to identify clues for further exploration. It would seem quite unwise to use the results of the study directly with the counselee or to let him know that such a study had been made.

Time Schedule

The time schedule is a detailed record kept by the counselee of his activities (usually for a period of one week) which shows both what he did and how much time he put on it. It is a useful source of data about the counselee, particularly when he appears to use his time unwisely or ineffectively. Often, however, this source of information is neglected when it could possibly be of great value.

When to Use a Time Schedule. The time schedule would be most helpful when the counselee is having difficulty with schoolwork or when he appears to have an unbalanced program of work and recreation, for example, too many school activities. Thus the counselor would usually decide whether or not to have the counselee keep a time schedule after he had some idea of the nature of the problem. Of course, he might use this technique in an exploratory way as he would any of the others, if he were searching for clues as to the problem rather than being actually aware of the specific difficulty that the counselee was having. Then, later on, he might use the same technique to estimate improvement in budgeting time. That is, the preparation of a balanced time schedule could be a task for the counselee in the planning phase of counseling.

How to Collect the Data. Usually the counselor will give the counselee a form such as the one shown on page 199. The counselee is asked to enter activities as soon as possible after they take place rather than wait until later, for example, until the end of the day. Other forms for a time schedule are shown in Refs. [176, pp. 58, 61–62; 257, pp. 28–29].

It may be useful to summarize the data from the time schedule on a sheet similar to that shown on page 200. The counselee can do this himself at the end of the week. It will show in concise form just where the time is expended. The bottom half of the form can also be filled in by the counselee and the counselor could have his own comments as reminders of points to discuss.

Interpreting the Data. The primary purpose of the time schedule is to show accurately how the counselee is using his time. The counselor might gain

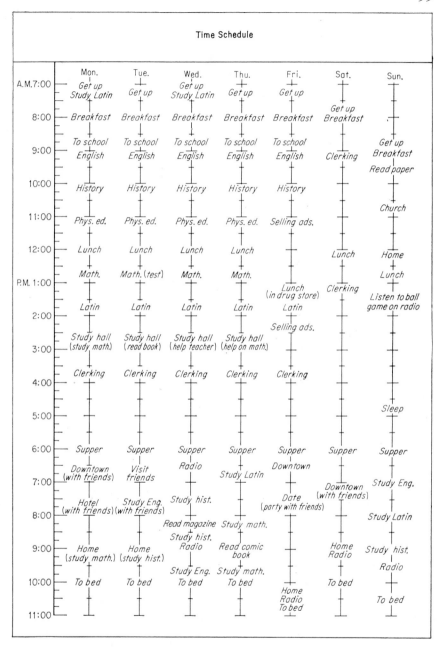

Time Schedule

	Mon.	Tue.	Wed.	Thu.	Fri.	Sat.	Sun.
A.M.7:00	Get up Study Latin	Get up	Get up Study Latin	Get up	Get up		
8:00	Breakfast	Breakfast	Breakfast	Breakfast	Breakfast	Get up Breakfast	
9:00	To school English	To school English	To school English	To school English	To school English	Clerking	Get up Breakfast Read paper
10:00	History	History	History	History	History		
11:00	Phys. ed.	Phys. ed.	Phys. ed.	Phys. ed.	Selling ads.		Church
12:00	Lunch	Lunch	Lunch	Lunch		Lunch	Home
P.M. 1:00	Math.	Math. (test)	Math.	Math.	Lunch (in drug store)	Clerking	Lunch
2:00	Latin	Latin	Latin	Latin	Latin Selling ads.		Listen to ball game on radio
3:00	Study hall (study math.)	Study hall (read book)	Study hall (help teacher)	Study hall (help on math.)			
4:00	Clerking	Clerking	Clerking	Clerking	Clerking		
5:00							Sleep
6:00	Supper	Supper	Supper	Supper	Supper	Supper	Supper
7:00	Downtown (with friends)	Visit friends	Radio Study Latin	Study Latin	Downtown	Downtown (with friends)	Study Eng.
8:00	Hotel (with friends)	Study Eng. (with friends)	Study hist.		Date (party with friends)		Study Latin
9:00	Home (study math.)	Home (study hist.)	Read magazine Study hist. Radio	Study math. Read comic book		Home Radio	Study hist.
10:00	To bed	To bed	Study Eng. To bed	Study math. To bed	Home Radio To bed	To bed	Radio
11:00							To bed

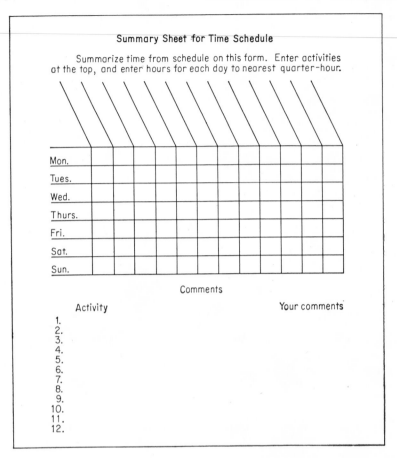

Summary Sheet for Time Schedule

Summarize time from schedule on this form. Enter activities at the top, and enter hours for each day to nearest quarter-hour.

some information about interests by noting what he does and how much time he spends on it. The counselor might also learn whether or not the counselee spends a reasonable amount of time in study, and check to determine if grades are in line with time spent on lessons, considering the counselee's level of ability. Other demands made upon the counselee's time could be noted, for example, a part-time job. The results of keeping the record may be compared with what the counselee has previously said he does and the comparison may aid him in understanding just how he perceives various activities; for example, he may have said that he puts little time on a hobby in which he has a great deal of interest, without realizing that interest makes the time pass quickly and that he actually spends a great deal of time on it. The data may be compared and synthesized with other data about the counselee obtained from other sources.

Using the Technique and Data in Counseling. The completed time schedule is a type of data that the counselor and counselee may consider together in the counseling process. The counselee may bring the time schedule and summary to the counseling session and together they may look it over. It is usually a good idea to give the counselee time to react to what the time schedule shows and help him to arrive at an interpretation, rather than interpret it for him. For example, suppose that a counselee, who complained, "I spend all my time studying," actually shows a very moderate amount of time spent in study. He may be genuinely surprised by the situation. It would be expected that in the permissive counseling situation he would be able to admit that his previous estimate was somewhat incorrect and that he was getting fair returns in school marks considering the small amount of time he actually devoted to study. He could then evaluate his use of time and the counselor could assist him in making needed changes.

SUMMARY

The counselor can obtain valuable information about the counselee from a number of sources and by means of a number of techniques such as anecdotal records, autobiographies, comments of others, informational forms, informal projective methods, sociometric procedures, and time schedules. The data obtained are not used alone but are compared and synthesized with other data. The collection of data by these procedures is primarily for the inference-making and synthesizing process. Thus the information, or the technique by which it is collected, is not usually brought into the counseling process directly. There are exceptions, however, such as the use of the time schedule during the counseling process.

CHECKS ON UNDERSTANDING

1. What sorts of data may the counselor obtain from the anecdotal record?
2. What cautions should be kept in mind by the counselor as he uses the anecdotal records?
3. What is the chief value of autobiographical data in counseling? What specific sorts of data about the counselee might it provide?
4. How would you use "others who know the counselee" as a source of data for counseling?
5. What is meant by the projective approach to understanding the counselee? What "projective" techniques might be used by the teacher or the counselor to learn more about the counselee?
6. What do sociometric data tell about the counselee? How might the counselor obtain this type of information?
7. When might you ask the counselee to keep a time schedule?

THINGS TO DO

1. Obtain from school records or some other source some anecdotal records and prepare an interpretation of them. Do the same for an autobiography.
2. Select a particular pupil whom you know fairly well and prepare questions

that you would ask parents and others who know him, in order to collect information for counseling. If you are actually working with a pupil, follow through with your questions and obtain information from parents, teachers, and others. Evaluate the information and interpret it.

3. Obtain an information form filled out by a pupil and interpret the data it contains. Evaluate the form from the standpoint of whether or not it calls for useful data.

4. Observe pupils in some situation, such as a class or activity period, and see if you can detect examples of projection. You might observe an example of sociodrama for the same purpose. Or the in-service or counselor-trainee group may actually put on a demonstration of sociodrama such as the following:

Two or three teachers may take roles and play them out before the group, or all members of the group may take roles so that the entire group is participating in the sociodrama. One person explains the problem or situation and identifies each of the persons who will take part. An example of a situation might be as follows:

Mrs. Smith, whose daughter has been kept in by Miss Jones, an eleventh grade teacher, has made a phone call demanding to know why the teacher "picks on her Mary." When told very politely that Mary Smith was late arriving in class and refused to explain her tardiness, Mrs. Smith replied that her daughter didn't have to explain her actions. She then mentioned that her husband was a member of the school board, and concluded by saying that she would see Miss Jones immediately after school.

When the sociodrama starts, Miss Jones is seated at her desk and Mrs. Smith is entering the classroom door. The teachers playing the roles start from this point and continue for a short time, probably five or six minutes.

It is not necessary to arrive at a solution to the problem. In the above illustration the main purpose is to help each player see the other side of the issue. Members of the in-service group should observe and at the conclusion may discuss how they would have reacted.

More appropriate situations can be based on local school or community problems, for example, pupils discussing the school. The situation should be described briefly by a member of the group, and the players identified.

5. Discuss the results of observation made by each member of the class or in-service group. Either use a written description of some behavioral incident or some material written by a pupil. Each member of the class presents the material in several minutes. The discussion that follows should be aimed at detecting the projections and analyzing their significance for the particular pupil. If most of the members of the class do not know the pupil, the one presenting the material should furnish a brief description of him.

6. Obtain one of the following from a pupil and prepare an interpretation of it: a series of anecdotal records, an autobiography, or a time schedule. Obtain sociometric data from a group or a class and present what it tells about one particular pupil. Plan how you might use the data in counseling.

7. Analyze John Doe's time schedule shown on page 199. What do you think of the way he is using his time? Summarize his activities on the summary sheet on page 200. What do the results tell about him? Should he make any changes?

CHAPTER 9

Occupational and
Educational Information

I N THIS AND the next chapter the use of information in
counseling is taken up. The major emphasis is on
occupational information, but other types of information, such as educational,
social, and personal, will also be considered. These sorts of information may
be used during the actual face-to-face process or by counselor and counselee
outside of it. Some introductory background material is covered in this chapter
while the next is devoted to the use of information in the counseling process.

The subject of information used in counseling, particularly occupational
information, is an extensive and complex one [13, p. 8; 87, pp. 1–2]. This
chapter provides only a brief introduction of some of the most important
aspects with which the counselor should be familiar. Extensive use of the
references is strongly recommended. If you have already had some training
and experience in the use of these materials you may find this a helpful
review and be in a better position to use the materials with the counselee in
the ways discussed in the next chapter.

Counselor Competencies

Tyler [240, pp. 170–171] points out that the counselor cannot expect to
know all the facts about occupations and educational opportunities, but he
should know how to obtain and use the information. Ordinarily the counselor
would know more about what has been classified as social and personal information, that is, information about dating, physical development, getting along
with others, and so on. But here, too, he would not be an expert in all these

areas and would usually need to know where to obtain the information and how to help the counselee use it.

Counselor competencies concerning the sort of information with which the counselor should be familiar have been developed in some detail in the occupational and educational information area. One example is *Counselor Competencies in Occupational Information* [152]. Others are Refs. [132, 158]. Texts on occupational information by Baer and Roeber [13], Greenleaf [87], Hoppock [102, ch. 2], and Shartle [201] indicate, by their contents, what the counselor should know. For counselors in special areas, Refs. [140, 159] describe particular competencies for these specialists.

From these references a brief list of counselor competencies in occupational and educational information may be drawn. Mahoney [132] gives a more detailed discussion. The counselor, then, should know

1. Something about the ways in which occupational information is obtained
2. In what forms occupational information is available
3. Indexes and other aids for obtaining occupational information
4. Sources of information about all types of education and training, as well as aptitude and abilities required for the training
5. Ways of classifying occupations and industries which will aid in understanding the occupational and industrial structure and in filing information for ready use
6. Criteria for evaluation of occupational and educational information
7. The specific details about an occupation which must be considered in making an occupational choice, such as the training required and the aptitudes needed
8. Something about sociological and psychological aspects of the occupation which have significance for the counselee; for example, what sort of persons usually work on the job, how it ranks in prestige
9. Something about trends and factors affecting trends, and how to obtain and analyze data about trends
10. How to synthesize data of various sorts into a meaningful picture of the occupation and industry for his own use and for the counselee's use
11. Something about labor legislation of the sort that affects the counselees with whom he is working

What the counselor should know about other types of information is not generally given in as much detail nor does it appear to have been as thoroughly studied as occupational and related types of information. Counselor knowledge in this area is closely related to his understanding of growth, development, and personality formation. There are materials, especially designed for the high school pupil, which can be given to the counselee to read. The counselor should know where to locate these, what they contain, and how to provide them for the counselee where necessary. He should know enough about each of the areas to discuss the readings with the counselee. Some of the areas covered by publications are dating and heterosexual adjustment; how to be popular; manners and etiquette; physical growth and health; emotional problems; dress and grooming; use of alcohol, drugs, and narcotics; personality traits such as honesty, dependability, and the like; how to get along with others; prejudice; military service; how to understand parents; how to read; and effective study. The list could be extended to include other topics, but those just listed should give an idea of the sorts of pamphlets available. One of the most extensive sources of pamphlet material is Science Research Associates, Inc., which publishes such pamphlets as *You and Your Health* [79], *Understanding Yourself* [138], and *Study Your Way through School* [81]. Another source is the New Public Affairs Press [160], which publishes such pamphlets as *So You Think It's Love, The Shy Child,* and *Too Young to Marry.* Information is also prepared by the Child Study Association of America, for example, a pamphlet entitled *Our Children Today* [45]; and the National Association for Mental Health [150]. A number of other publishers offer useful books and pamphlets; for example, McGraw-Hill Book Company, Inc., publishes *Ways to Improve Your Personality* [14]; and Arthur C. Croft Publications distributes such pamphlets as *Think of Others* [19].

Types of Information

Occupational and educational information is available in a number of different forms, some suitable for the counselor only, some useful to both counselor and counselee, and some particularly aimed at the counselee but generally also helpful to the counselor. To assist the counselor in gaining some understanding of the tremendous variety of information and what may be obtained from each type, the following brief descriptions are presented. References such as [13, 201] should be consulted for gaining a better understanding of what is available.

The Occupational Monograph. The most widely used and probably the most helpful type of occupational information for both the counselor and counselee is the occupational monograph. As the name indicates, this is a publication, usually booklet size, devoted to one topic, which in this case is one occupation or closely related group of occupations. It usually gives a description of the occupation and the work done, needed qualifications of the worker, compensation, prospects for employment, where the work may be found, and sources of additional information. There may be some added features such as history of the occupation, but those named above are the most important. A more detailed listing of the contents may be found in Refs. [13, pp. 63–66; 201, pp. 90–94]. Most monographs are designed for counselee use, but they are, of course, useful for the counselor. They are the best sources of detailed information about an occupation, more complete than any other single source, and usually represent a synthesis from many different sources. The best way to understand the contents is to look over several, such as may be obtained from sources listed in Ref. [73] and other indexes described later in this chapter.

Briefer Publications about a Particular Occupation. There are a number of other types of occupational information that the counselor will find useful, which are similar to the occupational monograph but much briefer, and which may cover only certain aspects of the occupation. The *occupational description* [201, p. 89] is highly condensed information in pamphlet form, which contains most of the important data about an occupation abstracted from other sources. Often short magazine articles may be found which present information about an occupation in narrative form and which may contain essentially the same information as the monograph or abstract but not in complete detail or in orderly sequence.

Except for the magazine article, the types of information that have been discussed are usually prepared specifically for commercial use by persons and organizations that make a business of publishing occupational information. However, some mention should be made of the great quantity of occupational literature published by business and industry, educational institutions, professional organizations, colleges, labor unions, and the like, which is often in a form similar to the monograph, brief, or abstract. Various branches of the Federal government also prepare and distribute materials of this sort. In the section on obtaining materials is an explanation of how to obtain samples of all these materials.

Book on Occupations. There are a number of book-length publications that provide information about occupations. They may include information in some detail about a limited number of occupations or may cover more briefly a much larger number. They may include material on other topics, such as how to select a job, how to go about applying for it, and the like. Many of these are designed as textbooks for the high school course in occupations [149]. Splaver [213] provides a helpful listing of such books.

The Occupational Outlook Handbook. While it is impossible in one chapter to deal with the many individual publications that contain occupational information, several are of such importance that they merit individual attention. One of these is the *Occupational Outlook Handbook* [247]. This publication of the United States Department of Labor, which covers over 500 of the more popular occupations, is revised at intervals, the first one being published in 1948, the next in 1951, and the current one in 1957. This handbook, which is extremely useful for high school pupils, college students, and counselors, combines in one source background information about the world of work, trends and patterns in major occupational and industrial areas, and trends, nature of the work, employment opportunities, training, and sources of additional information. It is a publication with which all counselors should be familiar, and which should be available in the school, and on the counselor's desk.

The Dictionary of Occupational Titles. Another publication of enough importance to merit individual attention is the *Dictionary of Occupational Titles* [246], which comes in three parts, each of which has a particular value for the counselor. These parts are discussed below.

Volume I contains definitions of 22,028 jobs, arranged in alphabetical order in the same manner as an ordinary language dictionary. Volume II contains information about the classification system, occupational titles arranged by industry, and other useful information. Part III is no longer available, as this was an earlier supplement that was combined with Part I in the most recent publication. Part IV deals with entry occupations, and is quite helpful in counseling with persons who have little or no work experience. The *Dictionary* should be available in every school, and the counselor should know how to use it. In the Things to Do section at the end of this chapter there is a short exercise to help you become familiar with various parts of the *Dictionary of Occupational Titles,* or "DOT," as it is usually called. You may also find an exceedingly helpful reference and exercise in [201, pp. 151–171].

Volume I, "Definition of Titles," may be used by both the counselor and the counselee. One useful way the counselor may use it is to look through the book to gain an idea of the large number of occupations that exist and to learn something about the nature of the work of selected occupations, as a brief definition is given for each one. He may also find the classification of the occupation, for example, professional, clerical, skilled, and so on, and the industry in which the occupation occurs. If the counselee has had work experience, the counselor can gain some idea of what this experience consisted of by looking the occupation up in the *Dictionary.* Or if the counselor hears of certain occupations about which he knows little or nothing, he can obtain at least a minimum of information about them by looking them up in the *Dictionary.* There are other uses of Volume I about which the counselor should know. These are covered in detail in Shartle [201, pp. 151–171]. As the counselor gains familiarity with Volume I he will find it a valuable aid to counseling.

The counselor will find that Volume II provides the most detailed classification of occupations available today. The use of this volume will enable him to gain an understanding of a very helpful classification system as well as the most widely used one. A great number of occupational pamphlets and monographs are coded to correspond with this system. The classification system itself shows several very helpful things about the occupations. First, the counselor is able to gain some idea of the level of the occupation, as to some extent the occupations are arranged from low to high according to the level of mental ability and amount of training required, that is, professional at the top and unskilled at the bottom.

Next, the counselor is able to gain a general understanding of characteristics of the occupation by knowing its classification. Detailed definitions of the classifications are given at the beginning of each section, for example, "sales and kindred" [246, vol. II, pp. 53–54].

Another use of the classification system is to learn the relationship among jobs in which there are unskilled, semiskilled, or skilled levels. The classification system allows the counselor to do this, as certain codes are the same for different levels [201, pp. 157–158]. Thus he can see lines of advancement which will help him and the counselee in planning for a suitable job.

Volume II also shows groups of related jobs or job families. In a sense, related occupations on different levels are occupational families, but the more common families are those in which occupations are rather closely related on the basis of important characteristics such as work done, experience and training needed, and the like. This is a particularly important concept for the counselor, as it enables him to assist the counselee to learn about a number of related occupations or an occupational area rather than center his attention on just one occupation. Shartle has a helpful discussion of this concept [201, pp. 155–156].

Volume II also contains several other helpful features. There is an "index of commodities" which is useful in classifying sales personnel and which will give the counselor some idea of the many types of sales jobs [246, vol. II, pp. 425–438]. Then on pages 439–505 there is a glossary of terms that defines specialized words with which most counselors are not familiar, for example, "dobby loom," "feed dog," or "jump saw." On pages 507–738, occupational titles are grouped by industry, such as the air transportation industry. Thus it is possible to gain an understanding of the great variety of occupational opportunities that occur in a particular industry. There is an index on pages 739–743.

The high school counselor will find Part IV of the DOT of especial interest, as it provides help in determining what occupations are suitable for the inexperienced worker. One section provides a classification and listing of entry jobs, or those occupations for which no previous work experience is necessary. While it is beyond the scope of this book to explain Part IV in detail, you will find helpful explanations in Part IV itself and also in Refs. [13, pp. 91–95; 201, pp. 204–218]. It should be pointed out that the major occupational groupings are defined in a way that is quite helpful to the counselor in locating an area of interest for the inexperienced counselee. Related occupations are grouped in such a way as to give an idea of the different occupational possibilities in a field of work. Then nonentry jobs, for which the counselee could qualify after he had gained some experience, are also shown.

The next section of Part IV provides help in evaluating factors such as personal traits, leisure-time activities, casual work experience, and military and civilian training courses for entry jobs. This section is particularly useful for the counselor as he attempts to make some judgments about the occupational significance of what the counselee is like and what he has done.

The *Dictionary of Occupational Titles* is a very helpful counseling tool. While it may appear rather complex at first, the counselor will find that use of the references, as well as the *Dictionary* itself, will enable him to learn about it rather quickly. Only through use will its potentialities for counseling be realized.

Estimates of Worker Trait Requirements. A publication that should be of help to the counselor along with the *Dictionary of Occupational Titles* is *Estimates of Worker Trait Requirements for 4,000 Jobs as Defined in the Dictionary of Occupational Titles* [249]. Worker trait requirements on six components are given. Representative components are training, aptitudes, and temperaments.

The Census. The census [244], taken every ten years by the U.S. Department of Commerce, has particular value for the counselor if he has access to it and is willing to do a little searching for data. The counselee would not, however, be able to make much effective use of this publication; it will thus be up to the counselor to extract information for use by himself and by the counselee. The counselor can analyze census data to almost any extent he desires, starting with determining the number of workers in the major occupational groups, such as "sales workers" or the industrial groups such as "manufacturing." Then he may find both occupations and industries broken down further. For example, in the occupational group, "sales workers," will be found such occupations as auctioneers, insurance agents and brokers, and advertising agents. In the industrial group, "manufacturing," will be found more specific industries such as "logging," "aircraft and parts," and "structural clay products." The more detailed data may be found for the nation, for the state, and for large cities. Less detailed information is available for towns and counties. The counselor will also be able to find data on worker characteristics such as age, sex, and amount of education.

The census is a source of considerable data to the counselor about distribution of workers, characteristics of workers, and trends of occupations and industries. It does not provide information, however, about activities on the job, needed training and experience, and the like. Thus the census data complement those in such sources as occupational monographs. While the census provides rather coarse groupings of occupations, such as "authors," within which many specific occupations may occur, it does help the counselor to know what kinds of occupations exist in a given area, the trends, and something about the workers in these occupations. A more detailed discussion of how to use the census is contained in Shartle [201, pp. 322–326].

A further value of the census is that it provides the counselor with a way of classifying occupations and industries that will be of help in making some order out of the extremely complex world of work, in organizing materials, and in collecting local information.

Journals That Provide Occupational Information. Another type of occupational information is the journal that contains articles about occupational trends, wages, industrial changes, and the like. Many of the articles will be quite useful to the counselor, although they would not, as a rule, be helpful to the counselee.

The Employment Security Review. This is a monthly publication of the Employment Service of the U.S. Department of Labor, which deals with current problems in employment.

The Labor Market. This is a monthly publication of the Bureau of Employment Security, U.S. Department of Labor. It contains current information on industrial trends, employment trends, and other similar information. In it the counselor may find such information as rise of employment in the air transportation industry, survey of current occupational shortages, and the like.

The Monthly Labor Review. This is a monthly publication of the U.S. Department of Labor. It deals with such topics as working conditions and economic outlook for specific occupations. The counselor will find that it contains articles such as issues relating to shorter working hours, studies of earnings in various industries, and current labor statistics, such as total labor force classified by employment status and other factors.

The Occupational Outlook. This is a new publication of the Bureau of Labor Statistics, U.S. Department of Labor, issued four times a year. Articles include summaries of the Bureau's research program in the occupational outlook field and reports of relevant research in other government agencies. It enables the counselor to keep current on occupational trends between biennial editions of the *Occupational Outlook Handbook.*

Occupational Wage Surveys. These are not journals as those discussed above; they are published as a series by the Bureau of Labor Statistics of the U.S. Department of Labor. If the counselor is in the area near the city in which the survey is made, he will find useful data about such aspects of the occupation as number employed, wages, and the like. Leading occupations in the area are covered.

Your Future Occupation. This is a relatively new publication edited by Max M. Baer and available from the Randall Publishing Company, Washington 4, D.C. It is published twice each month and contains information about occupations, trends, requirements, and similar data. Its format is attractive and it appears to be well suited for high school and college students.

Other Types of Printed Occupational Information. There are a great number of additional types of occupational information which, for the lack of space, will not be mentioned here. Happily for the counselor, several excellent publications describe these publications and indicate how they may be obtained [13, chs. 8, 9; 73; 87; 201, ch. 3].

Local Occupational Information. Up to this point the discussion has been about occupational information of the sort that is national in scope, although it may contain data that apply to a particular section of the country or even a state or city, for example, the census or the *Occupational Outlook Handbook*. Also, information of the sort that has been taken up is usually printed. The counselor needs also to be familiar with information about the particular town, county, or section of the state in which he is working. Strictly speaking, local information is just that which applies to the particular occupations in the counselor's community. But somewhere between this type and the national level are those materials which are available from state agencies and which contain data about the state as a whole or sections of the state. The number and types of publications vary from state to state; information about them may be obtained from the various departments in the state government, for example, the State Department of Labor. Emphasis in this section, however, is on that type of information which the counselor may obtain locally by his own original study or from others who have assembled the information.

The counselor may employ a number of ways to obtain local occupational information, such as interviews with local employers, reports of local groups such as Chambers of Commerce, articles in local newspapers, and want ads in local papers. The local office of the State Employment Service in the community may also be able to provide information about local opportunities and may be particularly helpful as a source of information about trends.

A useful guide for obtaining local information, which also shows the significant data that the counselor should know about an occupation, is the following form: *

Local Occupational Study

1. Title of the occupation_____
2. Other titles_____
3. Work done in the occupation
   (a) Duties (describe in detail)_____
   _____
   _____
   _____

   (b) Examples of articles made or services performed_____
   _____
   _____
   _____

4. Number of workers employed
   Male_____ Female_____ Total_____
5. Working conditions
   (a) Wages_____
   (b) Hours_____
   (c) Surroundings_____

* Adapted from Misc. 2923, Occupational Information and Guidance, U.S. Office of Education, "Occupational Studies Leaflet," by Franklin R. Zeran (used by permission of the author).

Local Occupational Study (*Continued*)

(d) Is this seasonal work? (check) Yes_____ No_____
If the work is seasonal, give:
Length of time of year of peak period_____
Length of time of year of slack period_____

(e) Trend in employment_____

(f) Hazards and safety measures_____

6. Requirements for entrance into the occupation
(a) Preferred age of entrance_____ Sex required (check)
M_____ F_____ Either_____
(b) General Education
Required: Complete_____th grade
(c) School subjects and other activities
Subjects that are essential_____

Subjects that are desirable_____

Hobbies that have a relationship to the occupation_____

7. Licenses_____
8. Bond_____
9. Kinds of tests that must be passed_____

10. Physical examination_____
11. How to get started in the occupation
(a) As a learner
Describe briefly what the worker is taught_____

Duration of training period_____
(b) As a helper
Describe briefly the work performed and any training that the helper may receive

Length of time before helper can be a fully qualified worker_____
(c) As an apprentice
Length of apprenticeship_____
Indenture (check) Yes_____ No_____
Subjects taught on job_____

Subjects taught on related vocational courses_____

12. Comments and information not covered elsewhere_____

Directories of Schools, Colleges, and Other Training Opportunities. Probably the most useful source of educational and training information are directories which contain basic data about colleges, universities, junior colleges, trade schools, business schools, and other types of training. Several helpful references of colleges and universities are *American Universities and Colleges* [110], *The College Blue Book* [109], and the widely used *Lovejoy's College Guide* [123]. These and other similar reference books are described in Baer and Roeber [13, pp. 258–269]. The counselor should look over these references to learn what they contain, both for his own use and for referring the counselee to them for study. Junior colleges are described in *American Junior Colleges* [28]. Trade and technical schools are described in such directories as *Approved Technical Institutes,* published by the National Council of Technical Schools, Washington, D.C. Home study courses are listed in *Home Study Blue Book* available from the National Home Study Council. Many colleges offer correspondence courses, which are described in bulletins that may be obtained from the institutions. A very complete description of sources of training and educational information is [13, pp. 258–269].

Related to this sort of information is that about financial aid such as scholarships, fellowships, and loans. A helpful reference in this area [67] now includes three volumes.

While pupils would not gain much help from publications such as *Retention and Withdrawal of College Students* [245], the counselor could extract useful information which he could provide to the counselee, for example, ". . . 60 percent of all students who enter degree granting institutions receive degrees" [245, p. 99], and much that would give him a better understanding of college-bound pupils, for example, "It was found that high ratings on item 16 were generally associated with poor persistence records for all groups of students" (item 16 was "I felt I could live an easier life if I had a college education") [245, p. 31].

Publications of Colleges, Professional Societies, and Other Organizations. Besides the directories, the counselor may obtain training and educational information from the catalogues and bulletins of schools and colleges. Usually a post card to the institution will be sufficient to obtain the publication and to be put on the mailing list. Current publications should be obtained, as courses and programs are frequently changed.

Professional organizations often publish lists of approved colleges and universities along with other material such as occupational pamphlets. An extensive list of organizations is contained in Ref. [13, pp. 232–250]. Usually a post card will be sufficient to obtain information from the organization.

Information about state and local trade and technical schools may be obtained from the State Department of Education. Depending upon the state, the department or division that distributes this information will be designated as occupational information service, guidance and counseling service, or a title with similar connotation. The National Council of Technical Schools (already mentioned) issues an annual list of approved schools containing standards for practice, entrance requirements, description of the schools, and courses offered.

This brief and incomplete survey of occupational and educational information hardly does justice to the great volume of data available to the counselor. The counselor should use Refs. [13, 87, 201] extensively, have these references on his desk, and obtain samples of information for study and use. As he actually utilizes and becomes familiar with these materials he will find that it becomes increasingly easy to decide what materials are needed, how to find them, and how to extract pertinent data.

Locating and Obtaining Occupational, Educational, and Other Information

As is apparent by now, a vast amount of occupational and educational information is available and more is becoming available each day. To learn what exists and to keep up with new materials, the counselor has several extremely valuable aids. Probably the most useful single reference is Forrester's book, *Occupational Literature* [73]. This publication contains a listing of many pamphlets with annotations. Materials are arranged in order of alphabetical listing of occupations, such as accountant, clothier, designer, and linotype operator. The counselor may quite easily locate occupational information on almost any field of work. Information is also given about publishers of pamphlet series. Other features of value to the counselor include criteria for evaluating occupational literature; directions for indexing and filing literature; and materials such as the following: publications describing more than one occupation, bibliographies, lists of charts and posters, labor law publications, and publishers' addresses.

Baer and Roeber [13, pp. 195–217] give an extremely helpful discussion of publications of governmental agencies. Using this reference along with Forrester's book, the counselor could gain a thorough knowledge of what information is available from what publisher or agency.

Another useful reference is *Guide to Career Information* [43], which gives complete information on over 800 books and pamphlets published in the last five years. The New York Life Insurance Company, one of the leaders in the publishing of occupational information, has distributed a number of complimentary copies to counselors.

The counselor needs to keep up with specific current publications as well as have information about those published in the past. To do this, he has several very useful indexes which are published at regular intervals. These are:

1. *Guidance Index,* an annual list of guidance materials, published by Science Research Associates, Inc. It contains annotated listings of occupational

materials as well as other types of information, including those for use by the counselor.

2. *Occupational Index,* published quarterly by Personnel Services, Inc., Peapack, New Jersey. A helpful feature is listing of materials by cost, including a "free" classification.

3. *Career Index,* published nine times a year by the Chronicle Press, Moravia, New York, each month during the school term. Printed post cards for ordering material are included.

4. *Counselor's Information Service,* a bimonthly guide to guidance literature, published by B'nai B'rith Vocational Service Bureau, Washington, D.C.

5. *NVGA Bibliography of Current Occupational Literature* [88], published by the National Vocational Guidance Association, and a regular annotated listing in each issue of the *Vocational Guidance Quarterly* [89]. Material is evaluated and classified.

A regular review of one or more of these indexes will be of great assistance in helping the counselor to keep abreast of current publications. The school should subscribe to at least one. Further description and samples may be obtained from the publishers before purchasing.

Arranging Occupational Information for Use

The counselor needs to be able to keep a rather large amount of occupational information ready for quick and easy reference for himself and for the counselee. Thus it is important to select a filing system that is easily understood by all who use the file and yet at the same time is complete enough so that all materials can be filed accurately and located quickly. A resource file of some sort is an indispensable tool for the counselor. A carefully selected one should be set up so that it may be expanded without having to be revised or changed. It would be a good idea for the counselor to look over several files to decide which type he would prefer. The following are widely used systems:

1. Alphabetical. Make up manila folders or some other type of container, such as expansion folders, to include the titles of the occupations, for example, accountant, actor, advertising agent, and so on. The breakdown of Forrester [73] may be used as a guide for making up folders. When additional information is obtained, additional folders are made up and inserted in the proper place. This method has the advantage of simplicity and of making information about a particular occupation easy to locate. It does not give the student a chance to see the occupations in a broad field of work as he looks through the file; for example, a student interested in clerical work would have to look up separate folders for typist, stenographer, file clerk, and so on, rather than finding these groups in the broader classification of clerical occupations.

2. The *Dictionary of Occupational Titles* classification. This method is more

complicated, but at the same time it allows for more accurate location of material and furnishes some homogeneous groupings, such as professional, clerical, and sales, and still finer groupings, for example under professional, social and welfare workers, teachers, and so on. To use this system one should be familiar with the *Dictionary of Occupational Titles* and its classification and coding system. Forrester [73, pp. 21–24] gives a description of this system and classifies all occupational information in her book with *Dictionary* code numbers and titles so that the counselor can file material obtained from her book correctly. A set of folders already made up for this system can be purchased from the Chronicle Press, Moravia, New York.

3. Fields of work. This system offers the counselor the opportunity to file material according to broad fields, for example, health, youth work, and the like. A commercial filing system of this type may be obtained from the Sturgis Printing Company, Inc., Sturgis, Michigan. Another plan of this type may be obtained from Science Research Associates, Inc.

A helpful description of these plans, together with factors that should be considered in setting up a filing system, is contained in Ref. [13, pp. 369–376]. The same reference also contains helpful suggestions for the counselor in setting up his own plan [13, pp. 376–385].

Occupational material, such as books, would usually be kept on shelves. College catalogues and similar publications may also be placed on shelves, or in file boxes that can be arranged on a shelf. It is helpful to separate the different types of training institutions, for example, colleges, junior colleges, trade schools, business schools, special schools such as those for handicapped individuals, and home-study opportunities. Suggestions for arranging these and other materials such as resource information needed by the counselor are given in Ref. [13, pp. 385–399].

Evaluating Occupational Information

The counselor needs to evaluate the occupational information that he obtains to decide whether or not it should be retained and used and to decide how suitable it is for the counselee. Inaccurate, biased, or otherwise poor material will probably do the counselor and counselee more harm than good. The major points the counselor should keep in mind in evaluating material are the following:

1. Accuracy. This may be difficult to check, but a comparison with other published information or help in evaluating by someone who knows the occupation will enable the counselor to obtain an estimate of the accuracy of the material. In *Occupational Literature* [73], Forrester gives an evaluation of many of the materials she lists.

2. Objectivity. Some materials give a biased description of the occupation. The counselor can probably detect such things as glowing descriptions of the

work, appeals to the emotions, and statements that seem to lack factual backing. Publications describing the work of a particular concern (often for recruiting workers) should particularly be checked for bias; this does not mean that the information would have no value, but the counselor and the counselee should both be aware that the publication may have the primary purpose of "selling" the particular type of work.

3. Recency. The date of the publication should be checked to determine whether it is recent enough to be of value. Employment opportunities change rapidly in some areas, and a publication several years old may give incorrect information. The actual nature of the work may have also changed in the past year or so. The counselor will have to use his judgment and what he knows of trends in employment and changes in the characteristics of various occupations to decide what should be eliminated from the files and what should be kept. Some materials are not dated; this adds to the counselor's problem of determining how well they apply to the present situation.

4. Suitability for the high school group. Some materials are not suited to the group that will be using them. The vocabulary may be difficult or the format may be unattractive. Occupational publications should be interesting, easy to read and understand, and appealing in appearance.

5. Reasonable cost. Some excellent materials are available at rather high costs, but their purchase might limit the coverage of the occupational information file. Unless the school has ample funds for extensive purchases, the counselor would do well to consider carefully whether or not cheaper materials would serve the same purpose. For example, for the dollar or so spent on a monograph, ten or fifteen pamphlets might be purchased.

In order to provide the counselor with more specific points by which to evaluate occupational literature, a rating or evaluation sheet is provided.* A preliminary review of this form will indicate the important aspects of occupational literature which should be considered in assessing its value.

Criteria for Judging an Occupational Study

1. Title of Book or Monograph: _____
2. Job Title as given in the Dictionary of Occupational Titles: _____

3. Code Number in Dictionary: _____
4. Author, if given: _____
5. Author's position and experience, if given: _____

6. Publisher: _____ Publisher's address: _____
7. Date of publication: _____ Date of revision: _____
   of reprinting: _____
8. Number of pages_____ Price_____ Number of illustrations (approximately)_____
9. Is there a table of contents?_____ With sub-headings?_____
10. Is there an index?_____ Bibliography?_____ Annotated bibliography?_____

* Prepared by Gertrude Forrester, Head Counselor, West Side High School, Newark, N.J. (used by permission of the author).

Criteria for Judging an Occupational Study (*Continued*)

11. Does bibliography include references to occupational material?_____
12. Check the topics discussed:

Adequate	Inadequate	Omitted	
_____	_____	_____	History of the occupation
_____	_____	_____	Importance of the occupation and its relation to society
_____	_____	_____	Number of workers engaged in the occupation
_____	_____	_____	Need for workers
_____	_____	_____	Duties
_____	_____	_____	Qualifications
_____	_____	_____	Preparation
_____	_____	_____	Methods of entering
_____	_____	_____	Length of time before skill is attained
_____	_____	_____	Advancement
_____	_____	_____	Related occupations to which job may lead
_____	_____	_____	Earnings
_____	_____	_____	Hours
_____	_____	_____	Regularity of employment
_____	_____	_____	Health and accident hazards
_____	_____	_____	Organizations (for employers_____, for employees_____)
_____	_____	_____	Typical place for employment
_____	_____	_____	Supplementary information
_____	_____	_____	Suggested readings
_____	_____	_____	Films, magazines, or trade and professional journals
_____	_____	_____	Other visual aids
_____	_____	_____	List of key firms and persons who may be contacted for further information
_____	_____	_____	List of research organizations or foundations
_____	_____	_____	Total number of topics adequately treated

13. What methods were used in gathering the facts?

Adequate	Inadequate	
_____	_____	Library work performed
_____	_____	Number and location of establishments visited
_____	_____	Number and kinds of schools visited
_____	_____	Number and kinds of organizations studied
_____	_____	Number of other persons interviewed

14. Is there unbiased, accurate presentation of information?_____
    Note exceptions and pages: _____
15. Is the scientific approach manifest throughout?_____
    Note exceptions and pages: _____
16. Do the text or footnotes indicate the source of quoted or paraphrased material?_____
    Note exceptions and pages: _____
17. Is there indication that the findings have been validated or checked?_____
18. Is there indication of means of validation or checking?_____
19. Is the U.S. Census data used the latest available?_____
20. Is the occupation presented in its social and economic setting so as to portray the "way of life" or other aspects of living (in addition to activities on the job) which are determined by the peculiarities of the job?_____
21. Style and format. Check the following:

Adequate	Inadequate	
_____	_____	Statements are specific and exact, not general and misleading
_____	_____	Clear style

———————	———————	Concise style
———————	———————	Interesting
———————	———————	Vocabulary and manner of presentation adapted to readers to whom the material is addressed
———————	———————	Format is pleasing and attractive
———————	———————	Typography
———————	———————	Illustrations of workers engaged in typical work
———————	———————	Charts, graphs, and other visual aids

Please write a brief annotation indicating your opinion (favorable or adverse) of this publication:

_____

_____

_____

_____

Name of Reviewer_____

Address_____

Student's name_____   Course_____

To enable you to gain a better understanding of the factors to be considered in evaluating occupational literature, references such as [13, ch. 4; 201, pp. 99–103] will be useful. Practice in evaluation will enable you to judge new material quickly and accurately and to keep your file up to date and uncluttered.

Interpreting the Information

Now let us suppose that the counselor knows about various sources of occupational information and that he has pamphlets, monographs, and other data about occupations available. The problem now becomes one of extracting and bringing together data about an occupation, a field of work, or an industry so that it will provide the counselee with what he needs to know to make a choice of an occupation. The counselor also needs to know enough about the occupation to be in a position to evaluate the quality of the counselee's decision, to estimate whether or not he has considered all factors that he should consider, and whether or not he has considered them realistically. To do these things, the counselor needs to be able to interpret and synthesize data in printed materials, to bring in pertinent local information, and to have adequate background information about the world of work upon which to draw. Background information includes aspects of the occupational world such as the following: the meaning and importance of work to an individual in our society and in various subcultures; the changing nature of the world of work; how the particular occupation ranks in prestige with other occupations; limiting factors in occupational mobility; and the characteristic of those who do the work as compared with the same characteristics of the labor force as a whole. The counselor is then able to understand the occupation in the context in which it occurs.

It is helpful to think of essential information about the occupation as primarily psychological, sociological, physiological, and economic. These categories of information are now taken up in detail.

Psychological Aspects. Let us consider first what is meant by the psychological aspects of an occupation. The counselor needs to be able to estimate what psychological characteristics or traits are required by the occupation, how much is needed, as well as the more subtle psychological aspects of work, such as the work atmosphere, types of rewards, and the like. Typical occupational literature gives some information about the crucial aspects of an occupation but it is usually not specific enough. For example, it is difficult for the counselor to judge how much mental ability, manual dexterity, or linguistic ability is needed for a particular occupation. Levels are determined, to a large extent, by the people who work on the job and with whom the counselee may be competing.

A publication opening up a new approach to the understanding of psychological factors in selection of occupations is Super's *The Psychology of Careers* [227]. Of particular value to the counselor are the concepts of *career patterns* and stages in occupational choice or *development*. The effects of various forces or conditions on vocational development are examined, for example, aptitude, interest, the family, and economics.

Other psychological characteristics needed for the work are even more difficult to specify, for example, amount of initiative, leadership ability, amount of responsibility the individual must take, or what significance this work has for the individual. The counselor needs to know what the occupation itself requires rather than the characteristics of a particular worker or a small group of workers on the job. A person, or a group of persons, may not actually possess the crucial characteristics to be suitable workers, or they may have much more of the characteristics than needed.

Thus as the counselor collects, abstracts, and synthesizes the information about the occupation, he will often need to use other data to help him estimate psychological characteristics. There are several helpful sources of data on mental ability levels and occupations [91, pp. 133–163; 179; 214; 230, pp. 286–310]. Roe gives a helpful new classification of occupations by level of work and primary type of activity [179, p. 151], a useful discussion of the variability of psychological traits with occupational groups [179, chs. 6, 7] and a rather detailed discussion of psychological characteristics of workers in occupational groups and occupations [179, chs. 13–20]. Super [227, p. 48] gives a three-dimensional classification of occupations.

A counseling tool that should prove useful to the counselor in estimating levels of several traits required in 432 occupations, such as academic ability, mechanical ability, social intelligence, artistic ability, musical talent, clerical ability, and physical agility, is the *Minnesota Occupational Rating Scale* [165]. Test manuals and research studies that give norms for various worker groups will also help the counselor determine the type and quantity of traits that are important for the work.

The counselor has a more difficult job when he begins to analyze occupational data to determine what psychological aspects such as initiative, responsibility that must be taken, working harmoniously with others, and ability to make quick and correct decisions are required. Then too, he wants to be able to understand just what meaning the occupation has for others, as a basis for understanding the meaning it *may* have for the counselee and how well he may be suited for it. The way an occupation is regarded by people in general appears to have some relation to the intellectual and other requirements of the occupation [41]. The occupational designation of a person is increasingly a determiner of status [42, p. 30]. What the worker finds attractive about his job and other aspects of the work that may not be in the typical occupational literature may be gathered from what workers on the job say about it [175; 181, pp. 553–554; 231; 74].

The usual occupational literature does not provide much help to the counselor in understanding the psychological atmosphere of the occupation or constructing a picture of the occupation. But the case history or "diary" of a worker, showing what he does in a representative period of time, can be quite helpful [57, 208, 226]. We also find little in the literature about how the worker gets out of the occupation [225]. Perhaps these are reasons why counselors seem to be able to do a better job of providing or helping the counselee obtain occupational information about the kind of work that they themselves have done. They can give the "occupational literature facts" and also interpret other psychological (and sociological) aspects of the occupation. The detailed study of one or a few workers mentioned above has limitations, but it does help the counselor and counselee get the "feel" of the occupation.

Sociological Aspects. In discussing the psychological aspects of the occupation, we have already included some things that would more properly be labeled sociological. It is difficult to classify many aspects as either psychological or sociological and no practical purpose would be served by doing so. However, in this section we will consider some of the aspects that are predominantly sociological. Many counselors have appeared to be little concerned with these sociological factors when using occupational information in counseling. There is, however, a growing body of literature that is of great significance for the counselor [15; 20; 41; 42; 57; 70; 139; 164; 175; 181; 208; 225; 226; 230, pp. 165–230, 389–403; 231; 252].

The importance of this area for the counselor is evident. As Miller and Form say [139, p. 3]: "The rise of industrial sociology may be identified with the failure of certain experiments. . . ." These experiments had to do with *physical* conditions of work, but it was found there were aspects ". . . far more important than hours, wages, or physical conditions of work." These aspects were "feelings" about the work. These feelings had to do with how well the worker realizes the importance of what he is doing, how important he feels, and how much a part of the group and larger industrial organization he feels himself to be.

What then are the important aspects of the occupation that should be considered by the counselor? The following are illustrative. First of all, with what sort of group will the worker be associated? Will this be the sort of group with which he will be satisfied to be associated? We need to keep in mind that a great part of our waking hours is spent on the job, and the work group has a pervasive influence. What sort of group is this in recreational activities, in attitudes, mores, and so on? See, for example, the chart of formal and informal groups * shown on page 223.

Next we might ask how the occupation is regarded by others. What is its level of prestige? Will the worker have the status that he desires?

Then we would want to know just what sort of relationships or social group organizations there are on the job. How do the workers act toward each other? Will the counselee feel at home in this situation?

We would want to be able to infer the social group or social level in which the work places the individual. In connection with this we would want to know something about the social role that the occupation sets for the worker. Is this role similar to his desired role?

We would also want to understand the career patterns of those in the occupation [227, ch. 5]. What factors operate to influence them to enter the occupation? What sort of occupational patterns do workers in the occupation exhibit [139, pp. 25–26]? A number of studies have been made of specific occupations [139, p. 26]. We may refer back to the discussions in Chapter 7 on the matter of stages in occupational choice or development. Here, in our study of a particular occupation, we are concerned with the pattern, and the factors affecting the pattern, in a particular occupation. What does this tell us about the occupation that will help us to help the counselee?

Another aspect with which we are concerned is mobility, both vertically and horizontally. What sort of promotions and advancements can the worker expect? What sorts of shifts to other occupations may be made?

Knowledge of occupational organizations, such as professional and labor, including factual information about regulations, is important. Information is also needed about informal organizations.

Economic and Trend Data. Along with those aspects already discussed above, the counselor needs to be able to interpret data in the occupational literature about economic aspects (salary, wages, other benefits) and to bring in background data from other sources. What do people in the occupation earn? What does it mean in terms of what they can buy and in terms of the type of economic status that they will have in the community? What may they

* Delbert C. Miller and William H. Form, *Industrial Sociology,* Harper & Brothers, New York, 1951 [139]. By permission of the publishers.

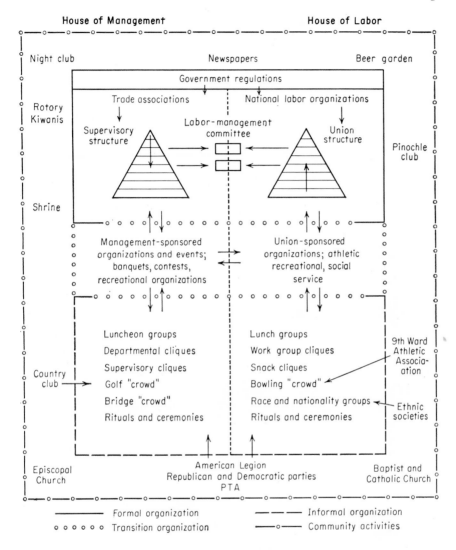

expect to earn after some years of work? What are the life earnings? What are the effects of seasonal variation? What other benefits are there that may be classified as economic, for example, retirement plans?

Of crucial importance is the way the occupation is affected by economic conditions in the nation. What factors operate to produce a greater need for workers and an increase in income? What does a knowledge of these factors enable the counselor to predict for this occupation?

Economic data are closely tied to trends in the number and type of workers. Trends in occupations show the effect of economic and other factors operating to cause an increase here, a decrease there, and a static situation in another area [8, pp. 51–63; 247]. While typical occupational literature has some data on trends and economic factors, the counselor needs additional background to interpret the data for himself and to help the counselee understand it. Baer and Roeber provide a helpful discussion of factors affecting trends and distribution of workers [13, pp. 156–182] and economic returns [13, pp. 182–191]. Shartle [201, pp. 320–359] provides a helpful discussion of trends, factors affecting trends, and materials that the counselor may use in predicting trends.

Vertical and horizontal mobility are two types of occupational mobility, but there are other types, such as becoming a member of a labor force or withdrawing from it, changes in jobs, and changes in place of work [15, p. 11]. Many factors tend to encourage or limit mobility, and an understanding of these factors is important to the counselor.

Physiological Aspects. In addition to psychological and sociological aspects, the counselor needs to understand physiological aspects such as the physical demands of the work. For many occupations, some physical qualities such as size and strength are becoming less important; dexterity, coordination, and agility are assuming more significance. For example, the unskilled labor group is decreasing while semiskilled operatives are increasing. Quite often the typical occupational materials give an estimate of physical abilities required, but not in much detail. As a rule, this problem is not acute, until the counselor deals with persons with physical handicaps; then he has to know the specific physical demands. A useful reference on using occupational information with handicapped persons is [201, ch. 10]. With the physically handicapped person, the counselor needs specific information about the *particular* job. Requirements vary in different organizations, and other conditions besides those on the job may be crucial; for example, having to climb stairs to the place of work may cause the job to be impractical for a handicapped person.

Thus the physiological aspects of the job, including some that may be classified as "psychophysical," need to be used in fully understanding the occupation.

Working Conditions. Closely related to the physical requirements of the work are the working conditions [13, pp. 96–98]. These may be rather well described in the typical literature (other than psychological and sociological aspects already considered). But to understand them and get the work "atmosphere," it is usually necessary actually to visit the place of work. Some characteristics are so obvious that they can be easily observed (for example, the pounding of a stamping machine), while others may not be so obvious (for example, electrical hazards). Conditions vary to some degree in each place or establishment in which the occupation occurs. The job analysis form [201, p. 41] shows working conditions often checked in the detailed study of a job. Unfavorable working conditions such as noise, dust, hazards, or working outdoors might cause some counselees to be unable or unwilling to do a job that appealed to them otherwise.

The counselor thus needs to assess the physical working conditions as accurately as possible and supplement occupational literature with firsthand observation where practical.

Legal Aspects. Occupational information includes laws and legislation that regulate such things as minimum age of workers, licensing requirements, and the like. This is a type of information that is often contained, at least in part, in the typical occupational literature. The counselor will need additional information, however, particularly state laws. Usually such material may be obtained from the State Department of Labor and the State Department of Education. Journal articles frequently provide useful interpretations [129]. Pamphlets published by the Federal government, such as *Employment Certificates Help You to Help Youth* [248], may be quite helpful.

Related Occupations. Usually the counselor, in working with a counselee, would approach the matter of learning about occupations through a consideration of the level (based on level of ability and amount of education required) and type (based upon major types of activities on the job, such as dealing with people) and then would deal with groups of related occupations or occupational families [91, p. 144]. Thus the counselor should be able to determine what occupations exist at a certain level and in a specific field, and then which ones make up a family. He can help the counselee to avoid focusing on one specific occupation too soon, and instead to learn about and consider a number of similar occupations. Helpful discussions of occupational families are in Refs. [13, pp. 84–96; 201, pp. 172–200]. The concept of occupational families is also useful with experienced workers who are seeking employment.

Studying an Occupation

Now suppose that the counselor is aware of all the aspects of an occupation that should be investigated and understood. He wishes to gain a better understanding of an occupation so that he may help the counselee in the ways described in the next chapter. How might he go about doing this?

First he would want to have one or more good monographs, and possibly several pamphlets and other sorts of information describing the job. It would be well to have several different sorts of materials because he will often find that one may include material that the other does not contain, and that there may be conflicting evidence that he will have to weigh. From the materials he will be able to make notes on what one does on the job, where the work is found, wages and salary, other benefits, related occupations, sources of additional information, and the like. Then he may add local data, if some are available, to show the local variations in the work. Local data about the job itself, such as work done, would be helpful, but he would also use data about the number of workers, the age of workers (to help anticipate openings), and trends in local businesses and industries that would affect opportunities.

The counselor would also draw upon his knowledge of national trends and distribution of workers, the number employed, data about the adequacy of the supply of workers, where the work is found, and future prospects. These and other questions would enable him better to understand the present status and opportunities in the occupation.

To this information he could add his knowledge about other aspects that would help him construct a picture of the occupation. He might draw upon the available data about particular individuals who do the work, keeping in mind, of course, that they represent only one or a few examples. Then he might use other material for clues as to what this work means for those who do it, what satisfactions it offers, and what status it gives. He might consider what sort of people do the work, and what they are like, socially, educationally, and otherwise.

Notice that we are not considering our counselee or his characteristics now. Instead, we are trying to round out our understanding of the occupation. We realize, however, that we are learning about the occupation *in general*, not about the specific job that the counselee might obtain. We can make some assumptions, however, about the similarity of the counselee's job (if he takes it) to our "picture" of the occupation.

Also notice that we are obtaining information that may be more useful for helping the counselee plan and decide upon a job that he will enter at some later time, rather than helping him decide whether or not to apply for (or take) a particular job right now. The same procedure could be used for a specific job, as in the placement process, although in an educational institution we should be helping the counselee plan for the future rather than assisting him *only* at that point when he is ready for employment.

Thus the counselor needs to know and use a variety of information in order to learn about occupations. When he needs to learn about a specific occupation, a field of work, or an industry he pulls together various sorts of data to get a well-rounded picture. He does this as a cumulative process, adding to his information as he has needs in working with counselees and through reading more general background information. As his knowledge of occupations and the world of work increases, he finds it easier to fit in new information. He may add to his information by visits, by actual work experience, by studying occupations, and by survey methods or job analyses. Each type of information, if synthesized with what he already knows, will enable the counselor better to comprehend the increasingly complex world of occupations.

SUMMARY

The counselor uses occupational information and other materials to (1) learn about occupations, educational opportunities, and personal and social problems; (2) obtain data that he will share in one way or another with the counselee; and

(3) assist the counselee to use the materials to obtain needed information for himself. Thus the counselor needs to know, first, what sorts of information are available; second, how to obtain the materials; and third, how to evaluate, classify, and file the materials for easy use both by himself and the counselee. Finally, and most important to all, the counselor must be able to interpret accurately the data contained in the occupational, educational, and other literature.

CHECKS ON UNDERSTANDING

1. What is an occupational monograph?

2. What publications can you use to locate sources of current occupational information?

3. Why is local occupational information essential for the counselor?

4. What cautions should the counselor observe when interpreting the information distributed by a particular business or industry to describe its own jobs?

5. Why would you evaluate an occupational pamphlet? How would you do it?

6. What are the economic aspects of occupational information that are of concern for the counselor?

7. What is meant by psychological and sociological aspects of an occupation? How is this sort of information about an occupation or industry obtained?

8. What should you know about an educational or training opportunity to help the counselee determine its suitability for him?

THINGS TO DO

1. Assume that you were preparing for a counseling session with a counselee who you knew was interested in a specific occupation, for example, industrial engineering, but who knew little or nothing about it. What facts about the occupation would you wish to have in mind so that you could help him understand the general nature and scope of the work?

2. Select a particular occupation and locate several different sorts of material about it, for example, a monograph, a pamphlet, and recruiting pamphlet. Then extract, compare, and synthesize data to present a comprehensive picture of the occupation.

3. Practice using the *Dictionary of Occupational Titles*, by doing the following exercise:

a. In Volume I, look up the description of an occupation that is widespread in your area but about which you know little or nothing. For example, if there is a garment factory in your community, do you know what a "bonnaz-machine operator" is? If you cannot think of the name of some occupation to look up, turn to page 507 of Volume II of the *Dictionary* where titles are arranged by industry.

b. To get some idea of the way occupations can be grouped by industry, turn to pages 507–743 in Volume II and look over the arrangements according to this type of classification. Pick out an industry that is widespread in your community and count the total number of occupations listed for it. Also count the ones that you know something about.

c. Occupations may be grouped on various bases, such as skills needed or similarity of activities performed. *The Dictionary of Occupational Titles* represents one type of grouping into what are called "Occupational Families." For example, look on page 110 of Volume II of the *Dictionary* where the occupation "Machinist" is given in bold-face type. In this family there are a number of jobs. What machinist's jobs are found in the following industries (one job in each): Firearms? Tinware? Radio manufacturing?

d. Part IV of the *Dictionary* is quite useful with high school students because it gives information about entry occupations. For example, on page 39 you will find entry occupations in computing work. Could a student without previous work experience, but with requisite school training, expect to begin as a comptometer operator? An insurance dividend deposit checker? In another section in Part IV, on pages 168–173, are listed casual work experience and entry occupations for which such experience is useful. For example, on page 170 the casual work experience of house-to-house canvassing is given, together with a number of entry occupations related to this type of work. Select one of the entry occupations suggested and look up the name of the occupation in the section on entry occupations, pages 17–156.

4. Use the rating sheets to evaluate an occupational pamphlet, monograph, or book.

5. Use Forrester's book and one or more of the indexes to obtain samples of occupational information.

6. Examine several occupational file systems to judge which appears to be most useful for the counselor and the counselee.

7. Interview several workers to determine what they like about their job, how they would rank it compared with other jobs, and what they think about other aspects of the work.

8. Select a particular occupation and describe the customs, beliefs, and attitudes of those who do the work. Describe the sort of home, family, recreational activities, and so on that appear to be characteristic of workers. Include the meaning of this work to the individual. To do this, use the references, interviews, observations, and other means of gathering data.

CHAPTER 10

Using Occupational, Educational, and Social Information in Counseling

I N THE PREVIOUS chapters we have discussed the types of information about occupations, training and educational opportunities, and social and related problems, and indicated how such information should be obtained, filed, and interpreted. In this chapter we shall discuss ways the counselor uses these sorts of information in the counseling process. If information is to be of help to the counselee, the counselor must be able to present it to him and help him accept and make use of it. The counselor provides the learning situation in which the counselee becomes aware of his need for information; he then helps the counselee to obtain the information and to determine its meaning for help in making plans and decisions.

Purposes of Using Occupational and Other Information in Counseling

As has already been pointed out, the counseling process is essentially a learning situation. It is of primary importance that this situation be such that the counselee can make practical plans and decisions and learn more effective behavior. Often in the process there is a need for specific sorts of information to enable learning to proceed. A distinction may be made between *purposes* of using information of various sorts and *ways* or *techniques* of using it. Purposes are summarized in this section, while techniques are taken up later.

The counselor needs to know what sort of information is needed for a specific problem and how and when it should be used in the counseling process [33]. He selects information to help the counselee in a way which he has decided will be beneficial. The purposes which the counselor has in mind are usually one or more of the following types.

A typical use of information is *instructional* [13, p. 425; 46]. Information may be provided to help the counselee to confirm an occupational choice, to decide among several possible choices, or to obtain a job. Within the scope of this purpose would come information getting to serve as exploration or to help the counselee to learn about various occupations and to search for suitable work roles [191].

A second purpose of using information may be called *readjustive* [31]. When the counselee has made inappropriate occupational plans, information may be used for the purpose of helping him arrive at more practical plans. In a sense this is a "therapeutic" use [46].

A third purpose of using information would be *motivational* [13, p. 425; 31; 46]. It may be necessary to help the counselee to realize the need to do something about selecting an occupation or about making occupational plans. The counselor may arouse interest by helping him to become aware of the possibilities that he may consider. In some cases the counselee may profess an interest only in learning about occupations when he actually needs more comprehensive counseling help [13, p. 425; 31]. The counselor provides occupational information to motivate the counselee to continue in the counseling relationship. This purpose is a very important one in counseling with high school youth; quite often they seem to feel that the future will take care of occupational planning, and it is pushed into the background by the multitude of other interests and activities.

A fourth purpose may be described as *evaluative* [13, p. 426]. In this use of information, the counselee is helped to determine the accuracy of information which he has obtained from many sources. For example, most counselees have some concept of occupations gathered from movies, television, and popular magazine articles. This information may be accurate but it is more likely to be biased and unrealistic.

Information may also be used for *assurance* purposes [13, p. 425]. The counselee is helped to satisfy himself on the appropriateness of his vocational choice and on the inappropriateness of alternative choices that he has given up.

In order to test the counselee's certainty or uncertainty about a choice that he has made, information may be used for *startle purposes* [13, p. 426].

An important purpose, not yet mentioned, is that of helping the counselee select a specific job and adjust to it. This is substantially a placement use. Christensen [46] describes it as a *distributional* use of information.

If the counselee has made an impractical plan, various sorts of information may be given to dissuade [92] him from holding to his obviously unsuitable intentions.

Providing information to the counselee may help him to learn something about self-directed problem solving as well as learn about occupations [116].

Information about educational and training programs is, of course, closely related to information about occupations. The occupational plans are made before the formulation of plans to obtain the training, but the information about the required training is considered along with other data for the purpose already discussed.

Information which might be described as more personal or social serves, to some extent, the same purposes as information about occupations. These types, personal and social, describe and interpret various environments for which the counselee has to make plans and decisions. For example, the counselee may need to learn what is essential to get along with others, to become a member of the group, or to establish satisfying relationships with the opposite sex. Information about personal and social aspects of life is not necessarily more "emotional" than that concerning occupational plans. As a matter of fact, the three areas, occupational, personal, and social, are so inextricably bound together that it is practically impossible to give information about one area without touching on the other two.

Principles of Using Information

For whatever purpose information may be used in counseling, there are certain general guides or principles which the counselor should observe. These apply specifically to occupational information but would also appear to apply when the counselor is using personal and social information, such as that concerned with building self-confidence, getting along with parents, or improving emotional health. These principles or guides are now discussed.

The Counselee's Desires. There is not much point in the counselor using occupational or other information in counseling until the counselee wants it. The counselor can, however, stimulate the feeling of need; he might help the counselee to become aware of the fact that his choice of school courses should be based upon occupational plans. Even though the counselee does not say, in so many words, that he wants information, the counselor may infer that he does. For example, the counselor may decide from the counselee's comments and questions that he really desires to know what different types of engineering occupations there are.

The Counselee's Needs. In addition to wanting information, the counselee should want it for a good reason, or really need it. The information should serve some useful purpose in counseling. For example, a rather immature counselee requested more and more information about unusual and, to him, glamorous occupations, apparently hoping for some "ideal" work and at the same time avoiding a careful and serious consideration of plans for the future. He did not actually need the information requested; he was using it to hold off the matter of actually making occupational plans.

The Counselee's Understanding of Himself. Probably the most important guide of all as to whether or not it is time for occupational information to be introduced into the counseling process is whether or not the counselee has an understanding of his assets, potentialities, liabilities, and occupational role so that he can make use of the information. Without this sort of understanding the information is likely to be of little use or may even be harmful.

This principle does not mean that the counselee must arrive at rather complete understanding of his interests, abilities, and needs prior to the use of occupational information. The counselor will be helping the counselee to gain self-understanding along with the occupational information; for example, the counselee may not really understand his role in the world of work until he has learned about some possible occupational roles. Of course, the goal of complete self-understanding by the counselee is probably never completely reached.

The Counselee's Desire to Obtain the Information. The more actively the counselee participates in the counseling process and in activities connected with counseling, the more effective a learning situation counseling will be. Thus it is quite desirable that he actually obtain needed information himself. Some counselees will need support, help, and supervision to do this, while others will be able to work more independently.

The Counselee's Readiness for the Information. The counselee will need some sort of preparation to do an effective job of obtaining information, whatever sources he uses [33, 46, 116, 211]. The most frequently used source is probably the occupational file or library; observing workers on the job, interviewing workers, viewing films on occupations, and tryout work experiences are other ways that might be utilized [211].

The counselee should have an understanding of the kinds of information he plans to obtain. The counselor can help him prepare a list of important items of information [101]. The form "Local Occupational Study" in Chapter 9 lists types of information that should be obtained.

Where to look for information is a question that also should be answered in the "getting ready" process. For example, the counselee may use the occupational file, write to a professional organization for information, and interview a worker.

Deciding upon which occupations to study is also important. Even in exploratory reading or other activities, the counselee should have a rather definite idea of occupations that will be covered. The counselee may bring up some, while the counselor, based on his knowledge of the counselee, may suggest others. The counselor should help the counselee to broaden his occupational horizon, without, however, giving the counselee the impression that he is telling him what he should do or recommending a particular occupation or occupational field [216].

In some cases the counselor provides the information during the counseling session. Prior to this, the counselee should be helped to identify those aspects of the occupation that he needs to consider. Otherwise, the information will probably not have much significance for him. For example, suppose that the matter of income is being discussed. If the counselee has not thought about what he wants from his life's work and has not considered the relative importance of income to other factors, he will probably not be able to evaluate the income in relation to what he expects from a job.

Counselee Abstracting and Synthesizing. It is helpful for the counselee himself to collect bits of information from various sources and bring them together to formulate a picture of an occupation rather than for the counselor to do it for him. While the counselee may not be able or willing to do a thorough and complete job, he should be able to go a long way in assembling and interpreting information from reading, observation, interviews, and the like. Aids such as the form shown on page 236 and in Ref. [206, p. 99] should assist the counselee in the abstracting and synthesizing process.

The Counselee's Level of Understanding. When the counselor presents information during the counseling process, he puts it in terms that are meaningful to the counselee. Since the counselee usually has had limited occupational experience, many terms will be quite unfamiliar to him, for example, semi-skilled occupation, skilled work, professional level, and the like.

Relating Self and Occupational Information. Prior to the use of occupational or other types of information, the counselee has gained some understanding of himself. He is helped to understand how these two types of data are related. He is also helped to accept the significance of the relationship. For example, he may know that his mental ability level is in the lowest one-fourth of those in the occupation, but he may not realize or accept what this may mean if he enters that occupation. Other self-data would be information about interests, abilities, achievement, finances, goals, occupational roles, and other aspects of the individual.

To help the counselee relate self and environmental information and accept the meaning of the relationship, the counselor provides the opportunity for the counselee to react freely. In the permissive counseling atmosphere the counselee's expression of feeling will help the counselor to understand him and assist him in clarifying his attitudes toward various work roles.

Fitting the Information into the Counseling Process. Whether the counselee obtains information by his own efforts or the counselor provides it, there is no break in the continuity or climate of counseling [240, p. 187]. Information is brought in as needed to supply what is required for progress and for making plans and arriving at decisions. A great deal may be introduced at one time or it may be brought in bit by bit over a period of time. As in the case of any information, the counselee should not be overwhelmed by a mass of data but rather should be allowed to proceed slowly, understanding each item of information as he goes along. The counselor may easily forget that this is new and complex information for the counselee and not realize that he understands little or nothing about it.

As in other aspects of the counseling process, the counselor does not take over but rather introduces information when the counselee sees that it is needed or understands the purpose of occupational information. There is a definite counseling value in the counselee's participating in the process of obtaining and using information. For example, he helps decide when it is needed; he plans how to obtain it; he locates it himself; and he discusses it with the counselor.

Counselor Checking and Clarification. While a great deal of information may be obtained by the counselee, this does not relieve the counselor from the responsibility of determining if it is accurate and complete. It may often be necessary for the counselor to explain or clarify information that the counselee has obtained, and to answer questions about it that the counselee may have. Completeness of information includes coverage of all appropriate occupations as well as adequate data about each occupation.

Of particular concern to the counselor is the matter of correcting biased or unreliable information about an occupation which the counselee may have obtained, for example, from a disgruntled worker or from a piece of persuasive recruiting literature about an industry.

Action by the Counselee. The purpose of using occupational information in counseling is to assist the counselee to do something that he needs to do. The "doing something" may be coming to conclusions about whether or not he would like the way of life determined by the occupation, or it may be estimating how well he could perform on the job. Possibly he might decide on particular occupational plans and actually apply for a job.

Principles Applicable to All Types of Information. In the preceding discussion of principles of presenting information, stress has been placed on information about occupations. The same principles would apply to materials about environments and relations with others. Thorne [232, pp. 417–418] points out desirable counselee attitudes when psychological information is given [232] and ways of actually providing the information [232]. The counselee needs information about ". . . social relationships, citizenship, occupational pursuits, avocational activity" [135, p. 101]. These are aspects of the environment which the counselee needs to understand and in which he needs to adjust. While the occupational environment is a major one, it is by no means the only one; it is part of the pattern of related life areas in which the counselee operates.

From this review of principles or guides for the use of various sorts of information, the matter of how the counselor actually uses information, what he says, and how he says it will be taken up.

A helpful summary of the principles of using occupational information in counseling may be found in Senick [198]. Tyler provides a useful discussion of occupational information and describes ways of using it in counseling [240, pp. 169–192]. Another useful reference is Baer and Roeber [13, pp. 418–473].

Hoppock summarizes the statements of forty-eight other authors on the use of occupational information in counseling [102, ch. 10] and then presents suggestions for ways of working with several types of counselees [pp. 150–157]: counselees with no preference; the counselee who has set up impractical goals; and those who are changing jobs [102]. Chapter 12 in the same reference gives some very helpful suggestions for the counselor on ways of providing occupational information to the counselee, particularly in answering his questions.

Techniques for Using Occupational Information

The counselor often feels puzzled as to what to say to the counselee about information, or how much and what to give in the counseling session, even though he is familiar with the principles of using information. This section describes and illustrates ways the counselor provides information or helps the counselee obtain it.

Using the Occupational File. One of the chief sources of occupational information for the counselor and counselee is the occupational file. It may be supplemented by books, catalogues, and the like, but the file of pamphlets, monographs, and other brief publications gives the most timely and extensive coverage of occupations. How to help the counselee use it effectively is often a problem. Many counselees thumb listlessly through the material without learning anything of interest to them, while others may be so overwhelmed by the number of occupations represented and the variety of material that they never settle down to learning anything about particular occupations.

To introduce the counselee to the use of the file the counselor might say, "We have a file that you can use to find out just what one does on the jobs, and other things too, like what training is needed, how to get a job, what sort of places jobs may be found, and other things that are important for a person who is thinking about work. You can look through it and find out about these things, and then we can talk about them later."

The counselor might ask a question or lead into the matter of what things the counselee should look for as he uses the file. Together they might list the important items, or the counselor might have a worksheet, such as on page 236, to help the counselee. As this sounds like (and is) hard work, sometimes the counselee's interests falls off rather sharply. It may be better to use the file first for a rather limited study; for example, to find what the principal duties are in one type of work. If the counselee is able to get the information without too much difficulty and if it is something that he feels a need to know, he may be interested enough to make a more extensive study.

Occupational Study Guide

Name of occupation_____

Use words or phrases only. This is for your benefit and sentences or paragraphs are not necessary.

Job side	My side
Description of the work preferred	Why I think I'd like this job

Job side	My side

Qualifications
  1. Training or education needed
    (a) What kind?
    (b) How much?
  2. Abilities needed
  3. Personal qualifications
	1. What related courses have I liked?
	    (a) Done well in?
	    (b) Can I arrange for the necessary training?
	2. What have I done to show I have these abilities?
	3. How do I rate myself on these?

Is moving or traveling necessary?	Am I willing to move or travel?

Compensation
  1. Income
  2. Other returns
	1. What income would satisfy me?
	2. What other returns from a job do I want?

Demand for people in this vocation
  1. Present
  2. Future
	How good will I have to be to
	  1. Enter?
	  2. Advance?

Advantages	What things do I like most about this vocation?
Disadvantages	What things do I like least about this vocation?

If the counselee is going to do exploratory reading, the counselor may help him select broad areas, such as sales work or social service work. He may have the counselee look through the file without any specific occupation or field of work in mind. The object of this use of the file is to find some areas for more intensive study. This sort of study is made at the counselee's level and in keeping with decisions he has to make. For example, as a high school freshman he usually needs only to make a definite choice among the school curriculum.

The next step would be to go with the counselee to the occupational file and explain how he may find materials in it. Several folders may be taken out and the counselee shown the kinds of material in the file. Then he is allowed to work on his own. The counselor will have to be the judge of how much he can do by himself. In some cases the counselor may actually have to find the pamphlets and other materials for the counselee. The counselor will also have to be the judge of how strongly motivated the counselee is to use the file. He may consider it "too much work" and only glance at a few pamphlets. Or he may show resistance at having to take some responsibility for the activity.

If the material were more of the type that deals with personal or social problems, for example, a booklet on getting along with others, the counselor would, after helping the counselee realize the need for such information, give him the pamphlet. These materials are not so extensive or complex that they require any special kind of filing system.

Obtaining Information by Interview, Observation, or Direct Experience. In addition to the occupational file and library, the counselee may obtain valuable information by interviewing workers and employers, by observing the worker on his job and the setting in which he works, or by actual tryout experience on the job. The counselor helps him to prepare for the experience so that he will obtain needed information and then helps him to evaluate the information and understand its meaning for him in the light of his capacities, interests, and goals. Also, the counselor helps the counselee evaluate work experience that he has already had, for example, afterschool work and summer jobs.

In preparing for this method of obtaining information, the counselor helps the counselee decide what he needs to know about the occupation. It is desirable for the counselee to bring out the points himself. Usually, however, the counselor will have to assist him in making up a list. In the following excerpt, the counselor is helping the counselee to realize the need for more information about an occupation (school principal) that he is seriously considering and to make plans to talk to persons in that occupation.

COUNSELOR: How much do you feel you know about what a person studies in college, the kinds of activities he does in training, and the kinds of things that he does when he really gets out and starts work?

COUNSELEE: I don't know much about that. . . . I haven't had time to really talk with anybody about it. I've gone to our principal but we didn't talk about that.

COUNSELOR: In other words you might want to explore that a little bit, by talking to people, by er, getting some literature. . . . If your principal doesn't have any, I'm sure he can get some, because most all of the schools do publish a lot of literature on different occupations and different lines of specialization in their particular area. . . . What would you think about taking the time sometime to visit, say, a rural school, a small school, and talk to the principal?

COUNSELEE: That'd be my chance to talk to Mr. Smith who lives out near me. I think his school is just about that size. It's very small. . . .

The counselee appears to be sufficiently motivated to do some interviewing. But, so far, not much has been said about what sorts of information the counselee would obtain. In the following excerpt the counselor and counselee are identifying the sorts of information that the counselee would need to know about an occupation.

COUNSELOR: There are some things about it. . . . You don't know whether you could do it?

COUNSELEE: I don't know too much. . . .

COUNSELOR: What the work involves. Also, the question of the length of training is not too much in favor of it exactly.

COUNSELEE: I think I could stand the length of training but it would just be the money . . . to get me through.

COUNSELOR: The actual financing of that schooling is a problem, I believe you mentioned?

COUNSELEE: Yes.

COUNSELOR: Well, maybe you could get some information. Maybe you could talk to a person who does that sort of work.

COUNSELEE: I don't. . . . I think that'd be nice. . . . I don't know anyone who does that.

COUNSELOR: Do you suppose the teacher who has that course would know?

. . . .

COUNSELOR: You might call the city health department and find someone whom you could go and talk to, and go and get them to tell you a little more about it. Then you'd know what the work involves, the requirements, er . . . the amount of training, and evaluate how much you think you'd like it.

In both this and the previous excerpt the counselor is helping the counselee to decide on or locate a person to interview, as well as prepare a list of questions that will be asked. The counselor may have to make the actual arrangements for the interview, depending upon how much initiative the counselee has.

In the following excerpt the counselee has done some thinking about needed information and has some definite questions in mind. Note that this process is not a straightforward listing of questions but involves, in this particular instance, discussion of the counselee's feeling about questions. After the counselee has obtained the information there will be time to discuss the data, bring out feelings about them, and relate them to data about the counselee.

COUNSELOR: Well, then, what kinds of questions were you going to ask the school people when they come for the college day and the others for the career day?

COUNSELEE: I don't have any idea of what kind of course I would follow in college. I don't know if I would go along the first year just like a regular college course. I was going to ask them about that . . . and the chances. . . . I know you can quit and it isn't so hard to get a job again.

COUNSELOR: You mean after you have graduated, you can work, and stop, and go to work somewhere else?

COUNSELEE: And then, the disadvantages I've heard about. . . . It's depressing, and it's hard work. I think any work's hard, so it couldn't be much worse than anything else. And I've heard that they have pretty irregular hours. . . . The lab technician would have definite hours where you'd go and come home.

COUNSELOR: What do you think of those irregular hours that they might have— different shifts?

COUNSELEE: I think you'd more or less get used to it. That's why I definitely didn't decide on . . . you know. . . . If I decided I liked something better I could branch out into it.

COUNSELOR: But you feel like you're interested in the medical field. Is that it?

COUNSELEE: I think so.

COUNSELOR: . . . Definitely decided on? . . .

It may be that the counselee does not need a complete list of all the topics that are usually contained in the occupational monograph to use as questions. Some of the needed data can be obtained from printed material in the library. Also, the counselor helps the counselee to be aware that the person being interviewed might present a biased picture of the occupation.

Evaluating the Information. Whatever way the counselee has obtained occupational information, whether by reading, talking to or observing workers, actual work experience, viewing films, or listening to talks, it is necessary that he and the counselor go over it in the counseling session so that the counselee can obtain the best possible understanding of it and so that he can use it in making plans.

First, the counselor checks to determine whether or not the counselee has covered the different occupations decided upon and the needed types of information about each. At the same time he is estimating the accuracy of the information. Knowing the source of information will assist the counselor in determining its accuracy. For example, if the counselee has taken notes from a monograph of a dependable publisher the counselor can assume that the information is correct. Also, while the counselor may not have the time to check on each detail about the occupations which he and the counselee plan to discuss, he can make a quick survey of particularly crucial information, such as the length of apprenticeship in sheet metal work, the nature of the work of the ceramic engineer, or the physical requirements for an airline hostess.

Next the counselor fills in gaps in information or helps the counselee to get the missing information. The counselor might very well supply a brief bit of information himself; if the amount of needed information is large, the counselee should obtain it.

Quite often the counselee will have questions about what he has read or observed. The counselor should attempt to answer these questions or help the counselee to find the answer. Not infrequently the counselor does not know the answer; he should admit it rather than try to avoid answering one way or another. Counselees can pose some rather difficult questions; for example, one counselee wanted to know what training was required for a diplomatic courier, and another wanted to know how an archeologist gets started in his work.

As the counselee has prepared a list of questions about which to collect information, his answers to them are discussed in the counseling session. Some of the questions call for factual data while others get at the counselee's reactions to the data. Examples of the latter type of questions are as follows: "What do I particularly like about the occupation? What parts of it could I do well? Would I have the chance to reach my goal?"

In the following counseling excerpt, the counselor is attempting to help the counselee express his feelings about some material he has read. Note also that, to some extent, the discussion deals with the relation of the information or facts about the occupation to counselee characteristics. This latter point is covered in more detail later on.

COUNSELEE: I've been reading. I read a book two or three days ago. It's about a girl who is a commercial artist in a store. It was interesting, but I don't think I'd like to do that.

COUNSELOR: It does sound interesting, but you don't think you'd want to do that?

COUNSELEE: Yes. It just goes into more experience and talent than I've ever had or will have.

COUNSELOR: You mean you think the job, er, would be more than you could handle . . . something like that?

COUNSELEE: Yes, the girl in this book had experience, . . . a talent for drawing and sketching, and things like that before she ever went into it. . . . Wouldn't suit me.

COUNSELOR: How do you know? What makes you think you don't have the talent . . . in doing that sort of thing?

COUNSELEE: I just don't think I'd be able to design . . . draw what they would be willing to buy. I don't think I could . . . what the demand is for.

COUNSELOR: Well, yes, but everybody has to learn these things. The question is do you think you could learn?

COUNSELEE: I think I could learn it.

COUNSELOR: But you'd estimate . . . as you think about it, you'd estimate your ability as probably not so good. You just wonder how you could ever do anything like that.

COUNSELEE: I wonder about it. I think if I knew the basic things that you'd have to do and had the experience that the girl in the book had I think I'd be a better success at it.

COUNSELOR: Supposing you could get training and whatever experience that you need for that—not starting out as you are right now . . . do you think you could do it?

COUNSELEE: I think I could in that case.

COUNSELOR: It appeals to you? It's something you think you might like to do?

COUNSELEE: I'd considered that before. That's the reason I read the book.

. . . .

COUNSELOR: Well, how would you estimate it? How much ability do you think you have in that . . . making appropriate layouts, what the store wants, what people will notice?

COUNSELEE: In just working as a clerk you don't have to do that. . . . But I've planned displays and done windows. . . .

COUNSELOR: You did that?

COUNSELEE: I did some of that . . . all along.
COUNSELOR: Did you get by?
COUNSELEE: Yes, I didn't try to sell them.

What feelings is the counselee expressing? To some extent there appears to be a defense of felt inadequacies for the work. It may be that the counselee felt a strong pull toward this sort of work but also felt a need to reject it.

The counselor also helps the counselee relate the information about occupations to information about himself. One way he can do this is to ask if the counselee sees any connection between the two kinds of information. He might ask him if he sees any connection between a hobby of repairing motors and the things an auto mechanic does on the job. Or the counselor may ask if the counselee sees any relationship between his liking to take responsibility in school clubs and work with people, and what he would do as an accountant as compared with a public relations worker. This procedure can be used with test data, school marks, and other types of counselee information.

Another way that the counselor can help the counselee to recognize the relationship between self and work factors is to use some graphic or written aid, showing the things required for the work and how the counselee rates on these characteristics. Much of this would have to be counselor judgment based on the best available evidence.

Still another way that the counselor can help develop this understanding or insight is to be particularly alert to the counselee's comments that show an attempt to relate work factors to self factors. As the counselee discusses information gained through reading or in some other way, he will often be comparing it with what he thinks or feels about himself. He may be testing the reality of his concept of his occupational role. By responding to those comments in a neutral, reflective way, the counselor can aid the counselee in exploring the relationship further and gaining a realistic concept of his occupational role and relating it to possible work roles. In the following excerpt the counselee is discussing a part-time work experience and the counselor is attempting, by his responses, to help the counselee gain some insight as to his need for work that would allow initiative and reward it.

COUNSELOR: You did a lot of things that you didn't have to do. You took it on your own to do things. . . .
COUNSELEE: A lot of the clerks would just stand around. . . . I noticed that those were the ones who didn't stay on so long. . . .
COUNSELOR: Just put in the time and that was all.
COUNSELEE: They just waited on them when they wanted something, and when there wasn't they just did what they wanted to do.

It may be difficult to determine how these comments would help the counselee to see the relationship between self and occupations. But by this sort of

discussion the counselee finally arrived at a better understanding of the role
that he preferred and whether or not it could be found in this sort of work.

It may be necessary for the counselor to point out the connection, keeping
in mind that this is not telling the counselee what to do about it and recognizing that the counselee may not "see" it or accept it just because the counselor says it.

Providing information or helping the counselee use what he has collected
should be a natural part of the ongoing counseling process. It would seem best
for the counselor to play the same role that he has been playing and make no
abrupt change in the counseling atmosphere. It may be that this relating of
self and job data would be left and returned to again and again; it would not
be something that had to be completed without a break in a certain amount of
time. The ultimate objective is to assist the counselee to make suitable and satisfying plans. Thus the long-range objective of counseling should not be lost
sight of as the counselor and the counselee become involved in this particular
process; the counselor should not take responsibility away from the counselee
at this point.

Providing Information in the Counseling Process. As has already been mentioned, the counselor may provide information to fill gaps in what the counselee has obtained. He may also, in many cases, actually provide a great deal of
the needed information in the counseling process himself. The counselor will
have to judge in what situations it is best to do this. If the counselee is strongly
motivated and appears to be so thoroughly involved in counseling that he will
not feel that the counselor is taking over, the counselor may facilitate the
progress of counseling by supplying the information himself. If the counselee
appears to be too dependent to take any responsibility and lacks initiative, the
counselor might, at least at first, provide the information. Then, in other cases
where there may be no suitable sources that the counselee can readily use, the
counselor may have to provide the information directly.

In the following excerpt, the counselee brings out questions about an occupational area and the counselor attempts to supply the information. At the
same time he makes an effort to help the counselee to react to the information
given.

COUNSELEE: Let me get to music first. Can I . . . can I ask you some questions?
Well, tell me . . . I mean. . . . This is just what my music teacher told me.
. . . Is it very tough? I mean the competition?
COUNSELOR: Is it tough? In music?
COUNSELEE: Yes, sir.
COUNSELOR: Well, how do you feel about it?
COUNSELEE: She said it was. So I just took her word for it.
COUNSELOR: It's pretty tough competition.
COUNSELEE: Well . . . are there fields in which it isn't tough? . . . In music?
COUNSELOR: Other fields in music in which there wouldn't be so much competi-

tion? Well . . . what would you think about it yourself? Now, you have music as a career, . . . in which you are a concert artist, and you have the people who teach in public schools or junior colleges . . . teach music there. Or you could give private lessons. Now what would you think about the different . . . how much competition there'd be in those different areas? First, take . . . suppose we take teaching first.

COUNSELEE: Don't look like there'd be much in that. I don't know . . . just doesn't. I don't know why. . . .

COUNSELOR: Well, perhaps you're not dependent upon selling in a competitive market, selling the work that you do.

COUNSELEE: Do music teachers make the same as regular teachers, or do they make more . . . or less?

COUNSELOR: Well, that depends upon where you would teach. In the public schools I think that generally their salary scale would be the same as the others.

. . . .

(*Further discussion about salary and advancement in teaching.*)

COUNSELOR: Now how about the others . . . in an orchestra? What do you think of the competition there?

COUNSELEE: Think it'd be rougher . . . than a teaching job.

COUNSELOR: Feel like it'd be a little hard to get that sort of job?

COUNSELEE: Yes. I don't know if it'd be as hard . . . the work . . . the skill.

COUNSELOR: Uh huh.

COUNSELEE: Guess it would.

COUNSELOR: Well, depending upon the kind of job. . . . Routine carrying out of someone else's plans . . . that might not demand as much in skill and probably not give as much in pay. But if you were in charge, say, had the responsibility of planning something, it would probably demand higher skill. . . .

COUNSELEE: If I got in music I'd want to go all the way with it. I'd want to plan it and direct it.

Was this the sort of information that the counselee needed? Was it in enough detail? It would appear that the counselee might now be ready to go into more specific information about one of the areas.

In providing information directly, the counselor may find it helpful to bring the pamphlet or other printed material to the counseling session, lay it on the desk, and look it over with the counselee. He could point out passages of particular significance; he might add information about the local situation. Charts and graphs such as those in the *Occupational Outlook Handbook* may be helpful.

In any sort of information giving, the ultimate aim is to help the counselee use the information to make plans. To make some effective use of it, he needs to have it as well as his feelings about it in some organized form. He should not come from the session with a miscellaneous assortment of disconnected information; he should be helped to bring together the loose ends and to organize what has been covered. For example, in the following excerpt, the counselor is attempting to help the counselee see the relationships among various sorts of data and to bring the data together in an orderly pattern.

COUNSELEE: I think that would be something that would come in with learning of a vocation itself. You'd realize that you couldn't let things upset you.

COUNSELOR: But you feel like you do . . . sometimes get right annoyed with people?

COUNSELEE: Once in a while. It doesn't last. . . .

COUNSELOR: But they do things that sort of annoy you. . . . Something like that?

.   .   .   .

(*Further discussion of incidents in which counselee becomes annoyed at those who "pick on someone."*)

COUNSELOR: Had you ever thought. . . . Well, does this tell you anything about yourself, what kind of person you are?

COUNSELEE: I never had thought about it . . . as being important, I mean. I just felt that way about it, and I took it for granted. I never had put it in line with any vocation.

COUNSELOR: Well, just in general, without thinking about a vocation, what kind of a person would you say you are?

COUNSELEE (*laughs*): That's hard to say. . . . I don't like people to be left out. I like for everybody to be included.

We see that the counselee might recognize this personality aspect and relate it to occupational life. But this and other aspects should be drawn together so that the counselee will not be like the one who first said, "I don't like to study. I'd rather do anything than that!" and then a little later said, "I plan to work for a graduate degree after I complete college." There had apparently been no bringing together of all the varied data that had been discussed over a number of sessions.

Principles and illustrations apply to all types of information as well as occupational. In the following illustration, the counselor is discussing some of the problems of getting along with others. The counselee has expressed intolerance of the habits and attitudes of others. He has been reading a booklet that the counselor gave him after the first conference. This counselee earlier expressed a desire for help in learning to understand why he antagonizes others but has also shown strong defensive attitudes (as might be expected) toward material suggesting that he might be the cause of the difficulty. After some preliminary discussion, the counselee brought up a point from the booklet.

COUNSELEE: I was reading in that booklet. . . . It's interesting. I hadn't seen any of those before.

COUNSELOR: What did you think of it? Any particular points?

COUNSELEE: Well, not exactly. . . . Nothing that I didn't know. Everybody knows those things. I didn't see much . . . much about myself . . . about how I rub people the wrong way like that.

COUNSELOR: Doesn't apply to you, as you see it.

COUNSELEE: Sure, I know, er . . . that sometimes I dispute what other people say. But that's only when they're wrong. Somebody has got to correct them! This book, er . . . said a person who's liked . . . well, listens to the other person's opinion. Here, let me show you. (*Opens pamphlet and reads short paragraph.*) That's so much hogwash! Some people are so dumb!

COUNSELOR: Uh huh. . . . You feel very positive about how other people need this . . . this correcting. It's up to you to do it.

COUNSELEE: Yeah!

COUNSELOR (*long pause*): Let's look at this a moment. Just what did this booklet say? Let's look at that statement again.

This counselee was not ready to accept psychological information that provided some threat to him and the way he felt he should act. Thus he became quite defensive. The counselor suggested further reading in the booklet and made an appointment for a later conference to discuss counselee reactions.

John Doe's Need for Occupational Information

There have been a number of indications that John Doe needed occupational information; the following examples are typical and are suggestive of what the counselor should look for in deciding whether or not occupational information might be useful and what should be obtained.

1. From the interview.

JOHN: You know that guidance day, last month, when all the people spoke on different jobs? Well, I listened to all the speeches, and they all sounded good. When I heard Mr. Smith from the bank, I thought I liked that. Then I heard the fellow from the telephone company and I thought I liked that. It sounded like each one was trying to make his work sound best. Then I went to some of the interviews and talked to some of the college people. I found out that you have to go to college eight years to become a doctor! . . . Then I asked if there were some courses that took only four years. He—this fellow from State U—said that you could take a liberal arts course, whatever that is.

MR. DOYLE: You'd like it better if you were preparing for a specific job, with some definite thing you could do?

JOHN: Something definite. Now suppose I was going to be a carpenter like my father. Well, if I was a carpenter, I'd know what I'd do. . . .

2. From the cumulative record. In the spaces for educational and vocational plans the entries are as follows:

1948: college, doctor or lawyer
1949: college, doctor perhaps

3. From the test profile. Interest test scores which indicate high measured interest in persuasive and clerical activities, and above-average interest in computational activities. Also, low measured interest in scientific activities.

4. From the autobiography.

. . . I have never thought very seriously about plans for the future. I guess I thought things would just happen. Part of it, I think, is having other people make choices for me, like taking the college preparatory course. I never thought about going to college in a practical way. In fact, when I think about it now, I guess I thought it meant not having to make any definite plans for work for another four years, and having a good time.

The counselor obtained several pamphlets from the occupational file on department store work, office machine operator, general office work, saleswork, and several other occupations. He felt that it would be just as effective to hand the materials to John as to have him look for them. John took them home and read them before the next session.

SUMMARY

Occupational, educational, and other types of information are frequently needed in the counseling process to help the counselee make the sort of plans and decisions that he needs to make. Such information may be used in ways that may be identified as instructional, readjustive, motivational, exploratory, evaluative, and therapeutic. Principles which the counselor should keep in mind in using information are: first, the counselee wants the information; second, he needs it at the time it is used; third, the counselee has gained an understanding of himself; fourth, the counselee participates in obtaining the information and does as much organizing of it as possible; fifth, information is used or given which the counselee can understand; and sixth, the counselee is helped to relate information about occupations to information about himself. Also, using information should be a natural part of counseling, helping the counselee to bring out his feelings about it.

In the counseling process the counselor may help the counselee consult sources of information such as the occupational file, workers, or employers, or he may furnish most or all of the needed information in the counseling session. Whatever way the information is obtained, the counselor helps the counselee to understand it, accept it, relate it to himself, and use it to make plans and decisions.

CHECKS ON UNDERSTANDING

1. How can the counselor determine when information, such as occupational information, is needed?

2. What is the difference between using occupational information in an informational way as compared with a therapeutic way?

3. Why is it important that the counselee understand himself before he attempts to use occupational information? Would you say that it is only important that the counselor understand him rather than requiring that he have self-understanding?

4. How do you prepare a counselee to use an occupational file?

5. How does the counselor help the counselee relate information about an occupation to information about himself?

6. What is meant by saying that the counselee should be given or should use occupational information that he can understand?

THINGS TO DO

1. Interview a counselor or several counselors to discover whether or not they use occupational information, and if they do, how they determine when to use it and just how they use it with the counselee.

2. Listen to a recording of counseling (or observe a session in a one-way-vision room) in which some use is made of occupational information. Evaluate the effectiveness of the interview, or use cases in books, such as Callis [39].

3. By using a case study or some other material, identify a pupil's problem that calls for occupational information. Prepare a plan for helping him obtain the needed information.

4. Assume that you have decided to provide occupational information to a counselee who needs it. Obtain the materials (pamphlets and so on) and extract and organize the information for presentation in the counseling session.

5. Role-play the use of occupational information with a particular counselee. To do this you will need the sort of data about the counselee which may be obtained from a case study. Record the session and evaluate it.

6. If occupational or other information is to be used with an actual counselee, you should first know something about him. Thus it would be impractical actually to provide information or help the counselee obtain it unless you were counseling him. If you are counseling a pupil who needs occupational and other information, make plans for its use, record your techniques in using it, and play back the recordings for evaluation.

CHAPTER 11

Synthesis and Interpretation of Data

O NE ASPECT of counseling that needs more emphasis than it has yet received is the process of synthesis and interpretation of data; it is a crucial but often neglected part of the counseling process. What has been said about it is scattered throughout the book and the dynamic nature of the activity may have been missed; also, some additional points need to be made. Then too, as the discussion of counseling moves to that phase which emphasizes more planning and decision making, synthesis and interpretation become more crucial to progress.

The Nature of Synthesis and Interpretation

It has been emphasized a number of times in this book that the counselor is continuously synthesizing and interpreting data about the counselee, from the first contact of any kind with him, on to the conclusion of counseling. Much of this activity takes place when the counselee and counselor are actually working together. The counselor is doing this when he brings together the bits of data in the following example. The counselee says: "I don't like that teacher! She is too bossy!" Earlier the counselee had stated, "I've always been told what to do at home! I'm treated like a baby!" The counselor brings together or synthesizes these feelings *during the counseling session* at the time the last remark is made and responds to the counselee in a way determined by his quick mental interpretation. He may say, "You resent autocratic persons, as you've experienced this in your family." Or he may not actually respond to the statement in a way based on this synthesis, but instead mentally combine these comments and fit them together with what he already knows about the counselee to increase his understanding of him.

Of necessity, then, much of this synthesizing and interpreting actually take place as the counselee and counselor work together in the counseling process. Any sort of data may be used, including those obtained from other sources such as cumulative records and tests. For example, the counselor may be thinking of a low measured interest in clerical work (which he has not discussed with the counselee) and have to compare it with the counselee's comment, "I know I'd like to do office work, but I don't think I'd like to type or take shorthand. I don't know why I'd like it, but I know I would!" He knows further that the counselee is primarily interested in getting a job where she will have the opportunity to meet eligible men and find a husband. From these data, synthesized at this moment, the counselor is better able to understand the counselee and to help her clarify her goals.

No amount of note taking could get down all the data that are brought out by the counselee, but even if it were possible to do so, it would not be practical because the counselor must relate data rapidly and move along with the counselee, inferring meanings, noting gaps and inconsistencies, and checking his conclusions with the counselee.

As is apparent by now, synthesis and interpretation is not a "one-person" activity but a dynamic aspect of the ongoing counseling process. What the counselee says and does (facial expressions, movements, and silences are important too) and what the counselor says and does determine what comes next; the product of each participant is the result of his own synthesis and interpretation. It is possible, too, that both work jointly on synthesizing data and interpreting them; this, of course, is an important process in planning and decision making. One has only to listen to recorded counseling sessions or read verbatim typescripts to be aware of this.

Now where does this leave counselor study of data when he is alone, between counseling sessions? (Obviously the counselee is also thinking and organizing data after the session with the counselor.) This process has already been discussed in connection with specific sources of information, cumulative records, tests, and other techniques; it is also essential for combining data from all sources. Both the face-to-face and the between-session syntheses are part of one total process of understanding and helping the counselee; needless to say, the latter as well as the former goes on all through counseling.

For ease of explanation, the between-sessions synthesis is taken up separately. Separating the two types implies a difference between them that does not exist in practice; what is done in one merges with what is done in the other until there is no clear dividing line. For example, the counselor uses reactions in the face-to-face session as he reviews data after the session; he also submits interpretations that he has derived in the aftersession study to the counselee. As an illustration of one way of doing this, some counselors prefer to make hasty and brief running notes (partly written or sometimes completely written after the session), then jot down a brief summary of two or three lines, and finally note significant trends, insights, and progress of the session compared with previous sessions, based on a quick review.

Why does the counselor carry out the aftersession study of data? He is not making a diagnosis nor deciding upon treatment or decisions to recommend. Instead, he wishes to understand the whole person [168, p. 198; 224], and to understand him in relation to the conditions in which he lives or may live. White [260], in a brief but very helpful book on studying the individual, points out that ". . . there must be an attempt through the synthesis of data to see the child as a complete individual struggling toward certain goals, in a certain way, because of particular life circumstances" [260, p. 123]. The process employs the sorts of data used in the case study [58; 133, p. 101], although the purpose is different from that of the case study. The counselor wants to derive as much meaning as possible from the information he has obtained about the counselee, to aid the counselee in planning [192, p. 112] but not to give him a plan. All sorts of data are used, including data about the counselee's environment [168, pp. 147–149] and the way he sees himself and his environment [192, p. 112; 218, p. 210]. He wishes, further, to help the counselee foresee the consequences of possible courses of action. He cannot do all the synthesizing and interpreting needed while he is face to face with the counselee, as he may not be able to concentrate on varied details to the extent needed and he cannot have the objective and matter-of-fact attitude needed for this type of study [240, p. 86].

While this synthesis and interpretation process helps the counselor check his own thinking about the counselee and enables him to determine whether he has reached hasty and ill-founded conclusions, he should be careful not to use stereotyped or "pet" interpretations, nor should he place ready-made labels on the counselee [218, p. 229].

With these cautions and principles in mind, particularly that the between-session synthesis is only part of the total process, let us now turn to a step-by-step discussion of how a counselor might carry out this process, and then go over an illustration using data from the counseling case that runs through the book. The time-consuming appearance of the procedure is due to the fact that it is explained in detail for clarity; the counselor would do it quickly as a more or less automatic process or way of thinking about the counselee. Too, the process is presented here only as a guide to the beginning counselor for the same purposes as the "interview guide" in Chapter 3; as the counselor becomes more experienced, he would discard an aid of this sort and develop his own way of drawing the most meaning possible from information. The counselor should keep in mind, too, that while this explanation and illustration might suggest that synthesis and interpretation is a "one-shot" act, that is not the case; it is an ongoing process, continuing all through counseling.

Begin with Information about the Counselee. The counselor has various sorts of data about the counselee, such as initial impressions; information about activities, feelings, problems, goals; school achievement and other information from cumulative records; work history; and psychological test results. Data may be described as direct or indirect data or observations [168, pp. 153–155], for some can be obtained directly, such as what the counselee does while he is sitting in the chair across from the counselor, and some indirectly, such as what the counselee's autobiography tells about his home conditions and his parents' attitudes. Some of the data are more objective than others; more dependence may be put on the more objective type. Some, of course, provide meaning that is quite tentative. The counselor should rely more heavily on the more dependable data [224]; however, he does make some guesses based upon relatively unsubstantiated or rather tenuous data [78, p. 403].

The counselor is limited in interpretation not only by the sort of data that he has but also by just how much meaning he can draw from them. For example, school marks vary with different teachers and with different schools. This is a limitation of the data when the counselor is trying to infer the counselee's level of achievement compared with his own group and with other groups. However, unless the counselor has some idea of how school marks are related to success in college or success in certain occupations, he cannot obtain the most possible information from the data. For example, is achievement in mathematics related to success in electronics work?

Estimate Relevance; Compare, Evaluate, and Infer Meaning.* As the counselor looks over the data, he groups types which relate to the same point, for example, all data about school achievement, home situation, or getting along with others in and out of school. He may mentally group data or actually make notes about them in a rough form. At this time he may be questioning the pertinence and validity of each datum; he has to make a judgment as to whether or not he needs to include it in the synthesis. Does it tell him anything? Then he has to make a judgment about its accuracy. This will probably be a matter of determining its relative accuracy rather than an all-or-none judgment. For example, he may have an obviously biased anecdotal record that shows the teacher's dislike for the pupil, but he uses it because it gives a clue as to how *one* person reacted to the counselee.

In the synthesis and interpretation process, the counselor keeps in mind the fact that some data are significant for a particular counselee with a particular problem. For example, in looking over information about a counselee who appeared to be having great difficulty in planning what to do after high school, the counselor noted that both parents had attended college, that there were ample indications that the family was economically able to send the counselee to college, and that it was assumed that he would follow a technical course.

* These terms and the process have been adapted from "The Preliminary Appraisal in Vocational Counseling," a talk made at the American Personnel and Guidance Association meeting by Donald E. Super, reprinted in Veterans Administration *Information Bulletin* 7–118, Sept. 21, 1956 [224] (used by permission of the author).

There was also evidence that the counselee's interests were not very well formed, that he had no really definite concept of an occupational role, but that he felt a strong need to assert some independence from his family. He could assert himself by rejecting their plan for what he should take in college; then he could further demonstrate his independence by taking any other course just so it was quite different from his parents' preferences. The data about vocational interests were conflicting, and most of them ran counter to what the counselee indicated he was determined to do, that is, take the most nontechnical course he could find in college. Thus, data about the relationships in the home and family were of crucial importance for the counselee; the same data might be of much less significance with another counselee.

Sometimes it is difficult to detect which data are the most significant and which should be given the most weight in the interpretation, but the more careful the study of data (assuming that they are adequate) the better the chance the counselor has of weighing them properly.

In determining which data are more dependable, the counselor needs to use his understanding of personality development, measurement, and other areas that provide bases for evaluating them. As far as possible, research evidence should be available to support the meaning drawn from the data. For example, how much can the counselor count on the high school sophomore's interests remaining about the same through high school? Does overbearing behavior always cover some inner feeling of weakness or insecurity? Does inability to concentrate on lessons and excessive daydreaming indicate frustration? Evaluation of the validity of data would include evaluation of the efficiency of the particular technique for obtaining it as well as evaluation of the specific information that was obtained. To illustrate the point, it may be said that the counselor needs to have an understanding of the *type* of information that is obtained by the pupil autobiography as well as some idea of what a specific bit of content may mean. If the counselee blames others for all his difficulties, is this more likely to be projection of needs or objective reporting of the facts?

The process of inferring the meaning of data would go on as the counselor studied, evaluated, and sifted it, but it should be done as a conscious process. The counselor asks himself such questions as, "What do these comments about himself mean?" "What do school marks tell me about achievement?" "Does the fact that his parents express little appreciation for education have an effect on this achievement?" "What does the fact that both parents completed the fifth grade indicate to me about the counselee?" "Why does this girl spend most of her spare time in solitary activities?" The ever-present question in the counselor's mind as he reviews each bit of information is, "What does it *really* mean?" Some meanings will be much more obvious than others. In some cases, the meaning may be inferred with considerable confidence; in other cases, the counselor might as well admit that he can make only the most tentative kind of guess. But the job, while not an easy one, needs to be done before the counselor can move ahead in the process of understanding and helping the counselee.

Write Ideas Down. A technique that is often helpful in organizing data and obtaining meaning from them is for the counselor actually to write out his ideas about the counselee. The act of writing something down tends to force one to crystallize his thinking and to recognize fuzzy and half-formed ideas. It may often lead to new insights about the counselee and help the counselor to see new relationships, patterns, and trends. He may note down the basic data and the meaning that he draws from them on one sheet of paper, using abbreviations that retain for him the full meaning or substance of the data. These notes could be used in the process of organizing meaning or inferences, the next step in the process of synthesis and interpretation.

Synthesize and Reduce the Number of Inferences. Now the counselor is ready to begin to bring together the inferences or best meanings that he can derive from the data. These inferences are compared, some are changed or rejected, and a relatively smaller number emerge [224]. The counselor is not forgetting that the counselee is a whole person and that behavior is complex, nor is he breaking him up into isolated bits. He is, instead, looking for a consistent pattern of meanings, of assets and liabilities [264, p. 179]. It is not, however, an additive process [264, p. 178] in which items of information are summed, but rather one in which they are related to describe the unique dynamic pattern of the counselee.

As the counselor compares inferences, he finds that some are at odds with the preponderance of evidence; he may find it necessary to modify his interpretation of some of the information. For example, he may have inferred that the low level of education of parents and low socioeconomic level would result in low motivation for education in the counselee. When this interpretation is compared with conflicting data about high goals, parents' ambitious plans, and measured scientific interests, the counselor might discard his inference of low level of educational aspiration. For another illustration, the counselor may have judged, on the basis of school marks and teachers' ratings, that a counselee had adequate ability for successful college work. When he compares the counselee's poor performance on academic ability and achievement tests with those of college freshmen, he may revise this inference downward. If the counselor finds that the counselee spends an inordinate amount of time on preparation, that would be added evidence that he would have difficulty with college work.

The counselor relates to each other those inferences that bear on the same point, emerging with an inference or inferences about larger areas of the counselee's life. From these he hypothesizes or makes "best guesses" about the counselee.

Set Up Hypotheses. The counselor is now in a position to go about setting up tentative hypotheses about the kind of person the counselee is, what he is likely to do, what success he will achieve in various areas of endeavor, what he needs to do to solve his problem, or what the basic source of difficulty is. These hypotheses represent the counselor's understanding of the counselee, what he is like now, how he got that way, what he can do, and what he will do. The counselor may hypothesize that the counselee is a person of considerable mechanical ability and interest; one who would be "at home" in a shop, such as an auto repair shop; a person who wants to be at the level of work that he labels "engineer"; one who knows little or nothing about such engineering but who has picked up from family and friends the belief that "success" is based on whether or not you wear a "white collar" to work as opposed to wearing a blue collar and "carrying a lunch pail." The counselor may also hypothesize that the counselee will be extremely resistant to changing his concept of his work role, that he will actually enter an engineering school, and that he will soon find it uninteresting and much too difficult. The counselor may even go farther and say that when the counselee is unsuccessful he will be ready to discuss more practical or realistic possibilities.

As another illustration of hypothesizing, the counselor may see the counselee as an immature person who feels a strong need for the approval and support of others and who at the same time fights against this feeling; thus he is torn between a desire to be independent and self-sufficient and a need to be childish and immature. The counselor may feel that the counselee will demand support and approval and that it will be difficult for him to face the fact that he is immature and even more difficult for him to do anything about it. With each hypothesis the counselor has constructed a "person" and is making tentative statements about him that might begin, "He seems to be the sort of person who . . ." [127].

In order for the counselor to evaluate the accuracy of his hypotheses about the counselee, it is necessary that they be put in testable form. For example, if the counselor says, "John appears to be able to use inner resources to solve his problem," he cannot verify this hypothesis very well because he is not going to be able to determine whether or not John has used "inner resources" or solved all his problems. But if the counselor says, "If John joins that club he will drop out of it in a few weeks," he can test the hypothesis by checking to discover whether or not John dropped out of the club. The counselor could also state that if he helped John get ready for participation in the club and supported him in his attempts to make a go of it, the counselee would stay in it.

Besides setting up hypotheses about the counselee, the counselor also formulates them for the results of what he does to help the counselee. In fact, each statement the counselor makes or each activity that he engages in with the counselee is based on a hypothesis that it will have a certain effect. For example, the counselor decides that the counselee needs occupational information to help him make a more realistic vocational choice. The counselor is hypothesizing what the counselee needs and what it will help him to do.

Make Predictions. Several kinds of predictions are made in counseling. Each response that the counselor makes carries an implicit prediction that the counselee will react to it in a certain way; each choice of procedures or materials is made because the counselor predicts that it will have the desired effect on counselee behavior, both in and out of the counseling session. The specific types of prediction now considered, however, are those made about how the counselee will perform *outside* of counseling in various courses of action open to him, about his present and future behavior, what he is likely to do, and with what success he is likely to do it. These predictions are not absolute and final statements. The counselor does not say, "John will succeed in college," but rather, "It appears likely that John has the ability, drive, and maturity to be able to do successful college work." The counselor might also predict that if the counselee does enter college, he will stick at it until he graduates. With another counselee, the counselor might predict that, knowing what he knows about him, he will drop out of school as soon as he is sixteen years of age.

The counselor needs to be quite cautious in making predictions because he does not *know* what the counselee will do, nor does he have any method of computing precise probability statements about what he will do in most of the life situations in which he will engage. The counselor's predictions are of a *clinical* sort [78, ch. 18; 220, p. 533]. He makes this type of prediction, not because it is best, but because he does not have the data to make statistical ones; that is, he does not have tables that will allow him to combine all he knows about the counselee into a number or several numbers, do some computation, and then state in precise terms what the counselee may be expected to do. The counselor does, however, use as much of statistical prediction as is available to him, for example, that which may be derived from test data. While the counselor is dealing with a unique person and while he has brought data together to formulate a picture of the one individual about whom he will make predictive statements, he cannot and should not avoid considering statistics that provide data about individuals similar to the counselee (for example, test results and college success). It would be desirable for the counselor to have validity coefficients for each type of data that he has, such as data about the predictive efficiency of the autobiography. Such research data are just not available, however.

The issues of clinical versus statistical prediction are discussed in Refs. [127; 136; 137; 168, pp. 166–169; 193]. While this is a rather complex matter, the counselor should be familiar with problems involved in making predictions and recognize what assumptions he makes when he predicts counselee behavior.

A further illustration of the clinical type of prediction may be helpful. The counselor may say, "It is probable that the counselee will do poorly in the diversified occupations program and will drop out of it." He cannot be absolutely sure that he will, but he can put varying degrees of confidence into his statement. The degree of confidence is a judgment, not a statistical statement such as saying that the chances are 20 to 1 that he *will* pass (not can pass) and remain in the course. If the counselor had data on previous pupils in the diversified occupations program and could determine the frequency with which pupils similar to the counselee remained in the program, he could make a statistical prediction. But he usually does not have these data, and if he does, he will have additional data about the counselee to consider which are not included in the statistical computation. Then he has the problem of determining if all aspects of the situation (teacher, equipment, work opportunities, and so on) are the same as when the statistical data were obtained.

In making predictions it might be well to set up several statements as to what the counselee may do, under what conditions he may do each, and which one he is the most likely actually to do [168, p. 169]. For example, the counselor may say that the counselee will stay in the diversified occupations program, or that he will drop out of it, or that he will drop out of school, and give the conditions for each of these actions. These alternative predictions help the counselor to think in terms of the different sorts of action open to the counselee and also prepare him to discuss these different possibilities with the counselee.

As has already been pointed out, this total process seems unduly detailed and time consuming. As the counselor tries it out, he will find, however, that it is not as complex as it seems and that it becomes easier with each new counselee.

Synthesis and Interpretation by John Doe's Counselor

The counselor, Mr. Doyle, used a definite outline to aid him in his synthesis and interpretation. This is one way to learn to synthesize data, and the outline used is one kind that may serve as a guide in the learning process. The counselor has entered data in a rather abbreviated form, but adequate for his purposes. He often uses only words and phrases to remind him of a particular point, though he uses complete sentences where they are needed.

1. The problem
   (a) As counselee sees it: What he should take in college. Also seems to have some doubts as to whether he wants to go to college or would be able to do the work.
   (b) As counselor sees it: Confused about future, partly because of lack of planning, and partly because of conflict between him and parents as to future plans. For some reason, he just became seriously concerned about the future. Is doubtful about college as suitable training.
2. Home situation
   Father, carpenter; mother, housewife. One sibling, younger sister, better academic achiever. Mother active in community affairs, ambitious for son. Family lifelong residents of town, respected. Moderate means, some luxuries, own home. Mother rather overprotective, domineering. Some conflict about independence, use of car, etc. Financing college might be difficult. In general, seems to be a rather harmonious family. Parents' education limited. Father thinks high school enough. Mother in favor of college.

3. Personal characteristics, aptitudes, abilities, handicaps
Neat appearance, likable manner, no unusual mannerisms. Seems to be able to make a good impression in face-to-face situations, though somewhat shy at first. Some leadership qualities, and can influence others. Gets along well with peers. Physical condition seems to be good, athletic. Seems to like to be with other people more than alone. Goes out of his way to get others to like him. Somewhat dependent.

Test results indicate mental ability above average. Better clerical aptitude than technical. Aptitude for routine clerical work above average. Seems to have aptitude for persuading others, selling. Lack of interest in reading—reason? Studying a difficult task. Works hard at something he likes. Would rather be "on the go" than sedentary.

4. Achievements
(a) Social: Well liked. Sometimes a leader. Normal heterosexual adjustment. Adequate social skills in peer group. Seems to be liked by most teachers.
(b) Academic: Grades about average or below, except for history (this term). Seem to be improving slightly. Achievement tests below average, except for social studies. Weakest in scientific subjects. Taking academic course which he does not like. Has come close to failing several subjects.
(c) Vocational: Delivered papers, worked as clerk. Puts in about twenty hours a week working. Likes the responsibility of a job. Work at swimming pool.

5. Attitudes, values, interests
Likes others to think well of him. Cooperative. Sincere. Respects feelings of others. Appears to like responsibility. Serious about planning future. Ambitious, but thinks in terms of immediate rather than distant goals. Puts income as high as prestige of job, if not higher. Feels a need to become more independent, and to make his own decisions. Will probably take responsibility for making own plans. Seems to be interested in activities in which he deals with people in some sort of business capacity. Measured persuasive interest high, clerical fairly high. Scientific, literary, mechanical, low. Seems to have some persuasive ability.

6. Plans
Undecided about future. Talks about going to college and studying for a profession like medicine, but is not too enthusiastic about this. Vague on requirements, training, cost, whether or not he would like the work. Also, talks about own business, such as filling station, but feels parental disapproval (mother). Seems to like some aspects of retail selling, if there were possibility of getting advancement to managerial position. May be drafted in several years, and would prefer to join Navy where he would try to learn a trade. Whatever plans he makes, will probably have some conflict at home about them.

After making up this summary, the counselor put down several tentative conclusions about the counselee. These are as follows:

1. College—liberal arts
John could find a college suited to his level of academic ability, but poor achievement and study habits handicap him. Does not appear to be interested in this type of education, but wants training for specific vocation. Personality might be in favor. Financing might be a problem. Mother would approve—father might not. Measured and expressed interests not in line with this course of action. He might gain a great deal from the activities, associations, and some of the classes. Does not seem to be a suitable plan.

2. College—premedical and medical training
Academic aptitude, achievement in school subjects indicate that he would have difficulty. Lack of interest in scientific subjects, low measured interest in this area are unfavorable signs. Goal too far in the future to be appealing. Vague about requirements, training, nature of work, and has probably not been interested enough to try to obtain information about the work. Lack of interest in intensive studying. Finances would probably be serious problem. Liking for people and ability to get along with them might be helpful, but seems to prefer business or social relationships, rather than doctor-patient type. No hobby or avocational interest in medical or scientific area. Would not provide the opportunity for

him to capitalize on persuasive ability and interest. In general, does not seem to be a
suitable course of action.

3. Sales work—outside

Personality, measured and expressed interest, avocational interests all seem suitable for
this work. Mental ability adequate, and achievement would not be handicap. Additional
schooling would not be required. Could approach through company training program for
salesman, or by means of semiskilled or clerical job to learn product. Would satisfy desire
to be earning own way. Amount of income might vacillate, depending upon plan of re-
muneration, and this might not appeal to him. Parents would probably go along with
this although mother might not be satisfied. Could probably get some part-time experience before finishes school. Does not seem to mind hard work if interested, and could
probably meet frustrations of the job.

4. Sales work—inside

Has had some experience and apparently has done satisfactory work. Would satisfy desire to go to work soon. Would have chance for advancement. Likes to work with people,
gets along with them, and has some aptitude for routine clerical work. Mental ability
adequate for work and advancement in this area. Seems to make use of John's assets, that
is, good relationships with others, hard worker at absorbing task, energy, aptitude for
clerical work. Weak points would not handicap him in this area. Could probably continue
part-time job now, and work into full-time job after finishing school. Would have to work
out some agreement with mother. Probably satisfactory to father.

5. Office work—with business school training

Learning ability, special aptitudes adequate for mastery of subjects. Personality would
be asset. Makes good impression on others. Would offer a period of training beyond high
school that would probably satisfy mother. Financing might not be difficult at some nearby
school. Would meet desire for specific vocational training, and employment usually available. Qualities such as getting along with others, leadership, would help him to advance
to supervisory position. Might not like the idea of putting in more time in school, but
should find some of the subjects interesting. The type of work might satify mother's desire
for "prestige" job. By exercising some selection, could get a job that would have several
possible avenues of advancement such as to sales, administrative, supervisory, or publicity. Another year or so in school would give him a chance to mature a little more before
beginning full-time work. Training would be helpful in military service.

Evaluation of the Counselor's Synthesis. After going over this synthesis, do
you think that it adequately summarizes the information about John Doe? If
you were another counselor in the same school and were asked your opinion
about the counselor's tentative conclusions, what would you say? Did he build
up his interpretation by the process of inferring the meaning of data, hypothesizing about the counselee, and making predictive statements about him?

Note that this synthesis and interpretation could be largely a mental process
and not written out to this extent. Also, note that much of it was obviously
made while the counselor and counselee were together in the conference and
affected what the counselor did at that time; the counselor, to some extent, is
simply reviewing what he has already inferred.

The Case Conference. The case conference may help the counselor to
check on the soundness of his thinking about the counselee and to get new
ideas about him. In the typical case conference, those who know something
about the case may contribute new information, may help the counselor to see
old information in a new way, or may assist him in evaluating his interpretations. Each member of the group discusses the counselee as he understands
him from the data or knows him personally.

In the typical case conference, the counselor presents the data about the counselee. So that all participants can easily follow the discussion and have needed data available, it is a good idea to have copies of pertinent information for everyone or to put essential data on a blackboard. Either the counselor or the chairman of the group may call for the discussion of the case. Participants are encouraged to add data about the case, to make interpretations, and to suggest what may be done to help the counselee. In the informal sort of case conference that is usually held in the school, the counselor might first give his interpretation and ask others what they think of it. He then might indicate what he has tentatively planned to do and get the reaction of others to the plan. In a school where the counselor may be the only person who is able to obtain much meaning from data and the only one who has some knowledge of counseling, the conference may be primarily for gaining information and providing in-service education. Good "counseling" ideas from those who are not counselors should not be overlooked. The process of discussing data seems to facilitate the development of insights that the counselor had previously failed to develop. If the case conference is with other workers who are specialists in various sorts of help to the pupil, a more formal type of case conference would probably be used. Each member, including the teacher, would have a contribution to make from his professional point of view.

SUMMARY

The counselor is continuously synthesizing and interpreting data about the counselee both while talking to him and after the counseling session. What is done in the face-to-face situation calls for rapid mental activity on the part of the counselor; it actually determines the success of counseling. Some, of course, is done outside the session and after each session; for this type, a systematic plan may be used in learning how to go about it. Each counselor, however, with experience will develop his own procedure. The total process of synthesis and interpretation becomes more significant as planning and decision making become major activities.

CHECKS ON UNDERSTANDING

1. What is meant by synthesis and interpretation?
2. Why should a hypothesis about the counselee be subject to revision? Under what circumstances is it revised?
3. How would you define clinical prediction as compared with statistical prediction?
4. What might be the major points around which to organize a summary or synthesis?
5. Describe the synthesis and interpretation process that makes up an aspect of the face-to-face counseling session. Why is this called a *dynamic* process?
6. In what ways can you check or test a hypothesis about the individual? What is a testable hypothesis?

THINGS TO DO

1. Describe the process through which the counselor goes in synthesis, from the basic data to predictive statements.

2. Evaluate the counselor's synthesis and interpretation about John Doe with the following check list. Several of the answers may be suitable but there is one best answer. Select the one that you think is the best response to the question.

1. The counselor's statement of the problem and the counselee's statement are
   (a)_____Really the same
   (b)_____Only slightly different
   (c)_____Different in that the counselee is puzzled about what to take in college, and the counselor is sure he should not go to college
   (d)_____Different in that the counselee is puzzled by his confusion and lack of enthusiasm for what he had thought were his plans, and the counselor puts main emphasis on lack of careful planning and his rejection of his mother's plan

2. The counselor's notes on the home situation give one the impression of
   (a)_____An extremely unhappy and strife-ridden family
   (b)_____A home where the younger child is much more highly thought of than the older
   (c)_____An average home, where the adolescent is normally seeking more independence
   (d)_____An extremely autocratic home situation, where the parents are the law

3. The evidence that the counselor has for John's ability to get along with others is
   (a)_____Very slight
   (b)_____Based on his impression in the interview
   (c)_____Based on information from a number of sources and could be considered dependable
   (d)_____Conclusive beyond any doubt

4. By describing John as "somewhat dependent," Mr. Doyle probably means that he
   (a)_____Asks others to make all his decisions for him
   (b)_____Has to have the approval of others for everything that he does
   (c)_____Seems to feel some need to have others, who represent authority, tell him what to do
   (d)_____Cannot take the responsibility for his actions

5. The counselor has noted that John seems to be liked by most teachers. He is probably basing this opinion on
   (a)_____His observation of John around the school
   (b)_____His impressions of John in the interview
   (c)_____The comments of teachers in anecdotal records and entries in the cumulative record
   (d)_____The fact that John has not failed a school subject

6. When comparing grades and measured academic ability, the counselor might come to the conclusion that John
   (a)_____Should rank at the top of his class
   (b)_____Has been getting much better grades than one would expect
   (c)_____Has earned grades a little lower than one would expect
   (d)_____Has done as well as one would expect of a person of his academic ability

7. The counselor's general opinion of college training for John seems to be that he
   (a)_____Should at least try it
   (b)_____Could never succeed in any kind of college work
   (c)_____Could probably find a college in which he would compare favorably with the average student in ability but that other factors are against college training
   (d)_____Would not benefit at all from college

8. The counselor might well consider John's wanting to be a doctor as
   (a)_____A carefully thought out plan
   (b)_____His mother's idea
   (c)_____An interest in scientific work
   (d)_____A practical vocational goal
9. As for saleswork
   (a)_____There is no reason for even considering this a possibility
   (b)_____There is some evidence that it might be suitable, but much more that it would not.
   (c)_____There seem to be some fairly substantial reasons for considering this area
   (d)_____He should rule it out because of potential parental objections
10. John might be handicapped in any kind of office work because he
   (a)_____Might not actually be interested in it
   (b)_____Is too ambitious
   (c)_____Has a poor school achievement record
   (d)_____Has more aptitude for an entirely different type of work

The best responses are as follows: 1 (d), 2 (c), 3 (c), 4 (c), 5 (c), 6 (c), 7 (c), 8 (b), 9 (c), 10 (a).

3. Using data from a counseling case or case study, make a synthesis and interpretation. You may use data from an actual counseling case or from case studies in the references, including those in textbooks. Where planning and follow-up are included, do not use this information until after you have made your synthesis and interpretation.

4. Ask a counselor to "think aloud" as he synthesizes information. How does he go about it? Record the sessions and play back for further study.

5. Interview several counselors to learn, first, whether they make a synthesis of information, and second, how they go about it.

6. Prepare a synthesis for a counselee with whom you are working. If possible, get at least one or two other persons to review your work.

7. Sit in on a case conference in which a counselee is discussed (in school, community agency, or clinic).

8. Carry out a case conference by role playing. Use an actual case and have each member of the case conference group play the role of a member of the school staff or some other professional worker (if he is familiar with the worker's area).

9. Listen to a recorded counseling session to detect examples of counselor synthesis and interpretation.

The counselor should establish an atmosphere in which the counselee can talk freely. Before the interview begins, the counselor should put his other work to one side so that he can give his full attention to the counselee.

The counselor's duties are not limited to discussion of the counselee's problem. The beginning counselor should be concerned with improving his interviewing methods and may find it helpful to play back recordings of the counseling sessions. He must also obtain further information about the counselee from sources such as the cumulative record and the teacher, and from aids like the standardized test.

If the problem is a serious one, a visit to the counselee's home may bring needed information. The counselor can also discover a great deal about the counselee's relationships with other people by observing him in informal situations such as decorating for the school dance. With all this information the counselor should be better able to guide him toward a more realistic appraisal of himself and his goals.

After the counselee has narrowed his vocational choices to those which seem most compatible with his interests and abilities, he is ready to investigate the requirements for specific jobs. The counselor's file will provide him with facts about the necessary qualifications, descriptions of duties, and a general picture of opportunities in the areas under consideration. In addition, he can learn a great deal by interviewing people in various jobs which interest him.

CHAPTER 12

The Planning Phase

W<small>E HAVE NOW</small> moved along in our discussion of the counseling process to the point where we are ready to begin the phase which is primarily planning and decision making. The counselor has reviewed his data as discussed in the previous chapter, he has made plans, and he has put down some notes for the next session. There may be only one planning conference, or there may be a series of counseling sessions devoted primarily to planning and decision making.

The purpose of this chapter is to highlight what the counselor aims to do in the planning phase and how he may do it; it is thus only a brief introduction to the more detailed treatment of "how" in the next chapter. Some of the points covered have already been brought up and discussed in previous chapters; for these points this chapter is a review. At this time, however, a review and pulling together of many points scattered through the preceding chapters seems highly desirable. Some new principles and techniques are introduced; these are illustrated and discussed in more detail in the following chapter.

Nature of the Planning Phase

As has been pointed out several times, counseling is a continuous process and there is no break or abrupt change when information getting ends and planning begins. The planning phase is simply that part of the total process when use of information is emphasized more than the obtaining of it, and the major concern of both counselor and counselee is planning. Certain kinds of planning and decision making have been going on, to some extent, all through counseling. For example, the counselee has decided that he will continue to see the counselor.

The counselor does not now change his role of helper (as it may appear that he does) but provides the sort of help that the counselee needs at this stage. The counselee is ready for and wants a *different sort* of counselor help.

Accomplishments in the Planning Phase. It would seem advisable at this point to review just what should be accomplished in this phase of counseling, before taking up the specific techniques. The concept of adjustment discussed in Chapter 7 serves as the basis of these points.

1. The counselor helps the counselee to understand his capabilities and limitations. With his skill and experience the counselor is able to help the counselee estimate what he can do well and what he is weak in and thus make a reasonably accurate inventory of his potentialities.

2. The counselor helps him to understand subjective as well as factual and objective aspects of his environment. The counselee needs to understand both the factual and objective aspects of the school, factory, or office, and also what might be described as subjective aspects. For example, objective information might be the type of material worked with and the aptitudes needed to handle small metal parts in assembly work. Subjective aspects might be the kind of group the worker becomes a member of, and the attitudes they have toward work, toward supervisors, and toward unions.

3. The counselor helps the counselee recognize and develop potentialities and make the most effective use of them. It is important for the counselor to help the counselee recognize potentialities, decide on satisfying ways to develop and make use of them, and plan for a happy and productive life rather than merely help him remedy the mistakes he has made and replan bad decisions.

4. The counselor helps the counselee to understand the goals, needs, and attitudes that make up his concept of himself. The counselor falls short of helping the counselee understand himself if he deals only with the more objective aspects of his personality, such as school achievement or mental ability, without considering how the counselee feels about these things and what kind of a person he considers himself to be.

5. The counselor helps him to comprehend the roles he is playing and the roles he wants to play. The counselor does not stop with assistance to the counselee in determining what he thinks of himself and the way he sees himself, but helps him to bring out or develop the roles he wants to fill in various situations such as in work, recreation, community life, social groups, and so on. He is helped to crystallize the preferred roles in various situations and to estimate the practicality of these roles.

6. The counselor wants to help the counselee make good plans and decisions. Closely tied in with the objective of helping the counselee to make a realistic appraisal of himself is that of helping him to make decisions that are good in the sense that they are practical, satisfying, and will enable the counselee to make a contribution to society.

7. The counselor helps the counselee to learn problem-solving and adjustment skills and how to deal with new problems and developmental needs. In the counseling process the counselee does not learn a formula for handling all problems, difficulties, or situations requiring decisions that he may encounter in the future, but he does learn how to approach new problems, such as deciding whether or not to change jobs, analyzing the difficulties he is having with a situation or persons, or understanding the motives or needs that are influencing his behavior. This problem-solving approach transfers from what is done in the present counseling situation to future events. He is also helped to understand how he may make use of counseling services as part of his problem-solving technique in dealing with future situations.

8. The counselor helps the counselee obtain the kind of assistance he needs. Quite often the most important activity of the planning phase is to help the counselee learn about and avail himself of sources of specialized help which he needs but which he knows little about or which he finds difficult to accept. For example, he may need speech therapy, visual examination and treatment, psychotherapeutic help, or rehabilitation services.

9. The counselor helps the counselee to accept the responsibility for his plans, choices, and decisions. In the planning phase of counseling, the counselee is helped to make plans, decide on ways to put them into effect, and actually get started on carrying them out. The counselor also helps him to accept responsibility for plans and decisions and for evaluating appropriateness.

Techniques Used in Helping the Counselee Plan

The counselor needs to know *how* to help the counselee achieve the objectives of counseling as well as what the objectives are; this calls for techniques by which the counselor may assist the counselee accomplish what is considered to be desirable. The techniques for building rapport and promoting a desirable counseling relationship, which were discussed in chapters on information getting, apply in the planning phase. Ways of providing test results and other sorts of information, already described, are actually techniques to help the counselee plan. In addition, other techniques and procedures are used in this phase. These techniques, discussed in the following paragraphs, may be employed in any order and in any combination that the counselor feels desirable. Knowing what techniques are available is important, but judging when and how to use them is of much greater importance.

In the following paragraphs, specific techniques are grouped according to the sort of help provided to the counselee. For example, giving information includes neutral statements, reflection of feeling, some questioning, and so on.

Presenting Information. In order to help the counselee gain insight, make plans, or learn a needed skill, the counselor may provide him with information of one sort or another. It has been suggested that information be given in a

neutral way, whether it be results of a mental ability test, the entrance requirements of a college, or data about the needs of adolescents for asserting some
independence from home. The counselee can react to it in terms of his own
needs.

Often the counselee needs help in determining the meaning of information
that the counselor has presented or that he has obtained for himself. This
information may include descriptions of incidents, circumstances, and the like
that have been brought up in the counseling session. The counselor may do
several things to assist the counselee in comprehending meaning. By accepting
the counselee's reactions, he may provide the atmosphere in which the counselee can freely search for meaning. For example, the counselee may say, "It
sounds like that work requires more dealing with all kinds of people than I
like," or, "When I always argue with other people or take exception to what
they say, it may not always be because they're wrong." Because the counselee
is able to talk about these feelings and events, he may begin to grasp their real
significance and meaning for him.

Quite often the counselor may need to do more than simply provide a free,
nonthreatening setting for the counselee to talk about his feelings and behavior. The counselor may ask an interpretative question in a tentative form, for
example, "Could this mean that your parents are not always unreasonable?"
or, "Is it possible that you want to go to college because the others in your
group plan to go?" For these kinds of interpretations to be helpful, the counselee should be ready to accept them and resistance should be low [30, p. 164].
Otherwise the counselee may need to defend himself against them and may
distort what was said [30, p. 165]. Th counselor should be aware of how he
phrases these interpretative questions, his tone of voice, what he emphasizes,
and his facial expressions, because all these factors will have an effect on the
counselee [48, p. 88]. The counselor should avoid giving the impression that
he is making a final pronouncement about the counselee and forcing him to
accept it [48, p. 88].

If resistance is aroused, the counselor may have to turn to a topic about
which there is little resistance or even deal with the resistance itself. He may
guide the discussion from the sensitive area and then wait for an opportunity
to return to it again. Or he may deal with the resistance directly by questions,
reflection, or interpretation. He may say, "It's hard to look at your abilities
squarely," or, "Do you have the feeling that this is just the opposite of what
you think is right and it's hard to talk about it?" As resistance is lessened, the
counselor and counselee can continue the process of determining the meaning
and significance of information, events, and attitudes, including, of course, the
meaning of the resistance itself.

The counselor frequently needs to help the counselee see the relationship
between past experience and present attitudes [27, p. 109]. For example, the
counselee may feel that he cannot succeed in anything because of past failures.

A useful technique is "comparison interpretation" [48, p. 84]. The counselor may first describe the counselee's mechanical ability and then point out the requirements of an occupation that he is considering. He simply states the information and allows the counselee to decide what it means for him. He may be pointing out a "connection" that the counselee has not thought of, or he may be focusing attention on a comparison that the counselee does not want to recognize because it is unacceptable to his self-concept.

The counselor may have to do more than this to indicate the relationship among data, though it would usually be best if the counselee himself discovered it. Thus the counselor may phrase a tentative question about the connections among various data; he may suggest what the connection appears to be; or, if necessary, he may point out the relationship, for example, "You seem to get upset when you do something that puts you in competition with others and you get this same feeling when you take a test." This rather strong interpretation may not work well if the situation is emotionally charged and the connection is derogatory to the counselee. If, however, he has just not understood the connection before, it might be a useful procedure.

Questions may also be used to help the counselee see relationships among data. The counselor might ask, "Do you see anything about the sort of activities that you prefer, the things you've liked in school, and the scores on this interest test that indicate anything to you?" By a question, the counselor is attempting to make a pattern of preferences stand out so that the counselee will see them, perhaps for the first time.

The counselor may suggest relationships by more direct statements. For example, he might say, "It seems as though you feel resentment toward persons in authority. In these incidents we have discussed you seem to act as if you were singled out for blame. . . ." The counselor might then mention the specific incidents. It would seem best to help the counselee detect and describe the pattern, and next best to interpret it for him in a tentative way.

Presenting a Hypothesis. In Chapter 11 the counselor activity of setting up hypotheses about the counselee was discussed. One of the reasons for formulating hypotheses is to submit them to the counselee for his consideration, evaluation, and use. It would seem best to present the hypothesis to the counselee when he seems to be ready for it, when he feels a need for it, and when he probably would be inclined to discuss it. What the counselor has hypothesized should be stated in tentative form (even though he is sure that he is right) so that the counselee will feel free to evaluate it critically, accept it, or reject it. He should be able to reject the hypothesis without having to reject the counselor [171, pp. 109–110]. Suppose that the counselor has formulated a concept of the counselee as a girl with good mental ability, strong artistic interests, and other indications of promise in artistic work, who nevertheless does not have the motivation to work for a professional career but rather looks forward to being a homemaker in several years. The counselor feels that she would not do the required amount of work to achieve success in the artistic field. He might then present this hypothesis in a planning session, "You appear to have more interest in looking forward to married life and a home than a career in art." The counselor might, of course, go into more detail, but the hypothesis should be clearly and simply stated so that the counselee will be able to follow him and to respond directly to the main idea.

The counselee is helped to react to and evaluate the hypothesis. He may reject it because it is actually out of line with his thinking, because he does not want to admit that it is accurate even if it is, or because he may have an unrealistic concept of the sort of person he is. In accepting it, he may add to it or modify it. He may use it as a steppingstone to further self-understanding and planning. His response provides the counselor with clues as to desirable next steps in counseling. For example, the counselee may need help to revise an unrealistic self-concept. It would seem ideal for the counselee to formulate his own hypotheses and bring them up for consideration in the counseling session. He may sometimes do this, but often he will not. Providing information, such as that about high school achievement, academic ability, and college requirements, may help him do it. The counselee may raise a question in this way: "I wonder if I would be satisfied to make a lot of money in business," or, "I can pass if I try," or, "I seem to have a preference for doing things in which I work with people who need help."

When the counselee formulates and brings out a hypothesis, the counselor accepts it and approves the counselee's effort but not the merits of the specific hypothesis. For example, if the counselee says, "I think that, all things considered, I would prefer to go to a small college where I would feel more at home, get to know more people, and get used to being away from home," the counselor might say, "You've come out with an idea that shows you're doing some thinking about yourself and what to do." He would then help the counselee evaluate the merits of this hypothesis. He might say, "Would doing this also give you the opportunity to take the kind of courses that you've decided you need?" Further discussion would be aimed at helping the counselee weigh all implications of the hypothesis.

Helping the Counselee to Plan. As the counselee moves toward deciding what he wants to do, what steps he will take to solve his problem, or how he can make the best use of his potentialities, the counselor helps him to look ahead and foresee what might happen as a result of possible courses of action. This help should come before he makes a definite choice among alternatives. It is a process of making tentative predictions. Either the counselor or counselee may do this, but it would be desirable for the counselee to participate as much as possible.

As a first step in predicting outcomes, the counselor might ask the counselee what he thinks the outcome will be. If, for example, the counselee has, among several alternatives, one of attending business school, the counselor might ask,

"How do you think you will do in those courses? Would you like the things you take up? Would you like the work?"

The counselor may bring in his own predictions in a tentative way, referring to specific data on which they are based. Thus he may say, "There appears to be a likelihood that you would find the work of the industrial arts teacher suitable, based on your interests, your ability to get the necessary training. . . ." He may be bringing up a possibility that the counselee has not thought of or he may be putting into words what has been clearly implied in the counselee's comments. When the counselee makes predictions that appear to be quite improbable, the counselor may challenge his conclusions [62, p. 16] to enable him to revise his estimation of outcomes.

How may the counselor help the counselee actually choose a course of action? It would seem that, first of all, the counselor should be accepting and permissive, show keen and sincere interest in what the counselee is trying to do, recognize that it is difficult, and be ready to provide the sort of help the counselee needs. The counselee may tend to make a decision too soon or he may find it quite difficult to face the fact that he has to decide something. He may decide, reconsider, change his mind, and this process may go on over a period of time.

If the counselee appears to be thinking about and carefully weighing various possibilities, the planning may go along rather easily without the counselor having to do much other than provide the setting in which the counselee can critically evaluate and accept or reject possibilities. The counselee may, of course, need support and reassurance in making up his mind. If he appears to be reluctant to make any kind of decision, the counselor may need to help him search for the causes of the difficulty. Decision making is a process that cannot and should not be hurried, but when there appear to be blocks to the counselee deciding anything, the counselor may need to look for unexplored attitudes or unresolved conflicts that prevent productive planning.

Does the counselee have the right to make obviously poor decisions and impractical plans? It seems important that he should be able to make his own decisions, even if they are poor ones. But it would appear that the counselor has not fully done his job unless he has used all his resources to help the counselee realize what is likely to happen should he follow a plan or a course of action that appears to be unsuitable. It would appear, too, that the counselor could justifiably use pretty strong suggestions to get the counselee to evaluate his choice more carefully and to be fully aware of its disadvantages.

The counselor may also use suggestions to help the counselee become aware of and undertake steps that should help him arrive at a plan or decision. For example, he may suggest that the counselee talk to a worker or workers who are on jobs which the counselee is considering [27, p. 107]. It would also appear helpful to reassure the counselee if he appears to be very unsure of himself or timid about trying something new. The counselor might say, "You seem to be able to do that as well as others, and might even do better than average."

The counselor may help the counselee in carrying out plans, either directly or indirectly. In the direct way, the counselor actually does something *for* or *with* the counselee to help him carry out plans, such as writing to a college for information, making out a job application and selecting places to send it, or contacting a club that he wants to join. In general, it would be better if the counselee did these things for himself. If he appears to need a great deal of support, however, the counselor may find it advisable to help him directly.

Indirect help, which is more in keeping with the process of counseling, is the sort which puts the responsibility for carrying out plans on the counselee. For example, the counselor may give the counselee needed information which he then uses to locate placement agencies; he may help him rehearse the job application interview or practice what to do when called on in class. The active steps which the counselee will take are planned in the counseling session, with the counselor only offering what help is needed. He may make suggestions or offer advice or reassurance to the degree needed to help the counselee do something he has decided to do and wants to do [27, pp. 107–108].

After the counselee has put plans or decisions into effect, he needs to evaluate their suitability. The way is left open for him to return for one or more conferences for this purpose. He may or may not take advantage of the opportunity; the decision to do so or not is his. If he does not come in the counselor may decide to contact him to find out how plans are working out and to indicate that further help is available. This offer may provide needed stimulation for him to return to evaluate plans. Quite often the counselee has done some additional thinking between the final counseling meeting and the evaluative session, and may be ready to do a much better quality of planning. He may bring out ideas that have not been mentioned before and that are a sort of "delayed reaction" to counseling.

Helping the Counselee Obtain Additional Information. As the planning phase of counseling progresses, the counselor may find quite often that additional information is needed, for example, occupational requirements, college entrance requirements, or information about the counselee and his environment. The counselor may obtain it or may help the counselee obtain it in ways already discussed. It may be helpful to give the counselee an assignment of something specific that he will do prior to the next meeting. Information may be from some sort of tryout experience or other activity that will take some time. It should not be felt that because counseling has moved well into planning, new information may not be obtained.

Helping the Counselee Accept Referral. It may be apparent, as the counseling process moves along, that referral for specialized help is needed. In many cases it might be possible at the first contact to judge that the counselee needs this kind of help. If this were the case, the counselor would make the referral then. Quite often, however, he is not in a position to make a definite judgment about the need for referral until he has obtained a fairly substantial amount of data about the counselee. He then can better estimate whether his help will be limited by some condition that he does not have the skill or training to handle.

To make use of specialized help, the counselor needs to be aware of the available resources to which the counselee may be referred and to know just what sorts of services these agencies, institutions, and specialists provide. He then must be able to help the counselee see the value of the referral.

The counselor might wait to bring up the matter of referral at a time when the counselee appeared to feel quite keenly the need for the type of help provided by the specialized source. For example, the counselee becomes aware that the difficulty, physical, emotional, economic, or otherwise, is an obstacle to progress in counseling; he may voice this awareness or it may be inferred by the counselor. The counselor may then bring up the matter of referral by saying, for example, "I believe that that's something that requires some special help. Would you be interested in checking up on that by talking to someone who is a specialist at helping people clear up those kinds of problems?" The counselor moves slowly in the discussion, maintaining a permissive manner and allowing the counselee to react to each new idea. Threatening labels are avoided and what is said is phrased in language that is familiar to the counselee.

When referral for emotional problems comes up, some counselees feel so threatened and anxious that they will break off counseling. It would appear appropriate for the counselor to provide as much support and reassurance as needed to help the counselee actually go through with the referral, including making an appointment and otherwise assisting the counselee to get to the referral resource. In the counseling framework, these helps would be given when the counselee gave indications that he wanted and needed them. It would appear unwise to attempt to force referral upon a counselee.

When the referral is for the purpose of obtaining information, for example, information about an occupation, the counselor may not have to deal with emotional reactions, such as resistance. Instead, he may have to motivate the counselee to follow through and get the needed information.

It should be pointed out that the counselor needs to know the policies of the school or institution in which he is working and make referrals in keeping with these policies. The counselor will need to have some plan worked out for those rare cases where he decides some sort of referral or special help is needed for the safety of the counselee or society.

Helping the Counselee See the Need for More Counseling. The counselee may need help, but for one reason or another he may terminate counseling. What does the counselor do when this happens?

Failure to return for counseling may result from resistance or other adverse emotional reactions to counseling and the counselor, from a general lack of interest and low level of motivation, or from finding a solution to the problem outside of counseling. The counselor could be at fault. He may be using the wrong techniques or he may have failed to establish a good counseling relationship. More probably the counselee is at fault, however.

To help the counselee continue, the counselor might bring out, or help the counselee to bring out, that problems were still unsolved or that the solutions arrived at might not be what seem to be needed. The counselor might also give the counselee some specific activities to carry out if he felt that active participation in counseling would help him to become more interested and continue. In some cases he might attempt to make the counselee uncomfortable enough so that he would want to return, for example, by pointing out problems of which he did not appear to be aware. However, very little would usually be gained by attempting to persuade or force the counselee to stay in counseling if less directive techniques did not help.

SUMMARY

The planning or decision-making phase of counseling represents an emphasis in the total process instead of a sharply defined stage. Some planning and decision making is always done early in counseling. Certain new techniques, in addition to the ones employed in the information-getting phase, are of particular value in the planning phase. The use of these techniques does not, however, change the counselor's role; they enable him to emphasize that aspect of his helping role which the counselee needs. These specific techniques assist the counselee to obtain needed information; determine meaning of information; see relationships, patterns, and trends; arrive at tentative conclusions and plans; and foresee the probable outcome of plans. Planning is not a systematic step-by-step process but one in which various techniques are used in any sequence and combination, and in which there may be backing up and moving forward slowly and tentatively.

CHECKS ON UNDERSTANDING

1. What would be the dangers of using suggestion and persuasion in the planning phase of counseling?

2. How can the counselor judge when the counselee is ready to move into planning and decision making?

3. Does the counselor take over responsibility for what is done in counseling when planning is taking place? If not, what is his role?

4. What, specifically, is the counselor trying to do in the planning phase?

5. What are specific techniques which the counselor may use to help the counselee plan and follow through in carrying out plans?

6. What pattern or sequence of techniques might be used in the planning phase?

7. What is the purpose in the planning phase of techniques and attitudes such as acceptance, providing a permissive atmosphere, and responding to central meaning and feeling?

8. What does the counselor do with the results of his synthesis to help the counselee plan?

THINGS TO DO

1. Listen to a recording of the latter part of a counseling case and note methods that the counselor used to help the counselee plan. Evaluate the suitability of the techniques and how they helped (or hindered) the counselee's planning.

2. Read a verbatim typescript of a counseling case [39], and identify and describe techniques the counselor used to facilitate planning. How successful were they?

3. Interview a counselor to learn what he considers to be effective ways to help the counselee plan, make choices and decisions, and evaluate his decisions.

4. Use role playing to practice some of the techniques of the planning phase. Record the practice and play it back for discussion.

5. Using data from an actual counseling case or from cases in books or other sources [39], prepare a tentative plan for what you will do in the planning phase. (If you are working with an actual counselee, use the data that you have collected.)

6. Prepare a check list to serve as a guide for carrying out and evaluating the planning phase.

CHAPTER 13

Objectives and Techniques
of the Planning Phase

I N CHAPTER 12 objectives and techniques of the planning
phase of counseling were discussed briefly. In this
chapter, some of the techniques will be illustrated and discussed further. Also,
some suggestions will be made as to possible patterns and sequences of techniques in helping the counselee plan.

With this chapter, the discussion of the counseling process is concluded.
The following and final chapter presents some suggestions for the evaluation
and improvement of counseling.

The Planning Phase and the Counseling Process

The discussion of the planning phase up to now may have left the counselor with the feeling that it is a complex process that cannot be described or
"pinned down" to a degree that will help him begin to work with a counselee.
To some degree, however, the planning phase has already been located in the
total counseling process. It is possible and desirable to show what might be a
method of working through the planning phase itself, keeping in mind that
the method should be flexible rather than fixed, and that what is done is based
on the counselee and his needs.

The counselor may be better prepared to provide effective help if he has in
mind some general guide or procedure to use when working with a counselee
in the planning phase. Such a procedure should be rather simple in its basic
elements. With such a guide in mind, the counselor will have "something to
do" when he is face to face with the counselee and can use techniques more

274

systematically and purposefully. If, instead, the counselor has only vague ideas about what he considers the counseling process to be, is not quite sure where he is going or how to get there, he quite likely will have difficulty in providing much help to the counselee. Thus it is possible, without doing violence to a concept of counseling based on counselee needs, to describe a general procedure for the planning phase in terms of what the counselor is trying to help the counselee do and the techniques that are designed to help him do it. First, however, the total counseling process will be reviewed briefly to show again just how the counselor leads up to the planning phase.

In the early stages of counseling, the counselor has been collecting information during conferences with the counselee and from other sources. He has established a relationship with the counselee and has helped him to bring out factual data and feelings and possibly gain some insight and make some progress by talking about himself and his problems. The counselee has decided that the counselor can help him, and the counselor had decided that he can be of assistance to the counselee. Very likely the counselee has been given some information, for example, test results (if he took the test during the counseling process), or perhaps some occupational or educational information. So far, this information giving has been more or less incidental to the major emphasis of gaining all sorts of information about the counselee and the setting in which he lives. It is important to keep in mind that both counselor and counselee are accumulating data for use in the later stages of counseling.

At about this point, the emphasis in the counseling process shifts from information getting to planning. The counselor maintains about the same sort of relationship and he uses many of the same techniques and procedures that he used in the earlier stages. In addition, he employs some different techniques that are designed to help the counselee make plans and decisions, to follow through on a plan, and to evaluate its effectiveness. He may appear to be taking a different role in the counseling process, but in fact he is not; rather he is doing what his role of helper requires that he do.

In this more active helping role the counselor has some idea of what he wants to help the counselee do, for example, to select a suitable college course, to make an occupational choice, to learn to study effectively, or to feel at ease in social situations with others. This goal, which is based on counselee needs, serves to give definite purpose and direction to the helping process. Then the counselor needs to plan how he will help the counselee reach the desired goal. His plans are flexible, but he goes to the conference with something to do to help the counselee. He may change, modify, or drop his plans if it appears that the counselee wants something else or is ready to do something else. For example, the counselor may have planned to talk about the gap between achievement and ability but then may discard this plan when the counselee appears to be more concerned about a conflict with parents over the choice of a college.

The counselor has a number of techniques that he can use to help the counselee reach his goal or to assist in carrying out the counselor-help plan. The use of a technique is based on what it contributes to the counseling process rather than on some logical sequence or preplanned pattern. However, it might be expected that, in the usual planning phase, the counselor would use techniques in somewhat the following way: giving information; discussing the meaning of information; helping the counselee react to and accept information; developing the patterns, trends, and relationships in information; and helping the counselee react to and accept these larger groups of data about himself and about situations which he is now in or which he may enter. As the counselee begins to understand himself better and to accumulate needed environmental data, the counselor may help him formulate general statements or hypotheses about himself, for example, what he can do best, what role or roles he would like to carry out in work, or what the bases are of his difficulty in getting along with others. The counselor has formulated hypotheses about the counselee which he may bring out for joint consideration by himself and the counselee. Hypotheses are tentative and may be modified if new data are brought out.

Now the counselor and counselee have a fairly complete picture of a person and how this person might behave in various situations, for example, as a student in engineering school. The counselee is ready to move into thinking about what he might do and what will be the results of his doing it. The counselor helps formulate predictive statements or provides some tentative predictions himself as to what probably would happen if various alternatives are followed. While the counselee may be supported or approved in his effort to plan, he is responsible for actually making the plans. Other alternatives may be suggested by the counselor if they are ones that the counselee should consider. The counselee is helped to make a decision or a choice among alternatives, but he makes it himself and takes the responsibility for it. He is given whatever help he *needs* to follow through on something he has decided to do.

There should then be an evaluation after the counselee has actually tried out what he decided to do. Whether or not there is an evaluative session is up to the counselee. Also, if further help is needed, it is the counselee who decides whether or not it will be accepted.

Reviewing Progress and Planning for the Next Conference

As counseling is a continuous and systematic learning situation, the counselor needs to take stock as to just where he and the counselee are and what next steps should be taken. Taking inventory of progress and planning for future steps give continuity and direction to counseling.

Reviewing Progress. Between conferences, particularly those of the planning stage, the counselor takes a look at where he and the counselee have come from, how far along in the process they have gone, where they appear to be going, and where they ought to go. This brief review may be done mentally or may be put in writing. The counselor attempts to identify which factors have promoted progress and which ones have been responsible for lack of it. For example, the counselor may feel that they are not working on the real problem, that he has been using the wrong techniques or using techniques in the wrong way, that resistance has been aroused, or that the counselee is poorly motivated to do anything. He then has a basis for deciding whether or not to continue along the same lines or to make some changes.

This stock taking is one form of evaluation of counseling which is discussed in more detail in the next chapter. It is extremely important in improving counseling and specifically in improving the quality of help to the particular counselee with whom the counselor is working.

Planning for the Next Conference. Counselor activities such as synthesis and stock taking provide help in planning for the next counseling conference. Counseling usually consists of several conferences, although it may consist of only one session. On the basis of what the counselee appears to need, the counselor makes some specific plans for the next meeting. He may prepare a summary of important data in convenient shorthand on a card or sheet of paper. He may carefully review data, particularly the synthesis. He may also have some particular question that he plans to ask, some needed information to give, several hypotheses to present to the counselee, or some activities to suggest. It would appear to be a good idea for the counselor to have plans written down on a sheet of paper which he would have before him in the conference. He would also have a reminder of things that the counselee was supposed to do for this conference. A few lines might be all that the counselor would need to write to remind him of plans for the conference.

Part of the plan would be the tentative selection of a starting point and a general approach for the conference. With these points in mind, the counselor is ready to begin the session and has some idea of what may be accomplished during the conference. It is essential, however, that the counselee have the opportunity to decide on the starting point, direction, and content of the session. Thus the counselor begins in a permissive way and helps the counselee bring out what is on his mind. This may mean scrapping the counselor's "plan." Often the most significant counselee thinking has gone on since the last session and thus the counselee himself may provide the most useful starting point for the conference and leads as to what should be taken up. It may be that the counselor and counselee should discard a plan that they had made jointly. For example, a counselee had taken several tests and he and the counselor had planned to discuss results in the next session. The counselor began the discussion of test results as planned; almost by accident he asked the counselee if he had had any ideas since the last meeting. The counselee immediately said that he had made a vocational choice. He had, in fact, decided on a vocation that had not been previously discussed. Several years later he was doing outstanding work in this vocation. The test results were never discussed. This is, of course, just one example, but it emphasizes the importance of what the counselee has been doing or thinking between sessions.

Examples of Planning

The following examples illustrate, with varying degrees of effectiveness, the use of techniques to assist the counselee in planning. Other counseling techniques, such as those used during the information-getting phase, are also shown. It would also be helpful to read and evaluate other examples of the planning phase of counseling.

In the following example, the counselor is attempting to help the counselee see the relationships among various data, to understand what he wants to get out of an occupation, and to begin to formulate an occupational role. The counselor appears to feel that the counselee has not fully thought through his basic values about work. Notice that the counselor uses tentative interpretations in many of his responses and also confronts the counselee with questions that deal with the relationships among various data. Note, too, that some tentative and partial hypotheses are advanced by both counselee and counselor and some predictive statements are made. We also find in this excerpt indications of counselee thinking between sessions.

COUNSELOR: What would be your ambitions in that sort of work?

COUNSELEE: You mean what I plan on doing and everything?

COUNSELOR: Yeah, I mean what would you hope to work up to, or be after you'd worked in it some years?

COUNSELEE: Well, er . . . after I'd done that I guess I'd like to get a bigger school or something like that. . . . I haven't thought much about that.

COUNSELOR: What would be your idea of success? The highest success you could achieve in educational work?

COUNSELEE: Well, er . . . helping others.

COUNSELOR: Could it be helping others in a very small situation? Or if you were doing a good job there, would you feel that you were successful, even though maybe . . . ?

COUNSELEE: Yes.

COUNSELOR: . . . Even though you didn't get in a large school, say?

COUNSELEE: . . . Yes.

COUNSELOR: I wonder if you would aspire to be in a large school that would pay more. . . .

COUNSELEE: No, I don't think that would matter.

COUNSELOR: How do you account for the fact that the income business is not nearly as important, or important at all, as it was when we talked before?

COUNSELEE: Well, er . . . I've changed a lot of ideas . . . since I last saw you,

since I thought about it, and er . . . it isn't as important to me now. . . . I
mean, I've just changed.

COUNSELOR: You . . . you mean you've changed your goals and things. . . .

COUNSELEE: Yeah. . . . Yeah.

COUNSELOR: . . . And some things that were important are just not important
now. . . .

COUNSELEE: Yeah. . . . That's right.

COUNSELOR: . . . And so you're going to investigate at college day the kinds of
colleges that you can go to?

Evaluate the counselor's use of techniques in this excerpt. Did he actually
help the counselee clarify his occupational goals? Do the questions appear to
be in keeping with what the counselee is saying? Note too the use of simple
acceptance and reflection along with questions. Would the counselor's question about future satisfaction appear to be an effort to help the counselee make
a predictive statement?

In the next excerpt, the counselor reflects what the counselee is saying but
goes beyond this technique and uses interpretation in an attempt to help the
counselee understand her concept of the way she thinks people make an
occupational choice. He feels that she is not utilizing important data, such as
interests and hobbies, and does not see relationships among various data that
should serve as a basis for making a choice. At this stage the counselee is probably not ready to formulate or consider statements about the kind of person
she is, what directions she may take, or the probable outcomes of the plans.

COUNSELOR: Have you ever thought about how you could use these interests in a
lifework or an occupation?

COUNSELEE: I don't know. I always just thought about picking out a career and
working toward it, more than actually basing it on feelings or interest.

COUNSELOR: You'd thought . . . thought maybe you'd have a sort of a sudden
glimpse of the "occupation for me," and then it'd all be settled?

COUNSELEE: I expect that's why I've never gotten any farther with it than I have
(laughs).

COUNSELOR: You feel that a person . . . that there is just one . . . occupation
for you, and it's up to you to find that right one? Or that you could probably do
a number of different things—it's just a matter of selecting . . . ?

COUNSELEE: I think it's a matter of selecting. I don't think you could ever right
away find one that you'd want to do. . . . You might get into one and you
might realize that you might like a certain thing just a little bit better and
you might develop it into what you wanted. . . . I don't think that you can
just pick one out of the sky . . . and start working right on it.

COUNSELOR: Sometimes people feel like there is for them *one* special thing. If they
can't find that, they want somebody to tell them.

What do you think of the counselor's use of interpretation in this excerpt?
Would you say that he put more into his interpretation than may be drawn

from the counselee's remarks? Does the counselee appear to be ready for the interpretations?

Referral has been mentioned as a technique that may be used in the planning and decision-making stage of counseling. It may come quite early in counseling, however, or just as soon as the counselor feels that the help of a specialist is needed. In the following excerpt the counselor is making an effort to refer a counselee for specialized help on an emotional problem. It has appeared that the counselee is having difficulty in making a good adjustment in school because of emotional problems of more complexity and severity than those with which the counselor has the training and skill to deal. Up to this point the counselor and counselee have been discussing how various symptoms interfere with doing satisfactory work.

COUNSELOR: Now maybe some of these things . . . maybe you could get some help, uh . . . to . . . well, get some of these things settled—these things that are bothering you.

COUNSELEE: They bother me . . . I could do better (tensely).

COUNSELOR: You'd be able to see things . . . apply yourself . . . if you didn't have these feelings. . . .

COUNSELEE: If I could just get that settled. I found out how I compare with those [other students] and I know how much I can do. . . . But sometimes I think I'll do something. . . . I've thought about it . . . something rash. . . .

COUNSELOR: Do something like . . .

COUNSELEE: Yeah, do that. . . . I get so . . . I feel like I could . . . well, just end it.

COUNSELOR: You feel that it's pretty bad, and you'd do most anything . . . to . . .

COUNSELEE: Yeah, . . . but I don't know any answer.

COUNSELOR: . . . And if someone . . . if we could find someone to help you . . . help you work these things out . . . could help you to . . . well, feel better, how would you feel about that?

COUNSELEE: Someone? . . . Who? . . . Uh. . . .

COUNSELOR: Well, I know . . . there are several people who help with just the sorts of things that are bothering you. I can give . . . help you find one.

COUNSELEE: Uhmmm. . . . I don't know. . . .

COUNSELOR: . . . One person in particular . . . I thought of. . . .

COUNSELEE: Do you mean a psychiatrist! Is that . . . what you mean? You think I'm . . . I'm off (laughs) . . . need that?

COUNSELOR: No, . . . I don't mean that. . . . But you have these difficulties. . . . Just like when you have a broken arm, you want a special person, a physician to fix it. Well, now, problems are sort of like that. . . .

COUNSELEE: I'm not crazy . . . nothing wrong with me that way (laughs). They told me that once. . . . I went to see this man. He asked me some silly questions.

COUNSELOR: Well, . . . it's a case of what you want. If you don't want to do something like this . . . if you don't feel the need, er . . . it won't help.

COUNSELEE: Well. . . . (Long pause while counselee toys with a pencil.)

COUNSELOR: Well, it's up to you. I can help you get to this person, . . . if you'd like to just go and talk a little. . . . Maybe you could get some of the things settled in your thinking, then we could get back to the matter of these courses and what to take. . . .

COUNSELEE: I don't know. . . . You think . . . you think . . . this would help?

COUNSELOR: It may. . . . It's helped others with the same sort of questions you have. It's just sort of a special help people need sometimes . . . just like . . .

COUNSELEE: Well, it can't hurt . . . much. . . . I suppose . . . I can stop if I want. . . . I don't think I need that. . . . It sounds . . .

COUNSELOR: . . . Sounds sort of like you're . . . you're bad off . . . ? But it doesn't mean that. . . . Well, here's a fellow who knows about these things . . . and . . .

COUNSELEE: People think about you, "He's going for that!"

COUNSELOR: You feel that people will think that, . . . and yet here's something that you might get a lot from. You have to decide . . . weigh these things. . . .

COUNSELEE: I don't . . . I might try that. If you think it'd help. . . . Would I see you then . . . I mean, at the same time?

The counselor is introducing the matter of the counselee getting relief from an emotional problem that is making it impossible to proceed with vocational and educational planning. He does not come right out and tell the counselee that he needs the help of a therapist but suggests that this sort of assistance is available and that it would seem to be helpful to the counselee. The counselee is somewhat appalled at the idea although he undoubtedly feels that he needs this sort of help. He shows various sorts of resistance, for example, denying that he needs therapy, laughing, or toying with objects on the desk. This brief excerpt does not show the complete referral, however. The closer the counselor came to actually making it, the more resistance and ambivalence the counselee showed. Eventually, however, the counselor named the therapist that the counselee would see, told something about his work, and made the first appointment. Then it had to be worked out with the therapist whether or not the counselee would continue to see the counselor regularly during therapy or wait until it had been concluded.

John Doe's Planning Interview. The counselor has been going over his notes and has them and his other material ready for the planning session with the counselee. It is about time for John to arrive and Mr. Doyle has just mentally reviewed his plan for the session. As you read over the typescript keep in mind what you already know about the counselee and what techniques the counselor has available for helping the counselee to plan. Evaluate what the counselor says. How effective is his use of techniques? Would you have done the same thing?

MR. DOYLE: Hello, John. Come in and have a seat. You're here right on the dot

JOHN: Yeah. I'm anxious to get started. Er . . .

MR. DOYLE: You really want to get going on this.

JOHN: I sure do. I don't mind coming in like I did the first time. What I mean is that . . . well . . . I didn't know what to expect. You know, I walked up and down the hall a couple of times before I got up the nerve to come in.

MR. DOYLE: You feel a lot better about it now.

JOHN: Yeah. I was worried about these tests, too. But they don't seem so bad now. I don't know when I had to think so much, though. It was almost like a month of school in a couple of hours. . . . I don't guess I did so good. I had a lot of trouble with that one with those little pictures. . . . I don't see how you can turn those things around. What was that one for?

MR. DOYLE: Let's see. You mean the one with the pictures of drawings that you had to mentally fold up into different shapes?

JOHN: Yeah, that one. It sure was tough. I think I did worst on that. Whatever kinds of jobs that's for I don't want any part of. That would drive you crazy! . . . What is it for? You said something about visualizing or something like that.

MR. DOYLE: Yes, that one is supposed to get at how well you can visualize how things work—how machines work, or how parts fit together—how well you can manipulate these things in your mind. You need that kind of ability in . . . well, work with machines, mechanical work, or in some technical work like engineering.

JOHN: I could have told that! I'm not interested in mechanical work. I guess you have to be able to do that in something like carpentry? I don't like that. I told you about that already.

MR. DOYLE: You're not surprised that you had some trouble with that? Well, the truth is, you came out about like you felt. You dropped down on that. It's not one of your best areas.

JOHN: Well, I don't mind that. If it was something I wanted to do I'd be out of luck. What about the others? What about college? I know I won't get an answer on what to take in college, but how do I look for college? You know I read that article about medicine, about studying to be a doctor, and it said that you had to be a good student and high up in your class. Tops in ability too. The competition is pretty tough too.

MR. DOYLE: What do you think about how you measure up for that, John? How does it look to you?

JOHN: That's hard to say. I mean, if I really was determined to do it. . . . But since I found out about the time it takes. . . . Then I read about the subjects that you take, chemistry, biology, and some like that, it doesn't sound so good. In fact I don't think I'd like the training at all. I never thought of it that way— what you'd have to study. I guess I just thought of the position the doctor has. He makes a lot of money too!

MR. DOYLE: Uh huh.

JOHN: But I've been thinking about it a lot. I would say right now that I couldn't do it. I never really thought about it seriously. I don't mind giving up that idea!

MR. DOYLE: From what you know about it, you don't think that you'd particularly like to be a doctor, considering the preparation, the time, and so on?

JOHN: That's right. Why doesn't somebody tell you about this stuff . . . I mean this stuff about jobs? I could have told earlier that I wouldn't like that if I read some of those things. I ought to take it home and have my sister read it. It would enlighten her!

MR. DOYLE: You didn't have much factual information about what the work actually was before now.

JOHN: Yeah, that's right. I read those others too. . . . Well, I don't know. . . . I'm still confused. I mean I may have some idea about what not to do, but what I want to know is what to do!

MR. DOYLE: What did you think about them? Did any of those jobs interest you? As I said, I didn't mean those as suggestions as to what you should do, but I thought they might be interesting. We can spend some more time looking over the information in the files.

JOHN: Yes, . . . I guess so. . . . That one about selling, I liked that. But I don't know how it'd be for a job. I've already said that I like to do it, what little I've tried. But it said that sometimes the pay is low, and you have to depend on commissions. I don't know whether I'd like to do that . . . earn a living that way. You can starve. How do I know I can sell anything?

MR. DOYLE: What about your experience in selling ads? Does that seem like the kind of thing you'd like to do?

JOHN: Yeah, that's interesting. I sort of like that. I guess you could call that selling. . . . What about those tests? Did they tell anything about that?

MR. DOYLE: Well, this might be of some help. These are the results of the interest test . . . not what you can do necessarily, or where you have special ability, but just the kinds of activities you seem to prefer. You remember marking that one?

JOHN: Yeah. Where you had to make a choice of three things. Sometimes I couldn't decide—I liked all of the things, or I didn't like any of them. What does that tell about me? Does it tell about selling?

MR. DOYLE: It might give a little help. . . . These are the areas at the top, and down here are the ratings you made. This line in the middle indicates about an average amount of interest—about the same as most people have. You don't feel much one way or the other about these that are near this middle line. These that are up here are above average, above this dotted line are high. Persuasive—getting people to agree with you, convincing others of something, well, like selling something to them—that's pretty high. Then over here, clerical, that's fairly high. . . .

JOHN: Uh huh. . . . Then these down there are low, I guess. I probably don't like these. Let's see—mechanical, scientific, literary—that's easy to see. I remember marking those questions "no" all the time. This is about what I'd expect. . . . What's this—music? I don't know why that's high. Music?

MR. DOYLE: What about that? Why do you think that is up there?

JOHN: Music? . . . I don't know. All I do is listen to the radio. That's all the music I like. I don't think I'd like to be a musician. I can't even play on the linoleum!

MR. DOYLE: That's probably it. Liking to listen to music sometimes shows up.

JOHN: I guess it could. . . . Well, that's a pretty good picture. It's what I thought. But let's see, how about this clerical? How does that fit in? I mean I have persuasive here pretty high, and clerical is the other high one. What does this mean—that I like typing?

MR. DOYLE: It could be that, but it includes the kinds of activities that you do in a business office or some similar type of place. It could be keeping records, running office machines, making up reports, checking accounts—activities that are somewhat routine.

JOHN: That kind . . . that might come from checking inventories in the store, or the accounts I keep on the ads. I have to keep account of the funds, and the printing costs. I checked things like that on the test.

MR. DOYLE: Those are somewhat clerical. How do you feel about work like that?

JOHN: It's part of the main job. I don't do that kind of work all the time. Checking inventories or taking them is only part of clerking. I don't know whether I'd like to do something like that all of the time, though. I do like it; I get sort of a kick out of getting records and having them check out right. It would be all right as part of another job.

MR. DOYLE: What does this tell you? What can you get from this about yourself?

JOHN: It looks like I should do clerical and persuasive work.

MR. DOYLE: What does this mean to *you*? The test doesn't tell you what you should do. Your own opinion is the most important thing. Do you see any connection between these things on the test, the kinds of things you enjoy doing, and those that you do best?

JOHN: That persuasive does. I think I would like work of that kind. I like to work around other people. I like to get them to do things—not argue them into it—but get them to work along with me. It doesn't seem like work though. I believe I could do that all day and not be tired.

MR. DOYLE: How good do you think you are at that? How would you rate yourself?

JOHN: Rate myself? Oh, I don't know. I might sound like I was bragging. I think I can convince others pretty well. On a job where that was necessary, I think I could hold my own.

MR. DOYLE: Uh huh.

JOHN: But what's the connection between doing office work and that? I don't see it.

MR. DOYLE: Did you find anything in the pamphlets that would help you fit these interests together?

JOHN: Well, I don't know. In the one about saleswork it said something about having to make reports and keep accounts. You'd have to do that. Then office work—some kinds of office work—might lead to selling a product that the company made. I guess there is some connection. I can see where one would go with the other pretty well. In a way, having a job in an office might be pretty good. You'd have a regular income and know how much you'd make. But from what I read I don't think you get so much—at least not to start with. But the thing I want to do is use my best ability. I want to do the thing that I could do best.

MR. DOYLE: Where do you think you can perform best? Where would you be making the most use of your abilities?

JOHN: Oh, I might . . . well, I would say that I might be at my best in dealing with people. Suppose you asked whether I could make something, like a shelf, better or conduct a meeting better. I would say I could conduct the meeting better. Then on that interest test it was the same. Those things tell you what you already know, but they make you realize it better.

MR. DOYLE: Considering the things you like to do and those you can do best might give you better ideas of the kinds of jobs to think about.

JOHN: Yes, but I don't know much about what I can do best. What else did those tests say? What is my IQ? I've heard that tests find that. How dumb am I?

MR. DOYLE: Of the other tests, one was specifically designed to get at your learning ability. Sometimes it's called IQ, but this is a score or number that means different things for different tests. But you did a little better than average. You should be able to learn about as well as the next fellow. For example, you might be expected to do satisfactory work in high school.

JOHN: I should tell my teachers that. I . . . some don't think I can, er . . . that's not bad, is it?

MR. DOYLE: No, you're about the same as most other fellows.

JOHN: I never thought that I was a "brain" or anything like that. But I can usually catch on to things. I guess I could do better in high school. Maybe I have better learning ability for history than math. People can be that way, can't they? You can learn some things easier than others?

MR. DOYLE: Interest may have a lot to do with it. Learning ability, as we're talking about it, usually applies to all of the regular school subjects. Why do you think you find history easier than math?

JOHN: Well, I can study history easier, for one thing. You can read it over once and have a pretty good idea of what it is all about. But math—you can read it over and not get a thing out of it. I guess part of my trouble is that I put it off until last, and then sometimes I don't get to it.

MR. DOYLE: Well, now we've talked about some different things, and you've brought out some pretty important things about yourself. . . .

JOHN: Yeah. . . .

MR. DOYLE: What does it mean to you? Do you see your situation any better now? Do you feel that you've moved along the way to making plans?

JOHN: I see that I still have some planning to do. I have another year in school, so I have some time to think about it. I still wonder about going to college. You know my mother is pretty strong for that. . . . I guess I want to myself, in a way. But I don't know what I'd take, and I can't see too much point in it.

MR. DOYLE: You haven't given up the idea entirely?

JOHN: No. I can't decide between going to work full time as soon as I finish school or going away to school. You see, if I could find something I liked, I would start in next summer. On the other hand, I'd like to have some special training. I'd still like to feel that I could do something . . . that I had a special skill.

MR. DOYLE: You'd like to get some special training in something?

JOHN: Yeah. . . . I think I would like to look into this selling some more. I might not be able to get a job like that right off. But if I had some training that would help me get started. . . . I got an idea from that interest test. I could get some training along the lines of office work, and then I could probably get a job working in a place, and when I get the chance, I could get some kind of sales job. . . . What I want now is some information about the kinds of schools I might go to.

MR. DOYLE: I think I can help you with that. . . . Right after we finish up here, we can take a look at the files and get something about schools.

JOHN: That's what I want now. . . . Maybe you can help me find something about some kinds of work, too. I'd like to sort of look over the field before I do any definite deciding. There may be others I don't know about. . . . Do you think that's a good idea?

MR. DOYLE: A very good one. I'll be glad to help you find whatever kind of information you like. . . . You think this information is helping you? You're getting something out of it?

JOHN: It's a lot of help. It never occurred to me to look at it before. A file full of papers doesn't look very interesting. You ought to tell more people about it.

MR. DOYLE: We're trying to do that. Maybe you can give it a little publicity, seeing that it's been of use to you.

JOHN: You bet I will. I know of several fellows right now who could use it. . . . But let's see, I had something else. . . . Oh, yes. What I'm wondering about is this course I'm taking in school. I'm having trouble with it, but maybe I'll be able to get by. But what I'd like to do is take something more in line with what we've been talking about. Something connected more with business. The question is do I need these courses in case I go on to school, and what else can I take?

MR. DOYLE: We can check the school requirements when we look at the school catalogue. Then there are some other courses in school that you might want to consider. You mentioned the economics course last time as one you thought would be helpful.

JOHN: That's one that I was thinking about. Maybe we can talk about that after I find out a little more about these schools. . . . I don't have any plan yet, but I see what to do. Could I talk to you some more about these things after I've done some more reading?

MR. DOYLE: Certainly. I'll be glad to go over them with you. You feel that you've made some definite progress?

JOHN: I sure do. It's not such a confusing business as it looks like at first. I'm beginning to see how you go about this business of deciding what you're going to do.

MR. DOYLE: Well, if you'd like to, we can go in the library and take a look at some of the information we have been talking about.

JOHN: OK, and I want to thank you for all the help you have given me.

Note that the counselee is given the opportunity to start the session off on a topic of concern to him. He seems to be primarily interested in test results. Remember that he thought of counseling as mostly "taking some tests." Also, the fact that he was given a battery of tests at one time may have reinforced this concept of counseling although the counselor tried to place test results in their proper perspective with other data. This meeting will probably not be the last counseling session with the counselee. He needs more information and will undoubtedly require help in relating it to what he knows about himself. He will return later, perhaps, to talk over plans. At a still later date he may ask the help of a counselor in evaluating the results of his decision.

SUMMARY

In the planning phase of counseling the counselor uses a variety of specific techniques as well as many of those previously employed in the information-getting phase to provide the counselee with needed information, to help him learn and accept the meaning of all sorts of data; to aid him in evaluating and formulating hypotheses about himself; to enable him to foresee probable outcomes of plans; to assist him to choose among plans, put a plan into effect, and evaluate its suitability. During the planning phase the counselor takes stock of progress and makes plans for the next session. Counselor plans are kept flexible and may be changed, modified, or even discarded depending upon counselee needs.

CHECKS ON UNDERSTANDING

1. Does it appear reasonable to describe the planning phase of counseling as a systematic and orderly process? What is the value of such a description?

2. Why should the counselor have a plan for an upcoming session with the counselee?

3. What is meant by the counselor taking stock of progress (or lack of it) in the counseling process?

4. How can you judge when the counselee is ready to begin planning? Does emphasis on planning change the counselor-counselee relationship or the counseling atmosphere?

5. Why should the counselor have the ultimate goal of counseling for the specific counselee in mind? How is this goal formulated?

6. What are the dangers of the counselor having a plan for a counseling session?

THINGS TO DO

1. Conduct a planning interview with a counselee. You may use the counselee with whom you have been working. As already suggested, the counselee should be someone who has no serious problems or difficulties, is not a discipline problem, and is cooperative and willing to work with you.

If possible, record the session and play it back for evaluation. What were you trying to do? Was this what the counselee needed? Evaluate in terms of the techniques discussed in the previous chapters. What things do you think you did well? What things would you do differently? How would you do them?

2. Read over and evaluate typescript material in the references. All of them will be helpful, but Ref. [39] will be particularly so.

3. Role-play a planning session with another person. This will give you the opportunity to try out techniques with more freedom than in an actual counseling session. Emphasize that the counselee should actually play his role. Be sure to set up the situation realistically. State what information has been obtained. Plan what you propose to do in the session. Record the session, discuss, and evaluate it.

4. Using verbatim case data, select some point before the final session, take stock of progress, and make plans for the next session. Decide what the counseling goal would be. Prepare your notes for the session.

CHAPTER 14

Evaluation and Research

IN THIS FINAL chapter, evaluation of counseling is con- sidered primarily from the point of view of what the practicing counselor on the job can do and the techniques and procedures he may use to improve his counseling. Evaluation and research by the counselor should enable him to do a better job of counseling and help him to appreciate the importance of checking up on himself as well as making use of the research of others. The complex research study which involves a rather large amount of time, money, and planning, and which may often be a cooperative enterprise, is of crucial importance in the progress of counseling as a profession but is beyond the scope of this chapter.

The point of this chapter is this: the counselor should use a research approach in his day-to-day work. He can put this approach into effect regard- less of how much or how little time and facilities he has available.

Action Research by Counselors

The concept of action research described in Corey [51] is the basis for the type of on-the-job research and evaluation suggested here. Research is carried out by practitioners, in this case counselors, to solve educational problems and improve educational practices. Thus the researcher is personally involved in the problems that he is studying and he is the one to put the results of the research into effect. The data for research come, to a large extent, from the typical day-to-day activities of the counselor (researcher). He may vary his counseling procedures and try something new, or he may do some rather exten- sive planning and carry on a study with others as a joint project. In any case, the purpose is to help him do a better job.

The dual role of the counselor as practitioner and scientist is thoroughly developed in Pepinsky and Pepinsky [168, particularly pp. 11–14]. The concept of self-evaluation and research on the job was suggested by this reference and by Corey [51].

The Counselor's Role in Formal Research Studies

It is not suggested here that the practicing counselor refrain from taking part in what may be classified as formal research studies. He should do this to the degree possible. There will be opportunities in the school for him to encourage a research program or to work with others in his city or county, or perhaps on a state-wide basis. Regional studies, which are broader in scope, are made also. The school counselor can play an important role in such research programs [190].

The Counselor's Use of Research of Others

The counselor needs to make use of the research of others to improve his work. This is a rather large order because the literature is extensive and the results are often presented in rather complex form. To make the most effective use of research the counselor needs to be able to *understand* and *evaluate critically* what was done and what the results are. There is, unfortunately, no short cut to being able to do this. He may find that summaries of research such as those included in the *Annual Review of Psychology* [9] and the *Review of Educational Research* [174] will be helpful, although he will need some counseling and research background to derive the most from these publications. *The Personnel and Guidance Journal* [172] presents useful studies and is relatively easy to understand. *The Journal of Counseling Psychology* [115] is probably the most valuable single source of research studies on counseling, but the counselor will need a fairly good understanding of research and counseling to understand and make use of the results.

Counseling Research and Evaluation on the Job

Why does the counselor want to study and evaluate his own work? He does it to find out if what he is doing is actually helping the counselees. He also wants to discover which specific things he is doing are helpful and which are not, and under what conditions they are or are not helpful. When he collects evidence about these points, he should be better able to improve his help to counselees.

What questions does the counselor ask about his counseling to serve as guides in the collection of data? Pepinsky and Pepinsky raise the following questions about which the counselor should be concerned [168, p. 276].

1. What is the client like?
2. How did the client get that way?
3. What is the counselor doing during counseling?
4. What is the client doing during counseling?
5. How do the counselor and client interact during counseling?

Assuming that these questions have been answered, the authors then say that the following two questions need to be asked [168, p. 277]:

6. How has the client changed?
7. What is the relationship between (a) the client's behavior *subsequent* to counseling and (b) the previous behavior of the counselor and client *during* and *prior* to counseling?

What do these questions suggest for the counselor to do to evaluate and improve his counseling? It would appear that they indicate, among others, the following two kinds of activities:

1. The counselor should check on how effective he is at understanding the counselee.

2. The counselor should check on how effective his actual counseling is in helping the counselee achieve suitable goals.

A word needs to be said about goals. They are not the subject of investigation in the evaluation of counseling; they are to some extent based upon counselor judgments about what is *good* for the counselee [170]. What is good for the counselee, however, is not discovered through research on the counseling process; it is drawn from other sources such as the study of the individual in his culture [170].

Now that the general types of activity in which the counselor may engage to evaluate and improve his counseling have been given, the next question is, What does the counselor do to carry out these activities? What, specifically, does the practicing counselor on the job do in his day-to-day work?

Checking Inferences about the Counselee. Counselor Smith, as he works with a counselee, collects data from which he makes inferences and hypotheses about the counselee. Since these inferences provide, in part, the basis of what he does to help the counselee, they should be accurate. Counselor Smith wants them to be as good as possible. He asks himself "How good are they?" He decides to study his effectiveness in actually understanding the counselee; he feels that perhaps he is not doing as well as he would like.

Counselor Smith writes down his inferences and hypotheses about the counselee and puts them aside for a later check. He may write, for example, "The counselee has ability to do average work but is performing poorly because he has no goal and because parents care little about how well he does." The statement may be longer than this, but it needs to contain only the most significant aspects as he sees them.

The counselor then checks his inferences or statements about what the counselee is like against additional data that are obtained later. For example, evidence for or against the above hypotheses may be obtained by talking to the counselee's parents and by giving the counselee an academic aptitude test.

These inferences and hypotheses about the counselee are never final but are subject to revision and modification as new data are obtained, as was pointed out earlier in the discussion of the counseling process. All that has been added here is a technique to study them as objectively as is possible under the conditions of day-to-day work. In this way the counselor is able to determine just how good a job he is doing in understanding the counselee. He may have missed important clues; he may have jumped to unwarranted conclusions; he may have overlooked an area of information that should have been tapped.

This is one way that the research approach may be used with day-to-day problems. It is a modification of the action research approach in which the worker attempts to improve his day-to-day practices.

Checking the Effectiveness of Counseling. The second type of day-to-day activity in which the counselor may engage to evaluate his work is more in keeping with the usual type of counseling research. Counselor Smith illustrates the need for it when he asks himself, "Am I actually helping counselees?"

There are several different methods that Counselor Smith, or any other counselor, may use to find answers to this question. They are as follows [76]:

1. He may check what he is doing against a standard of what is considered to be good counseling.

2. He may follow up counselees to determine what they are doing as a result of counseling.

3. He may find out what former counselees think of the help they have received.

4. He may have experts evaluate the suitability of the counselee's plans, decisions, adjustments, and the like.

5. He may evaluate the effects of specific techniques, such as providing occupational information in a certain way or interpreting test results in a particular way.

6. He may compare the status of counselees before counseling with their status after counseling. Status may involve school marks, occupational plans, social adjustment, and the like.

7. He may compare a group of individuals who received counseling with a group who did not receive counseling, to determine the effect of help given.

A great many methods and techniques may be used to carry out these types of evaluation. But obviously adaptations need to be made in typical research procedures so that the counselor may evaluate his day-to-day work without setting up an elaborate and time-consuming research study.

Let us return to Counselor Smith and his question about the effectiveness of his help. He is deciding upon a simple evaluation procedure. He makes decisions about what he will do to help each particular counselee with whom he works. Suppose that he made a brief note describing what he plans to do, why he plans to do it, and what he expects his plan to help the counselee do. Then he checks his expectations against what the counselee does later in counseling or after counseling has been completed. Would not this help him to evaluate and improve his work?

An illustration may point out how this procedure could be helpful. Counselor Smith is working with a counselee who has asked for help in planning what to take in college. The counselee may be described as a person with low academic interests and ability but with white-collar aspirations. His parents have saved all their lives so that he can be a "professional man" rather than do the same sort of semiskilled mill work that they do. The counselee would feel that he had let his parents down if he decided upon other than college work; a lower-level occupational choice would cause unpleasant guilt feelings.

The counselor decides that he will explain to the counselee the wide gap between ambitions and abilities. He makes a note of his plan and predicts that it will cause the counselee to adjust his educational goals so that they will be more in line with reality. His plan does not work. The counselee, instead, becomes quite defensive and asserts that he can do it if he tries.

Counselor Smith realizes that he has not been successful and decides on another approach; he will attempt to help the counselee explore the reasons for his unrealistic plans. He feels that the counselee is uncertain and anxious about his ability and that, given a chance, he will bring these feelings out. This is his next statement about his decision, his reason for making it, and what he thinks will happen.

Counselor Smith then tries out this approach. The counselee gains some insight, begins to consider some mechanical trades (for which he has considerable ability), and concludes counseling with plans to get some part-time exploratory work experience. Counselor Smith's plan has been successful. He will follow the counselee up later after he has had an opportunity to learn something about his suitability for mechanical trades to check further on the effectiveness of the way he tried to help the counselee.

What has the counselor learned? He has evaluated his decision against the results it obtained. He is able to estimate how much he has helped the counselee. He has sharpened his ability to work with and help future counselees.

Has the counselee been helped? In the counselor's judgment he has because he concluded counseling with what the counselor considers practical plans, and because he expressed the opinion that he had been helped. In addition to following up the counselee, the counselor may also have someone else (an expert) judge the appropriateness of the counselee's plans.

The possibilities for other types of action research by the counselor are numerous. Gordon [86, pp. 331–332] suggests problems of particular concern to the teacher, teacher-counselor, and counselor, and describes the action research approach for the teacher [86, pp. 321–328]. Emphasis so far has been put upon evaluating counseling process and outcomes. The counselor could also study other phases such as his role in the school, effective ways of serving teachers and working with them, record systems, data-gathering techniques, ways of offering maximum services to pupils with available resources.

It is possible, too, for the counselor to set up a more formal action study than the type discussed here. For example, he may select one group for intensive counseling and another group for a minimum of counseling help, or he may attempt to vary the type of counselor-counselee relationship with two or more groups. He may also work cooperatively with other members of the school staff on a research study that aims to discover such things as who needs help, how it should be given, when, and by whom. In a later section of this chapter, there are additional suggestions for research studies.

Stating "Why" as Well as "What." In any type of evaluation, the source of the counselor's hypotheses is important. To formulate a hypothesis, the counselor has to have some point of view about individuals, the way they behave, and how they may be helped. Bases or points of view were discussed in Chapter 7. The counselor formulates, from his point of view, "best guesses" or hypotheses about the counselee and the sort of help that should be given. He should ask himself "why?" If he can determine the "why" of the results that he has obtained, he can then do a better job of applying results to new counselees. For example, he may say that the counselee becomes upset and ineffective when taking a test because he fears situations in which he must compete with others. He further states that strong emotions interfere with intellectual activities.

The counselor is not testing the validity of his point of view about behavior; he is using it to explain why. Having an explanation for the way the counselee behaves, he is in a position to decide upon a type of counseling help and to predict what it will enable the counselee to do. The counselor does test or evaluate the effectiveness of the help he gives. If it works, he assumes that it works for the reasons which he has set up. He is, in a sense, building a theory of counseling. He is attempting to explain and predict behavior. This would seem to be an essential process for the counselor to undertake.

The point of this discussion is simply this—the counselor should state "why" as well as "what." He is then able to explain the reasons for his success (or lack of it) in understanding the counselee and in helping him. He wants to know what works in counseling; he also wants to know why it works.

It may appear to be a large order to suggest that the counselor have reasons for what he does and be able to express these reasons verbally. But the counselor does have reasons, whether or not he can tell himself or anyone else about them. All that is asked here is that he make himself be coherent and specific about his reasons, as well as his specific choices and decisions about counseling procedures.

Research Procedures and Techniques

In planning and conducting research studies that go beyond the two types suggested for the day-to-day work of the counselor on the job, several points should be kept in mind by the researcher. These are as follows:

1. Keep the counselee's welfare foremost. Do not try something that you have reason to consider harmful or that will deny a needed service to a counselee.

2. Keep your results in the form of hypotheses. What you come out with will be a hypothesis for which you have no support, or only a degree of support as to its *probability* of being true. You will not have established unchanging or irrefutable facts. In most cases you will only have some evidence to suggest that one procedure *may* be better than another or that something works. The more carefully designed your study and the more clear-cut the results, the greater the degree of confidence you may put in your conclusions about hypotheses. You may, of course, come out with new and better hypotheses.

3. Use as large a number of cases as practical. There is no set number that you should use, but, other factors being equal, the larger the number of cases, the more confidence you may put in your results. The ones you use should be a representative sample of those about whom you wish to generalize.

4. Carefully and specifically define what you are investigating. One of the greatest difficulties in evaluating the success of counseling is establishing a criterion [76]. What should counseling accomplish? How do you measure it? How do you determine if changes in the counselee are the result of counseling and not the result of other experiences? It is necessary to define, in terms that can be "observed," just what the results should be. The criterion of the opinion of the counselee has already been mentioned, as has judgments of experts about him. Suggestions for other criteria may be found in Ref. [76], and by reviewing research studies such as those in Refs. [115, 172, 190].

The criteria that you use, however, should be based upon what you want your counseling to do. You may set up any criteria you wish; the only requirement is that they be put in operational terms. For example, if you use social adjustment, an operational definition might be: "Social adjustment *is when* the counselee goes to the class parties." While this definition may not cover what he does at the party or how he feels about it, it names behavior that can be observed.

5. Use appropriate statistics. A consideration of statistics in the planning stages of the study will enable you to obtain the most possible information from the data you collect. There is no need to overanalyze data statistically; the apparent exactness of statistics cannot put more accuracy in the data than is already in them. Guilford [90] is a helpful reference for planning the statistical analysis.

6. Use controls as much as possible. When we study the results of trying

out something in counseling, we need to know what happens to those who do not have the treatment. Thus we need to have a control group that is similar in important aspects to those on whom we are trying the new or experimental procedure. Then we need to keep in mind that we cannot rule out, or even know about, all the conditions that affect the subjects. We need to be alert for factors that may affect our study and distort results. We wish to have as much evidence as possible that changes in counselees are due to counseling and not the result of other factors.

Actual methods of setting up or designing studies were mentioned earlier. Several additional comments, which elaborate on the seven procedures discussed, are now given.

The counselor may try out a procedure or technique on a group of counselees and immediately, or soon after, check on the results. For example, the counselor may give occupational information in a certain way, and then ask the counselee to complete a check list about his reactions to this procedure. Instead of an immediate check, the counselor may wait until the end of counseling or until a later time.

Another example of an evaluation study would be one in which immediate in-counseling results are compared with later information about the counselee. For example, the counselor may compare the counselee's expressed satisfaction with an immediate occupational choice with expressions of satisfaction after he has been on the job selected long enough to form some opinions about it.

Still a third procedure would be to provide counseling to one group and compare changes with those in a similar group of pupils who had no counseling. The groups should be as alike as possible to eliminate or reduce the effects of other variables besides counseling. A variation of this procedure would be to provide both groups with different sorts of counseling; results would indicate which type of counseling was the more effective.

One or several counselees could be studied intensively during the counseling process to determine what changes take place. For example, after each session the counselor may ask the counselee to describe his occupational goal. The desired goal might then be compared with what the counselor considers to be a realistic goal. Other methods could be used to assess change [54, 124]. Verbatim recordings may be studied to determine changes in such things as the counselee's concept of himself.

Data-gathering Materials and Techniques for Counseling Research

The research study will necessitate the collection of some sort of data and they must be collected by a dependable instrument or technique. The data collected must, of course, be based on the criterion of the study. For example, if the counselor decides to use occupational adjustment as the criterion, he needs to decide just what he means by occupational adjustment and how it can be observed or inferred. Then he needs to select, adopt, or formulate an instrument or technique for collecting the data and to decide on ways to apply it. Quite often the counselor would make up his own data-collecting forms. Some useful examples may be found in Refs. [13, pp. 286–287, 292–296; 65, pp. 530–542; 77, pp. 317–324]. Other instruments besides informational forms could be used; these will be discussed later. Furthermore, the counselor would often use several of the following data-gathering techniques in combination.

1. Mailed questionnaires. The counselor may prepare a questionnaire to be sent to the counselee, which he is to check and return. Questions of fact or opinion may be used. For example, he may be asked the name of his job (a fact), and how he likes it (an opinion). References already mentioned provide various forms that may serve as guides in preparing a questionnaire. In general, the questionnaire should be brief and easy to answer, for example, by checking a multiple-choice item. The questionnaire is appropriate when it is necessary to contact a large number of counselees who are scattered over a wide area. Young [266] is a particularly helpful reference for the use of this technique.

2. The structured interview. If the interview is used for research purposes, it is necessary to have it standardized so that results obtained from different counselees will be comparable. The counselor may prepare a form containing the questions which he will ask. Some questions may call for specific answers; others may provide for the counselee to express his feelings and opinions. Techniques already discussed may be used for establishing rapport. The interview technique may be employed during and after counseling, but the time that it will take will limit the number of counselees that may be contacted in the study. It should be kept in mind, also, that the person conducting the research interview has an effect on what the counselee says. For example, suppose that the counselor asked one of his former counselees whether or not counseling had helped him.

3. Rating scales. The counselor may prepare a rating scale to rate the counselee, which the counselee uses to rate himself or which others use to rate the counselee. The techniques of "Q sorts" is a method of having the counselee describe himself or of having others describe him. Ratings may be used during counseling, after it is completed, or later on when the counselee is on the job or in school.

4. Sociometrics. In getting at the results of counseling, the counselor may find that information about the individual's status in the group is needed. Sociometric procedures may be used to provide the needed data, which may be obtained before, during, shortly after counseling, or after a longer period of time has elapsed. Obviously, many factors may affect sociometric ratings besides counseling. Sociometric data, however, would appear to be quite useful when counseling aims to help the individual improve social adjustment and the counselor wants to assess the adjustment.

5. Anecdotal records. A series of anecdotal records made of the counselee may be used as indications of change that takes place during counseling. The counselor, or other teachers, could make the records to provide objective descriptions of behavior in various situations, such as in the classroom, in recreational activities, or in clubs. The counselor could then analyze them for patterns or trends in behavior. The results could be used to estimate adjustment, progress in improving adjustment, and trends in behavior.

6. Autobiographical writings. In writing about himself in short essays or the more lengthy autobiography, the counselee gives a view of how he sees himself and the world about him. Results of counseling may be evaluated by studying such writings, either to get a total impression of the counselee or to evaluate some particular aspect, such as his degree of self-confidence.

7. Tests and inventories. A great number of psychological instruments are available for use in evaluating results of counseling. Tests may be given *before* and *after* counseling, and the results compared. Personality and interest tests are probably the most useful and widely used. Instruments of this sort should be carefully selected and should provide data about the criterion that has been set up for the study. References already given in the chapter on testing will be useful here.

8. Analysis of recorded counseling sessions. Counseling may be evaluated by using verbatim recordings and typescripts made from these recordings. Numerous studies of this sort have been made [178]. The effect of counselor techniques could be studied to determine which techniques had the desired result.

9. The critical incident technique. This is a relatively new technique that is useful in setting up criteria of what is critical behavior in various situations [71]. Eilbert [64] applies a variation of the procedure to define more clearly the term emotional immaturity. The procedure would appear to be particularly useful in setting up criteria by which to evaluate counseling and counselee behavior.

Counseling Records and Reports

Among the counselor activities that go along with the work done in the counseling process are the keeping of records of counseling and making reports to others. Neither deals directly with the matter of evaluating counseling, although records may furnish data for research. In a report to someone else, the counselor hypothesizes what sort of person the counselee is and what he will do.

Counseling Records. The counselor must set up a system of records in which data may be recorded quickly and easily, which will enable the counselor to make a quick review of information, and which, nevertheless, will contain all the essential data. It is quite easy to allow the record system to become so complex and lengthy that the counselor may get lost in a maze of detail.

To make the most effective use of record-keeping time, it is best to avoid recopying notes and transferring data from one record to another. Thus the notes that the counselor makes during the counseling session would be left as they are, with perhaps a few additions after the session. There should be a place in the record for the counselor to pull together the session as an aid to his thinking and to serve as a quick refresher for the next session. A suggested form is shown below.

Counseling Session Record Form

Session no. _____
Date _____

1. Counselor activities for the next session
    (a) Tests to be given_____
    (b) Occupational or other information to be obtained_____
    (c) Persons to be called, etc. _____
2. Interview notes to include
    (a) Brief account of interview
    (b) Specific things to be done by counselee before next session
    (c) One-paragraph summary of the session (emphasize insights and progress)
    (d) Test results, when given and scored as part of sessions (attach profile sheet)

This form is not suitable for research or teaching, as it provides space only for the essential data. It would seem advisable to include a separate sheet for each contact, no matter how brief. The completed forms might be kept in order, with synthesis notes included. Little time would be needed to complete this form and the entire series could be quickly reviewed just before the counselee arrives.

Data that are needed in the central file in the school could be extracted and entered in the school record. The type of record just discussed would be in the counselor's personal file.

Reports to Others. Counselors find it necessary to make a number of different kinds of reports, both *formal* and *informal*. Formal reports include written reports to colleges, employers, parents, referral agencies, and the like. Informal reports are those made verbally to teachers, the principal, parents, and others. Informal reports may be supplemented by written reports.

Reports often suggest changing or modifying the counselee's environment. For example, a report to a teacher may suggest a different way of dealing with the counselee. Thus, in his reports, the counselor needs to be able to make suggestions that would result in help for the counselee. While ways of modifying or changing the environment are not taken up in this book, the counselor needs to be familiar with procedures and practices used so that he can be specific in his recommendations.

The actual system of reporting will, of course, be based upon the policy of the institution in which the counselor is working. However, it is usually up to the counselor to determine the form and content of formal reports and the approach and content of informal reports. A useful reference on formal reports is Hammond [93]. One of the most important points in reporting is to write the report so that the recipient can understand it [93, pp. 28–36]. Thus a report to a parent will be quite different from one to another counselor.

Informal reports are adapted to the level of understanding of the recipient. The counselor also needs to keep in mind the degree of personal involvement of the one to whom the report is made. For example, in talking with parents, the counselor would want to use a different approach than he would with a teacher.

Whatever type of report the counselor is making, it is essential to have the data organized into meaningful statements and hypotheses about the counselee, including examples. It is also helpful, if appropriate, to provide suggestions for what can be done to help the counselee. With parents, major emphasis may need to be put on helping them accept what has been concluded about the counselee and on agreeing to do what is suggested. In conferences with parents, it may be best to be permissive and accepting, to begin the conference by bringing up the counselee's strong points and let them react to these points, and then go on to those things that parents may not regard so favorably. The counselor would ask the parents what *they* think of each point that is introduced. A helpful reference on reports to parents and conferences with parents is [120, pp. 66–87].

SUMMARY

The counselor evaluates his work to improve his counseling skill and to provide more effective help to individuals. Evaluation is a continuous process, with the counselor checking up on the effectiveness of the help he provides the counselee. He may also plan and carry out relatively simple research studies on the job and may take part in more formal and basic research studies. Use is made of the research of others to improve the quality of counseling. Record keeping is a part of the counselor's job. Records should be easy to maintain and use and should contain adequate information. The counselor will frequently make reports to others. These reports may be formal or informal and should be understandable to the person for whom they are made.

CHECKS ON UNDERSTANDING

1. Why should the counselor write down his hypotheses and predictions about the counselee and then check on them later? What is the relation of the counselor's assumption about bases of counseling and his hypotheses and predictions?

2. How does the counselor apply the concept of action research to his work?

3. In doing a research study, why are "controls" a problem to the counselor?

4. How do you formulate a criterion with which to evaluate your counseling?

5. What are the purposes of keeping records of counseling?

6. What factors would you have to keep in mind in preparing a report to others on the counselee?

THINGS TO DO

1. In your work with a counselee, record your hypotheses and predictions, and check up on them.

2. Select a research article from one of the journals mentioned and describe how the results could be used to help the counselor improve his work (or why it provides no help).

3. Design a research study of the sort that the counselor could do along with his regular job. Prepare the data-collecting instrument that would be used and describe how you would use it.

4. Prepare a form that could be used to keep a record of counseling.

5. Prepare directions and needed forms for making reports to others, for example, parents, educational institutions, therapists.

References

1. Aldrich, Margaret C.: "An Exploratory Study of Social Guidance at the College Level," *Educational and Psychological Measurement,* vol. 2, pp. 209–216, 1942.

2. Alexander, Franz, and Thomas Morton French: *Psychoanalytic Therapy,* New York, The Ronald Press Company, 1946.

3. American Psychological Association, Committee on Counselor Training, Division of Counseling Psychology, "Recommended Standards for Training Counseling Psychologists at Doctorate Level," *American Psychologist,* vol. 7, pp. 175–181, June, 1952.

4. American Psychological Association, Committee on Ethical Standards for Psychology, *Ethical Standards for Psychologists: A Summary of Ethical Practices,* Washington, 1953.

5. American Psychological Association, Committee on Ethical Standards for Psychology, *Ethical Standards of Psychologists,* Washington, 1953.

6. American Psychological Association, Committee on Subdoctoral Education of the Education and Training Board, "The Training of Technical Workers in Psychology at the Subdoctoral Level," *American Psychologist,* vol. 10, pp. 541–545, September, 1955.

7. American Psychological Association, Committee on Definition, Division of Counseling Psychology, "Counseling Psychology as a Specialty," *American Psychologist,* vol. 11, pp. 282–285, June, 1956.

8. Anderson, Hobson Dewey, and Percy E. Davidson: *Occupational Trends in the United States,* Stanford, Calif., Stanford University Press, 1940.

9. *Annual Review of Psychology,* Palo Alto, Calif., Annual Reviews, Inc.

10. Arbuckle, Dugald S.: *Teacher Counseling,* Reading, Mass., Addison-Wesley Publishing Company, 1950.

11. Arsenian, Seth, and Francis W. McKenzie: *Counseling in the YMCA,* New York, Association Press, 1954.

12. Association for Supervision and Curriculum Development: *Fostering Mental Health in Our Schools,* Washington, National Education Association, 1950.

13. Baer, Max F., and Edward C. Roeber: *Occupational Information,* Chicago, Science Research Associates, Inc., 1951.

14. Bailard, Virginia, and Ruth Strang: *Ways to Improve Your Personality,* New York, McGraw-Hill Book Company, Inc., 1951.

15. Bakke, E. Wright, et al.: *Labor Mobility and Economic Opportunity,* New York, John Wiley & Sons, Inc., 1954.

16. Baller, W. R.: *The Case of Mickey Murphy,* rev. ed., Lincoln, Nebr., University of Nebraska Press, 1945.

17. Barr, A. S., R. A. Davis, and P. O. Johnson: *Educational Research and Appraizal,* Philadelphia, J. B. Lippincott Company, 1953.

18. Barry, Ruth, and Beverly Wolf: *Modern Issues in Guidance-Personnel Work,* New York, Bureau of Publications, Teachers College, Columbia University, 1957.

19. Beckley, John, and Robert Baldwin: *Think of Others,* New London, Conn., Arthur C. Croft Publications.

20. Beilin, Harry, and Kay V. Bergin: "The Social Mobility of a Limited Urban Group and Some Implications for Counseling," *Personnel and Guidance Journal,* vol. 34, pp. 544–552, May, 1956.

21. Bennett, George K., Harold G. Seashore, and Alexander G. Wesman: *Manual: Differential Aptitude Tests,* 2d ed., New York, The Psychological Corporation, 1952.

22. Bennett, George K., Harold G. Seashore, and Alexander G. Wesman: *Counseling from Profiles,* New York, The Psychological Corporation, 1951.

23. Berdie, Ralph F. (ed.): *Concepts and Programs of Counseling,* Minneapolis, University of Minnesota Press, 1951.

24. Berg, Irwin A.: "Comment" to "Career Patterns as a Basis for Vocational Counseling," by Donald E. Super, *Journal of Counseling Psychology,* vol. 1, p. 19, February, 1954.

25. Blos, Peter: *The Adolescent Personality,* New York, Appleton-Century-Crofts, Inc., 1941.

26. Blum, Gerald S.: *Psychoanalytic Theories of Personality,* New York, McGraw-Hill Book Company, Inc., 1953.

27. Blum, Milton L., and Benjamin Balinsky: *Counseling and Psychology,* Englewood Cliffs, N.J., Prentice-Hall, Inc., 1951.

28. Bogue, Jesse P. (ed.): *American Junior Colleges,* Washington, American Council on Education, 1956.

29. Bordin, Edward S. (ed.): *Training of Psychological Counselors,* Ann Arbor, Mich., University of Michigan Press, 1951.

30. Bordin, Edward S.: *Psychological Counseling,* New York, Appleton-Century-Crofts, Inc., 1955.

31. Brayfield, Arthur H.: "Putting Occupational Information Across," *Educational and Psychological Measurement,* vol. 8, pp. 485–495, Autumn, 1948.

32. Brayfield, Arthur H. (ed.): *Readings in Modern Methods of Counseling,* New York, Appleton-Century-Crofts, Inc., 1950.

33. Brayfield, Arthur H.: "Dissemination of Occupational Information," *Occupations,* vol. 29, pp. 411–413, March, 1951.

34. Bureau of Research and Service, College of Education, Michigan State University, *How to Make Referrals,* Professional Series Bulletin 12, East Lansing, Mich., 1956.

35. Buros, Oscar Krisen (ed.): *The Third Mental Measurements Yearbook,* New Brunswick, N.J., Rutgers University Press, 1949 (earlier volumes were published in 1938 and 1940).

36. Buros, Oscar Krisen (ed.): *The Fourth Mental Measurements Yearbook,* Highland Park, N.J., Gryphon Press, 1953.

37. Burton, Arthur, and Robert E. Harris: *Case Histories in Clinical and Abnormal Psychology,* New York, Harper & Brothers, 1947.

38. Burton, Arthur, and Robert E. Harris: *Clinical Studies of Personality,* New York, Harper & Brothers, 1955.

39. Callis, Robert, Paul C. Polmantier, and Edward C. Roeber: *A Casebook of Counseling,* New York, Appleton-Century-Crofts, Inc., 1955.

40. Cameron, Norman: *The Psychology of Behavior Disorders,* Boston, Houghton Mifflin Company, 1947.

41. Canter, Ralph R.: "Intelligence and the Social Status of Occupations," *Personnel and Guidance Journal,* vol. 34, pp. 258–260, January, 1956.

42. Caplow, Theodore: *The Sociology of Work,* Minneapolis, University of Minnesota Press, 1954.

43. Career Information Service, New York Life Insurance Company, *Guide to Career Information,* New York, Harper & Brothers, 1957.

44. Cattell, Raymond B.: "Principles of Design in 'Projection' or Misperception Tests of Personality," in Harold H. Anderson and Gladys L. Anderson (eds.), *An Introduction to Projective Techniques,* Englewood Cliffs, N.J., Prentice-Hall, Inc., 1951.

45. Child Study Association of America, *Our Children Today,* New York, The Viking Press, Inc., 1952.

46. Christensen, T. E.: "Functions of Occupational Information in Counseling," *Occupations,* vol. 28, pp. 11–14, October, 1949.

47. Clark, Florence E., and Cleo Murtland: "Occupational Information in Counseling: Present Practices and Historical Development," *Occupations,* vol. 24, pp. 451–475, May, 1946.

48. Colby, Kenneth Mark: *A Primer for Psychotherapists,* New York, The Ronald Press Company, 1951.

49. Cole, Luella: *Psychology of Adolescence,* 4th ed., New York, Rinehart & Company, Inc., 1954.

50. Cooperman, Irene G., et al.: "Counseling and the Counseling Record," *Personnel and Guidance Journal,* vol. 34, pp. 333–339, February, 1956.

51. Corey, Stephen M.: *Action Research,* New York, Bureau of Publications, Teachers College, Columbia University, 1953.

52. Cottle, William C.: "A Form for Evaluating Standardized Tests," *Occupations,* vol. 30, pp. 188–194, December, 1951.

53. Council of Guidance and Personnel Associations, "Job Analyses of Educational Personnel Workers," part II, Special Report, *Occupations,* vol. 30, pp. 1–22, October, 1951.

54. Cronbach, Lee J.: "Correlation between Persons as a Research Tool," in O. Hobart Mowrer (ed.), *Psychotherapy, Theory and Research,* New York, The Ronald Press Company, 1953, pp. 376–388.

55. Cushman, Jack L., and Walter F. Johnson: *Paul, a Case Study Unit.* East Lansing, Mich., Institute of Counseling, Testing and Guidance, Michigan State College.

56. Danielson, Paul J., and J. W. M. Rothney: "The Student Autobiography: Structured or Unstructured," *Personnel and Guidance Journal,* vol. 33, pp. 30–33, September, 1954.

57. Danskin, David G.: "Occupational Sociology in Occupational Exploration," *Personnel and Guidance Journal,* vol. 34, pp. 134–136, November, 1955.

58. Darley, John G.: "The Structure of the Systematic Case Study in Individual Diagnosis and Counseling," *Journal of Consulting Psychology,* vol. 4, pp. 215–220, 1940.

59. Department of Guidance and Counselor Training, Michigan State College, *Charles, a Case Study Unit,* East Lansing, Mich.

60. Division of Vocational Education, *Course Selection and Career Planning,* Columbus, Ohio, State Department of Education, 1955.

61. Dollard, John, and Neal E. Miller: *Personality and Psychotherapy,* New York, McGraw-Hill Book Company, Inc., 1950.

62. Dollard, John, Frank Auld, and Alice Marsden White: *Steps in Psychotherapy,* New York, The Macmillan Company, 1953.

63. *Educational and Psychological Measurement,* Durham, N.C.

64. Eilbert, Leo R.: "A Tentative Definition of Emotional Immaturity Utilizing the

Critical Incident Technique," *Personnel and Guidance Journal,* vol. 35, pp. 554–563, May, 1957.

65. Erickson, Clifford E. (ed.): *A Basic Text for Guidance Workers,* Englewood Cliffs, N.J., Prentice-Hall, Inc., 1947.

66. Erickson, Clifford E.: *The Counseling Interview,* Englewood Cliffs, N.J., Prentice-Hall, Inc., 1950.

67. Feingold, S. Norman: *Scholarships, Fellowships, and Loans,* vol. III, Cambridge, Mass., Bellman Publishing Company, 1955 (also vols. I and II).

68. Festinger, L., and D. Katz: *Research Methods in the Behavioral Sciences,* New York, The Dryden Press, Inc., 1953.

69. Fiedler, Fred E.: "Quantitative Studies on the Role of Therapists' Feelings toward Their Patients," in O. Hobart Mowrer (ed.), *Psychotherapy, Theory and Research,* New York, The Ronald Press Company, 1953, pp. 296–315.

70. Fine, Sidney A.: "What Is Occupational Information?" *Personnel and Guidance Journal,* vol. 33, pp. 504–509, May, 1955.

71. Flanagan, J. C.: "The Critical Incident Technique," *Psychological Bulletin,* vol. 51, pp. 327–358, June, 1954.

72. Forrester, Gertrude: *Methods of Vocational Guidance,* rev. and enl., Boston, D. C. Heath and Company, 1951.

73. Forrester, Gertrude: *Occupational Literature,* New York, The H. W. Wilson Company, 1954.

74. Friedmann, Eugene A., and Robert J. Havighurst: *The Meaning of Work and Retirement,* Chicago, University of Chicago Press, 1954.

75. Froehlich, Clifford P., and Arthur L. Benson: *Guidance Testing,* Chicago, Science Research Associates, Inc., 1948.

76. Froehlich, Clifford P.: *Evaluating Guidance Procedures: A Review of the Literature,* Washington, U.S. Office of Education, 1949.

77. Froehlich, Clifford P.: *Guidance Services in Schools,* 2d ed., New York, McGraw-Hill Book Company, Inc., 1958.

78. Froehlich, Clifford P., and John G. Darley: *Studying Students,* Chicago, Science Research Associates, Inc., 1952.

79. Gallagher, J. Roswell: *You and Your Health,* Chicago, Science Research Associates, Inc., 1950.

80. Garrett, A.: *Counseling Methods for Personnel Workers,* New York, Family Service Association of America, 1945.

81. Gerken, C. d'A.: *Study Your Way through School,* Chicago, Science Research Associates, Inc., 1949.

82. Ginzberg, Eli, et al.: *Occupational Choice: An Approach to a General Theory,* New York, Columbia University Press, 1951.

83. Gluck, Samuel, et al.: "A Proposed Code of Ethics for Counselors," *Occupations,* vol. 30, pp. 484–490, April, 1952.

84. Good, Carter V., and Douglas E. Scates: *Methods of Research,* New York, Appleton-Century-Crofts, Inc., 1954.

85. Goodenough, Florence L.: *Mental Testing: Its History, Principles, and Applications,* New York, Rinehart & Company, Inc., 1949.

86. Gordon, Ira J.: *The Teacher as Guidance Worker,* New York, Harper & Brothers, 1956.

87. Greenleaf, Walter J.: *Occupations,* Washington, Superintendent of Documents, 1951.

88. Guidance Information Review Service. *NVGA Bibliography of Current Occupational Literature,* Washington, National Vocational Guidance Association, 1956.

89. Guidance Information Review Service, "Current Occupational Literature," *Vocational Guidance Quarterly,* vol. 5, pp. 27–33, Autumn, 1956. (Each issue following this one will contain a section on occupational literature.)

90. Guilford, J. P.: *Fundamental Statistics in Psychology and Education,* 2d ed., New York, McGraw-Hill Book Company, Inc., 1950.

91. Hahn, Milton E., and Malcolm S. MacLean: *Counseling Psychology,* 2d ed., New York, McGraw-Hill Book Company, Inc., 1955.

92. Hale, Peter P: "Dissuasive Tools in Counseling," *Personnel and Guidance Journal,* vol. 31, pp. 451–452, April, 1953.

93. Hammond, Kenneth R., and Jeremiah M. Allen: *Writing Clinical Reports,* Englewood Cliffs, N.J., Prentice-Hall, Inc., 1953.

94. Hamrin, Shirley A., and Blanche B. Paulson: *Counseling Adolescents,* Chicago, Science Research Associates, Inc., 1950.

95. Hardee, Melvene Draheim (ed.): *Counseling and Guidance in General Education,* Yonkers, N.Y., World Book Company, 1955.

96. Harsh, Charles M., and H. G. Schrickel: *Personality,* New York, The Ronald Press Company, 1950.

97. Havighurst, Robert J., and H. Taba: *Adolescent Character and Personality,* New York, John Wiley & Sons, Inc., 1949.

98. Hilgard, Ernest R.: *Theories of Learning,* 2d ed., New York, Appleton-Century-Crofts, Inc., 1956.

99. Hillway, Tyrus: *Introduction to Research,* New York, Houghton Mifflin Company, 1956.

100. Hollingshead, August B.: *Elmtown's Youth,* New York, John Wiley & Sons, Inc., 1949.

101. Hoppock, Robert: "A Check List of Facts about Jobs for Use in Vocational Guidance," *American Psychologist,* vol. 3, pp. 417–418, September, 1948.

102. Hoppock, Robert: *Occupational Information,* New York, McGraw-Hill Book Company, Inc., 1957.

103. Horrocks, J. E., and M. E. Troyer: *A Study of Barry Black,* Syracuse, N.Y., School of Education, Syracuse University, 1944.

104. Horrocks, J. E., and M. E. Troyer: *A Study of Connie Casey,* Syracuse, N.Y., School of Education, Syracuse University, 1945.

105. Horrocks, J. E., and M. E. Troyer: *A Study of Sam Smith,* Syracuse, N.Y., School of Education, Syracuse University, 1945.

106. Hulslander, S. C.: *Referring Counselees to Specialists,* Boston, Research Publishing Company, 1950.

107. Hunt, J. McV. (ed.): *Personality and the Behavior Disorders,* New York, The Ronald Press Company, 1944.

108. Hunt, J. McV.: "Measuring Movement in Casework," *Journal of Social Casework,* vol. 29, pp. 343–351, 1948.

109. Hurt, N. W., and C. E. Burckel: *The College Blue Book,* 6th ed., Yonkers, N.Y., Christian E. Burckel, 1950.

110. Irwin, Mary (ed.): *American Universities and Colleges,* Washington, American Council on Education, 1956.

111. Jennings, Helen Hall: *Sociometry in Group Relations,* Washington, American Council on Education, 1948.

112. Jesness, R.: "To Refer or Not to Refer," *Occupations,* vol. 30, pp. 521–524, April, 1952.

113. Johnson, Palmer O., and Robert W. B. Jackson: *Introduction to Statistical Methods,* Englewood Cliffs, N.J., Prentice-Hall, Inc., 1953.

114. Joint Committee of the American Psychological Association, American Educational Research Association, and National Council on Measurements Used in Education, "Technical Recommendations for Psychological Tests and Diagnostic Techniques," *Psychological Bulletin,* vol. 51, part 2, March, 1954.

115. *Journal of Counseling Psychology,* Columbus, Ohio, Ohio State University.

116. Kelley, Richard W.: "Some Vocational Counseling Methods," *Educational and Psychological Measurement,* vol. 9, Summer, 1949.

117. Kirk, Barbara, and Marjorie E. Michaels: "A Study of Counselee Reading of Occupational Materials," *Occupations,* vol. 28, pp. 446–450, April, 1950.

118. Klineberg, Otto: *Social Psychology,* rev. ed., New York, Henry Holt and Company, Inc., 1954.

119. Krech, David, and Richard S. Crutchfield: *Theory and Problems of Social Psychology,* New York, McGraw-Hill Book Company, Inc., 1948.

120. Leonard, Edith M., Dorothy D. Vandeman, and Lilliam E. Miles: *Counseling with Parents,* New York, The Macmillan Company, 1954.

121. Lindgren, Henry Clay: *Psychology of Personal and Social Adjustment,* New York, American Book Company, 1953.

122. Louttit, C. M.: *Clinical Psychology,* rev. ed., New York, Harper & Brothers, 1947.

123. Lovejoy, Clarence E.: *Lovejoy's College Guide,* 4th ed., New York, Simon and Schuster, Inc., 1956.

124. Luborsky, Lester: "Intraindividual Repetitive Measurement (P Technique) in Understanding Psychotherapeutic Change," in O. Hobart Mowrer (ed.), *Psychotherapy, Theory and Research,* New York, The Ronald Press Company, 1953.

125. Lynd, Robert S., and Helen M. Lynd: *Middletown,* New York, Harcourt, Brace and Company, Inc., 1929.

126. Lynd, Robert S., and Helen M. Lynd: *Middletown in Transition,* New York, Harcourt, Brace and Company, Inc., 1937.

127. McArthur, Charles: "Analyzing the Clinical Process," *Journal of Counseling Psychology,* vol. 1, pp. 203–207, Winter, 1954.

128. McCabe, George E.: "How Substantial Is a Substantial Coefficient?" *Personnel and Guidance Journal,* vol. 34, pp. 340–344, February, 1956.

129. McComb, W. R.: "Changes in the Fair Labor Standards Act Affect Young Workers," *Occupations,* vol. 28, pp. 429–432, April, 1950.

130. McDaniel, Henry B.: *Guidance in the Modern School,* New York, The Dryden Press, Inc., 1946.

131. McKinney, Fred: *Counseling for Personal Adjustment,* Boston, Houghton Mifflin Company, 1958.

132. Mahoney, Harold J.: *Occupational Information for Counselors,* Yonkers, N.Y., World Book Company, 1952.

133. Marzolf, Stanley S.: *Psychological Diagnosis and Counseling in the Schools,* New York, Henry Holt and Company, Inc., 1956.

134. Mathewson, Robert H.: "The General Guidance Counselor," *Personnel and Guidance Journal,* vol. 32, pp. 544–547, May, 1954.

135. Mathewson, Robert H.: *Guidance Policy and Practice,* rev. ed., New York, Harper & Brothers, 1955.

136. Meehl, Paul E.: *Clinical versus Statistical Prediction,* Minneapolis, University of Minnesota Press, 1954.

137. Meehl, Paul E., David Tiedeman, and Charles McArthur: "Symposium on Clinical and Statistical Prediction," *Journal of Counseling Psychology,* vol. 3, pp. 163–173, Fall, 1956.

138. Menninger, William C.: *Understanding Yourself,* Chicago, Science Research Associates, Inc., 1951.

139. Miller, Delbert C., and William H. Form: *Industrial Sociology,* New York, Harper & Brothers, 1951.

140. Miller, Leonard M., James F. Garrett, and Nathaniel Stewart: "Opportunity Rehabilitation Counseling," *Personnel and Guidance Journal,* vol. 33, pp. 444–447, April, 1955.

141. Miller, Neal E., and John Dollard: *Social Learning and Imitation,* New Haven, Conn., Yale University Press, 1941.

142. Morris, C. Eugene: *Counseling with Young People,* New York, Association Press, 1954.

143. Morris, Glyn: *Practical Guidance Methods for Principals and Teachers,* New York, Harper & Brothers, 1952.

144. Mowrer, O. Hobart: "Anxiety Theory as a Basis for Distinguishing between Counseling and Psychotherapy," in Ralph F. Berdie (ed.), *Concepts and Programs of Counseling,* Minneapolis, University of Minnesota Press, 1951.

145. Mowrer, O. Hobart (ed.): *Psychotherapy, Theory and Research,* New York, The Ronald Press Company, 1953.

146. Mowrer, O. Hobart: "Q Technique: Description, History, and Critique," in O. Hobart Mowrer (ed.), *Psychotherapy, Theory and Research,* New York, The Ronald Press Company, 1953, pp. 316–375.

147. Mowrer, O. Hobart, et al.: "Further Studies Utilizing the Discomfort-relief Quotient," in O. Hobart Mowrer (ed.), *Psychotherapy, Theory and Research,* New York, The Ronald Press Company, 1953, pp. 257–295.

148. Murphy, Gardner: *Personality,* New York, Harper & Brothers, 1947.

149. Myers, George E., Gladys M. Little, and Sarah A. Robinson: *Planning Your Future,* 4th ed., New York, McGraw-Hill Book Company, Inc., 1953.

150. National Association for Mental Health, New York.

151. National Association of Guidance Supervisors and Counselor Trainers, *Duties, Standards, and Qualifications of Counselors,* Misc. 3314–1, Washington, Office of Education, 1949.

152. National Association of Guidance Supervisors and Counselor Trainers, *Counselor Competencies in Occupational Information,* Misc. 3314–3, Washington, Office of Education, 1949.

153. National Association of Guidance Supervisors and Counselor Trainers, *Counselor Competencies in Analysis of the Individual,* Misc. 3314–4, Washington, Office of Education, 1949.

154. National Association of Guidance Supervisors and Counselor Trainers, *Counselor Competencies in Counseling Techniques,* Misc. 3314–5, Washington, Office of Education, 1949.

155. National Association of Guidance Supervisors and Counselor Trainers, *In-service Preparation for Guidance Duties,* Misc. 3314–7A, part 1, Washington, Office of Education, 1950.

156. National Association of Guidance Supervisors and Counselor Trainers, *Enlisting and Coordinating Resources for In-service Education,* Misc. 3314–7B, part 2, Washington, Office of Education, 1950.

157. National Association of Guidance Supervisors and Counselor Trainers, *Administrative Relationships of the Guidance Program,* Misc. 3314–8, Washington, Office of Education, 1949.

158. National Vocational Guidance Association, Joint Committee to Consider the Common Elements in Counselor Training, *Counselor Preparation,* Washington, 1949.

159. National Rehabilitation Association and National Vocational Guidance Association, *Rehabilitation Counselor Preparation,* Washington, National Vocational Guidance Association, 1956.

160. New Public Affairs Press, New York.

161. Newcomb, Theodore M., and Eugene L. Hartley (eds.): *Readings in Social Psychology,* New York, Henry Holt and Company, Inc., 1947.

162. OSS Assessment Staff, *Assessment of Men,* New York, Rinehart & Company, Inc., 1948.

163. Ohlsen, Merle M.: *Guidance: An Introduction,* New York, Harcourt, Brace and Company, Inc., 1955.

164. Palmer, Gladys Louise: *Labor Mobility in Six Cities,* New York, Social Science Research Council, 1954.

165. Paterson, Donald G., C. d'A. Gerken, and Milton E. Hahn: *Revised Minnesota Occupational Rating Scale,* Minnesota Studies in Student Personnel Work, no. 2, Minneapolis, University of Minnesota Press, 1953.

166. Pennington, L. A., and Irwin A. Berg: *An Introduction to Clinical Psychology,* New York, The Ronald Press Company, 1948.

167. Pepinsky, Harold B.: "The Selection and Use of Diagnostic Categories in Clinical Counseling," *Applied Psychology Monographs,* no. 15, 1948.

168. Pepinsky, Harold B., and Pauline Nichols Pepinsky: *Counseling, Theory and Practice,* New York, The Ronald Press Company, 1954.

169. Pepinsky, Harold B.: "Research Notes from Here and There," *Journal of Counseling Psychology,* vol. 3, pp. 145–147, Summer, 1956.

170. Pepinsky, Harold B.: "Research Notes from Here and There," *Journal of Counseling Psychology,* vol. 3, pp. 222–226, Fall, 1956.

171. Perry, William G., and Stanley G. Estes: "The Collaboration of Client and Counselor," in O. Hobart Mowrer (ed.), *Psychotherapy, Theory and Research,* New York, The Ronald Press Company, 1953, pp. 95–118.

172. *Personnel and Guidance Journal,* Washington, American Personnel and Guidance Association.

173. Porter, E. H.: *An Introduction to Therapeutic Counseling,* New York, Houghton Mifflin Company, 1950.

174. *Review of Educational Research,* Washington, American Educational Research Association, National Education Association.

175. Reynolds, Lloyd George, and Joseph Shister: *Job Horizons,* New York, Harper & Brothers, 1949.

176. Robinson, Francis P.: *Effective Study,* New York, Harper & Brothers, 1946.

177. Robinson, Francis P.: *Principles and Procedures in Student Counseling,* New York, Harper & Brothers, 1950.

178. Robinson, Francis P.: "The Dynamics of Communication in Counseling," *Journal of Counseling Psychology,* vol. 2, pp. 163–169, Fall, 1955.

179. Roe, Anne: *The Psychology of Occupations,* New York, John Wiley & Sons, Inc., 1956.

180. Roeber, Edward C., Glenn E. Smith, and Clifford E. Erickson: *Organization and Administration of Guidance Services,* 2d ed., New York, McGraw-Hill Book Company, Inc., 1955.

181. Roethlisberger, F. J., and W. J. Dickson: *Management and the Worker,* Cambridge, Mass., Harvard University Press, 1939.

182. Rogers, Carl R.: *Counseling and Psychotherapy,* Boston, Houghton Mifflin Company, 1942.

183. Rogers, Carl R., and John L. Wallen: *Counseling with Returned Servicemen*, New York, McGraw-Hill Book Company, Inc., 1946.

184. Rogers, Carl R.: *Client-centered Therapy*, Boston, Houghton Mifflin Company, 1951.

185. Rogers, Carl R., and Rosalind Dymond (eds.): *Psychotherapy and Personality Change*, Chicago, University of Chicago Press, 1954.

186. Rosenzweig, Saul: *Psychodiagnosis*, New York, Grune & Stratton, Inc., 1949.

187. Rothney, John W. M., and Bert A. Roens: *Counseling the Individual Student*, New York, William Sloane Associates, 1949.

188. Rothney, John W. M., and Bert A. Roens: *Guidance of American Youth*, Cambridge, Mass., Harvard University Press, 1952.

189. Rothney, John W. M.: *The High School Student: A Book of Cases*, New York, The Dryden Press, Inc., 1955.

190. Rothney, John W. M.: *Guidance Practices and Results*, New York, Harper & Brothers, 1958.

191. Rusalem, Herbert: "New Insight on the Role of Occupational Information in Counseling," *Journal of Counseling Psychology*, vol. 1, pp. 84–88, 1954.

192. Sanderson, Herbert: *Basic Concepts in Vocational Guidance*, New York, McGraw-Hill Book Company, Inc., 1954.

193. Sarbin, Theodore R.: "A Contribution to the Study of Actuarial and Individual Methods of Prediction," *American Journal of Sociology*, vol. 48, pp. 593–602, 1943.

194. Sargent, S. Stansfield: *Social Psychology*, New York, The Ronald Press Company, 1950.

195. Schwebel, Milton: "Some Ethical Problems in Counseling," *Personnel and Guidance Journal*, vol. 33, pp. 254–259, January, 1955.

196. *SRA Primary Mental Abilities*, Chicago, Science Research Associates, Inc., 1949.

197. Seeman, Julius: *The Case of Jim*, Nashville, Tenn., Educational Test Bureau, 1957.

198. Senick, Daniel: "Occupational Information in the Counseling Interviews," *The Vocational Guidance Quarterly*, vol. 4, pp. 145–149, Summer, 1956.

199. Shaffer, E. Evan: "The Autobiography in Secondary School Counseling," *Personnel and Guidance Journal*, vol. 32, pp. 395–398, March, 1954.

200. Shaffer, Laurance F., and Shoben, Edward J.: *The Psychology of Adjustment*, 2d ed., Boston, Houghton Mifflin Company, 1956.

201. Shartle, Carroll L.: *Occupational Information*, 2d ed., Englewood Cliffs, N.J., Prentice-Hall, Inc., 1952.

202. Shepard, Eugene L.: "The Role of the Faculty Counselor in General Education," in Melvene Draheim Hardee (ed.), *Counseling and Guidance in General Education*, Yonkers, N.Y., World Book Company, 1955, pp. 161–178.

203. Shoben, Edward J.: "Counseling and the Learning of Integrative Behavior," *Journal of Counseling Psychology*, vol. 1, pp. 42–48, February, 1954.

204. Shoben, Edward J., et al.: "Behavior Theories and a Counseling Case: A Symposium," *Journal of Counseling Psychology*, vol. 3, pp. 107–124, Summer, 1956.

205. Shoben, Edward J.: "Toward a Concept of the Normal Personality," *The American Psychologist*, vol. 12, pp. 183–189, April, 1957.

206. Shostrom, Everett L., and Lawrence M. Brammer: *The Dynamics of the Counseling Process*, New York, McGraw-Hill Book Company, Inc., 1952.

207. Small, Leonard: "Personality Determinants of Vocational Choice," *Psychological Monographs*, vol. 67, no. 1, 1953.

208. Smigel, Erwin O.: "Occupational Sociology," *Personnel and Guidance Journal*, vol. 32, pp. 536–539, May, 1954.

209. Smith, Glenn E.: *Counseling in the Secondary School,* New York, The Macmillan Company, 1955.

210. Snyder, W. V., et al.: *Casebook of Non-directive Counseling,* Boston, Houghton Mifflin Company, 1947.

211. Spear, George S., and Leslie Jasker: "The Influence of Occupational Information on Occupational Goals," *Occupations,* vol. 28, pp. 15–17, October, 1949.

212. Spear, George S.: "Counselors and Occupational Information," *Personnel and Guidance Journal,* vol. 32, pp. 339–342, February, 1954.

213. Splaver, Sarah: *Occupational Books,* Washington, Biblio Press, 1952.

214. Stewart, N.: "A.G.C.T. Scores of Army Personnel Grouped by Occupations," *Occupations,* vol. 26, pp. 5–41, October, 1947.

215. Strang, Ruth: *Behavior and Background of Students in College and Secondary School,* New York, Harper & Brothers, 1937.

216. Strang, Ruth: "Use in Counseling of Information about Vocations," *School Review,* vol. 53, pp. 526–529, November, 1945.

217. Strang, Ruth: *Every Teacher's Record,* rev. ed., New York, Bureau of Publications, Teachers College, Columbia University, 1947.

218. Strang, Ruth: *Counseling Technics in College and Secondary School,* rev. and enl., New York, Harper & Brothers, 1949.

219. Strang, Ruth: *The Role of the Teacher in Personnel Work,* 4th ed., New York, Bureau of Publications, Teachers College, Columbia University, 1953.

220. Super, Donald E.: *Appraising Vocational Fitness,* New York, Harper & Brothers, 1949.

221. Super, Donald E.: "A Dilemma for Test Users," *Occupations,* vol. 29, pp. 174–176, December, 1950.

222. Super, Donald E.: "Vocational Adjustment: Implementing a Self-concept," *Occupations,* vol. 30, pp. 88–92, November, 1951.

223. Super, Donald E.: "A Theory of Vocational Development," *American Psychologist,* vol. 8, pp. 185–190, May, 1953.

224. Super, Donald E.: "The Preliminary Appraisal in Vocational Counseling," address presented at the national meeting of the American Personnel and Guidance Association, Washington, 1956, reprinted in Veterans Administration *Information Bulletin* 7–118, Sept. 21, 1956.

225. Super, Donald E.: "Getting Out of an Occupation," *Personnel and Guidance Journal,* vol. 34, pp. 491–493, April, 1956.

226. Super, Donald E.: "It's All in the Day's Work," *Personnel and Guidance Journal,* vol. 34, pp. 541–543, May, 1956.

227. Super, Donald E.: *The Psychology of Careers,* New York, Harper & Brothers, 1957.

228. Symonds, Percival M.: *Dynamic Psychology,* New York, Appleton-Century-Crofts, Inc., 1949.

229. Terman, Lewis M., and Maud A. Merrill: *Measuring Intelligence,* Boston, Houghton Mifflin Company, 1937.

230. Thomas, Lawrence G.: *The Occupational Structure and Education,* Englewood Cliffs, N.J., Prentice-Hall, Inc., 1956.

231. Thompson, Albert S., and Junius A. Davis: "What Workers Mean by Security," *Personnel Psychology,* vol. 9, pp. 229–241, Summer, 1956.

232. Thorne, Frederick C.: *Principles of Personality Counseling,* Journal of Clinical Psychology, Brandon, Vt., 1950.

233. Thorne, Frederick C.: *Principles of Psychological Examining,* Journal of Clinical Psychology, Brandon, Vt., 1955.

234. Thorne, Frederick C.: "An Evaluation of Eclectically Oriented Psychotherapy," *Journal of Clinical Psychology,* vol. 21, pp. 459–464, 1957.

235. Thorne, Frederick C.: "Structuring Eclectic Psychotherapy for the Client," *Journal of Clinical Psychology,* vol. 4, 1958.

236. Thorpe, Louis P.: *Child Psychology and Development,* New York, The Ronald Press Company, 1946.

237. Toven, J. Richard: "Appraising a Counseling Program at the College Level," *Occupations,* vol. 23, pp. 459–466, 1945.

238. Traxler, Arthur E., et al.: *Introduction to Testing and the Use of Test Results in Public Schools,* New York, Harper & Brothers, 1953.

239. Traxler, Arthur E.: *Techniques of Guidance,* rev. ed., New York, Harper & Brothers, 1957.

240. Tyler, Leona E.: *The Work of the Counselor,* New York, Appleton-Century-Crofts, Inc., 1953.

241. Tyler, Leona E.: "The Initial Interview," *Personnel and Guidance Journal,* vol. 34, pp. 466–473, April, 1956.

242. Tyler, Leona E.: "Theoretical Principles Underlying the Counseling Process," *Journal of Counseling Psychology,* vol. 5, pp. 3–8, Spring, 1958, and "Comment" by Harold B. Pepinsky, pp. 8–10.

243. Tyler, Leona E.: "Counseling," *Annual Review of Psychology,* vol. 9, pp. 375–390, 1958.

244. U.S. Bureau of the Census, *Census of Population, 1950,* vol. IV, *Special Reports,* part 1, chap. B, Occupational Characteristics, Washington, 1956 (also vols. I and II, and other reports in vol. IV).

245. U.S. Department of Health, Education, and Welfare, *Retention and Withdrawal of College Students,* Washington, 1958.

246. U.S. Department of Labor, *Dictionary of Occupational Titles,* vols. I and II, 2d ed., and part IV (2d printing), Washington, 1949.

247. U.S. Department of Labor, *Occupational Outlook Handbook,* Washington, 1957.

248. U.S. Department of Labor, *Employment Certificates Help You to Help Youth,* Washington, 1955.

249. U.S. Department of Labor, *Estimates of Worker Trait Requirements for 4,000 Jobs as Defined in the Dictionary of Occupational Titles,* Washington, 1956.

250. Walker, Helen M.: *Elementary Statistical Methods,* New York, Henry Holt and Company, Inc., 1943.

251. Warner, W. Lloyd: *Democracy in Jonesville,* New York, Harper & Brothers, 1949.

252. Warner, W. Lloyd, and James C. Abegglem: *Occupational Mobility in American Business and Industry,* Minneapolis, University of Minnesota Press, 1955.

253. Warters, Jane: *Techniques of Counseling,* New York, McGraw-Hill Book Company, Inc., 1954.

254. Warters, Jane: *High School Personnel Work Today,* 2d ed., New York, McGraw-Hill Book Company, Inc., 1956.

255. Weaver, Glenn L.: *How, When, and Where to Provide Occupational Information,* Chicago, Science Research Associates, Inc., 1955.

256. Wechsler, David: *The Measurement of Adult Intelligence,* 3d ed., Baltimore, The Williams & Wilkins Company, 1944.

257. Weigand, George, and Walter S. Blake: *College Orientation,* Englewood Cliffs, N.J., Prentice-Hall, Inc., 1955.

258. White, Robert W.: *The Abnormal Personality,* New York, The Ronald Press Company, 1948.

259. White, Robert W.: *Lives in Progress,* New York, The Dryden Press, Inc., 1952.

260. White, Verna: *Studying the Individual Pupil,* New York, Harper & Brothers, 1958.

261. Willey, Roy DeVerl, and Dean C. Andrew: *Modern Methods and Techniques in Guidance,* New York, Harper & Brothers, 1955.

262. Williamson, E. G., and Edward S. Bordin: "The Evaluation of Vocational and Educational Counseling: A Critique of the Methodology of Experiments," *Educational and Psychological Measurement,* vol. 1, pp. 5–24, 1941.

263. Williamson, E. G. (ed.): *Trends in Student Personnel Work,* Minneapolis, University of Minnesota Press, 1949.

264. Williamson, E. G.: *Counseling Adolescents,* New York, McGraw-Hill Book Company, Inc., 1950.

265. Wrenn, C. Gilbert: "The Ethics of Counseling," *Educational and Psychological Measurement,* vol. 12, pp. 161–177, 1952.

266. Young, Pauline V.: *Scientific Social Surveys and Research,* Englewood Cliffs, N.J., Prentice-Hall, Inc., 1949.

Index